THE LOEB CLASSICAL LIBRARY

FOUNDED BY JAMES LOEB, LL.D.

EDITED BY

† T. E. PAGE, c.h., litt.d.

† E. CAPPS, ph.d., ll.d.   † W. H. D. ROUSE, litt.d.

L. A. POST, l.h.d. E. H. WARMINGTON, m.a., f.r.hist.soc.

MARTIAL

EPIGRAMS

II

MARTIAL
EPIGRAMS

WITH AN ENGLISH TRANSLATION BY
WALTER C. A. KER, M.A.
SOMETIME SCHOLAR OF TRINITY COLLEGE, CAMBRIDGE
OF THE INNER TEMPLE, BARRISTER-AT-LAW

IN TWO VOLUMES
II

CAMBRIDGE, MASSACHUSETTS
HARVARD UNIVERSITY PRESS
LONDON
WILLIAM HEINEMANN LTD
MCMLXI

First printed 1920
Reprinted 1927, 1930, 1950, 1961

CONTENTS

CONTENTS

THE
EPIGRAMS OF MARTIAL

M. VALERI MARTIALIS EPIGRAMMATON

LIBER OCTAVUS

Imperatori Domitiano Caesari Augusto Germanico Dacico Valerius Martialis S.

Omnes quidem libelli mei, domine, quibus tu famam, id est vitam, dedisti, tibi supplicant; et, puto propter hoc legentur. hic tamen, qui operis nostri octavus inscribitur, occasione pietatis frequentius fruitur; minus itaque ingenio laborandum fuit, in cuius locum materia successerat: quam quidem subinde aliqua iocorum mixtura variare temptavimus, ne caelesti verecundiae tuae laudes suas, quae facilius te fatigare possint quam nos satiare, omnis versus ingereret. quamvis autem epigrammata a severissimis quoque et summae fortunae viris ita scripta sint ut mimicam verborum licentiam adfectasse videantur, ego tamen illis non permisi¹ tam lascive loqui quam solent. cum pars libri et maior et melior ad maiestatem sacri nominis tui alligata sit, meminerit non nisi religiosa purificatione lustratos accedere ad templa debere. quod

---

¹ This book appears by internal evidence to have been published towards the end of A.D. 93. The epigrams are not, however, in chronological order.

THE EPIGRAMS OF MARTIAL

BOOK VIII

To THE EMPEROR DOMITIANUS, CAESAR, AUGUSTUS,
CONQUEROR OF GERMANY AND DACIA, VALERIUS
MARTIALIS SENDS GREETING [1]

Of a truth all my little books, Sire, to which you
have given fame, that is, life, are your suppliants,
and I think will, for this reason, be read. This one,
however, which is marked the eighth of my works,
enjoys more frequently the opportunity of showing
loyalty. Accordingly I had less occasion for the
labour of invention, for which the subject-matter
formed a substitute; that, however, I have here and
there attempted to diversify by some intermixture
of pleasantry, so that every verse should not heap
upon your divine modesty its meed of praise which
would more easily weary you than satiate me. And
although epigrams have been written in such a style,
even by men the most austere and of the highest
position, as apparently to have aimed at the verbal
licence of mimes, yet I have not allowed these to
speak with their usual playfulness. As part of my
book—and that the greater and better—is attached
to the Majesty of your sacred name, it should remember that it is unfitting to approach the temple
save cleansed by religious purification.[2] That readers

[2] An allusion to the Emperor's assumption of deity : *cf.*
VIII. ii. 6.

3

ut custoditurum me lecturi sciant, in ipso libelli
huius limine profiteri brevissimo placuit epigram-
mate.

I

LAURIGEROS domini, liber, intrature penates
disce verecundo sanctius ore loqui.
nuda recede Venus; non est tuus iste libellus:
tu mihi, tu Pallas Caesariana, veni.

II

FASTORUM genitor parensque Ianus
victorem modo cum videret Histri,
tot vultus sibi non satis putavit
optavitque oculos habere plures,
et lingua pariter locutus omni   5
terrarum domino deoque rerum
promisit Pyliam quater senectam.
addas, Iane pater, tuam rogamus.

III

" QUINQUE satis fuerant: nam sex septemve libelli
est nimium: quid adhuc ludere, Musa, iuvat?
sit pudor et finis: iam plus nihil addere nobis
fama potest: teritur noster ubique liber;
et cum rupta situ Messallae saxa iacebunt   5
altaque cum Licini marmora pulvis erunt,

---

[1] Because of the Emperor's recent victories on the Danube.
[2] The god Janus presided over the year and the public
records. He was represented with two faces turned in op-
posite ways, *i.e.* towards the past and the future; or with
four to represent the four seasons.

4

may know I shall regard this obligation, I have deter-
mined to make my profession on the very threshold
of this little book by a very brief epigram.

I

THOU, my book, who art purposed to enter my
Master's laurel-wreathed[1] abode, learn to speak more
reverently in modest speech. Undraped Venus, stand
back: this little book is not thine; do thou come
to me, thou, Pallas, patron of Caesar.

II

WHEN Janus, begetter and parent of our annals,[2]
of late saw Hister's conqueror, he deemed his many
faces were not enough for him, and wished to possess
more eyes; and, speaking alike with every tongue,
he promised the Lord of Earth and God of the
Universe a Pylian old age[3] four times over. Add,
Father Janus, we entreat, your own.

III

"FIVE were sufficient; for six or seven books are
too much: why do you want, Muse, to frolic still?
Let there be some stint and an end: now nothing
more can Fame give me; my book is thumbed everywhere; and when Messalla's[4] pavements shall lie
shivered by decay, and Licinus'[5] towering marble

[3] Nestor's.
[4] M. Valerius Messalla Corvinus, the patron of Tibullus:
cf. x. ii. 9. He repaired the *Via Latina*: cf. Tib. I. vii. 57.
Or " *saxa* " may perhaps refer to his tomb.
[5] A rich freedman of Augustus (*cf.* Juv. i. 109), who had
a magnificent tomb.

5

me tamen ora legent et secum plurimus hospes
    ad patrias sedes carmina nostra feret."
finieram, cum sic respondit nona sororum,
    cui coma et unguento sordida vestis erat :   10
"Tune potes dulcis, ingrate, relinquere nugas?
    dic mihi, quid melius desidiosus ages?
an iuvat ad tragicos soccum transferre coturnos
    aspera vel paribus bella tonare modis,
praelegat ut tumidus rauca te voce magister,   15
    oderit et grandis virgo bonusque puer?
scribant ista graves nimium nimiumque severi,
    quos media miseros nocte lucerna videt.
at tu Romanos lepido sale tingue libellos :
    adgnoscat mores vita legatque suos.   20
angusta cantare licet videaris avena,
    dum tua multorum vincat avena tubas."

IV

Quantus, io, Latias mundi conventus ad aras
    suscipit et solvit pro duce vota suo !
non sunt haec hominum, Germanice, gaudia tantum,
    sed faciunt ipsi nunc, puto, sacra dei.

V

Dum donas, Macer, anulos puellis,
    desisti, Macer, anulos habere.

---

[1] Thalia, the Muse of epigram.   [2] Hexameters.
[3] For Jan. 3, the day when vows were publicly offered for
the Emperor (*votorum nuncupatio : cf.* Suet. *Ner.* xlvi.).

shall be dust, yet me shall lips read, and many
a sojourner shall carry my poems with him to his
fatherland." I ended; when thus replied the ninth
of the Sisters,[1] her hair and vesture stained with
unguent : "Can you, ungrateful man, resign your
pleasant trifles ? Tell me, what better thing when
idle will you do? Wish you to adapt your comic shoe
to the tragic buskin, or in even-footed measures[2] to
thunder of rough wars, that a pompous pedagogue
may dictate you in hoarse tones, and tall girl and
honest boy hate you ? Let those themes be written
by men grave overmuch, and overmuch austere, whom
at midnight their lamp marks at their wretched toil.
But do you dip your little Roman books in sprightly
wit ; let Life recognize and read of her own manners. To a thin pipe you may appear to sing, if only
your pipe outblow the trump of many."

IV

Ho! How great a concourse of the world at Latin
altars makes and pays their vows[3] for their Chief!
These are not the joys of men only, Germanicus :
nay, the very gods now, I ween, offer sacrifice.

V

While you give rings to girls, Macer, you have
ceased, Macer, to possess rings yourself.[4]

---

[4] *i.e.* you have lost your qualification as a knight : *cf.*
Juv. xi. 43. The *ius anulorum* (right to wear a gold ring)
was possessed by senators, knights, and magistrates.

7

VI

Archetypis vetuli nihil est odiosius Aucti
  (ficta Saguntino cymbia malo luto),
argenti furiosa sui cum stemmata narrat
  garrulus et verbis mucida vina facit:
"Laomedonteae fuerant haec pocula mensae: 5
  ferret ut haec, muros struxit Apollo lyra.
hoc cratere ferox commisit proelia Rhoetus
  cum Lapithis: pugna debile cernis opus.
hi duo longaevo censentur Nestore fundi:
  pollice de Pylio trita columba nitet.   10
hic scyphus est in quo misceri iussit amicis
  largius Aeacides vividiusque merum.
hac propinavit Bitiae pulcherrima Dido
  in patera, Phrygio cum data cena viro est."
miratus fueris cum prisca toreumata multum,   15
  in Priami calathis Astyanacta bibes.

VII

Hoc agere est causas, hoc dicere, Cinna, diserte,
  horis, Cinna, decem dicere verba novem?
sed modo clepsydras ingenti voce petisti
  quattuor. o quantum, Cinna, tacere potes!

VIII

Principium des, Iane, licet velocibus annis
  et renoves voltu saecula longa tuo,

---

[1] In the battle between the Lapithae and the Centaurs.
[2] Achilles: *cf.* Hom. *Il.* ix. 203.

VI

THAN old Auctus' antiques nothing is more odious—I prefer drinking vessels moulded from Saguntine clay —when he prates of the crazy pedigrees of his silver plate, and by his chattering makes the wine vapid. "These are cups that once belonged to Laomedon's table: to win these Apollo by his harp-playing built the walls of Troy. With this mixing-bowl fierce Rhoetus joined battle with the Lapithae:[1] you see the workmanship is dinted by the fight. These two goblets are valuable because of aged Nestor: the dove is burnished by the rubbing of the Pylian thumb. This is the tankard in which the grandson of Aeacus[2] ordered a fuller draught and stronger wine be mixed for his friends. In this bowl most beautiful Dido pledged Bitias when her banquet was given to the Phrygian hero."[3] When you have much admired these ancient chasings, in Priam's cups you will drink Astyanax.[4]

VII

Is this your pleading of causes, is this eloquence, Cinna, in ten hours, Cinna, to say nine words? And just now in loud tones you asked for four water-clocks![5] Oh, what store of silence, Cinna, you possess!

VIII

ALBEIT thou, Janus, givest their beginning to the flying years, and dost with thy visage renew the

[3] Aeneas: cf. Verg. Aen. i. 738.
[4] i.e. something very young and immature. Astyanax was the grandson of Priam.   [5] cf. VI. XXXV. 1.

te primum pia tura rogent, te vota salutent,
  purpura te felix, te colat omnis honos:
tu tamen hoc mavis, Latiae quod contigit urbi   5
  mense tuo reducem, Iane, videre deum.

IX

SOLVERE dodrantem nuper tibi, Quinte, volebat
  lippus Hylas, luscus vult dare dimidium.
accipe quam primum; brevis est occasio lucri:
  si fuerit caecus, nil tibi solvet Hylas.

X

EMIT lacernas milibus decem Bassus
  Tyrias coloris optimi.   lucrifecit.
"Adeo bene emit?" inquis.   immo non solvet,

XI

PERVENISSE tuam iam te scit Rhenus in urbem;
  nam populi voces audit et ille tui:
Sarmaticas etiam gentes Histrumque Getasque
  laetitiae clamor terruit ipse novae.
dum te longa sacro venerantur gaudia Circo,   5
  nemo quater missos currere sensit equos.
nullum Roma ducem, nec te sic, Caesar, amavit:
  te quoque iam non plus, ut velit ipsa, potest.
10

long ages, albeit pious incense invokes thee, prayers salute thee first, to thee the consul's joyous purple, to thee every magistrate pays court, yet this thou countest more—it has been thy fortune, Janus, in thine own month to see our god [1] returning home!

IX

HYLAS, when blear-eyed, Quintus, was willing lately to pay you three-quarters of his debt; now he is one-eyed he is willing to give half. Take it at once: brief is the opportunity for gain; if he become blind, Hylas won't pay you a penny.

X

BASSUS has bought a cloak for ten thousand sesterces, a Tyrian of the best colour. He has made a bargain. "Did he buy so cheap?" you ask. Aye, he is not going to pay.

XI

THAT thou hast come to thy city Rhine knows already, for he too hears the voices of thy people: Sarmatian tribes as well, and Hister and the Getae, the very shout of our new-found gladness has affeared. While in the sacred Circus applause long sustained revered thee, no man perceived the steeds had four times been started. No chief has Rome so loved, nor thee so much, Caesar, as now; thee too, albeit she would, she cannot now love more.

[1] The Emperor.

XII

UXOREM quare locupletem ducere nolim
    quaeritis? uxori nubere nolo meae.
inferior matrona suo sit, Prisce, marito:
    non aliter fiunt femina virque pares.

XIII

MORIO dictus erat: viginti milibus emi.
    redde mihi nummos, Gargiliane: sapit.

XIV

PALLIDA ne Cilicum timeant pomaria brumam,
    mordeat et tenerum fortior aura nemus,
hibernis obiecta Notis specularia puros
    admittunt soles et sine faece diem.
at mihi cella datur non tota clusa fenestra,   5
    in qua nec Boreas ipse manere velit.
sic habitare iubes veterem crudelis amicum?
    arboris ergo tuae tutior hospes ero.

XV

DUM nova Pannonici numeratur gloria belli,
    omnis et ad reducem dum litat ara Iovem,
dat populus, dat gratus eques, dat tura senatus,
    et ditant Latias tertia dona tribus,

---

[1] Naturals or cretins were kept as curiosities: *cf.* III.
lxxxii. 24; XII. xciii. 3.

XII

" WHY am I unwilling to marry a rich wife?" Do
you ask? I am unwilling to take my wife as husband.
Let the matron be subject to her husband, Priscus;
in no other way do woman and man become equal.

XIII

HE had been described as an idiot;[1] I bought him
for twenty thousand sesterces. Give me back my
money, Gargilianus; he has his wits.

XIV

THAT your orchard trees from Cilicia may not grow
wan and dread the winter, nor too keen an air nip
the tender boughs, glass casements facing the wintry
south winds admit the clear suns and daylight undefiled. But to me is assigned a garret, shut in by
an ill-fitting window, in which even Boreas himself
would not care to abide. Is it in such a lodging you
cruelly bid your old friend dwell? Then as the
guest of one of your trees I shall be more protected.[2]

XV

WHAT time from Pannonian war new glory is added
to the tale, and every altar makes fair offerings to
greet returning Jove, while the people gives, the
grateful knights give, the Senate gives incense, and
a third largess makes rich the Latin tribes, Rome

[2] cf. a similar epigram, VIII. lxviii.

hos quoque secretos memoravit[1] Roma triumphos, 5
  nec minor ista tuae laurea pacis erat,[2]
quod tibi de sancta credis pietate tuorum.
  principis est virtus maxima nosse suos.

XVI

    PISTOR qui fueras diu, Cypere,
    causas nunc agis et ducena quaeris:
    sed consumis et usque mutuaris.
    a pistore, Cypere, non recedis:
    et panem facis et facis farinam.   5

XVII

EGI, Sexte, tuam pactus duo milia causam.
  misisti nummos quod mihi mille quid est?
"Narrasti nihil" inquis "et a te perdita causa est."
  tanto plus debes, Sexte, quod erubui.

XVIII

SI tua, Cerrini, promas epigrammata vulgo,
  vel mecum possis vel prior ipse legi:
sed tibi tantus inest veteris respectus amici,
  carior ut mea sit quam tua fama tibi.

[1] *memorabit* β.   [2] *erit* β.

---

[1] Domitian had waived a formal triumph, merely dedicating a laurel-wreath (*ista laurea*, l. 6) to Jupiter Capitolinus: Suet. *Dom.* vi.; Stat. *Sylv.* III. iii. 171.

has made memorable this triumph also, though concealed; [1] nor was the laurel that marks the peace thou bringest of less account, because touching thy people's reverent love thou dost trust thyself. [2] A Prince's greatest virtue is to know his own.

XVI

You who were long a baker, Cyperus, now conduct cases, and look to make two hundred thousand sesterces a year; but you squander them, and are continually raising loans. You do not part from your rôle of baker, Cyperus; you make your bread— and make your dust fly too. [3]

XVII

I have pleaded your case, Sextus, for an agreed fee of two thousand sesterces. What is the reason you have sent me one thousand? "You set out none of the facts," you remark, "and by you my case was ruined." You owe me all the more, Sextus; I blushed.

XVIII

Were you, Cerrinius, to issue your epigrams to the public, you might be read in rivalry with me, or even as my superior; but so great is your regard for your old friend that dearer to you is my fame than your

[2] *i.e.* thou canst rely on the people understanding the greatness of thy victory without a triumph.
[3] *i.e.* you dissipate your earnings, as grain is reduced to the dust of flour. Or perhaps the metaphor is taken from flour falling through the meshes of a sieve: *cf.* Pers. iii. 112.

sic Maro nec Calabri temptavit carmina Flacci,   5
  Pindaricos nosset cum superare modos,
et Vario cessit Romani laude coturni,
  cum posset tragico fortius ore loqui.
aurum et opes et rura frequens donabit amicus :
  qui velit ingenio cedere rarus erit.   10

XIX

PAUPER videri Cinna vult ; et est pauper.

XX

CUM facias versus nulla non luce ducenos,
  Vare, nihil recitas.   non sapis, atque sapis.

XXI

PHOSPHORE, redde diem : quid gaudia nostra moraris ?
  Caesare venturo, Phosphore, redde diem.
Roma rogat.   placidi numquid te pigra Bootae
  plaustra vehunt, lento quod nimis axe venis ?
Ledaeo poteras abducere Cyllaron astro :   5
  ipse suo cedet nunc tibi Castor equo.
quid cupidum Titana tenes ? iam Xanthus et Aethon
  frena volunt, vigilat Memnonis alma parens.
tarda tamen nitidae non cedunt sidera luci,
  et cupit Ausonium luna videre ducem.   10
iam, Caesar, vel nocte veni : stent astra licebit,
  non derit populo te veniente dies.

---

[1] Horace.
[2] It is fatal to appear poor : *cf.* v. lxxxi.
[3] The Constellation of the Lesser Bear.

own. So Maro did not even attempt the lyrics of
Calabrian Flaccus,[1] although his skill might have
surpassed the measures of Pindar, and he gave place
to Varius in the renown of the Roman buskin, though
he might have spoken in tragic tone with stronger
voice. Gold and possessions and lands many a friend
will bestow: he who is willing to yield in genius will
be rare.

XIX

Cinna wishes to appear poor, and he is poor.[2]

XX

Although no day passes but you compose two
hundred verses, Varus, you recite none of them.
You have no wit—and yet are wise.

XXI

Phosphor, bring us back day; why puttest thou
off our joys? Now Caesar comes, Phosphor, bring
us back day, Rome begs thee. Doth the sluggish
wain of slow-twisting Bootes[3] bear thee, that thou
comest with too slow an axle? Thou mightest have
withdrawn Cyllarus[4] from Leda's constellation; freely
will Castor now yield his steed to thee. Why stayest
thou eager Titan? Already Xanthus and Aethon[5]
look for the reins; Memnon's kindly Mother[6] wakes.
Yet the slow stars yield not to glowing light, and
the moon longs to see Ausonia's Chief. Now, Caesar,
come thou, even by night; let the stars stand still;
the people, when thou comest, shall not want for day.

[4] The horse of Castor: cf. VIII. xxviii. 8.
[5] Horses of the Sun: cf. III. lxvii. 5.
[6] Aurora, goddess of the morning.

XXII

INVITAS ad aprum, ponis mihi, Gallice, porcum.
　hybrida sum, si das, Gallice, verba mihi.

XXIII

ESSE tibi videor saevus nimiumque gulosus,
　qui propter cenam, Rustice, caedo cocum.
si levis ista tibi flagrorum causa videtur,
　ex qua vis causa vapulet ergo cocus?

XXIV

SI quid forte petam timido gracilique libello,
　inproba non fuerit si mea charta, dato.
et si non dederis, Caesar, permitte rogari:
　offendunt numquam tura precesque Iovem.
qui fingit sacros auro vel marmore vultus, 5
　non facit ille deos: qui rogat, ille facit.

XXV

VIDISTI semel, Oppiane, tantum
　aegrum me: male saepe te videbo.

XXVI

NON tot in Eois timuit Gangeticus arvis
　raptor, in Hyrcano qui fugit albus equo,
quot tua Roma novas vidit, Germanice, tigres,
　delicias potuit nec numerare suas.

---

¹ Hybrids were supposed to want sense. A hybrid pri-
marily meant the offspring of a sow and of a wild boar: *cf.*
Plin. *N. H.* viii. **79.**

XXII

You invite me to a boar; you set before me, Gallicus, a pig. I am a hybrid [1] myself if you can deceive me, Gallicus.

XXIII

I APPEAR to you cruel and over gluttonous because, on account of the dinner, Rusticus, I lash my cook. If that seem to you a slight reason for a beating, for what reason, then, do you wish a cook to be flogged?

XXIV

IF I may by chance ask for something in my bashful and slender little volume, if my page be not overbold, do thou grant it. And even if thou shalt not grant it, Caesar, allow the asking: incense and prayers never offend Jove. He who shapes sacred lineaments in gold or marble does not make gods: he makes them who prays.

XXV

You came to see me once only when I was ill. It will go badly with me if I see you often.[2]

XXVI

TIGRESSES not so many has the robber [3] dreaded in Eastern fields by Ganges' side, as he flies with pale face on his Hyrcanian steed, as but now thy Rome, Germanicus, has seen, nor could she count what gave

[2] cf. v. ix.
[3] i.e. of cubs.

vincit Erythraeos tua, Caesar, harena triumphos   5
  et victoris opes divitiasque dei :
nam cum captivos ageret sub curribus Indos,
  contentus gemina tigride Bacchus erat.

XXVII

Munera qui tibi dat locupleti, Gaure, senique,
  si sapis et sentis, hoc tibi ait "Morere."

XXVIII

Dic, toga, facundi gratum mihi munus amici,
  esse velis cuius fama decusque gregis?
Apula Ledaei tibi floruit herba Phalanthi,
  qua saturat Calabris culta Galaesus aquis?
an Tartesiacus stabuli nutritor Hiberi   5
  Baetis in Hesperia te quoque lavit ove?
an tua multifidum numeravit lana Timavum,
  quem pius astrifero Cyllarus ore bibit?
te nec Amyclaeo decuit livere veneno
  nec Miletos erat vellere digna tuo.   10
lilia tu vincis nec adhuc delapsa ligustra
  et Tiburtino monte quod albet ebur;
Spartanus tibi cedet olor Paphiaeque columbae,
  cedet Erythraeis eruta gemma vadis :
sed licet haec primis nivibus sint aemula dona,   15
  non sunt Parthenio candidiora suo.

---

[1] Bacchus, according to myth, made an expedition into
the East, where he taught the conquered nations the use of
the vine. He was represented as drawn by tigers.

her delight. Thy Arena, Caesar, has surpassed Indian
triumphs and the wealth and riches of the victor
god ;[1] for Bacchus, while he drove beneath the yoke
the captive Indians, was content with two tigresses
alone.

XXVII

HE who gives presents, Gaurus, to you, a rich man
and old, if you have wit and sense, says this to
you—"Die."

XXVIII

SAY, Toga, welcome gift to me of my eloquent
friend, of what flock wouldst thou be the fame and
glory? Did the Apulian herbage of Spartan Phalan-
thus flourish for thy sake, where Galaesus[2] floods the
tilth with Calabrian waters? or did Tartessian Baetis,
nurse of Hiberian flocks, wash thee too on the back
of a Spanish sheep?[3] or has thy wool counted the
mouths of many-cleft Timavus, whereof trusty Cyllarus,[4] now amid the stars, once drank? Thee it
beseemed not to darken with Spartan dye, nor was
Miletus worthy to stain thy fleece. Lilies thou
dost outshine, and privet yet unfallen, and the ivory
that gleams white on Tibur's mount; Sparta's swan
shall yield to thee and Paphian doves, there shall
yield the pearl plucked out from Eastern shoals.
Yet, albeit this gift vies with new fallen snow, 'tis
not more dazzling white[5] than Parthenius its giver.

[2] A river near Tarentum founded by the Spartan Phalan-
thus. The district was famed for the fine fleeces of its
sheep: cf. Hor. Od. II. vi. 10.
[3] cf. v. xxxvii. 7. [4] cf. IV. xxv. 6.
[5] An allusion to the etymology of Parthenius' name (παρ-
θένιος = virgin-white).

non ego praetulerim Babylonos picta superbae
    texta Samiramia quae variantur acu ;
non Athamanteo potius me mirer in auro,
    Aeolium dones si mihi, Phrixe, pecus.   20
o quantos risus pariter spectata movebit
    cum Palatina nostra lacerna toga !

XXIX

Disticha qui scribit, puto, vult brevitate placere.
    quid prodest brevitas, dic mihi, si liber est ?

XXX

Qui nunc Caesareae lusus spectatur harenae,
    temporibus Bruti gloria summa fuit.
aspicis ut teneat flammas poenaque fruatur,
    fortis et attonito regnet in igne manus !
ipse sui spectator adest et nobile dextrae   5
    funus amat : totis pascitur illa sacris ;
quod nisi rapta foret nolenti poena, parabat
    saevior in lassos ire sinistra focos.
scire piget post tale decus quid fecerit ante :
    quam vidi satis hanc est mihi nosse manum.   10

XXXI

Nescio quid de te non belle, Dento, fateris,
    coniuge qui ducta iura paterna petis.
sed iam supplicibus dominum lassare libellis
    desine et in patriam serus ab urbe redi :

---

[1] Phryxus' ram with the golden fleece : cf. VI. iii. 6.
[2] A hint for a new cloak.

I could not more prize proud Babylon's painted tapestry embroidered by Semiramis' needle; no more should I admire myself in gold of Athamas, if thou, Phryxus, wert to give me the ram of Aeolus' son.[1] Oh, what laughter will my worn cloak excite seen together with this toga from the Palatine![2]

XXIX

He who writes distichs wishes, I imagine, to please by brevity. What is the use of brevity, tell me, if it constitute a book?

XXX

What now entertains as a spectacle in Caesar's Arena was in Brutus' days their chiefest glory.[3] You see how the hand grasps the flame and relishes its punishment, and bravely lords it amid the astonished fire! His own spectator is he, and he admires his right hand's noble death; in the full sacrifice that hand delights. Had not, against its will, that penalty been denied it, his left hand—fiercer still—was ready to pass to the sated hearth. I care not, after such a feat, to learn what was its crime before: enough for me to have known the prowess of the hand I saw.

XXXI

'Tis not a pretty sort of confession, Dento, you make about yourself, who, after you have married a wife, ask for paternal rights.[4] Cease at last with suppliant petitions to weary our Master, and, though late, return from the city to your own country.

---

[3] cf. X. xxv., where a different view is taken of Mucius' heroism. [4] cf. II. xci. and xcii.

nam dum tu longe deserta uxore diuque   5
  tres quaeris natos, quattuor invenies.

XXXII

AERA per tacitum delapsa sedentis in ipsos
  fluxit Aratullae blanda columba sinus.
luserat hoc casus, nisi inobservata maneret
  permissaque sibi nollet abire fuga.
si meliora piae fas est sperare sorori   5
  et dominum mundi flectere vota valent,
haec a Sardois tibi forsitan exulis oris,
  fratre reversuro, nuntia venit avis.

XXXIII

DE praetoricia folium mihi, Paule, corona
  mittis et hoc phialae nomen habere iubes.
hac fuerat nuper nebula tibi pegma perunctum,
  pallida quam rubri diluit unda croci.
an magis astuti derasa est ungue ministri   5
  brattea, de fulcro quam reor esse tuo ?
illa potest culicem longe sentire volantem
  et minimi pinna papilionis agi ;
exiguae volitat suspensa vapore lucernae
  et leviter fuso rumpitur icta mero.   10
hoc linitur sputo Iani caryota Kalendis,
  quam fert cum parco sordidus asse cliens.

---

[1] Paulus (*cf.* VII. lxxii.) had sent M. a cup of such thin metal that it could hardly be called a cup. An epigram against paltry gifts.

Otherwise, after deserting your wife at such a distance and for so long, while you are seeking three sons you will discover four!

XXXII

GLIDING down through the still air, a winsome dove fluttered into Aretulla's very bosom as she sat. Chance might have played the freak had not the bird stayed, all unguarded, and refused to take the flight permitted to it. If a loving sister may hope for happier things, and prayers avail to move the Master of the World, belike from Sardinia's shores this bird came to thee, the exile's messenger, to herald thy brother's return.

XXXIII

FROM your praetor's crown, Paulus, you send me a leaf and require this to be called a bowl.[1] With this film your platform[2] was lately coated, and the pale stream of red saffron[3] washed it away. Or rather was it a flake—I think, belonging to the leg of your couch—scraped off by the nail of a cunning slave? It can from a distance feel the fluttering of a gnat, and be wafted by the wing of the very smallest butterfly; it floats in air, kept up by the heat of a tiny lamp, and, splashed with wine even lightly sprinkled, it dissolves. With such a layer is coated on the Kalends of January the nut[4] which a shabby client brings as a gift together with small coin. Pliant

[2] cf. *Lib. Spect.* ii. 2.   [3] cf. *Lib. Spect.* iii. 8.
[4] Symbolic gifts, like Easter eggs: cf. XIII. xxvii : **Ov.** *F.* i. 189.

lenta minus gracili crescunt colocasia filo,
  plena magis nimio lilia sole cadunt;
nec vaga tam tenui discurrit aranea tela,   15
tam leve nec bombyx pendulus urget opus.
crassior in facie vetulae stat creta Fabullae,
  crassior offensae bulla tumescit aquae;
fortior et tortos servat vesica capillos   20
  et mutat Latias spuma Batava comas.
hac cite Ledaeo vestitur pullus in ovo,
  talia nnata splenia fronte sedent.
quid tibi cum phiala, ligulam cum mittere possis,
  mittere oe n possis vel cocleare mihi,
(magna nimis loquimur), cocleam cum mittere possis,
  denique cum possis mittere, Paule, nihil?   26

XXXIV

Archetypum Myos argentum te dicis habere.
  quod sine te factum est hoc magis archetypum est?

XXXV

Cum sitis similes paresque vita,
uxor pessima, pessimus maritus,
miror non bene convenire vobis.

XXXVI

Regia pyramidum, Caesar, miracula ride;
  iam tacet Eoum barbara Memphis opus:

---

[1] A kind of soap giving the hair a light hue: cf. XIV.
xxvi.   [2] cf. II. xxix. 9.
[3] An ancient Greek artist, famous for working in silver:
cf. XIV. xcv. He was contemporary with Phidias.

Egyptian beans grow with a less slender filament,
of thicker mould are lily leaves that fall beneath the
overpowering sun; nor does the spider dart about
a web so slender, nor the pendulous silkworm ply
a work so light. Denser stands the chalk on old
Fabulla's face, denser swells the bubble in tumbled
water, and stronger is the bladder-net that confines
knotted locks, and the Batavian pomade [1] that trans-
forms Latin tresses. With skin like this is clothed
the chick in a swan's egg, such are the patches that
rest on a crescent-plastered [2] brow. What use have
you for a bowl when you can send me a tablespoon,
when you can send me even a snail-pick—I am sug-
gesting too great things—when you can send me a
snail-shell : in a word, when you, Paulus, can send
me nothing?

XXXIV

You say you have a piece of silver, a genuine
antique by Mys.[3] Is that which was made without
your assistance any the more an antique? [4]

XXXV

SEEING that you are like one another, and a pair
in your habits, vilest of wives, vilest of husbands,
I wonder you don't agree!

XXXVI

LAUGH, Caesar, at the regal wonders of the Pyramids : now barbaric Memphis speaks not of her

---

[4] Perhaps addressed to a silversmith who was in the habit
of "faking" his antiques. "You may not have faked this,"
says M., "but that does not prove it genuine."

pars quota Parrhasiae labor est Mareoticus aulae !
   clarius in toto nil videt orbe dies.
septenos pariter credas adsurgere montes ;   5
   Thessalicum brevior Pelion Ossa tulit ;
aethera sic intrat nitidis ut conditus astris
   inferiore tonet nube serenus apex
et prius arcano satietur numine Phoebi
   nascentis Circe quam videt ora patris.   10
haec, Auguste, tamen, quae vertice sidera pulsat,
   par domus est caelo sed minor est domino.

XXXVII

Quod Caietano reddis, Polycharme, tabellas,
   milia te centum num tribuisse putas ?
"Debuit haec" inquis. tibi habe, Polycharme, tabellas
   et Caietano milia crede duo.

XXXVIII

Qui praestat pietate pertinaci
sensuro bona liberalitatis,
captet forsitan aut vicem reposcat.
at si quis dare nomini relicto
post manes tumulumque perseverat,   5
quaerit quid nisi parcius dolere ?
refert sis bonus an velis videri.
praestas hoc, Melior, sciente fama,
qui sollemnibus anxius sepulti
nomen non sinis interire Blaesi,   10

---

[1] cf. VII. lvi.
[2] When the giants attempted to scale heaven in their war
with the gods, they piled Pelion upon Ossa, both mountains
in Thessaly.

Eastern work. How small a part of the Palatine hall [1] would Egypt's toil achieve! Nothing so grand the eye of day sees in all the world. You would believe the seven hills uprose all together; Ossa with Thessalian Pelion atop was not so high; [2] Heaven it so pierces that, hidden amid the lustrous stars, its peak echoes sunlit to the thunder in the cloud below, and is sated with Phoebus' mystic power ere Circe [3] views her sire's springing face. And yet, Augustus, this palace that with its pinnacle touches the stars, though level with Heaven, is less than its lord.

XXXVII

BECAUSE, Polycharmus, you return to Caietanus his bond, do you really imagine you have given him a hundred thousand sesterces? "He owed this sum," you say. Keep your bond, Polycharmus, and trust Caietanus with two thousand. [4]

XXXVIII

HE who with constant devotion bestows gifts on one who will feel the bounty's good, fishes perhaps or claims return. But if any man persist in giving to the name that survives death and the tomb, what profit seeks he but assuagement of grief? Wide is the difference 'twixt goodness and pretence. This gift, as fame knows, you, Melior, make; who, in your care, by solemn rites forbid to perish the name of buried Blaesus, and that his birthday should be

---

[3] Daughter of the Sun, which was said to strike first upon her island. Here put for Circeii in Latium.

[4] cf. a similar epigram, IX. cii.

et de munifica profusus arca
ad natalicium diem colendum
scribarum memori piaeque turbae
quod donas, facis ipse Blaesianum.
hoc longum tibi, vita dum manebit, 15
hoc et post cineres erit tributum.

XXXIX

Qui Palatinae caperet convivia mensae
  ambrosiasque dapes non erat ante locus:
hic haurire decet sacrum, Germanice, nectar
  et Ganymedea pocula mixta manu.
esse velis, oro, serus conviva Tonantis: 5
  at tu si properas, Iuppiter, ipse veni.

XL

Non horti neque palmitis beati
sed rari nemoris, Priape, custos,
ex quo natus es et potes renasci,
furaces, moneo, manus repellas
et silvam domini focis reserves: 5
si defecerit haec, et ipse lignum es.

XLI

"Tristis Athenagoras non misit munera nobis
  quae medio brumae mittere mense solet."
an sit Athenagoras tristis, Faustine, videbo:
  me certe tristem fecit Athenagoras.

---

[1] He endows the guild of scribes with a fund out of which

kept, in your lavish bounty out of a princely coffer
to the school of scribes—a company that remembers
him and loves—yourself celebrate a feast to Blaesus.[1]
This shall be your long-enduring tribute while life
shall last, this also after you are dust.

XXXIX

Large enough to hold the revels of the Palatine
board and its ambrosial feasts, was no place hereto-
fore; here it beseems thee, Germanicus, to quaff
thy nectar divine, and cups blent by Ganymede's
hand. May it be late, I beseech thee, that thou
dost consent to be the Thunderer's guest; but do
thou, Jupiter, if thou art impatient, come hither
thyself.

XL

Priapus, guardian, not of parterre or blooming
vine, but of the thin wood wherefrom thou wert
born and canst be born again, keep off, I warn thee,
thievish hands, and preserve my copse for its master's
hearth. If this copse fail, thou also art wood![2]

XLI

"Athenagoras regrets he did not send me the
presents he is used to send in the middle of winter's
month." Whether Athenagoras regrets, Faustinus,
I will consider; me, at any rate, Athenagoras made
regret.

to celebrate annually the birthday of B. "In effect," says
M., "you do this yourself every year."
[2] i.e. and may be burned instead. Horace (Sat. I. viii. 2)
with like flippancy treats Priapus as little better than wood.

XLII

Sī te sportula maior ad beatos
non corruperit, ut solet, licebit
de nostro, Matho, centies laveris.

XLIII

Effert uxores Fabius, Chrestilla maritos,
    funereamque toris quassat uterque facem.
victores committe, Venus: quos iste manebit
    exitus, una duos ut Libitina ferat.

XLIV

Titulle, moneo, vive: semper hoc serum est;
sub paedagogo coeperis licet, serum est.
at tu, miser Titulle, nec senex vivis,
sed omne limen conteris salutator
et mane sudas urbis osculis udus,   5
foroque triplici sparsus ante equos omnis
aedemque Martis et colosson Augusti
curris per omnis tertiasque quintasque.
rape, congere, aufer, posside: relinquendum est.
superba densis arca palleat nummis,   10
centum explicentur paginae Kalendarum:
iurabit heres te nihil reliquisse,
supraque pluteum te iacente vel saxum,
fartus papyro dum tibi torus crescit,
flentis superbus basiabit eunuchos;   15
tuoque tristis filius, velis nolis,
cum concubino nocte dormiet prima.

---

[1] A hundred farthings (*quadrantes*) was the client's usual allowance (*cf.* III. vii. 1), and a *quadrans* was the price of a bath.

XLII

IF greater dole has not, as is usual, bribed you to court wealthy men, you may bathe, Matho, a hundred times at my expense.[1]

XLIII

FABIUS buries his wives, Chrestilla her husbands, and each of them waves the funeral torch over a marriage-bed. Match the victors, Venus; this is the end that will await them—one funeral to convey the pair.

XLIV

TITULLUS, I warn you, live your life: ever this comes late; though you begin under a pedagogue, 'tis late. But you, wretched Titullus, do not live even in old age, but wear out every threshold at levees, and sweat at daybreak beslavered with the kisses of the town; and in the three Forums, mud-bespattered in front of all the Equestrian statues, and the Temple of Mars, and the Colossus[2] of Augustus, you hurry ever from the third to the fifth hours.[3] Plunder, hoard, rob, possess: you must resign it all. Let your proud money-chest be yellow with crowded coins, an hundred pages of debts due on the Kalends be opened, your heir will swear you have left nothing. And even when you are laid out on bier or stone, while, stuffed with papyrus, your pyre is growing high, he will in insolence kiss the weeping eunuchs; and your mourning son, whether you wish it or not, will the first night sleep with your favourite.

[2] A bronze statue of Augustus in the Forum that bore his name.

[3] *i.e.* during the business hours of the day : *cf.* IV. viii. 2, 3.

33

XLV

Priscus ab Aetnaeis mihi, Flacce, Terentius oris
    redditur : hanc lucem lactea gemma notet ;
defluat et lento splendescat turbida lino
    amphora centeno consule facta minor.
continget nox quando meis tam candida mensis ?   5
    tam iusto dabitur quando calere mero ?
cum te, Flacce, mihi reddet Cythereia Cypros,
    luxuriae fiet tam bona causa meae.

XLVI

Quanta tua est probitas tanta est infantia formae,
    Ceste puer, puero castior Hippolyto.
te secum Diana velit doceatque natare,
    te Cybele totum mallet habere Phryge ;[1]
tu Ganymedeo poteras succedere lecto,   5
    sed durus domino basia sola dares.
felix, quae tenerum vexabit sponsa maritum
    et quae te faciet prima puella virum !

XLVII

Pars maxillarum tonsa est tibi, pars tibi rasa est,
    pars vulsa est.   unum quis putet esse caput ?

---

   [1] *Phryge* Brodaeus, *phryga* Codd.   Housman suggests
molli mallet habere Phryge.

              [1] *cf.* XIV. ciii. and civ.

XLV

TERENTIUS PRISCUS is given back to me, Flaccus,
from Etna's shore: this day let a milk-white pearl
mark! and let the wine-jar, shrunken through a
hundred consulships, be outpoured, and its dull-
ness grow bright, slowly strained through linen.[1]
When shall a night so fair again bless my board?
When shall I be allowed to warm with wine so justly
earned? When Cytherean Cyprus shall give thee,
Flaccus, back to me, as good a cause shall arise for
my revelry.

XLVI

EVEN as thy modesty is thy childish grace of form,
boy Cestus, than boy Hippolytus[2] more chaste.
Thee would Diana[3] wish, and teach, to swim with
her, thee, not unmanned, would Cybele prefer to the
Phrygian;[4] thou mightest have succeeded to the bed
of Ganymede,[5] but in thy hardness kisses only
wouldst thou have given thy lord. Happy the bride
that shall provoke her youthful spouse, the maid that
first shall make of thee a man!

XLVII

PART of your jaws are clipped, part is shaved, part
is plucked of hairs. Who would imagine this to be
a single head?

[2] Who rejected the solicitation of his stepmother Phaedra.
[3] The virgin goddess of chastity.
[4] The emasculated Attis: cf. v. xli. 2.
[5] cf. I. vi. 1.

XLVIII

Nescit cui dederit Tyriam Crispinus abollam,
    dum mutat cultus induiturque togam.
quisquis habes, umeris sua munera redde, precamur:
    non hoc Crispinus te sed abolla rogat.
non quicumque capit saturatas murice vestes   5
    nec nisi deliciis convenit iste color.
si te praeda iuvat foedique insania lucri,
    qua possis melius fallere, sume togam.

XLIX

Formosam sane sed caecus diligit Asper.
    plus ergo, ut res est, quam videt Asper amat.

L

Quanta Gigantei memoratur mensa triumphi
    quantaque nox superis omnibus illa fuit,
qua bonus accubuit genitor cum plebe deorum
    et licuit Faunis poscere vina Iovem,
tanta tuas celebrant, Caesar, convivia laurus;   5
    exhilarant ipsos gaudia nostra deos.
vescitur omnis eques tecum populusque patresque
    et capit ambrosias cum duce Roma dapes.
grandia pollicitus quanto maiora dedisti!
    promissa est nobis sportula, recta data est.   10

---

[1] A well-known fop: *cf. Cum verna Canopi | Crispinus,
Tyrias humero revocante lacernas*: Juv. i. 27.

XLVIII

CRISPINUS[1] does not know to whom he gave his Tyrian cloak while he was changing his dress and putting on his toga. Whoever you are who have it, restore to his shoulders their own endowment, we beg you : Crispinus does not ask this of you, but the cloak does. Not everyone sets off a robe steeped in purple : only daintiness that colour suits. If looting attract you, and a mad rage for disgraceful gain, to escape notice the better, select a toga ![2]

XLIX

ASPER loves a woman who is undoubtedly lovely, but he is blind; so Asper, as the fact is, loves more than he sees.[3]

L

GREAT as was the storied feast for triumph over the Giants, and great as was to all the High gods that night on which the good Sire reclined at table with the common crowd of gods, and Fauns had licence to call on Jove for wine ; so great a banquet, Caesar, celebrates thy laurels won : our joys make glad the very gods themselves. Every knight feasts along with thee, the people too, and the Fathers, and Rome together with her Chief partakes ambrosial fare. Large things didst thou promise : how much greater hast thou given ! A dole was promised us, a banquet has been given.

[2] As being universal wear.
[3] cf. v. xv.

LI

Quis labor in phiala? docti Myos anne Myronos?
  Mentoris haec manus est an, Polyclite, tua?
livescit nulla caligine fusca nec odit
  exploratores, nubila massa, focos.
vera minus flavo radiant electra metallo   5
  et niveum felix pustula vincit ebur.
materiae non cedit opus: sic alligat orbem,
  plurima cum tota lampade luna nitet.
stat caper Aeolio Thebani vellere Phrixi
  cultus: ab hoc mallet vecta fuisse soror;   10
hunc nec Cinyphius tonsor violaverit et tu
  ipse tua pasci vite, Lyaee, velis.
terga premit pecudis geminis Amor aureus alis;
  Palladius tenero lotos ab ore sonat:
sic Methymnaeo gavisus Arione delphin   15
  languida non tacitum per freta vexit onus.
imbuat egregium digno mihi nectare munus
  non grege de domini sed tua, Ceste, manus;
Ceste, decus mensae, misce Setina: videtur
  ipse puer nobis, ipse sitire caper.   20
det numerum cyathis Istanti[1] littera Rufi:
  auctor enim tanti muneris ille mihi:

---

[1] *Istanti* Munro, *instanti* β, *instantis* γ.

---

[1] All Greek artists of past days, renowned for chasing or
sculpture.
[2] The golden fleece of the ram that bore Phryxus and
Helle over the sea: *cf.* VIII. xxviii. 20.   [3] *cf.* VII. xcv. 13.

LI

WHOSE labour is in the bowl? was it of artist
Mys or of Myron? Is this Mentor's hand, or, Polyclitus, thine?[1] No darkness gives it a dull leaden
hue, nor is it a cloudy mass that shrinks from as-
saying fires. True amber is less radiant than its
yellow ore, and the fine frosted silver surpasses snow-
white ivory. The workmanship yields not to the
material: even so the moon rounds her orb when
she shines in fullness with all her light. There
stands a he-goat prankt in the Aeolian fleece of
Theban Phryxus[2]; by such his sister would more
gladly have been borne; such a goat no Cinyphian
barber[3] would deform, and thou thyself, Lyaeus,
wouldst consent to his cropping thine own vine.[4] A
Love in gold, two-winged, loads the back of the beast;
the pipe of Pallas sounds from his tender lips; in
such wise the dolphin, blithe with the burden of
Methymnaean Arion,[5] bore him, no unmelodious
freight, o'er tranquil seas. Let no hand from the
master's crowd of slaves, only thy hand, Cestus,
first fill this peerless gift for me with fitting nectar;
Cestus, the banquet's pride, mix thou the Setine:
the very boy, the very goat, methinks, is athirst. Let
the letters of Istantius Rufus'[6] name assign their
number to our measures of wine,[7] for he was the
source to me of so proud a gift. If Telethusa come,

---

[4] Juv. alludes to this : i. 76 (*stantem extra pocula caprum*).

[5] A celebrated harpist, who, to escape the crew of the
vessel carrying him to Corinth with his wealth, leaped, it is
said, into the sea after playing a last time on his harp : *cf.*
Herod. i. 23, 24.

[6] A friend of M.: *cf.* VIII. lxxiii. 1.

[7] As to this practice, *cf.* IX. xciii. 8 ; XI. xxxvi. 8.

si Telethusa venit promissaque gaudia portat,
    servabor dominae, Rufe, triente tuo ;
si dubia est, septunce trahar ; si fallit amantem,   25
    ut iugulem curas, nomen utrumque bibam.

LII

Tonsorem puerum sed arte talem
qualis nec Thalamus fuit Neronis,
Drusorum cui contigere barbae,
aequandas semel ad genas rogatus
Rufo, Caediciane, commodavi.   5
dum iussus repetit pilos eosdem,
censura speculi manum regente,
expingitque cutem facitque longam
detonsis epaphaeresin capillis,
barbatus mihi tonsor est reversus.   10

LIII

Formosissima quae fuere vel sunt,
sed vilissima quae fuere vel sunt,
o quam te fieri, Catulla, vellem
formosam minus aut magis pudicam !

LIV

Magna licet totiens tribuas, maiora daturus
    dona, ducum victor, victor et ipse tui,
diligeris populo non propter praemia, Caesar,
    te propter populus praemia, Caesar, amat.

---

[1] cf. I. cvi.

[2] M. intends to drink to the vocative, i.e. Rufe, Istanti, etc.

[3] Probably the Emperors Claudius and Nero, who bore this
name before they became Emperors.

and bring her promised joys, I will keep myself for
my mistress, Rufus, by drinking your four measures;[1]
if she be doubtful, I shall while away the time by
seven; if she fail her lover, then, to throttle care, I
will drink both your names.[2]

LII

A BARBER, young, but such an artist as not even
was Nero's Thalamus, to whom fell the beards of the
Drusi,[3] I lent, on his request, Caedicianus, to Rufus
to smooth his cheeks once. While at command he
was going over the same hairs, guiding his hand by
the judgment of the mirror, and rougeing the
skin, and making a second thorough clip of the
close-cut hair, my barber returned to me with a
beard.[4]

LIII

MOST beautiful of all women who have been or
are, but vilest of all who have been or are,[5] oh, how I
could wish, Catulla, you could become less beautiful
or more pure!

LIV

ALBEIT thou givest so oft great gifts, and shalt
give greater, O thou victor over Captains and victor
withal over thyself,[6] thou art loved by the people,
Caesar, not because of thy boons; 'tis because of
thee, Caesar, the people loves thy boons.

---

[4] *cf.* VII. lxxxiii.
[5] An echo of the style of Catullus: *cf.* xxi. 2 and xxiv. 2.
[6] *i.e.* whose virtues (or bounties) increase day by day.

LV

AUDITUR quantum Massyla per avia murmur,
    innumero quotiens silva leone furit,
pallidus attonitos ad Poena mapalia pastor
    cum revocat tauros et sine mente pecus,
tantus in Ausonia fremuit modo terror harena.   5
    quis non esse gregem crederet ? unus erat ;
sed cuius tremerent ipsi quoque iura leones,
    cui diadema daret marmore picta Nomas.
o quantum per colla decus, quem sparsit honorem
    aurea lunatae, cum stetit, umbra iubae !   10
grandia quam decuit latum venabula pectus
    quantaque de magna gaudia morte tulit !
unde tuis, Libye, tam felix gloria silvis ?
    a Cybeles numquid venerat ille iugo ?
an magis Herculeo, Germanice, misit ab astro   15
    hanc tibi vel frater vel pater ipse feram ?

LVI

TEMPORIBUS nostris aetas cum cedat avorum
    creverit et maior cum duce Roma suo,
ingenium sacri miraris desse Maronis
    nec quemquam tanta bella sonare tuba.
sint Maecenates, non derunt, Flacce, Marones   5
    Vergiliumque tibi vel tua rura dabunt.
iugera perdiderat miserae vicina Cremonae
    flebat et abductas Tityrus aeger oves :
risit Tuscus eques paupertatemque malignam
    reppulit et celeri iussit abire fuga.   10

---

[1] *i.e.* in the presence of the emperor.
[2] A yoke of lions was the sign of Cybele.

LV

Loud as is heard the roar through Massylian wilds, oft as the woodland riots with countless lion-hordes, what time the pale shepherd recalls to his Punic stead the startled bulls and flock dismayed, so great a terror roared but now on Ausonia's sand. Who but would deem it a herd? 'Twas a single beast, but one whose laws even the very lions would tremble at, to whom marble-dight Numidia would assign a crown. Oh, what glory, what dignity did not the tawny cloud of his curved mane, when it stood erect, shed upon his neck! How that broad breast became mighty spears, and how great joy he won by his noble death![1] Whence came, Libya, so blest an honour to thy woods? Had he come down from Cybele's yoke?[2] Or rather, did thy brother, Germanicus, or thy sire himself, send down this beast from Hercules' star?[3]

LVI

Although our grandsires' age yields to our own times, and Rome has waxed greater in company with her chief, you wonder divine Maro's genius is seen no more, and that no man with such a trump as his blows loud of war. Let there be many a Maecenas, many a Maro, Flaccus, will not fail, and even your fields will give you a Virgil. Tityrus,[4] sick at heart, had lost his lands nigh ill-starred Cremona, and was weeping for his plundered sheep: the Tuscan knight smiled, and dispelled malignant poverty, and bade it go in hurried

---

[3] Had Titus or Vespasian, now gods, sent down the Nemean lion slain by Hercules from the constellation Leo? *cf.* IV. lvii. 5.　　[4] Representing Virgil in the *Bucolics*.

"Accipe divitias et vatum maximus esto;
  tu licet et nostrum" dixit "Alexin ames."
adstabat domini mensis pulcherrimus ille
  marmorea fundens nigra Falerna manu,
et libata dabat roseis carchesia labris   15
  quae poterant ipsum sollicitare Iovem.
excidit attonito pinguis Galatea poetae,
  Thestylis et rubras messibus usta genas;
protinus "Italiam" concepit et "Arma virumque,"
  qui modo vix Culicem fleverat ore rudi.   20
quid Varios Marsosque loquar ditataque vatum
  nomina, magnus erit quos numerare labor?
ergo ego Vergilius, si munera Maecenatis
  des mihi? Vergilius non ero, Marsus ero.

LVII

Tres habuit dentes, pariter quos expuit omnes,
  ad tumulum Picens dum sedet ipse suum;
collegitque sinu fragmenta novissima laxi
  oris et adgesta contumulavit humo.
ossa licet quondam defuncti non legat heres: 5
  hoc sibi iam Picens praestitit officium.

LVIII

Cum tibi tam crassae sint, Artemidore, lacernae,
  possim te Sagarim iure vocare meo.

LIX

Aspicis hunc uno contentum lumine, cuius
  lippa sub adtrita fronte lacuna patet?

---

[1] *cf.* v. xvi. 12.
[2] Characters in the *Bucolics.*

flight. "Take wealth, and be greatest of bards:
you," he said, "may love even my Alexis."[1] That
boy most fair was standing by his master's board,
pouring the dark Falernian with hand marble-fair,
and offered the beaker tasted first by his rosy lips,
lips that might tempt Jove himself. Plump Galatea[2]
fell away from the inspired bard and Thestylis[2] with
her cheeks burnt red by harvest; at once "Italy"
he conceived, and "Arms and the man,"[3] he who
but now in song untrained had with effort wept for
a gnat.[4] Why should I speak of Variuses and Mar-
suses, and tell the names of poets enriched, whom
'twere a long task to number? Shall I then be a
Virgil if you give me the gifts of a Maecenas? I
shall not be a Virgil, a Marsus[5] shall I be.

LVII

PICENS had three teeth, all of which he spat out
at once as he was sitting by his own tomb; and he
gathered up in his lap the latest fragments of his
loosened jaws, and entombed them in piled-up earth.
His heir some day need not gather up the dead
man's bones: that office Picens has already per-
formed for himself.

LVIII

SEEING that your cloaks, Artemidorus, are so thick,
I might rightly call you Sagaris.[6]

LIX

You see this fellow who puts up with one eye,
under whose shameless brow a sightless socket gapes?

[3] Italy = *Georgics*, "arms, etc." = *Aeneid*.
[4] *Culex*, an early poem.   [5] *cf.* IV. xxix. 8.
[6] A play on words. *Sagum* was a thick military cloak.

ne contemne caput, nihil est furacius illo ;
    non fuit Autolyci tam piperata manus.
hunc tu convivam cautus servare memento :   5
    tunc furit atque oculo luscus utroque videt.
pocula solliciti perdunt ligulasque ministri
    et latet in tepido plurima mappa sinu ;
lapsa nec a cubito subducere pallia nescit
    et tectus laenis saepe duabus abit ;   10
nec dormitantem vernam fraudare lucerna
    erubuit fallax, ardeat illa licet.
si nihil invasit, puerum tunc arte dolosa
    circuit et soleas subripit ipse suas.

LX

Summa Palatini poteras aequare Colossi,
    si fieres brevior, Claudia, sesquipede.

LXI

Livet Charinus, rumpitur, furit, plorat
et quaerit altos unde pendeat ramos :
non iam quod orbe cantor et legor toto,
nec umbilicis quod decorus et cedro
spargor per omnes Roma quas tenet gentes,   5
sed quod sub urbe rus habemus aestivum
vehimurque mulis non ut ante conductis.
quid inprecabor, o Severe, liventi ?
hoc opto : mulas habeat et suburbanum.

---

[1] The son of Mercury, patron of thieves, and himself the typical thief.

Don't despise the man, he is thievishness itself; Auto-lycus'[1] hand was not so sharp. When he is your guest remember to watch him carefully : then he runs amok and, though one-eyed, sees with either. Cups and dessert-spoons the anxious servants lose, and there lurks many a napkin in his warm bosom ; nor is he ignorant how to withdraw by stealth even the mantle slipt from your elbow, and often he goes away clad in two cloaks ; and the cunning thief does not blush to rob a sleeping home-born slave of his lamp, although it is alight. If he has seized nothing, then with crafty skill he circumvents his slave and filches his very own slippers !

LX

You might reach to the top of the Palatine Colossus[2] if you, Claudia, were to grow shorter by a foot and a half.

LXI

CHARINUS is green with envy, is bursting, raging, weeping, and is looking out for high boughs to hang himself from ; not now because I am acclaimed and read through the whole world, nor because, smart with bosses and cedar oil, I am spread abroad over all the nations Rome sways, but because I have in the suburbs a summer country house, and am drawn by mules no longer, as before, hired. What curse shall I utter, Severus, on his green looks ? I wish him this : let him possess mules and a suburban property ![3]

[2] cf. Lib. Spect. ii. 1.
[3] With all their worries.

LXII

SCRIBIT in aversa Picens epigrammata charta,
  et dolet averso quod facit illa deo.

LXIII

THESTYLON Aulus amat sed nec minus ardet Alexin,
  forsitan et nostrum nunc Hyacinthon amat.
i nunc et dubita vates an diligat ipsos,
  delicias vatum cum meus Aulus amet.

LXIV

UT poscas, Clyte, munus exigasque,
uno nasceris octiens in anno
et solas, puto, tresve quattuorve
non natalicias habes Kalendas.
sit vultus tibi levior licebit   5
tritis litoris aridi lapillis,
sit moro coma nigrior caduco,
vincas mollitia tremente plumas
aut massam modo lactis alligati,
et talis tumor excitet papillas   10
qualis cruda viro puella servat,
tu nobis, Clyte, iam senex videris:
tam multos quis enim fuisse credat
natalis Priamive Nestorisve?
sit tandem pudor et modus rapinis.   15
quod si ludis adhuc semelque nasci
uno iam tibi non sat est in anno,
natum te, Clyte, nec semel putabo.

---

[1] Phoebus, who inspires poets.

LXII

PICENS writes epigrams on the backside of his paper, and complains that when he does so the god [1] turns his.

LXIII

AULUS is fond of Thestylus, and has no less warmth for Alexis; perhaps now he is fond of my Hyacinthus too. Go, now! doubt after that whether my friend Aulus loves the poets themselves, seeing that he loves poets' favourites.

LXIV

THAT you may demand, Clytus, and exact a present, you are born eight times in a single year, and only three or four Kalends, I think, you do not keep as birthdays. Smoother though your face be than the dry beach's wave-worn pebbles, blacker your hair than a mulberry ripe to fall, though you surpass feathers in fluttering softness, or a lump of newly curdled milk, and though such a rounded fullness swells a breast as the virgin bride keeps for her spouse, yet you seem to us, Clytus, already old; for who would believe so many birthdays were Priam's or Nestor's? Let there be at length some decent limit and measure to your rapine. But if you still play with us, and a single birth in one year is now not sufficient for you, I shall regard you, Clytus, as not having been born even once. [2]

[2] "To regard a person as not born" was a common phrase to express that the person alluded to was a nobody: *cf.* IV. lxxxiii. 4; x. xxvii. 4; Petr. 58

LXV

Hic ubi Fortunae Reducis fulgentia late
   templa nitent, felix area nuper erat:
hic stetit Arctoi formosus pulvere belli
   purpureum fundens Caesar ab ore iubar:
hic lauru redimita comas et candida cultu   5
   Roma salutavit voce manuque ducem.
grande loci meritum testantur et altera dona:
   stat sacer et domitis gentibus arcus ovat.
hic gemini currus numerant elephanta frequentem,
   sufficit inmensis aureus ipse iugis.   10
haec est digna tuis, Germanice, porta triumphis;
   hos aditus urbem Martis habere decet.

LXVI

Augusto pia tura victimasque
pro vestro date Silio, Camenae.
bis senos iubet en redire fasces,
nato consule, nobilique virga
vatis Castaliam domum sonare   5
rerum prima salus et una Caesar.
gaudenti superest adhuc quod optet,
felix purpura tertiusque consul.
Pompeio dederit licet senatus
et Caesar genero sacros honores,   10
quorum pacificus ter ampliavit
Ianus nomina, Silius frequentes
mavult sic numerare consulatus.

---

[1] A temple was built to *Fortuna Redux* in honour of
Domitian's Sarmatian campaign.

[2] The temple of Fortuna Redux being the other.

[3] The lictor, escorting the consul to his house, struck on
the door with his staff: Liv. vi. 34.

LXV

HERE, where far-gleaming shines the fane of Fortune that gives return,[1] was of late, happy in its lot, an open space; here, graced by the dust of Northern war, stood Caesar, shedding from his face effulgent light; here, her locks wreathed with bay, and white of vesture, Rome with voice and hand greeted her Chief. A second gift, too,[2] attests the high merit of the spot: a consecrated arch stands in triumph over the conquered nations; here stand two chariots and many an elephant; he himself in gold is master of the mighty cars. This gate, Germanicus, is worthy of thy triumphs: such an approach it beseems the City of Mars to possess.

LXVI

To Augustus bring, ye Camenae, pious incense and victims on behalf of your Silius. Lo! by a son's consulship Caesar, our chief and only ward, bids the twice six axes return, and the door of the poet sire resound to the lictor's noble staff.[3] Yet this remains for his joy to wish for, the blessed purple of a third consul.[4] Though to Pompeius the senate, to his son-in-law[5] Caesar, gave sacred honours, and peaceful Janus thrice enrolled their names,[6] yet *thus* would Silius rather reckon repeated consulships.

[4] M. hopes that Silius' second son (who, however, died shortly afterwards) may become consul, three consulships thus falling to one house. The father was consul A.D. 68. VII. lxiii. 9.

[5] Agrippa, who married Julia, Augustus' daughter.

[6] The consular Fasti were kept in the Temple of Janus.

LXVII

Horas quinque puer nondum tibi nuntiat, et tu
　　iam conviva mihi, Caeciliane, venis,
cum modo distulerint raucae vadimonia quartae
　　et Floralicias lasset harena feras.
curre, age, et inlotos revoca, Calliste, ministros;　5
　　sternantur lecti: Caeciliane, sede.
caldam poscis aquam: nondum mihi frigida venit;
　　alget adhuc nudo clusa culina foco.
mane veni potius; nam cur te quinta moretur?
　　ut iantes, sero, Caeciliane, venis.　　　　10

LXVIII

Qui Corcyraei vidit pomaria regis,
　　rus, Entelle, tuae praeferet ille domus.
invida purpureos urat ne bruma racemos
　　et gelidum Bacchi munera frigus edat,
condita perspicua vivit vindemia gemma　　　5
　　et tegitur felix nec tamen uva latet:
femineum lucet sic per bombycina corpus,
　　calculus in nitida sic numeratur aqua.
quid non ingenio voluit natura licere?
　　autumnum sterilis ferre iubetur hiemps.　　10

---

[1] cf. IV. viii. 2.
[2] i.e. adjourned the court. *Vadimonia* were bonds required of the parties to a suit to ensure their appearance.

LXVII

THE boy does not yet announce to you the fifth hour, and yet you, Caecilianus, come already as my guest, although the fourth hour, hoarse with pleading,[1] has only just enlarged the bail-bonds,[2] and the arena still wearies the wild beasts at Flora's games.[3] Come, run, Callistus, and call back the unwashed servants; let the couches be spread: Caecilianus, sit down. You ask for warm water: my cold has not yet arrived;[4] my kitchen is closed and chill, its fire unlaid. Come rather at daybreak; for why should the fifth hour keep you waiting? For a breakfast you come late, Caecilianus.

LXVIII

HE who has seen the orchards of Corcyra's king[5] will prefer, Entellus, the country your house contains. That jealous winter may not sear the purple clusters, and chill frost consume the gifts of Bacchus, your vineyard blooms shut in transparent glass, and the fortunate grape is roofed and yet unhid. So shine a woman's limbs through silk, so is the pebble counted in pellucid water. What power has not Nature wished for mind? Barren winter is bidden to bear autumn's fruits.[6]

---

[3] Hares and goats were hunted in the arena at the *Ludi Florales*.

[4] M. had no water laid on to his house: *cf.* IX. xix.

[5] Alcinous: *cf.* VII. xlii. 6.

[6] *cf.* a similar epigram, VIII. xiv.

LXIX

MIRARIS veteres, Vacerra, solos
nec laudas nisi mortuos poetas.
ignoscas petimus, Vacerra : tanti
non est, ut placeam tibi, perire.

LXX

QUANTA quies placidi tantast facundia Nervae,
  sed cohibet vires ingeniumque pudor.
cum siccare sacram largo Permessida posset
  ore, verecundam maluit esse sitim,
Pieriam tenui frontem redimire corona   5
  contentus, famae nec dare vela suae.
sed tamen hunc nostri scit temporis esse Tibullum,
  carmina qui docti nota Neronis habet.

LXXI

QUATTUOR argenti libras mihi tempore brumae
  misisti ante annos, Postumiane, decem ;
speranti plures (nam stare aut crescere debent
  munera) venerunt plusve minusve duae ;
tertius et quartus multo inferiora tulerunt ;   5
  libra fuit quinto Septiciana quidem ;
besalem ad scutulam sexto pervenimus anno ;
  post hunc in cotula rasa selibra data est ;

---

[1] Afterwards emperor. His poetical ability is also alluded
to in IX. xxvi.

LXIX

You admire, Vacerra, the ancients alone, and praise
none but dead poets. Your pardon, pray, Vacerra:
it is not worth my while, merely to please you, to
die.

LXX

GREAT as is the restraint, so great is the eloquence
of placid Nerva,[1] but modesty restrains his power
and genius. Though he might have drained sacred
Permessis[2] in full draughts, he chose to slake his
thirst with diffidence, content to wreathe his poet's
brow with a slender crown, and to leave his sail
unspread to the breeze of his own fame. Yet that
he is the Tibullus of our time each man knows who
keeps in mind the lays of learned Nero.[3]

LXXI

FOUR pounds of silver plate in winter's season you
sent me, Postumianus, ten years ago. While I hoped
for a greater weight—for gifts should stand fixed or
grow—there arrived two pounds more or less. The
third and the fourth year brought much inferior
presents: in the fifth was one pound, Septicius'[4]
work to boot. I came down to an eight-ounce
oblong dish in the sixth year; the next was given
me a bare half-pound in the shape of a small cup.

---

[2] A fountain (also called Aganippe) sacred to the Muses,
and arising in Mt. Helicon.

[3] Nero is said to have called Nerva his Tibullus.

[4] *i.e.* inferior: *cf.* IV. lxxxviii. 3.

octavus ligulam misit sextante minorem;
　　nonus acu levius vix cocleare tulit.　　　　　　10
quod mittat nobis decumus iam non habet annus:
　　quattuor ad libras, Postumiane, redi.

LXXII

Nondum murice cultus asperoque
　　morsu pumicis aridi politus
　　Arcanum properas sequi, libelle,
　　quem pulcherrima iam redire Narbo,
　　docti Narbo Paterna Votieni,　　　　　　5
　　ad leges iubet annuosque fasces:
　　votis quod paribus tibi petendum est,
　　continget locus ille et hic amicus.
　　quam vellem fieri meus libellus!

LXXIII

Istanti, quo nec sincerior alter habetur
　　pectore nec nivea simplicitate prior,
si dare vis nostrae vires animosque Thaliae
　　et victura petis carmina, da quod amem.
Cynthia te vatem fecit, lascive Properti;　　　　5
　　ingenium Galli pulchra Lycoris erat;
fama est arguti Nemesis formosa Tibulli;
　　Lesbia dictavit, docte Catulle, tibi:
non me Paeligni nec spernet Mantua vatem,
　　si qua Corinna mihi, si quis Alexis erit.　　　　10

---

[1] The full name appears to have been Colonia Julia Paterna
Narbo Marcia, now Narbonne. It was the capital of Gallia
Narbonensis.

The eighth sent me a dessert-spoon less than two ounces weight: the ninth produced—with difficulty —a snail-pick lighter than a needle. The tenth year now has nothing to send me: to your four pounds, Postumianus, return.

LXXII

THOUGH you are not yet smart with purple and smoothed by the rough bite of dry pumice, you haste, little book, to follow Arcanus, whom most lovely Narbo—Narbo Paterna[1] of the learned Votienus—now bids return to declare the laws and to yearly office. 'Twill be your lot—to be sued for with equal prayers—to see that spot and to have this friend. How I wish I could become my own little book !

LXXIII

ISTANTIUS,[2] than whom none other is held more true of heart, before whom is none in pure sincerity, if thou wouldst give strength and spirit to my Muse, and lookest for poems that shall live, give me something to love. 'Twas Cynthia made thee a poet, wanton Propertius; of Gallus the inspiration was fair Lycoris; tuneful Tibullus' renown sprang from lovely Nemesis; Lesbia prompted thee, learned Catullus. The Pelignians[3] will not spurn me, nor Mantua,[4] as a bard, if some Corinna, if some Alexis be my own.

---

[2] Istantius Rufus: *cf.* VIII. li. 21.
[3] Countrymen of Ovid.
[4] Birthplace of Virgil.

LXXIV

Oplomachus nunc es, fueras opthalmicus ante.
  fecisti medicus quod facis oplomachus.

LXXV

Dum repetit sera conductos nocte penates
  Lingonus a Tecta Flaminiaque recens,
expulit offenso vitiatum pollice talum
  et iacuit toto corpore fusus humi.
quid faceret Gallus, qua se ratione moveret?   5
  ingenti domino servulus unus erat,
tam macer ut minimam posset vix ferre lucernam :
  succurrit misero casus opemque tulit.
quattuor inscripti portabant vile cadaver,
  accipit infelix qualia mille rogus ;   10
hos comes invalidus summissa voce precatur,
  ut quocumque velint corpus inane ferant :
permutatur onus stipataque tollitur alte
  grandis in angusta sarcina sandapila.
hic mihi de multis unus, Lucane, videtur   15
  cui merito dici "mortue Galle" potest.

LXXVI

"Dic verum mihi, Marce, dic amabo ;
  nil est quod magis audiam libenter."
sic et cum recitas tuos libellos,
  et causam quotiens agis clientis,

---

¹ *cf.* similar epigrams, I. xxx. and xlvii.
² *cf.* III. v. 5.

LXXIV

You are now a gladiator: you were an eye-specialist before. You did as doctor what you do now as gladiator.[1]

LXXV

WHILE late at night a Lingonian—just returning from the Covered[2] and Flaminian Ways—was making for his hired lodging, catching his big toe, he put out his ankle, and lay upset all his length on the ground. What should the Gaul do? how could he move? The huge master had a single tiny slave, so thin that he could barely carry the smallest lantern: chance came to the rescue of the wretched man, and brought aid. Four branded slaves were carrying a common corpse—the pauper's burying-ground receives a thousand such—these slaves the weak attendant besought in a low voice to shift the lifeless body wherever they wished. The load is changed and the cargo is lifted high and crammed in—a huge cargo in a narrow bier. This fellow seems to me, Lucanus, to be the one of many to whom can justly be said, "Oh dead Gaul."[3]

LXXVI

"TELL me the truth, Marcus, tell me, please: there is nothing I would more gladly hear." Such, Gallicus, both when you recite your poems and whenever you plead a client's cause is your prayer

[3] "*Mortue Galle*" was the refrain of the verses with which the *retiarius* (net-caster) used to provoke his opponent, the *mirmillo* (who wore a Gaulish helmet).

oras, Gallice, me rogasque semper.   5
durum est me tibi quod petis negare.
vero verius ergo quid sit audi :
verum, Gallice, non libenter audis.

LXXVII

Liber, amicorum dulcissima cura tuorum,
  Liber, in aeterna vivere digne rosa,
si sapis, Assyrio semper tibi crinis amomo
  splendeat et cingant florea serta caput ;
candida nigrescant vetulo crystalla Falerno   5
  et caleat blando mollis amore torus.
qui sic vel medio finitus vixit in aevo,
  longior huic facta est quam data vita fuit.

LXXVIII

Quos cuperet Phlegraea suos victoria ludos,
  Indica quos cuperet pompa, Lyaee, tuos,
fecit Hyperborei celebrator Stella triumphi,
  o pudor ! o pietas ! et putat esse parum.
non illi satis est turbato sordidus auro   5
  Hermus et Hesperio qui sonat orbe Tagus.
omnis habet sua dona dies : nec linea dives
  cessat et in populum multa rapina cadit ;
nunc veniunt subitis lasciva nomismata nimbis,
  nunc dat spectatas tessera larga feras,   10
nunc implere sinus securos gaudet et absens
  sortitur dominos, ne laceretur, avis.

---

[1] cf. a very similar epigram, v. lxiii.

[2] For a similar sentiment, cf. x. xxiii. 7, 8.

[3] The victory of the gods over the giants in the Phlegraean
Plains in Campania : cf. VIII. l. 1.

and request to me continually. It is hard for me to refuse what you want. Hear, then, what is truer than truth; truth, Gallicus, you do not willingly hear.[1]

LXXVII

LIBER, of thy friends the care most sweet, Liber, worthy to live amid deathless roses, if thou art wise, let thy locks glisten alway with Assyrian balm and chaplets of flowers encircle thy head; let thy clear crystal darken with old Falernian, and thy soft couch warm with love's endearments. Whoever has so lived, to him, even did the end come in middle age, life has been made longer than was appointed.[2]

LXXVIII

SPORTS which a Phlegraean victory[3] might have craved for its own, which thy Indian pageant, Lyaeus,[4] might have craved to be thine, Stella, honouring the Northern triumph, has given; and yet—what modesty is his, what loyalty !—he holds them too small. Not for him suffices the wealth of Hermus, dark with tumbled gold, and of Tagus echoing in the Western world. Each day provides its own gifts; the cord's rich burden[5] fails not, and full-laden spoil falls upon the people; now come in sudden showers sportive tokens;[6] now the bounteous ticket assigns the beasts of the arena; now the bird is glad to fill a lap that gives it safety, and—that it be not torn asunder—

---

[4] cf. VIII. xxvi. 7.
[5] A cord hung with gifts for the populace.
[6] Entitling the holder to receive presents.

61

quid numerem currus ter denaque praemia palmae,
  quae dare non semper consul uterque solet?
omnia sed, Caesar, tanto superantur honore,   15
  quod spectatorem te tua laurus habet.

LXXIX

Omnis aut vetulas habes amicas
aut turpis vetulisque foediores.
has ducis comites trahisque tecum
per convivia porticus theatra.
sic formosa, Fabulla, sic puella es.   5

LXXX

Sanctorum nobis miracula reddis avorum
  nec pateris, Caesar, saecula cana mori,
cum veteres Latiae ritus renovantur harenae
  et pugnat virtus simpliciore manu.
sic priscis servatur honos te praeside templis   5
  et casa tam culto sub Iove numen habet;
sic nova dum condis, revocas, Auguste, priora:
  debentur quae sunt quaeque fuere tibi.

---

¹ Birds are, instead of being scrambled for and so torn to
pieces, assigned by lot. Statius (*Sylv.* I. vi. 75 *seq.*) describes
one of Domitian's Saturnalian shows, where huge clouds of
birds descend "*subito volatu*" among the people, birds supposed by Verrall (*Lit. Essays*, 82) to have been toy ones with
tickets for presents attached.

wins, while apart, by lot its owner.[1] Why should I
count the chariots, and victory's thrice ten prizes,
which both consuls are not always wont to give?[2]
But all, Caesar, is surpassed by this great glory, that
thy triumph hath thee a spectator.

LXXIX

ALL the female friends you have are either old
crones or ugly, and fouler than old crones. These, as
your companions, you conduct and drag about with
you through parties, colonnades, theatres. In this
way, Fabulla, you are lovely, in this way young.

LXXX

THOU restorest to us, Caesar, the wonders of our
honoured grandsires' age, and lettest not the times
of old die, now that the ancient fashions of the
Latin arena are renewed and valour fights with
more natural hand.[3] So also for the old-world fanes
is kept their honour while thou art Governor, and
the Cot[4] under a Jove so worshipped keeps its
sanctity ;[5] so, while thou dost found the new, thou
bringest back, Augustus, the former things : what is,
and what was, are owed to thee !

---

[2] There were thirty races. The consuls exhibited games
on their entrance into office.

[3] Domitian had restored pugilism in the amphitheatre.

[4] The Cot (*Casa Romuli*) was a straw-thatched cottage on
the Palatine, and was revered as the legendary dwelling of
the Founder of Rome : *cf.* Virg. *Aen.* viii. 654.

[5] Jove is magnificently honoured, yet the humble Cot is
hallowed.

LXXXI

Non per mystica sacra Dindymenes
nec per Niliacae bovem iuvencae,
nullos denique per deos deasque
iurat Gellia, sed per uniones.
hos amplectitur, hos perosculatur,   5
hos fratres vocat, hos vocat sorores,
hos natis amat acrius duobus.
his si quo careat misella casu,
victuram negat esse se nec horam.
eheu, quam bene nunc, Papiriane,   10
Annaei faceret manus Sereni!

LXXXII

Dante tibi turba querulos, Auguste, libellos
  nos quoque quod domino carmina parva damus,
posse deum rebus pariter Musisque vacare
  scimus et haec etiam serta placere tibi.
fer vates, Auguste, tuos: nos gloria dulcis,   5
  nos tua cura prior deliciaeque sumus.
non quercus te sola decet nec laurea Phoebi:
  fiat et ex hedera civica nostra tibi.

---

[1] Apis, the sacred Egyptian bull, representing Osiris, the husband of Isis, who was represented as a heifer: *cf.* II. xiv. 8.

[2] An obscure allusion. Perhaps S. was notoriously a wearer of pearls. Some commentators take him for a noted thief. But M. would then hardly have mentioned his name.

[3] Domitian had himself written poetry before he became emperor.

LXXXI

Not by the mystic rites of Dindymene, nor by the bull,[1] the spouse of Nile's heifer, in a word by no gods and goddesses does Gellia swear, but by her pearls. These she hugs, these she kisses passionately, these she calls her brothers, these she calls her sisters, these she loves more ardently than her two sons. If by any chance the unhappy woman should lose them, she says she would not live even an hour. Ah, how usefully now, Papirianus, would the hand of Annaeus Serenus be employed![2]

LXXXII

While the throng offers to you, Augustus, its querulous petitions, the reason why we too offer to our Master a few poems, is because we know that a god can have leisure at once for business and for the Muses, and that even this wreath of song pleases you. Bear with your bards, Augustus: we are your treasured pride, we are your earlier[3] care, and your delight. Not alone does the oak[4] beseem you, or Phoebus' laurel;[5] let there be made a civic crown for you of ivy[6] as well!

[4] The *corona civica* of oak-leaves given to one who had preserved the life of a citizen, afterwards given to the emperor as the general preserver.

[5] The crown of victory in war.

[6] The distinction of a poet: *cf.* Virg. *Ecl.* viii. 12.

BOOK IX

LIBER NONUS

Have, mi Torani, frater carissime. epigramma,
quod extra ordinem paginarum est, ad Stertinium
clarissimum virum scripsimus, qui imaginem meam
ponere in bybliotheca sua voluit. de quo scribendum
tibi putavi, ne ignorares Avitus iste quis vocaretur.
vale et para hospitium.

Note, licet nolis, sublimi pectore vates,
    cui referet serus praemia digna cinis,
hoc tibi sub nostra breve carmen imagine vivat,
    quam non obscuris iungis, Avite, viris:
"Ille ego sum nulli nugarum laude secundus,   5
    quem non miraris sed puto, lector, amas.
maiores maiora sonent: mihi parva locuto
    sufficit in vestras saepe redire manus."

I

Dum Ianus hiemes, Domitianus autumnos,
Augustus annis commodabit aestates,
dum grande famuli nomen adseret Rheni
Germanicarum magna lux Kalendarum,

---

[1] Addressed as Avitus also in I. xvi.
[2] *i.e.* a senator. S. was consul A.D. 92.

BOOK IX

GREETING, my Toranius, dearest brother. The epigram which is supernumerary to my pages I have written to Stertinius,[1] a most illustrious man,[2] who wished to place my bust in his library. Concerning whom I thought I ought to write to you, that you might not be ignorant who was the Avitus there addressed. Farewell, and get ready your hospitality.

Famed, though against thy will, as a bard of sublime invention, to whom death long hence shall pay thy fitting meed, let this short stanza abide, I pray thee, beneath that bust of me, which thou addest, Avitus, to those of not ignoble men :

"Lo! he am I whose light verse yields to none ;
Reader, thy love, not awe, methinks I've won.
Let greater men strike greater notes : I earn
Enough if my small themes oft to thy hands return."

I

WHILE Janus shall lend winters to the year, Domitianus autumns, Augustus summers ; while the great day of the Germanic Kalends shall claim a mighty name from the subservient Rhine ;[3] while

---

Domitian, copying Augustus, who named August, gave the names Germanicus and Domitianus to September and October respectively, because he was made emperor in the one and was born in the other : Suet. *Dom.* 13.

Tarpeia summi saxa dum patris stabunt,   5
dum voce supplex dumque ture placabit
matrona divae dulce Iuliae numen,
manebit altum Flaviae decus gentis
cum sole et astris cumque luce Romana.
invicta quidquid condidit manus, caeli est.   10

II

PAUPER amicitiae cum sis, Lupe, non es amicae
    et queritur de te mentula sola nihil.
illa siligineis pinguescit adultera cunnis,
    convivam pascit nigra farina tuum.
incensura nives dominae Setina liquantur,   5
    nos bibimus Corsi pulla venena cadi ;
empta tibi nox est fundis non tota paternis,
    non sua desertus rura sodalis arat ;
splendet Erythraeis perlucida moecha lapillis,
    ducitur addictus, te futuente, cliens ;   10
octo Syris suffulta datur lectica puellae,
    nudum sandapilae pondus amicus erit.
i nunc et miseros, Cybele, praecide cinaedos :
    haec erat, haec cultris mentula digna tuis.

III

QUANTUM iam superis, Caesar, caeloque dedisti
    si repetas et si creditor esse velis,

---

[1] cf. VI. iii. 6 ; VI. xiii.
[2] The temple built by Domitian in honour of the *gens*
Flavia : cf. IX. iii. 12.

the Tarpeian rock of the Sire Supreme shall stand;
while, suppliant with prayer, and with incense, the
matron shall propitiate the fair deity of Julia[1] now
divine: the towering glory of the Flavian race[2]
shall endure, coeternal with sun and stars, and with
the light that shines on Rome. Whatever an unconquered arm has founded, that is of Heaven!

II

ALTHOUGH you are a poor man to your friends,
Lupus, you are not so to your mistress, and only
your virility has no grievance against you. She, the
adulteress, fattens on lewdly shaped loaves:[3] black
meal feeds your guest. Setine wines are strained
to inflame your lady's snow;[4] we drink the black
poison of a Corsican jar. Her favours—not un-
shared—are bought at the price of your paternal
estate; your comrade, neglected, ploughs fields that
are not his own: the adulteress is bright and shining
with Eastern jewels; your client is committed and
dragged off to prison while you enjoy amours: a
litter poised on eight Syrian slaves is given to your
girl; your friend—a naked corpse—will be the
burden of a pauper's bier. Go now, Cybele! and
castrate wretched paederasts: here, here is matter
long since worthy of your knife!

III

WERE you, Caesar, to reclaim, and did you wish to
be creditor for all you have already given to the

[3] cf. XIV. lxix.
[4] cf. v. lxiv. 2; XIV. cxvii.

grandis in aetherio licet auctio fiat Olympo
  coganturque dei vendere quidquid habent,
conturbabit Atlans et non erit uncia tota   5
  decidat tecum qua pater ipse deum.
pro Capitolinis quid enim tibi solvere templis,
  quid pro Tarpeiae frondis honore potest?
quid pro culminibus geminis matrona Tonantis?
  Pallada praetereo : res agit illa tuas.   10
quid loquar Alciden Phoebumque piosque Laconas?
  addita quid Latio Flavia templa polo?
expectes et sustineas, Auguste, necesse est :
  nam tibi quod solvat non habet arca Iovis.

IV

AUREOLIS futui cum possit Galla duobus
  et plus quam futui, si totidem addideris,
aureolos a te cur accipit, Aeschyle, denos?
  non fellat tanti Galla. quid ergo? tacet.

V

NUBERE vis Prisco : non miror, Paula ; sapisti.
  ducere te non vult Priscus : et ille sapit.

VI

TIBI, summe Rheni domitor et parens orbis,
  pudice princeps, gratias agunt urbes :

---

¹ An *uncia* for every *as*, *i.e.* a penny in the shilling.
² *cf.* IV. i. 6 : IV. liv. 1.
³ Domitian regarded himself as being peculiarly under the
protection, and in fact the son, of Pallas.

high gods and to heaven, then, though a great
auction were held on skyey Olympus and gods were
forced to sell whatever they possess, Atlas will go
bankrupt, and there will not be a full twelfth[1]
wherewith the Sire of the gods himself may settle
with you. For what can he pay you in return for
Capitoline temples, what for the glory of the Tarpeian
oak crown?[2] What can the Thunderer's dame pay
for her two temples? Pallas I pass by: she is your
partner.[3] Why should I speak of Alcides and Phoebus, and the loving Spartan twins?[4] Why of the
Flavian fane, a new gift to the Latin heaven?[5] You
must wait and endure, Augustus; for to pay you
Jove's money-chest has not the wherewithal.

IV

ALTHOUGH Galla's favours may be secured for two
gold pieces, and special favours if you add as much
again, why does she receive ten pieces from you,
Aeschylus? Galla's evil practices are not so dear as
that. What is, then? Her silence.

V

You wish to marry Priscus; I don't wonder, Paula;
you are wise. Priscus does not wish to marry you:
he, too, is wise.

VI

To thee, Conqueror supreme of Rhine, and parent
of the world, O modest Prince, the cities give their

[4] Castor and Pollux.
[5] *i.e.* to the Roman Pantheon, the deified emperors: *cf.*
IX. xxxiv. 2.

populos habebunt; parere iam scelus non est.
non puer avari sectus arte mangonis
virilitatis damna maeret ereptae,   5
nec quam superbus conputet stipem leno
dat prostituto misera mater infanti.
qui nec cubili fuerat ante te quondam,
pudor esse per te coepit et lupanari.

VII

DICERE de Libycis redu-i tibi gentibus, Afer,
  continuis volui quinque diebus "Have":
"Non vacat" aut "Dormit" dictum est bis terque
    reverso.
  iam satis est.   non vis, Afer, havere: vale.

VIII

TAMQUAM parva foret sexus iniuria nostri
  foedandos populo prostituisse mares,
iam cunae lenonis erant, ut ab ubere raptus
  sordida vagitu posceret aera puer:
inmatura dabant infandas corpora poenas.   5
  non tulit Ausonius talia monstra pater,
idem qui teneris nuper succurrit ephebis,
  ne faceret steriles saeva libido viros.
dilexere prius pueri iuvenesque senesque,
  at nunc infantes te quoque, Caesar, amant.   10

---

[1] cf. II. lx. 4; v. lxxv.
[2] "Vale" was said when the survivors took leave of the

thanks: population shall they have; to bring forth is at last no crime.[1] The boy, mutilated by the grasping slave-dealer's art, does not lament the loss of his ravished manhood, nor does a needy mother give her prostituted infant the pittance which the haughty pander is to count out. The modesty which erewhile before thee not even the marriage-bed possessed, now by thy means even a brothel begins to show.

VII

When you had returned from the tribes of Libya, Afer, five days running I wanted to say "Good day!" "He is engaged," or "He is taking a siesta," was the message when I had returned twice and three times. Enough! Afer, you don't want a "Good day": "Good bye." [2]

VIII

As if it were small injury to our sex to prostitute our males to pollution by the people, the cradle was but now so the pander's own that a boy snatched from his mother's breast begged with infant wail for sordid coin; bodies immature suffered unutterable outrage.[3] The Father of Italy could not endure such enormities, even he who of late succoured [4] tender youths, that cruel lust might not make barren men. Boys loved thee before, and young men, and aged sires; but now infants, too, love thee, Caesar.

corpse at a funeral: cf. v. lxvi. 2. "I shall look upon you as dead in future," says M.

[3] Domitian revived the *Lex Scantinia* against unnatural crimes: Suet. *Dom.* viii.

[4] cf. IX. vi. 4.

IX

Nil tibi legavit Fabius, Bithynice, cui tu
  annua, si memini, milia sena dabas.
plus nulli dedit ille: queri, Bithynice, noli:
  annua legavit milia sena tibi.

X

Cenes, Canthare, cum foris libenter,
clamas et maledicis et minaris.
deponas animos truces monemus:
liber non potes et gulosus esse.

XI

Nomen cum violis rosisque natum,
quo pars optima nominatur anni,
Hyblam quod sapit Atticosque flores,
quod nidos olet alitis superbae;
nomen nectare dulcius beato,   5
quo mallet Cybeles puer vocari
et qui pocula temperat Tonanti,
quod si Parrhasia sones in aula,
respondent Veneres Cupidinesque;
nomen nobile molle delicatum   10
versu dicere non rudi volebam:
sed tu, syllaba contumax, repugnas.
dicunt Eiarinon tamen poetae,
sed Graeci quibus est nihil negatum
et quos Ἄρες Ἄρες decet sonare: 15
nobis non licet esse tam disertis
qui Musas colimus severiores.

---

[1] "You now save the sum you spent on him."
[2] The honey of Hybla, in Sicily, and of Hymettus respec
tively: cf. v. xxxix. 3; vii. lxxxviii. 8.

IX

FABIUS has bequeathed you nothing, Bithynicus, he to whom, if I remember, you used to give six thousand sesterces a year. More he gave to no man; don't complain, Bithynicus: he has bequeathed you six thousand sesterces a year.[1]

X

ALTHOUGH you gladly dine abroad, Cantharus, you bawl and abuse and threaten people. Discard such truculent spirits, I warn you; you can't be both independent and a glutton.

XI

A NAME born with the violets and the roses, after which the year's best part is called, that savours of Hybla and Attic flowers,[2] that smells of the nest of the lordly fowl;[3] a name, sweeter than nectar divine, by which Cybele's loved boy[4] and he who blends his draught for the Thunderer, would fain be called; whereto, shouldst thou sound it in the Palatine hall, Venuses and Cupids make answer; a name noble, soft, delicate—this I wished to utter in no rugged verse: but you, an obstinate syllable, rebel.[5] Yet poets speak of Eiarinos; but they were Greeks, to whom nothing is denied, and whom it becomes to sound Ares short as Ares long.[6] We cannot be so versatile, who court Muses more unbending.

[3] The phoenix : cf. VI. lv. 2.

[4] Attis : cf. v. xli. 2.

[5] The four short syllables in Earinos will not go into M.'s metre.

[6] Homer (*Il.* v. 31) uses both quantities in one line : Ἄρες, Ἄρες βροτολοιγέ, μιαιφόνε, τειχεσιπλῆτα.

XII

Si daret autumnus mihi nomen, Oporinos essem,
    horrida si brumae sidera, Chimerinos;
dictus ab aestivo Therinos tibi mense vocarer:
    tempora cui nomen verna dedere, quis est?

XIII

Nomen habes teneri quod tempora nuncupat anni,
    cum breve Cecropiae ver populantur apes:
nomen Acidalia meruit quod harundine pingi,
    quod Cytherea sua scribere gaudet acu;
nomen Erythraeis quod littera facta lapillis,   5
    gemma quod Heliadum pollice trita notet;
quod pinna scribente grues ad sidera tollant;
    quod decet in sola Caesaris esse domo.

XIV

Hunc quem mensa tibi, quem cena paravit amicum
    esse putas fidae pectus amicitiae?
aprum amat et mullos et sumen et ostrea, non te.
    tam bene si cenem, noster amicus erit.

---

[1] The Greek adjectives expressing autumn, winter, and
summer are respectively Ὀπωρινός, Χειμερινός, and Θερινός.
"Of spring" is similarly Ἐαρινός.

[2] Acidalia was a name of Venus from a fountain in
Boeotia. She was also called Cytherea from Cythera, an
island off the coast of Laconia.

XII

WERE Autumn to give me my name, Oporinus
should I be, or if rough winter's sky, Chimerinos;
named after summer's month, to you I should be
called Therinos: who is he to whom spring's season
has given his name? [1]

XIII

THOU hast a name that bespeaks the season of the
budding year, when Attic bees lay waste the brief-
lived spring; a name meet to be writ in colour by
Acidalia's [2] pen, which Cytherea joys to embroider
with her own needle; a name which letters strung
of Indian pearls, which a jewel of the Heliades [3]
rubbed by the fingers, should mark; which cranes
with wings that write upon the skies [4] should lift
to heaven; which it beseems to be in Caesar's house
alone.

XIV

THIS man, whom your table, whom your dinner
has made your friend—think you his heart one of
loyal friendship? 'Tis boar he loves, and mullet,
and sow's paps, and oysters, not you. Were I to
dine so well, he will be my friend.

[3] By amber, into which the tears of the H. for the death
of their brother Phaethon were turned. It became fragrant
by rubbing: cf. III. lxv. 5; XI. viii. 6.
[4] Palamedes was said to have invented the Greek Υ (the
Latin V) by observing the formation of cranes in flight.
V begins *ver* (spring), and represents Earinos: cf. XIII.
lxxv.

XV

Inscripsit tumulis septem scelerata virorum
  "Se fecisse" Chloe.   quid pote simplicius?

XVI

Consilium formae speculum dulcisque capillos
  Pergameo posuit dona sacrata deo
ille puer tota domino gratissimus aula,
  nomine qui signat tempora verna suo.
felix quae tali censetur munere tellus!   5
  nec Ganymedeas mallet habere comas.

XVII

Latonae venerande nepos, qui mitibus herbis
  Parcarum exoras pensa brevesque colos,
hos tibi laudatos domino, rata vota,[1] capillos
  ille tuus Latia misit ab urbe puer;
addidit et nitidum sacratis crinibus orbem,   5
  quo felix facies iudice tuta fuit.
tu iuvenale decus serva, ne pulchrior ille
  in longa fuerit quam breviore coma.

XVIII

Est mihi (sitque precor longum te praeside, Caesar)
  rus minimum, parvi sunt et in urbe lares.

------

[1] sua vota β, rata voce γ.

------

[1] The words are ambiguous.   "*Chloe fecit*" was intended
to mean "C. built this tomb."   M. suggests "wrought the
death of her husbands."

XV

ACCURSED Chloe inscribed the monuments of her seven husbands with "Chloe wrought this." What could be plainer? [1]

XVI

HIS mirror, beauty's counsellor, and his darling locks—gifts dedicated to the god of Pergamus [2]— that boy [3] has offered, who, in all the palace most dear to his master, by his name denotes the time of spring. Happy the land whose worth is gauged by such a gift! It would not choose instead even the tresses of Ganymede.

XVII

REVERED grandson of Latona, who with the magic of thy gentle herbs dost win over [4] the threads and brief distaffs of the Fates, these locks by his master praised thy [5] boy has sent, his vow's fulfilment, from Latium's city; and to his consecrated hair has he added the bright disk, by whose judgment his happy beauty was assured. Do thou preserve his youthful bloom, that he be no fairer with long curls than with shortened locks!

XVIII

I HAVE—and I pray I may have it long, Caesar, beneath thy guardianship—a tiny country house, and

[2] Aesculapius, the god of healing, who had a temple at Pergamus in Asia Minor.
[3] Earinos, Domitian's cupbearer, mentioned in Epp. xi.–xiii.
[4] *i.e.* who dost prolong human life.
[5] Perhaps Earinos came from Pergamus.

sed de valle brevi quas det sitientibus hortis
curva laboratas antlia tollit aquas :
sicca domus queritur nullo se rore foveri,   5
cum mihi vicino Marcia fonte sonet.
quam dederis nostris, Auguste, penatibus undam,
Castalis haec nobis aut Iovis imber erit.

XIX

LAUDAS balnea versibus trecentis
cenantis bene Pontici, Sabelle.
vis cenare, Sabelle, non lavari.

XX

HAEC, quae tota patet tegiturque et marmore et auro,
– infantis domini conscia terra fuit.
felix o, quantis sonuit vagitibus et quas
vidit reptantis sustinuitque manus !
hic steterat veneranda domus quae praestitit orbi   5
quod Rhodos astrifero, quod pia Creta, polo.
Curetes texere Iovem crepitantibus armis,
semiviri poterant qualia ferre Phryges :
at te protexit superum pater et tibi, Caesar,
pro iaculo et parma fulmen et aegis erat.   10

---

[1] The *Aqua Marcia* was one of the great aqueducts.
According to Strabo (v. 3) almost every house in Rome
had water laid on ; see also Hor. *Ep.* I. x. 20. M.'s was an
exception : *cf.* VIII. lxvii. 7.

[2] An epigram on the building of the Flavian Temple on
the site of the house in which Domitian was born : Suet.
Dom. i.

I have, too, a small dwelling in the city. But my
curved pole and bucket lift with labour from a
shallow valley water to bestow on the thirsty garden;
the arid house complains that it is freshened by
no moisture, though Marcia babbles in my ears with
neighbouring fount.[1] The water thou shalt give,
Augustus, to my household gods will be to me a
spring of Castaly or a shower of Jove.

XIX

You extol in infinite verse the baths of Ponticus
who gives good dinners, Sabellus. You wish to dine,
Sabellus, not to wash!

XX

This spot of earth, which now lies wholly open,
and is being covered with marble and with gold,
knew our lord's infant years.[2] O blessed spot! With
wailings of how great a babe it echoed, and what
hands it saw and upbore as they crept! Here
had stood the house august that made real to the
world what Rhodes, what duteous Crete[3] made real
to the starry heaven. Cybele's priests guarded Jove
with their rattling arms, such arms as Phrygians,
but half men, could wield;[4] but thee the Sire of the
gods safeguarded, and for thee, Caesar, thunderbolt
and aegis stood for spear and buckler.

---

[3] *i.e.* the birth of a god. Pallas (Pind. *Ol.* vii. 35) was
said to have sprung from the head of Zeus at Rhodes. But
some commentators think Poseidon is referred to. Zeus or
Jupiter was born in Crete.

[4] The Curetes (demi-gods) clashed their arms to drown
the infant's cries, lest his father Cronos should hear and
eat him.

XXI

Artemidorus habet puerum sed vendidit agrum;
    agrum pro puero Calliodorus habet.
dic uter ex istis melius rem gesserit, Aucte:
    Artemidorus amat, Calliodorus arat.

XXII

Credis ob haec me, Pastor, opes fortasse rogare
    propter quae populus crassaque turba rogat,
ut Setina meos consumat gleba ligones
    et sonet innumera compede Tuscus ager;
ut Mauri Libycis centum stent dentibus orbes   5
    et crepet in nostris aurea lamna toris,
nec labris nisi magna meis crystalla terantur
    et faciant nigras nostra Falerna nives;
ut canusinatus nostro Syrus assere sudet
    et mea sit culto sella cliente frequens;   10
aestuet ut nostro madidus conviva ministro,
    quem permutatum nec Ganymede velis;
ut lutulenta linat Tyrias mihi mula lacernas
    et Massyla meum virga gubernet equum.
est nihil ex istis: superos ac sidera testor.   15
    ergo quid? ut donem, Pastor, et aedificem.

XXIII

O cui virgineo flavescere contigit auro,
    dic ubi Palladium sit tibi, Care, decus.

---

[1] Wine was strained through snow: *cf.* v. lxiv. 2; xiv.
cxvii.   [2] *cf.* xiv. cxxvii. and cxxix.   [3] *cf.* x. xiii. 2.
[4] Possibly Pastor (like Gellius in ix. xlvi.) made "building"
an excuse for never "giving." Friedländer explains "carry
out public works for the general good"; but this is not in
the Latin.

XXI

ARTEMIDORUS possesses a young slave, but has
sold his land; the land Calliodorus possesses in exchange for the slave. Say, which of those two
made the better bargain, Auctus? Artemidorus has
his pleasure, Calliodorus his plough.

XXII

You believe, Pastor, I perhaps ask for riches for
the same reasons as the vulgar and the dense-witted
crowd ask, in order that Setia's glebe may wear away
my hoes, and Tuscan fields clank with countless fet-
tered slaves; that a hundred round Moorish tables
may stand on Libyan tusks, and golden plating
tinkle on my couches; that none but large crystal
cups be rubbed by my lips, and that my Falernian
darken the cooling snow;[1] that Syrian slaves in
Canusian[2] wool may sweat beneath my litter-pole,
and my chair be crowded by full-dressed clients;
that the tipsy guest may be hot for page of mine,
whom you would not barter even for a Ganymede;
that a mud-bespattered mule may soil my Tyrian
cloak, and the rod of a Massylian[3] guide my horse.
'Tis none of those things—I call to witness the high
gods and heaven! Then what? To make presents,
Pastor, and to build.[4]

XXIII

O THOU whose lot has been to gleam with the
Virgin's gold,[5] say, Carus, where is the prize Pallas

[5] C. had won the golden olive-wreath, the prize for poetry,
at the annual contest in honour of Minerva at Domitian's
Alban villa: cf. IV. i. 5. This he had transferred to the
Emperor's bust.

85

" Aspicis en domini fulgentes marmore vultus ?
 venit ad has ultro nostra corona comas."
Albanae livere potest pia quercus olivae,   5
 cinxerit invictum quod prior illa caput.

XXIV

Quis Palatinos imitatus imagine vultus
 Phidiacum Latio marmore vicit ebur ?
haec mundi facies, haec sunt Iovis ora sereni :
 sic tonat ille deus cum sine nube tonat.
non solam tribuit Pallas tibi, Care, coronam ;   5
 effigiem domini, quam colis, illa dedit.

XXV

Dantem vina tuum quotiens aspeximus Hyllum,
 lumine nos, Afer, turbidiore notas.
quod, rogo, quod scelus est mollem spectare ministrum ?
 aspicimus solem sidera templa deos.
avertam vultus, tamquam mihi pocula Gorgon   5
 porrigat atque oculos oraque nostra petat [1] ?
trux erat Alcides, et Hylan spectare licebat ;
 ludere Mercurio cum Ganymede licet.
si non vis teneros spectet conviva ministros,
 Phineas invites, Afer, et Oedipodas.   10

---

[1] tegam β, petat.

gave thee? "Seest thou there our master's face bright in marble? My crown unprompted passed to those locks." The patriot oak[1] may envy Alba's olive for that it first wreathed that unconquered brow.

XXIV

Who, portraying in a bust Imperial features, has in Latin marble surpassed Phidian ivory? This is the aspect of a world, this the countenance of Jove in calm: so thunders that god when he thunders in cloudless skies. Not a crown alone has Pallas granted thee, Carus; our master's effigy which thou dost worship has she given.

XXV

As often as we have glanced at your Hyllus while he is serving wine, 'tis with a somewhat troubled eye you regard us, Afer. What, what offence, I ask you, is it to gaze on a gentle cup-bearer? We look upon the sun, stars, temples, gods. Am I to turn away my face as if a Gorgon offered me the cup, and were assaulting my eyes and my face? Fierce was Alcides, and 'twas allowed to gaze on Hylas: Mercury is allowed to sport along with Ganymede. If you do not wish your guest to gaze on your youthful servants, Afer, you should invite Phineuses and Oedipuses.[2]

[1] The golden oak-leaf crown, the prize of the quinquennial contest in music, etc., in honour of Jup. Capitolinus: *cf.* IV. i. 6.

[2] Both Phineus and Oedipus were blind.

XXVI

AUDET facundo qui carmina mittere Nervae,
    pallida donabit glaucina, Cosme, tibi,
Paestano violas et cana ligustra colono,
    Hyblaeis apibus Corsica mella dabit.
sed tamen et parvae nonnulla est gratia Musae ;   5
    appetitur posito vilis oliva lupo.
nec tibi sit mirum modici quod conscia vatis
    iudicium metuit nostra Thalia tuum :
ipse tuas etiam veritus Nero dicitur aures,
    lascivum iuvenis cum tibi lusit opus.   10

XXVII

CUM depilatos, Chreste, coleos portes
et vulturino mentulam parem collo
et prostitutis levius caput culis,
nec vivat ullus in tuo pilus crure,
purgentque saevae cana labra volsellae,   5
Curios Camillos Quintios Numas Ancos
et quidquid usquam legimus pilosorum
loqueris sonasque grandibus minax verbis,
et cum theatris saeculoque rixaris.
occurrit aliquis inter ista si draucus,   10
iam paedagogo liberatus et cuius
refibulavit turgidum faber penem,
nutu vocatum ducis, et pudet fari
Catoniana, Chreste, quod facis lingua.

---

¹ The future emperor : cf. VIII. lxx.
² The celebrated perfumer : cf. III. lv. 1. *Glaucina* seems
to have been an unguent made from the plant *glaucium*
(? celandine).
³ *i.e.* will send things—and inferior things—where they
are not wanted. Corsican honey was bitter from the
abundance of yews in the island : cf. Verg. *Ecl.* ix. 30.

XXVI

He who ventures to send poetry to eloquent Nerva[1] will present you, Cosmus,[2] with pale glaucine unguent, will give to a Paestan gardener violets and white privets, to bees of Hybla Corsican honey.[3] Yet even a humble Muse possesses some charm ; a cheap olive gives relish to a bass upon the board. And do not wonder that, conscious of the slender powers of her bard, my Thalia shrinks from your judgment; even Nero himself[4] is said to have feared your critic ears when in youth he lightly touched for you some wanton theme.

XXVII

Although you carry about one part of your person, Chrestus, plucked of hair, and another matching a vulture's neck, and a head smoother than prostituted ——, and not a single bristle sprouts on your shanks, and pitiless pluckings clear your bloodless lips, you prate of Curii, Camilli, Quinctii, Numas, Ancuses, and of all the bristly philosophers we read of anywhere,[5] and you vociferate in loud and threatening words, and quarrel with the theatres and the age. But if, in the midst of that pother of yours, there meet you, now freed from his pedagogue, some sodomite di cui turgido membro abbia il fabro sfibbiato, tu lo conduci chiamato con un segno ; e mi vergogno dire, O Chresto, ciò che fai colla tua lingua da Catone.

---

[4] Who made verses easily : Suet. *Ner.* lii.
[5] M. constantly reviles the hypocrisy of dissolute scoundrels assuming the guise of philosophers : *cf.* i. xxiv.; ix. xlviii.; and Juv. ii. 3 *seqq.*

XXVIII

Dulce decus scaenae, ludorum fama, Latinus
    ille ego sum, plausus deliciaeque tuae,
qui spectatorem potui fecisse Catonem,
    solvere qui Curios Fabriciosque graves.
sed nihil a nostro sumpsit mea vita theatro   5
    et sola tantum scaenicus arte feror:
nec poteram gratus domino sine moribus esse:
    interius mentes inspicit ille deus.
vos me laurigeri parasitum dicite Phoebi,
    Roma sui famulum dum sciat esse Iovis.   10

XXIX

Saecula Nestoreae permensa, Philaeni, senectae
    rapta es ad infernas tam cito Ditis aquas?
Euboicae nondum numerabas longa Sibyllae
    tempora: maior erat mensibus illa tribus.
heu quae lingua silet! non illam mille catastae   5
    vincebant, nec quae turba Sarapin amat,
nec matutini cirrata caterva magistri,
    nec quae Strymonio de grege ripa sonat.
quae nunc Thessalico lunam deducere rhombo,
    quae sciet hos illos vendere lena toros?   10

---

[1] A celebrated mime or comic actor: *cf.* II. lxxii. 3. He was also a *delator*, or informer.

[2] Ben Jonson has evidently copied these lines in his tribute to Shakespeare, " Th' applause, delight, the wonder of our stage."   [3] *cf.* I. Intr. Epist.

[4] My art is that of a mime, not my morals.

[5] There appears to have been a fellowship of *mimi* (comic actors), called the " Parasites of Phoebus." At any rate *mimi* were so called: *cf. Grut. Corp. Inscr.* cccxxix. and cccxxx.

XXVIII

THE darling pride of the stage, the glory of the
games, that Latinus[1] am I, the favourite of your
applause,[2] who could have made a spectator of
Cato,[3] who could have dissolved in laughter the
stern Curii and Fabricii. But nought from Rome's
theatre did my life assume; and only through my
art am I accounted of the stage;[4] nor could I have
been dear to my master had I not character: that
God looks into the heart within. Call me, if ye
will, the parasite of laurelled Phoebus,[5] so Rome
but know that I am the servant of her Jove.[6]

XXIX

PHILAENIS, who hast measured to the full the ages
of Nestor's long life, hast thou been hurried so swiftly
to the nether waters of Dis? Not as yet wert thou
reckoning the long years of Euboea's Sibyl:[7] older
by three months was she. Alas, what a tongue is
silent! That tongue not a thousand slave-marts used
to drown, nor the throng that worships Serapis, nor
the curly-headed troop of the schoolmaster at morn,
nor the river bank that echoes to Strymon's flock of
cranes. Who now will be cunning with Thessalian
wheel to draw earthward the moon,[8] what bawd
to sell this or that marriage bed? May upon thee

[6] The emperor.

[7] The Sibyl of Cumae in Campania, a colony from Chalcis
in Euboea. Sibyls were women inspired with prophetic
power. The Cumaean Sibyl was said to have been 700 years
old when Aeneas landed, centuries before Martial.

[8] Witches were supposed to have this power: *cf.* XII.
lvii. 17.

sit tibi terra levis mollique tegaris harena,
ne tua non possint eruere ossa canes.

XXX

CAPPADOCUM saevis Antistius occidit oris
 Rusticus.   o tristi crimine terra nocens!
rettulit ossa sinu cari Nigrina mariti
 et questa est longas non satis esse vias;
cumque daret sanctam tumulis, quibus invidet, urnam,
 visa sibi est rapto bis viduata viro.   6

XXXI

CUM comes Arctois haereret Caesaris armis
 Velius, hanc Marti pro duce vovit avem.
luna quater binos non tota peregerat orbes,
 debita poscebat iam sibi vota deus:
ipse suas anser properavit laetus ad aras   5
 et cecidit sanctis hostia parva focis.
octo vides patulo pendere nomismata rostro
 alitis?   haec extis condita nuper erant.
quae litat argento pro te, non sanguine, Caesar,
 victima iam ferro non opus esse docet.   10

XXXII

HANC volo quae facilis, quae palliolata vagatur,
 hanc volo quae puero iam dedit ante meo,

---

[1] The last two lines are found in a Greek epigram (*Anth. Pal.* xi. 226) by Ammianus, a contemporary of M.
[2] Velius Paullus, who went with Domitian to the Sarmatian war.

earth be light, and thou be covered with crumbling sand, that thy bones dogs may not—be unable to root up![1]

XXX

ANTISTIUS RUSTICUS has died on Cappadocia's cruel shores: O land guilty of a dolorous crime! Nigrina brought back in her bosom her dear husband's bones, and sighed that the way was all too short; and when to the tomb she envies she was giving that sacred urn, she deemed herself twice widowed of her ravished spouse.

XXXI

VELIUS,[2] what time he looked to join Caesar's Arctic war, for his general's sake vowed this bird to Mars.[3] The moon had not rounded full her orb twice four times over[4] when the god was claiming the vow already due. Of its own accord[5] the goose gladly hasted to the altar, and fell, a humble victim, on the sacred hearth. See you eight coins hanging from the fowl's open beak? These were but now hid in its entrails. The victim, Caesar, that for thee gives fair omens with silver, not with blood, teaches us there is now no need for steel.

XXXII

HER I wish for who is willing, who gads about in a mantilla, her I wish for who has already granted

[3] A goose was representative of the safety of Rome.
[4] The Sarmatian war did not last eight months.
[5] It was a good omen when the victim went willingly to the sacrifice.

hanc volo quam redimit totam denarius alter,
    hanc volo quae pariter sufficit una tribus.
poscentem nummos et grandia verba sonantem   5
    possideat crassae mentula Burdigalae.

XXXIII

    Audieris in quo, Flacce, balneo plausum,
    Maronis illic esse mentulam scito.

XXXIV

Iuppiter Idaei risit mendacia busti,
    dum videt Augusti Flavia templa poli,
atque inter mensas largo iam nectare fusus,
    pocula cum Marti traderet ipse suo,
respiciens Phoebum pariter Phoebique sororem,   5
    cum quibus Alcides et pius Arcas erat,
" Gnosia vos " inquit " nobis monumenta dedistis:
    cernite quam plus sit Caesaris esse patrem."

XXXV

Artibus his semper cenam, Philomuse, mereris,
    plurima dum fingis, sed quasi vera refers.
scis quid in Arsacia Pacorus deliberet aula,
    Rhenanam numeras Sarmaticamque manum,

---

¹ Such women were called *diobolares* (worth two obols):
Plaut. *Poen.* I. ii. 58 ; and associated with slaves. Plaut.
(*ibid.* 53) thus calls them *servilicolas sordidas.*

her favours to my slave; her I wish for whom a
second sixpence purchases altogether;[1] her I wish
for whose single self suffices three lovers at once.
One who demands moneys, and who talks in a big
style, the stupid Gascon may possess.

XXXIII

IN whatever bath, Flaccus, you hear sounds re-
sembling applause, know that there Maron's yard is
to be found.

XXXIV

JUPITER laughed at the lying tale of his tomb on
Ida as he looked on the Flavian temple of the
Augustan heaven;[2] and amid the feast when now
full steeped in nectar, as with his own hand he
passed to Mars his son the beaker, looking back to
Phoebus and Phoebus' sister side by side, with whom
were Alcides and the leal Arcadian god,[3] he said:
"Ye have given me a monument at Gnossos: ye
see how much more it is to be Caesar's sire!"

XXXV

BY such arts as these, Philomusus, you always
earn your dinner: you invent much and retail it
as truth. You know what counsel Pacorus[4] takes
in his Arsacian palace; you estimate the Rhenish

---

[2] cf. IX. iii. 12.
[3] Hercules and Mercury respectively.
[4] King of Parthia, Rome's great rival in the East.

verba ducis Daci chartis mandata resignas,   **5**
    victricem laurum quam venit ante vides,
scis quotiens Phario madeat Iove fusca Syene,
    scis quota de Libyco litore puppis eat,
cuius Iuleae capiti nascantur olivae,
    destinet aetherius cui sua serta pater.   **10**
tolle tuas artes; hodie cenabis apud me
    hac lege, ut narres nil, Philomuse, novi.

XXXVI

VIDERAT Ausonium posito modo crine ministrum
    Phryx puer, alterius gaudia nota Iovis:
" Quod tuus ecce suo Caesar permisit ephebo
    tu permitte tuo, maxime rector " ait.
" iam mihi prima latet longis lanugo capillis,   **5**
    iam tua me ridet Iuno vocatque virum."
cui pater aetherius " Puer o dulcissime," dixit
    " non ego quod poscis, res negat ipsa tibi:
Caesar habet noster similis tibi mille ministros
    tantaque sidereos vix capit aula mares;   **10**
at tibi si dederit vultus coma tonsa viriles,
    quis mihi qui nectar misceat alter erit?"

XXXVII

CUM sis ipsa domi mediaque ornere Subura,
    fiant absentes et tibi, Galla, comae,

---

[1] *i.e.* you know whether corn, which comes from Egypt
and Libya, is likely to be plentiful.
[2] *cf.* IX. xxiii. 1.   [3] *cf.* IX. xxiii. 5.

and Sarmatian armies; the orders of Dacia's commander, committed to despatches, you unseal; victory's laurel ere it arrives you see; you know how often dusky Syene is drenched by Egypt's showers; you know how many ships set sail from Libya's shore;[1] for whose brow are growing Julian olives,[2] for whom Heaven's father designs his chaplets.[3] A truce to your arts! To-day you shall dine at my house on this condition, Philomusus, that you tell me no news![4]

XXXVI

THE Phrygian boy,[5] famed darling of the other Jove, had seen Ausonia's cupbearer[6] with locks lately shorn, and said: "What thy Caesar, behold, has allowed his young attendant, that do thou, almighty ruler, allow thy own. Already early down lies hid by my long hair, already thy Juno laughs at me and calls me man." To whom Heaven's sire: "O sweetest boy," he said, "'tis not I refuse thy asking: 'tis very need refuses thee. My Caesar hath a thousand servants like to thee, and his hall, mighty as it is, scarce holds his youths divinely fair. But if shorn hair shall give thee face of man, what other shall there be to mix nectar for me?"

XXXVII

ALTHOUGH, yourself at home, you are arrayed in the middle of the Subura, and your tresses, Galla,

[4] cf. a similar description of a woman in Juv. vi. 398-412.
[5] Ganymede.
[6] Earinos : cf. IX. xi. to xiii.; and, as to the cutting of the hair, IX. xvi. and xvii.

nec dentes aliter quam Serica nocte reponas,
    et iaceas centum condita pyxidibus,
nec tecum facies tua dormiat, innuis illo   5
    quod tibi prolatum est mane supercilio,
et te nulla movet cani reverentia cunni,
    quem potes inter avos iam numerare tuos.
promittis sescenta tamen ; sed mentula surda est,
    et sit lusca licet, te tamen illa videt.   10

XXXVIII

Summa licet velox, Agathine, pericula ludas,
    non tamen efficies ut tibi parma cadat.
nolentem sequitur tenuisque reversa per auras
    vel pede vel tergo, crine vel ungue sedet ;
lubrica Corycio quamvis sint pulpita nimbo   5
    et rapiant celeres vela negata Noti,
securos pueri neglecta perambulat artus,
    et nocet artifici ventus et unda nihil.
ut peccare velis, cum feceris omnia, falli
    non potes : arte opus est ut tibi parma cadat.   10

XXXIX

Prima Palatino lux est haec orta Tonanti,
    optasset Cybele qua peperisse Iovem ;
hac et sancta mei genita est Caesonia Rufi :
    plus debet matri nulla puella suae.

---

[1] An epigram on a juggler tossing a shield. A mistake,
says M., is impossible, unless intended.

are manufactured far away, and you lay aside your
teeth at night, just as you do your silk dresses, and
you lie stored away in a hundred caskets, and your face
does not sleep with you—yet you wink with that
eyebrow which has been brought out for you in the
morning, and no respect moves you for your outworn
carcass—which you may now count as one of your
ancestors.   Nevertheless you offer me an infinity
of delights.   But Nature is deaf, and although she
may be one-eyed, she sees you anyhow.

XXXVIII

Although, Agathinus, you deftly play a game of
highest risk, yet you will not achieve the falling of
your buckler.[1] Though you avoid it, it follows you,
and, returning through the yielding air, settles on
foot or back, on hair or finger-tip.   However
slippery is the stage with a Corycian saffron-shower,
and although rushing winds tear at the awning that
cannot be spread, the buckler, though disregarded,
pervades the boy's careless limbs, and wind and
shower baffle the artist no whit.   Although you try
to miss, do what you will, you cannot be foiled:
art is needed to make your buckler fall.

XXXIX

This day was the first that dawned upon the
Thunderer of the Palatine,[2] a day whereon Cybele
would have chosen to bring forth Jove; on this day,
too, was born Caesonia, my Rufus'[3] wife revered:
no maid owes to her mother more than she.   Her

---

[2] Domitian, born Oct. 24.
[3] Canius Rufus, the poet of Gades : cf. I. lxi. 9 ; III. xx.

laetatur gemina votorum sorte maritus,   5
  contigit hunc illi quod bis amare diem.

XL

Tarpeias Diodorus ad coronas
  Romam cum peteret Pharo relicta,
vovit pro reditu viri Philaenis
  illam lingeret, ut puella simplex,
quam castae quoque diligunt Sabinae.   5
dispersa rate tristibus procellis
mersus fluctibus obrutusque ponto
ad votum Diodorus enatavit.
o tardus nimis et piger maritus!
hoc in litore si puella votum   10
fecisset mea, protinus redissem.

XLI

Pontice, quod numquam futuis, sed paelice laeva
  uteris et Veneri servit amica manus,
hoc nihil esse putas? scelus est, mihi crede, sed ingens,
  quantum vix animo concipis ipse tuo.
nempe semel futuit, generaret Horatius ut tres;   5
  Mars semel, ut geminos Ilia casta daret.
omnia perdiderat si masturbatus uterque
  mandasset manibus gaudia foeda suis.
ipsam crede tibi naturam dicere rerum
  "Istud quod digitis, Pontice, perdis, homo est."   10

spouse rejoices in a twofold granting of prayer: this day it has fallen to him to cherish with a double love.

XL

WHEN Diodorus, leaving Egypt, was travelling to Rome to receive the Tarpeian crown,[1] Philaenis made a vow for the return of her husband that, as an innocent girl, she would put her lips to what[2] even chaste Sabine women love. His ship shattered by grim tempests, though plunged in the waves, and o'erwhelmed by the deep, Diodorus, to claim the vow, swam safe to land. Oh, what a very tardy and sluggish husband! If girl of mine had made this vow on the shore, I should have returned at once![3]

XLI

O PONTICO, il perche tu mai immembri, ma usi l'adultera tua sinistra, e l'amica mano serve a Venere, pensi tu che ciò sia niente? È una sceleragine, credimi, ma sì grande e tale, che appena tu stesso la concepisci nell'animo tuo. In fatti Orazio immembrò una volta sola perche generasse tre figliuoli; Marte una volta perche la casta Ilia dasse i gemelli. L'uno e l'altro avrebbe distrutto ogni cosa se quel masturbatore avesse abbandonato i sozzi piaceri alle sue mani. Credi che la natura stessa delle cose ti dice: "ciò che, O Pontico, distruggi colle dita è un uomo."

[1] cf. IX. xxiii. 5.   [2] i.e. mentulam.
[3] Without embarking from Egypt at all.

XLII

CAMPIS dives Apollo sic Myrinis,
sic semper senibus fruare cycnis,
doctae sic tibi serviant sorores
nec Delphis tua mentiatur ulli,
sic Palatia te colant amentque :   5
bis senos cito te rogante fasces
det Stellae bonus adnuatque Caesar.
felix tunc ego debitorque voti
casurum tibi rusticas ad aras
ducam cornibus aureis iuvencum.   10
nata est hostia, Phoebe ; quid moraris ?

XLIII

HIC qui dura sedens porrecto saxa leone
  mitigat, exiguo magnus in aere deus,
quaeque tulit spectat resupino sidera vultu,
  cuius laeva calet robore, dextra mero,
non est fama recens nec nostri gloria caeli ;   5
  nobile Lysippi munus opusque vides.
hoc habuit numen Pellaei mensa tyranni,
  qui cito perdomito victor in orbe iacet ;
hunc puer ad Libycas iuraverat Hannibal aras ;
  iusserat hic Sullam ponere regna trucem.   10
offensus variae tumidis terroribus aulae
  privatos gaudet nunc habitare lares,

---

[1] A town in Mysia, in Asia Minor. In the neighbourhood
was Grynium with a temple of Apollo.
[2] *i.e.* in vocal swans. Swans were supposed to sing just
before death : *cf.* XIII. lxxvii.   [3] The Muses.
[4] The insignia of the consul : *cf.* VIII. lxvi. 3.
[5] Hercules for a time took the place of Atlas in upholding
the sky : *cf.* VII. lxxiv. 6.

XLII

So mayst thou, Apollo, be rich in plains of Myrina,[1] so mayst thou alway delight in hoary swans,[2] so may thy learned Sisters[3] serve thee, and thy Delphic priestess speak not falsely to any man; so may the Palace court and love thee, if, at thy asking, our kindly Caesar's nod give quickly to Stella the twice six axes.[4] Then I, happy, and a debtor for my vow, will bring thee a victim to thy rustic altar, a steer with gold-gilt horns. The offering is born, Phoebus: why dost thou delay?

XLIII

He who seated makes softer the hard stones by a stretched lion's skin, a huge god in small shape of bronze, and who, with face upturned, regards the stars he shouldered,[5] whose left hand is aglow with strength, his right with wine[6]—no recent work of fame is he, nor the glory of Roman chisel: Lysippus' noble gift and handiwork you see.[7] This deity the board of Pella's tyrant displayed, he who lies in a world he swiftly subdued;[8] by him Hannibal, then a boy, swore at Libyan altars;[9] he bade fierce Sulla resign his power. Vexed by the boastful threats of fickle courts, he is glad now to dwell beneath a

[6] He has a club in one hand, a wine-cup in the other.

[7] This and the following epigram are on a statue by Lysippus, a contemporary of Alexander the Great, of Hercules reclining at the banquet of the gods (*epitrapezius*). Statius (*Sylv.* IV. vi.) has a poem on the same subject.

[8] Alexander the Great.

[9] H. when a boy swore undying hatred to Rome.

utque fuit quondam placidi conviva Molorchi,
sic voluit docti Vindicis esse deus.

XLIV

ALCIDES modo Vindicem rogabam
esset cuius opus laborque felix.
risit, nam solet hoc, levique nutu
"Graece numquid" ait "poeta nescis?
inscripta est basis indicatque nomen."   5
Λυσίππου lego, Phidiae putavi.

XLV

MILES Hyperboreos modo, Marcelline, triones
et Getici tuleras sidera pigra poli:
ecce Promethei rupes et fabula montis
quam prope sunt oculis nunc adeunda tuis!
videris inmensis cum conclamata querellis   5
saxa senis, dices "Durior ipse fuit."
et licet haec addas: "Potuit qui talia ferre,
humanum merito finxerat ille genus."

XLVI

GELLIUS aedificat semper: modo limina ponit,
nunc foribus claves aptat emitque seras,
nunc has, nunc illas reficit mutatque fenestras:
dum tantum aedificet, quidlibet ille facit,
oranti nummos ut dicere possit amico   5
unum illud verbum Gellius "Aedifico."

---

¹ The shepherd who entertained him unawares: cf. IV.
lxiv. 30.
² Prometheus, according to myth, moulded man out of
clay (cf. X. xxxix. 4), giving them the qualities of various

private roof; and, as he was of old the guest of
gentle Molorchus,[1] so has he now chosen to be the
god of learned Vindex.

XLIV

I asked Vindex lately whose art and happy toil
fashioned Alcides. He laughed—for this is his way
—and slightly nodding, said: "Don't you, a poet,
know your Greek? The base has an inscription and
shows the name." I read "of Lysippus": I thought
it was of Phidias!

XLV

A soldier, Marcellinus, you had endured of late
the cold of the Northern Wain, and the slow-circling
stars of Getic skies: behold, how near the compass
of your eyes are now Prometheus' crag, and the
fabled mount! When you shall have seen the rocks
that echoed with the old man's groans, you will say,
"He himself was harder still." And this you may
add: "He who could endure such things was fit to
mould the race of man."[2]

XLVI

Gellius is always building: now he lays down
thresholds, now he fits keys to doors and buys bolts,
now these, now those windows he repairs and alters;
provided only he be building,[3] Gellius does anything
whatever, that to a friend who asks for money he
may be able to say that one word: "Building."

animals: *cf.* Hor. *Od.* i. xvi. 13. Credulity in later times
saw in stones at Panope in Phocis (still smelling of human
flesh!) the remnants of P. clay: Paus. x. iv. 3.

[3] Friedländer punctuates "*fenestras, . . . aedificet. Quidlibet . . . facit,*"

XLVII

Democritos, Zenonas inexplicitosque Platonas
  quidquid et hirsutis squalet imaginibus,
sic quasi Pythagorae loqueris successor et heres;
  praependet sane nec tibi barba minor:
sed, quod et hircosis serum est et turpe pilosis,   5
  in molli rigidam clune libenter habes.
tu, qui sectarum causas et pondera nosti,
  dic mihi, percidi, Pannyche, dogma quod est?

XLVIII

Heredem cum me partis tibi, Garrice, quartae
  per tua iurares sacra caputque tuum,
credidimus (quis enim damnet sua vota libenter?)
  et spem muneribus fovimus usque datis;
inter quae rari Laurentem ponderis aprum   5
  misimus: Aetola de Calydone putes.
at tu continuo populumque patresque vocasti;
  ructat adhuc aprum pallida¹ Roma meum:
ipse ego (quis credat?) conviva nec ultimus haesi,
  sed nec costa data est caudave missa mihi.   10
de quadrante tuo quid sperem, Garrice? nulla
  de nostro nobis uncia venit apro.

XLIX

Haec est illa meis multum cantata libellis,
  quam meus edidicit lector amatque togam.

¹ *pallida* Dousa, *callida* codd.

XLVII

OF Democrituses, Zenos, and enigmatic Platos, and
of every philosopher shown, dirty and hirsute, on a
bust, you prate as if you were successor and heir of
Pythagoras; and before your chin hangs a beard certainly no less than theirs. Ma ciò che tardi si senti
agli ircosi, e turpemente ai pelosi, tu volontieri lo
comporti rigido nelle effeminate coscie. You, who
know the origins of the schools and their argu-
ments, tell me this: what dogma, Pannychus, is it
to be a pathic?

XLVIII

SEEING that you swore, Garricus, by your sacred
rites and by your head, that I was heir to a quarter
of your estate, I believed you—for who would
willingly damn his own wishes?—and I kept warm
my hope by continual presents, among which I
sent you a Laurentian boar of unusual weight: you
would imagine it came from Aetolian Calydon.[1]
But you at once invited both people and Senate; a
bilious Rome is still belching my boar. I myself—
who could believe it?—was not added even as your
last guest, aye, and not even a rib was given me or
tail sent me. Concerning that quarter-estate of yours,
what should I expect, Garricus? Not a twelfth of
my own boar came to me!

XLIX

THIS is that toga much sung of in my poems, which
my reader has heard of to the full, and loves.[2]

[1] i.e. it was as huge as the boar slain by Meleager: cf.
VII. xxvii. 2.   [2] cf. VIII. xxviii.

Partheniana fuit quondam, memorabile vatis
    munus : in hac ibam conspiciendus eques,
dum nova, dum nitida fulgebat splendida lana,   5
    dumque erat auctoris nomine digna sui :
nunc anus et tremulo vix accipienda tribuli,
    quam possis niveam dicere iure tuo.
quid non longa dies, quid non consumitis anni?
    haec toga iam non est Partheniana, mea est.   10

L

INGENIUM mihi, Gaure, probas sic esse pusillum,
    carmina quod faciam quae brevitate placent.
confiteor.   sed tu bis senis grandia libris
    qui scribis Priami proelia, magnus homo es?
nos facimus Bruti puerum, nos Langona vivum :   5
    tu magnus luteum, Gaure, Giganta facis.

LI

QUOD semper superos invito fratre rogasti,
    hoc, Lucane, tibi contigit, ante mori.
invidet ille tibi ; Stygias nam Tullus ad umbras
    optabat, quamvis sit minor, ire prior.
tu colis Elysios nemorisque habitator amoeni   5
    esse tuo primum nunc sine fratre cupis ;
et si iam nitidis alternus venit ab astris
    pro Polluce, mones Castora ne redeat.

---

[1] Parthenius (himself a poet : *cf.* XI. i.) was Domitian's
secretary, his name being derived from παρθένος (virgin), on
which M. plays.   The cloak was once young and unspotted :
now it is old.

[2] *i.e.* threadbare, and therefore chill : *cf.* IV. xxxiv. 2.

[3] It befits my poverty.

Parthenian was it once, a bard's memorable gift:[1] in
this I went conspicuous as a knight, while it was new,
while it brightly shone with glossy wool, and while
it was worthy of its giver's name. Now it is an old
crone, and one scarcely to be accepted by a dodder-
ing pauper, which you may without contradiction
call " snowy." [2] What does not length of days, what
do ye not consume, ye years? This toga is no longer
Parthenian: it is mine.[3]

L

You prove to me, Gaurus, that my genius is in this
way a puny one, because I make poems that please
by their brevity. I confess it. But you, who in
twice six books write of Priam's wars in grand style,
are you a great man? I make Brutus' boy,[4] I make
Langon live: you, great man as you are, Gaurus,
make a giant of clay.

LI

What thou didst alway crave of the High Gods,
though thy brother said nay, this has fallen to thee,
Lucanus—the earlier death. He envies thee; for
Tullus longed, though younger than thou, to go
before thee to the Stygian shades. Thou dwellest
in Elysian fields, and, denizen of that pleasant grove,
now for the first time desirest to be without thy
brother; and, if Castor [5] has now come alternate
from the lustrous stars in Pollux' stead, thou dost
counsel him not to return again.[6]

[4] A statuette admired by Brutus, the assassin of Caesar :
cf. II. lxxvii. 4. Of Langon nothing is known.
[5] cf. I. xxxvi. 2
[6] Another punctuation is a comma after *astris* and none
after *Polluce*. *Alternus* would then refer to Pollux, and not
Castor.

LII

Sı credis mihi, Quinte, quod mereris,
natalis, Ovidi, tuas Aprilis
ut nostras amo Martias Kalendas.
felix utraque lux diesque nobis
signandi melioribus lapillis!   5
hic vitam tribuit sed hic amicum.
plus dant, Quinte, mihi tuae Kalendae.

LIII

Natali tibi, Quinte, tuo dare parva volebam
    munera; tu prohibes: inperiosus homo es.
parendum est monitis, fiat quod uterque volemus
    et quod utrumque iuvat: tu mihi, Quinte, dato.

LIV

Sı mihi Picena turdus palleret oliva,
    tenderet aut nostras silva Sabina plagas,
aut crescente levis traheretur harundine praeda,
    pinguis et inplicitas virga teneret avis,
Care, daret sollemne tibi cognatio munus   5
    nec frater nobis nec prior esset avus.
nunc sturnos inopes fringillorumque querellas
    audit et arguto passere vernat ager;
inde salutatus picae respondet arator,
    hinc prope summa rapax milvus ad astra volat. 10

---

[1] M.'s friend and neighbour at Nomentum: *cf.* VII. xciii.
He addresses to him VII. xliv. and xlv., and the following
epigram.
[2] A cane smeared with birdlime, which could be elongated
like a fishing-rod: *cf.* XIV. ccxviii.

LII

If you believe me, Quintus Ovidius,[1] the kalends of your natal April I love—'tis your desert—as much as my own of March. Happy is either morn! and days are they to be marked by us with fairer stones. One gave me life, but the other a friend. Your kalends, Quintus, give me the more.

LIII

On your birthday, Quintus, I was wishing to give you a small present; you forbid me; you are an imperious person! I must obey your monition. Let be done what both of us wish, and what pleases both. Do you, Quintus, make *me* a present!

LIV

If fieldfares were fattened for me on Picenian olives, or Sabine woodland saw my gins stretched out, or a fluttering prey were drawn down by the lengthening reed,[2] and a limed rod held fast the entangled birds, Carus, my kinship[3] would give you the customary offering, and neither brother nor grandsire would come before you. As it is, my fields listen only to useless starlings and the plaint of chaffinches, and are vernal with the shrill sparrow; on that side the ploughman answers the magpie's call; on this, hard by, the ravening kite towers to

---

[3] On Feb. 22 was held the festival of the Caristia, when relations met and interchanged presents and arranged differences. It was a kind of family love-feast: *cf.* Ov. *Fast.* ii. 617; Val. Max. ii. i. 8.

mittimus ergo tibi parvae munuscula chortis,
    qualia si recipis, saepe propinquus eris.

LV

Luce propinquorum, qua plurima mittitur ales,
    dum Stellae turdos, dum tibi, Flacce, paro,
succurrit nobis ingens onerosaque turba,
    in qua se primum quisque meumque putat.
demeruisse duos votum est; offendere plures   5
    vix tutum; multis mittere dona grave est.
qua possum sola veniam ratione merebor:
    nec Stellae turdos nec tibi, Flacce, dabo.

LVI

Spendophoros Libycas domini petit armiger urbis:
    quae puero dones tela, Cupido, para,
illa quibus iuvenes figis mollesque puellas:
    sit tamen in tenera levis et hasta manu.
loricam clipeumque tibi galeamque remitto;   5
    tutus ut invadat proelia, nudus eat:
non iaculo, non ense fuit laesusve sagitta,
    casside dum liber Parthenopaeus erat.
quisquis ab hoc fuerit fixus morietur amore.
    o felix, si quem tam bona fata manent!   10
dum puer es, redeas, dum vultu lubricus, et te
    non Libye faciat, sed tua Roma virum.

---

[1] See note to preceding epigram.
[2] Stella, the poet mentioned in i. vii. and other epigrams,
and (perhaps) Valerius Flaccus, the author of the epic poem,
the *Argonautica*.

the lofty stars. So I send you the small tributes of my scanty poultry-yard; if you accept such things, you shall often be my kinsman.

LV

ON Kinsmen's Day,[1] when many a fowl is despatched, while I was preparing to send fieldfares to Stella, while also to you, Flaccus,[2] there came to my mind a big and burdensome crowd, of which each one thinks himself the chief, and my particular friend. To oblige two is my wish; to offend more is hardly safe; to despatch gifts to many is a heavy charge. In the only way I can I will earn their pardon : neither to Stella, nor to you, Flaccus, will I give fieldfares.

LVI

SPENDOPHORUS goes, his master's armour-bearer, to Libyan cities : get ready the shafts, Cupid, to give the boy—those wherewith thou dost pierce youths and soft girls ; yet in his tender hand let there be a smooth spear too. Cuirass and shield and helm I leave to thee ; that he may plunge amid the war unscathed let him go bare ; by no javelin, by no sword or arrow was Parthenopaeus [3] hurt when he was not disguised by a casque. Whoever shall be pierced by this boy shall perish of love—oh, happy he, over whoever so fair a fate impends ! While thou art boy, return, while thy face is perilously bright ; [4] and thee let not Libya, but thy Rome, make man !

---

[3] A young and handsome Greek warrior, one of the "Seven against Thebes" : cf. VI. lxxvii. 2 ; x. iv. 3.

[4] A reminiscence of Hor. Od. I. xix. 8 : et vultus nimium lubricus aspici.

LVII

Nil est tritius Hedyli lacernis:
non ansae veterum Corinthiorum,
nec crus compede lubricum decenni,
nec ruptae recutita colla mulae,
nec quae Flaminiam secant salebrae,   5
nec qui litoribus nitent lapilli,
nec Tusca ligo vinea politus,
nec pallens toga mortui tribulis,
nec pigri rota quassa mulionis,
nec rasum cavea latus visontis,   10
nec dens iam senior ferocis apri.
res una est tamen (ipse non negabit)
culus tritior Hedyli lacernis.

LVIII

Nympha sacri regina lacus, cui grata Sabinus
    et mansura pio munere templa dedit,
sic montana tuos semper colat Umbria fontes
    nec tua Baianas Sassina malit aquas,
excipe sollicitos placide, mea dona, libellos;   5
    tu fueris Musis Pegasis unda meis.
" Nympharum templis quisquis sua carmina donat,
    quid fieri libris debeat, ipse docet."

LIX

In Saeptis Mamurra diu multumque vagatus,
    hic ubi Roma suas aurea vexat opes,

---

[1] The slower the progress, the greater would be the friction
of the wheel, and its polish.

[2] Caesius Sabinus, of Sassina, in Umbria, to whom M.
presented his seventh book: *cf.* VII. xcvii. In IX. lx. he
sends him a wreath of roses.

LVII

NOTHING is worn smoother than Hedylus' mantles:
not the handles of antique Corinthian vases, nor a
shank polished by a ten-years-worn fetter, nor the
scarred neck of a broken-winded mule, nor the ruts
that intersect the Flaminian Way, nor the pebbles
that shine on the sea beach, nor a hoe polished by a
Tuscan vineyard, nor the shiny toga of a defunct
pauper, nor the ramshackle wheel of a lazy [1] carrier,
nor a bison's flank scraped by its cage, nor the tusk,
now aged, of a fierce boar. Yet there is one thing—
he himself will not deny it: Hedylus' rump is worn
smoother than his mantle.

LVIII

NYMPH, Queen of the sacred mere, to whom Sabinus [2] by pious gift has given a temple, welcome to
thee and destined to endure—so may hilly Umbria
ever honour thy fount, and thy Sassina prize not
more the waters of Baiae—receive with placid brow
my gift, these anxious [3] verses; then shalt thou be
to my Muse her spring of Pegasus. [4] " Whoever gives
his poems to temples of the Nymphs, himself declares
what should be done with his books." [5]

LIX

MAMURRA, long and often wandering in the Saepta,
here where Golden Rome flings about her wealth,

[3] *i.e.* as to its reception by the Nymph, or by Sabinus.
[4] Hippocrene, the fountain of the Muses, created by the
stroke of the hoof of Pegasus.
[5] *i.e.* to be thrown into the water. The supposed reply of
the Nymph. For the same idea, *cf.* I. v.; III. c. 4 ; IV. x. 6.

inspexit molles pueros oculisque comedit,
  non hos quos primae prostituere casae,
sed quos arcanae servant tabulata catastae   5
  et quos non populus nec mea turba videt.
inde satur mensas et opertos exuit orbes
  expositumque alte pingue poposcit ebur,
et testudineum mensus quater hexaclinon
  ingemuit citro non satis esse suo.   10
consuluit nares an olerent aera Corinthon,
  culpavit statuas et, Polyclite, tuas,
et, turbata brevi questus crystallina vitro,
  murrina signavit seposuitque decem.
expendit veteres calathos et si qua fuerunt   15
  pocula Mentorea nobilitata manu,
et viridis picto gemmas numeravit in auro,
  quidquid et a nivea grandius aure sonat.
sardonychas veros mensa quaesivit in omni
  et pretium magnis fecit iaspidibus.   20
ındecima lassus cum iam discederet hora,
  asse duos calices emit et ipse tulit.

LX

Seu tu Paestanis genita es seu Tiburis arvis,
  seu rubuit tellus Tuscula flore tuo,
seu Praenestino te vilica legit in horto,
  seu modo Campani gloria ruris eras,

---

[1] cf. II. xliii. 9.
[2] Connoisseurs professed to detect an odour in genuine
Corinthian bronze: Petr. 50.
[3] Of Sicyon, a celebrated sculptor of the fifth century B.C.

inspected and devoured with his eyes dainty boys,
not those the outer stalls made public, but those who
are guarded by the platforms of a secret stand, and
whom the people do not see, nor the crowd of such as
I. Then, sated with the view, he had tables and
round covered table-tops [1] laid bare, and must needs
have their high-hung glistening ivory supports brought
down; and, after four measurements of a tortoise-shell
couch for six, he said with a sigh that it was too small
for his citrus-wood table. He took counsel of his
nose whether the bronzes smelt of Corinth,[2] and
condemned even your statuary, Polyclitus;[3] and,
complaining that the crystal vases were disfigured
by a small piece of glass, he put his seal on ten
murrine [4] articles, and set them aside. He weighed
antique tankards, and any cups made precious by
Mentor's [5] handiwork, and counted the emeralds set
in chased gold, and every larger pearl that tinkles
from a snow-white ear. Genuine sardonyxes he
looked for on every table, and offered a price for
some big jaspers. When at the eleventh hour,
fagged out, he was at last departing, for a penny he
bought two cups—and bore them off himself![6]

LX

WHETHER thou wert born in fields of Paestum or
of Tibur, or the soil of Tusculum blushed with thy
flower; or a farmer's wife culled thee in a garden
at Praeneste, or thou wert erewhile the glory of

---

[4] Perhaps porcelain : *cf.* XIV. cxiii.
[5] A celebrated worker in embossed metal of the fourth
century B.C.: *cf.* III. xli. 1 ; IV. xxxix. 5.
[6] He had not even a slave of his own.

pulchrior ut nostro videare corona Sabino,   5
  de. Nomentano te putet esse meo.

LXI

In Tartesiacis domus est notissima terris,
  qua dives placidum Corduba Baetin amat,
vellera nativo pallent ubi flava metallo
  et linit Hesperium brattea viva pecus.
aedibus in mediis totos amplexa penates   5
  stat platanus densis Caesariana comis,
hospitis invicti posuit quam dextera felix,
  coepit et ex illa crescere virga manu.
auctorem dominumque suum sentire videtur :
  sic viret et ramis sidera celsa petit.   10
saepe sub hac madidi luserunt arbore Fauni
  terruit et tacitam fistula sera domum :
dumque fugit solos nocturnum Pana per agros,
  saepe sub hac latuit rustica fronde Dryas.
atque oluere lares comissatore Lyaeo,   15
  crevit et effuso laetior umbra mero ;
hesternisque rubens deiecta est herba coronis
  atque suas potuit dicere nemo rosas.
o dilecta deis, o magni Caesaris arbor,
  ne metuas ferrum sacrilegosque focos.   20
perpetuos sperare licet tibi frondis honores :
  non Pompeianae te posuere manus.

---

[1] Which produced nothing : *cf.* VII. xxxi. 8.
[2] The Guadalquiver.
[3] *cf.* V. xxxvii. 7 ; VIII. xxviii. 6.

Campanian meads; that thou mayst seem to my
Sabinus a chaplet the more fair, let him think thou
art from my Nomentan [1] farm.

LXI

A HOUSE renowned stands in the land of Tartessus
where rich Corduba woos tranquil Baetis,[2] where
fleeces are yellow-pale with native ore, and living
gold o'erlays the Western flock.[3] In the middle of
the house, shadowing all the abode, stands with
dense leafage Caesar's [4] plane, which an unconquered
Guest's propitious hand planted, and which—then
but a shoot—began from that hand to grow. It
seems to feel who was its creator and lord; so
green it is, and with its boughs it climbs high
heaven. Ofttimes under this tree sported Fauns [5]
flown with wine, and a late-blown pipe startled the
still house; and, while o'er lonely fields she fled by
night from Pan, oft under these leaves the rustic
Dryad [6] nestled hid. And fragrant has the dwelling
been when Lyaeus held revel, and more luxuriant
grown the tree's shade from spilth of wine, and the
blushing flower has been scattered down from last
night's wreath, and none could claim his own roses.
O thou dear to the gods! O tree of mighty Caesar!
fear not the steel and sacrilegious fires. Thou mayst
hope thy leafy honours shall endure for ever: it was
not Pompey's hands [7] set thee there!

[4] Julius Caesar.
[5] Rustic deities, half goat, half in human shape.
[6] The Dryads were nymphs of the woods.
[7] But those of his conqueror.

LXII

TINCTIS murice vestibus quod omni
et nocte utitur et die Philaenis,
non est ambitiosa nec superba :
delectatur odore, non colore.

LXIII

AD cenam invitant omnes te, Phoebe, cinaedi.
mentula quem pascit, non, puto, purus homo est.

LXIV

HERCULIS in magni voltus descendere Caesar
dignatus Latiae dat nova templa viae,
qua Triviae nemorosa petit dum regna, viator
octavum domina marmor ab urbe legit.
ante colebatur votis et sanguine largo,　　　　5
maiorem Alciden nunc minor ipse colit.
hunc magnas rogat alter opes, rogat alter honores ;
illi securus vota minora facit.

LXV

ALCIDE, Latio nunc agnoscende Tonanti,
postquam pulchra dei Caesaris ora geris,
si tibi tunc isti vultus habitusque fuissent,
cesserunt manibus cum fera monstra tuis,

---

[1] She wishes to drown her own peculiar odour.　Tyrian-
dyed garments had a rank smell : *cf.* IV. iv. 6.

[2] Domitian dedicated a temple to Hercules with a statue
bearing the features of the emperor.

LXII

Because Philaenis night and day wears garments dipped in every kind of purple, she is not ambitious or proud. She is pleased with the smell, not with the hue.[1]

LXIII

All the dissolute rascals invite you to dinner, Phoebus. He whom impurity feeds is not, I opine, a spotless person.

LXIV

Caesar, deigning to descend to the features of great Hercules,[2] gives a new temple to the Latin Way, where the traveller, on his journey to Trivia's woody realm,[3] reads the eighth milestone from the Queen City. Aforetime was Alcides worshipped with prayer and full blood of victims; now he, the lesser, himself worships a greater[4] Alcides. Of him, the greater, one man begs large wealth, another begs honours; to him, the lesser, carelessly he makes his more trifling prayers.

LXV

Alcides, worthy now to be owned by the Latin Thunderer,[5] after that thou wearest the features fair of Caesar our god, if thine had been then that face and guise when savage monsters yielded to thy arms, the nations had not seen thee the serf of the

[3] To the temple and grove of Diana of the Crossways (*Trivia*) at Aricia.
[4] The emperor. [5] Jupiter of the Capitol.

Argolico famulum non te servire tyranno   5
  vidissent gentes saevaque regna pati;
sed tu iussisses Eurysthea: nec tibi fallax
  portasset Nessi perfida dona Lichas;
Oetaei sine lege rogi securus adisses
  astra patris summi, quae tibi poena dedit;   10
Lydia nec dominae traxisses pensa superbae
  nec Styga vidisses Tartareumque canem.
nunc tibi Iuno favet, nunc te tua diligit Hebe;
  nunc te si videat Nympha, remittet Hylan.

LXVI

Uxor cum tibi sit formosa, pudica, puella,
  quo tibi natorum iura, Fabulle, trium?
quod petis a nostro supplex dominoque deoque,
  tu dabis ipse tibi, si potes arrigere.

LXVII

Lascivam tota possedi nocte puellam,
  cuius nequitias vincere nulla potest.
fessus mille modis illud puerile poposci:
  ante preces totas primaque verba dedit.

---

[1] Hercules was the serf of Eurystheus until he had accomplished his twelve labours.

[2] Lichas, the servant of Hercules, at the bidding of Deianeira, his wife, gave him the shirt of Nessus steeped in the poison of the hydra slain by H. It clung to him, and he burnt himself on a pyre on Mt. Oeta.

despot of Argos,[1] and enduring a cruel thrall, but thou wouldst have commanded Eurystheus; nor would false Lichas[2] have brought to thee the guileful gift of Nessus; without the ordeal of Oeta's pyre wouldst thou unvexed have won that heaven of thy Sire supreme which thy penance gave thee; nor wouldst thou have drawn out the wool of a haughty mistress,[3] nor have viewed Styx and the Tartarean hound.[4] Now to thee is Juno kind, now thy Hebe loves thee; now, should she see thee, the nymph will send Hylas[5] back.

LXVI

WHEN you have a wife beautiful, modest, young, what is the use to you, Fabullus, of the rights[6] three sons bestow? What you suppliantly ask of our Lord and God you will yourself supply—if you can play the man.

LXVII

POSSEDEI per tutta la notte una lasciva ragazza, le di cui malizie nessuna può sorpassare. Sazio in mille maniere, dimandai quel non so che alla fanciullesca: me lo accordò avanti d'esserne pregata, ed alle prime

---

[3] Omphale, queen of Lydia, who wore H.'s lion-skin while he spun her wool.

[4] It was one of the labours of Hercules to fetch Cerberus from the shades.

[5] A beautiful youth, the attendant of Hercules, carried off by the enamoured Nymphs: cf. v. xlviii. 5.

[6] Often given, as a compliment, even to childless persons: cf. II. xci. 6.

inprobius quiddam ridensque rubensque rogavi :   5
   pollicitast nulla luxuriosa mora.
sed mihi pura fuit; tibi non erit, Aeschyle, si vis
   accipere hoc munus condicione mala.

LXVIII

Quid tibi nobiscum est, ludi scelerate magister,
   invisum pueris virginibusque caput?
nondum cristati rupere silentia galli :
   murmure iam saevo verberibusque tonas.
tam grave percussis incudibus aera resultant,   5
   causidicum medio cum faber aptat equo :
mitior in magno clamor furit amphitheatro,
   vincenti parmae cum sua turba favet.
vicini somnum non tota nocte rogamus :
   nam vigilare leve est, pervigilare grave est.   10
discipulos dimitte tuos.   vis, garrule, quantum
   accipis ut clames, accipere ut taceas?

LXIX

Cum futuis, Polycharme, soles in fine cacare.
   cum pedicaris, quid, Polycharme, facis?

LXX

Dixerat "O mores! o tempora!" Tullius olim,
   sacrilegum strueret cum Catilina nefas,

---

[1] Some disgraceful complaisance was required in return,
which M. says he refused, but which Aeschylus would not.
[2] Successful lawyers were in the habit of erecting equestrian statues of themselves in their vestibules: *cf.* **Juv. vii.**
124.

ricchieste. Fra 'l riso e la vergogna dimandai qualche cosa d'assai nefando : me lo promise senza la menoma interessata dilazione. Ma fù da me lasciata pura ; non lo sarà da te, O Eschilo, se vuoi prendere questo dono ma a mala condizione.[1]

LXVIII

WHAT have you to do with us, accursed pedagogue, a fellow odious to boys and girls ? Not yet have crested cocks broken the hush of night, already with menacing voice and with thwacks you raise an uproar. So heavily re-echoes brass on smitten anvils when a smith is fitting a pleader's statue astride a steed ;[2] milder in the huge amphitheatre riots the shout when its own faction acclaims the small shield.[3] We neighbours don't ask for sleep all the night ;[4] for some wakefulness is a trifle, to wake all night is no joke. Dismiss your pupils. Are you willing, you blatant fellow, to accept for holding your tongue as much as you accept for bawling ?

LXIX

QUANDO immembri, O Policarmo, suoli dopo sgravarti. Quando sei sodomizzato, che fai, O Policarmo ?

LXX

"O MANNERS ! O times !" cried Tully once when Catiline was planning his sacrilegious crime,[5] when

---

[3] *Parma*, carried by gladiators called Thracians. Domitian favoured the *scutarii*, the carriers of the large shield. Hence a victory of the *parmularius* would be more unexpected.   [4] As to the noises of Rome, *cf.* XII. lvii.
[5] Cic. *Cat.* I. i. 2.

cum gener atque socer diris concurreret armis
　　maestaque civili caede maderet humus.
cur nunc "O mores!" cur nunc "O tempora!" dicis?
　　quod tibi non placeat, Caeciliane, quid est?　　6
nulla ducum feritas, nulla est insania ferri;
　　pace frui certa laetitiaque licet.
non nostri faciunt tibi quod tua tempora sordent,
　　sed faciunt mores, Caeciliane, tui.　　10

LXXI

Massyli leo fama iugi pecorisque maritus
　　lanigeri mirum qua coiere fide.
ipse licet videas, cavea stabulantur in una
　　et pariter socias carpit uterque dapes:
nec fetu nemorum gaudent nec mitibus herbis,　　5
　　concordem satiat sed rudis agna famem.
quid meruit terror Nemees, quid portitor Helles,
　　ut niteant celsi lucida signa poli?
sidera si possent pecudesque feraeque mereri,
　　hic aries astris, hic leo dignus erat.　　10

LXXII

Liber, Amyclaea frontem vittate corona,
　　qui quatis Ausonia verbera Graia manu,
clusa mihi texto cum prandia vimine mittas,
　　cur comitata dapes nulla lagona venit?
atqui digna tuo si nomine munera ferres,　　5
　　scis, puto, debuerint quae mihi dona dari.

---

[1] Pompey married Caesar's daughter Julia.
[2] The lion slain by Hercules and the ram that carried
Helle respectively, afterwards two of the signs of the Zodiac.

son-in-law and father-in-law[1] were clashing in dreadful war, and the weeping earth was drenched with civil carnage. Why do you now cry "O manners!" why now "O times!" What is it displeases you, Caecilianus? No savagery of captains is here, no frenzy of the sword : we may enjoy unbroken peace and pleasure. 'Tis not our "manners" that make your "times" despicable to you, but your own manners, Caecilianus, make them so.

LXXI

A LION, the renown of Massylian hills, and the husband of the fleecy flock, have allied themselves in wondrous confidence. You may yourself see them : they are stalled in one pen, and each with the other takes his social meal ; they relish not the breed of the woods, nor harmless herbs, but a young lamb sates their friendly hunger. What was the merit of the terror of Nemea, what of the carrier of Helle,[2] that they should glow, the tall sky's lustrous signs? If both sheep and wild beasts could win by merit to heaven, this ram, this lion were worthy to become stars.

LXXII

LIBER,[3] whose brow is wreathed with an Amyclaean[4] crown, who level with an Italian arm the Grecian boxer's blows, as you are sending me a lunch shut in a wicker basket, why does no flagon come attendant on the feast? And yet, if you were to produce a gift to match your name,[5] you know, I think, what present should have been given me!

[3] To whom also VIII. lxxvii. is addressed.
[4] *i.e.* Spartan. Pollux, the son of Spartan Leda, invented boxing.   [5] Liber was also a synonym of Bacchus.

LXXIII

DENTIBUS antiquas solitus producere pelles
    et mordere luto putre vetusque solum,
Praenestina tenes defuncti rura[1] patroni,
    in quibus indignor si tibi cella fuit;
rumpis et ardenti madidus crystalla Falerno   5
    et pruris domini cum Ganymede tui.
at me litterulas stulti docuere parentes:
    quid cum grammaticis rhetoribusque mihi?
frange leves calamos et scinde, Thalia, libellos,
    si dare sutori calceus ista potest.   10

LXXIV

EFFIGIEM tantum pueri pictura Camoni
    servat, et infantis parva figura manet.
florentes nulla signavit imagine voltus,
    dum timet ora pius muta videre pater.

LXXV

NON silice duro structilive caemento
    nec latere cocto, quo Samiramis longam
    Babylona cinxit, Tucca balneum fecit,
    sed strage nemorum pineaque conpage,
    ut navigare Tucca balneo possit.   5
    idem beatas lautus extruit thermas
    de marmore omni, quod Carystos invenit,
    quod Phrygia Synnas, Afra quod Nomas misit
    et quod virenti fonte lavit Eurotas.
    sed ligna desunt: subice balneum thermis.   10

---

[1] *decepti regna* β.

LXXIII

WONT with your teeth to stretch out ancient hides, and to gnaw a shoe-sole rotten with mud and worn out, you possess the Praenestan fields of your dead patron, in which I think it shame if you ever had a garret; and drunk, you fill to bursting your crystal with hot Falernian, and lewdly trifle with the cup-bearer of your master. But me foolish parents taught paltry letters: what is the use of teachers of grammar and rhetoric to me? Break your worthless pens, Thalia, and tear up your books, if a shoe can give a cobbler a gift like that.

LXXIV

CAMONIUS' picture preserves but the image of a child, and only an infant's tiny form survives. On the face of manhood's bloom[1] a father stamped no semblance: his love feared to see the lips that spake no more.

LXXV

NOT of hard flint or laid rubble, nor of burnt brick, wherewith Semiramis girt the long walls of Babylon, has Tucca made his bath; but of the havoc of the woods and of balks of pine, so that Tucca may go to sea in his bath! He also, luxurious man that he is! builds costly warm baths of every kind of marble that Carystos discovers, that Phrygian Synnas, that African Numidia has sent him, and of that which Eurotas has washed green[2] with his spring. But firewood is lacking. Put the bath under the warm bath![3]

[1] *cf.* IX. lxxvi. 3–5.
[2] *cf.* VI. xlii. 11. Laconian marble was green.
[3] The wooden bath might have made a boat (l. 5), but is now to make a fire.

E 2

LXXVI

Haec sunt illa mei quae cernitis ora Camoni,
    haec pueri facies primaque forma fuit.
creverat hic vultus bis denis fortior annis
    gaudebatque suas pingere barba genas,
et libata semel summos modo purpura cultros   5
    sparserat.   invidit de tribus una soror
et festinatis incidit stamina pensis,
    apsentemque patri rettulit urna rogum.
sed ne sola tamen puerum pictura loquatur,
    haec erit in chartis maior imago meis.   10

LXXVII

Quod optimum sit disputat convivium
    facunda Prisci pagina,
et multa dulci, multa sublimi refert,
    sed cuncta docto pectore.
quod optimum sit quaeritis convivium?   5
    in quo choraules non erit.

LXXVIII

Funera post septem nupsit tibi Galla virorum,
    Picentine: sequi vult, puto, Galla viros.

LXXIX

Oderat ante ducum famulos turbamque priorem
    et Palatinum Roma supercilium:

---

[1] The Fates.
[2] C. died in Cappadocia: *cf.* VI. lxxxv. 3.

LXXVI

THIS face you see is that of my Camonius: this
was his childish face and infant form. These features
had grown manlier in twice ten years, and his beard
gladly was tinging its native cheek, and darkening
down, shaved but once, had newly besprent the
scissors' tip. Jealous was one Sister of the Three,[1]
and she cut the thread from the wool too quickly
spun, and an urn gave back to the sire the ashes
from afar.[2] Yet, that not alone be the picture that
bespeaks a boy, in my lay shall this, a nobler likeness,
be found.

LXXVII

PRISCUS' pages fluently discuss what is the best
kind of entertainment, and he puts forward many
views in a pleasant, many in a lofty style, and all
with learning. Do you ask what is the best entertainment? One where there will be no flute-
player with his chorus.[3]

LXXVIII

AFTER burying seven husbands, Galla has married
you, Picentinus; Galla wants, I imagine, to follow
her husbands.[4]

LXXIX

ONCE Rome abhorred the henchmen and the old
retinue of her chiefs, and the haughtiness of the

[3] To drown conversation. The *choraules* accompanied a
chorus, as distinguished from the *auletes* or the *citharoedus*,
a single player on flute or harp : *cf.* v. lvi. 8.
[4] Both G. and P. were poisoners : *cf.* VIII. xliii.

at nunc tantus amor cunctis, Auguste, tuorum est
  ut sit cuique suae cura secunda domus.
tam placidae mentes, tanta est reverentia nostri,   5
  tam pacata quies, tantus in ore pudor.
nemo suos (haec est aulae natura potentis)
  sed domini mores Caesarianus habet.

LXXX

Duxerat esuriens locupletem pauper anumque :
  uxorem pascit Gellius et futuit.

LXXXI

Lector et auditor nostros probat, Aule, libellos,
  sed quidam exactos esse poeta negat.
non nimium curo : nam cenae fercula nostrae
  malim convivis quam placuisse cocis.

LXXXII

Dixerat astrologus periturum te cito, Munna,
  nec, puto, mentitus dixerat ille tibi.
nam tu dum metuis ne quid post fata relinquas,
  hausisti patrias luxuriosus opes,
bisque tuum deciens non toto tabuit anno.   5
  dic mihi, non hoc est, Munna, perire cito?

LXXXIII

Inter tanta tuae miracula, Caesar, harenae,
  quae vincit veterum munera clara ducum,
multum oculi sed plus aures debere fatentur
  se tibi, quod spectant qui recitare solent.

Palatine; but now, Augustus, all men so love those that belong to you that to each his own household is but a second care. So gentle are their tempers, so great is their respect for us, so unruffled is their calm, such modesty is in their faces! No servant of Caesar—such is the mood of an imperial hall—displays his own manners, but those only of his master.

LXXX

HUNGRY, and a pauper, Gellius married a rich and old woman. He now feeds and tickles his wife.

LXXXI

READER and hearer approve of my works, Aulus, but a certain poet says they are not polished. I don't care much, for I should prefer the courses of my dinner to please guests rather than cooks.

LXXXII

AN astrologer said that you would quickly come to an end, Munna, and he did not lie, I think, when he said it to you. For you, in your fear of leaving anything after your death, have in extravagance exhausted your father's wealth, and your two millions have melted away in less than a year. Tell me, is not this, Munna, quickly coming to an end?

LXXXIII

AMID the mighty wonders of your arena, Caesar, which surpasses the grand spectacles of former chiefs, there is much our eyes admit they owe you, but our ears still more, for the usual reciters are now spectators.[1]

[1] And cannot bore us: *cf.* Juv. i. 7–14.

LXXXIV

Cum tua sacrilegos contra, Norbane, furores
    staret pro domino Caesare sancta fides,
haec ego Pieria ludebam tutus in umbra,
    ille tuae cultor notus amicitiae.
me tibi Vindelicis Raetus narrabat in oris,   5
    nescia nec nostri nominis Arctos erat:
o quotiens veterem non infitiatus amicum
    dixisti " Meus est iste poeta, meus ! "
omne tibi nostrum quod bis trieteride iuncta
    ante dabat lector, nunc dabit auctor opus.   10

LXXXV

Languidior noster si quando est Paulus, Atili,
    non se, convivas abstinet ille suos.
tu languore quidem subito fictoque laboras,
    sed mea porrexit sportula, Paule, pedes.

LXXXVI

Festinata sui gemeret quod fata Severi
    Silius, Ausonio non semel ore potens,
cum grege Pierio maestus Phoeboque querebar.
    " Ipse meum flevi " dixit Apollo " Linon " :
respexitque suam quae stabat proxima fratri   5
    Calliopen et ait " Tu quoque vulnus habes.

---

[1] Appius Norbanus had been sent in A.D. 88 to crush the
revolt of Saturninus against Domitian : cf. IV. xi. He was
absent six years, and M.'s works would be Books IV.–VIII.

[2] i.e. is lost to me. *Porrigere pedes* was said of a corpse
when laid out with the feet pointing to the outer door :
Pers. iii. 105 ; Hom. *Il.* xix. 212.

LXXXIV

WHEN your inviolate loyalty, Norbanus, in defence of your master Caesar was withstanding impious frenzy, I, secure in the Pierian shade, the wooer, as men know, of your friendship, threw off these books. Me the Rhaetian quoted to you on Vindelicia's shores, and the North was not unknowing of my name. Oh, how often, not denying your old friend, you exclaimed: "My own is that poet, my own!" All work of mine, which during three years twice counted[1] your reader gave you before, its author will give you now.

LXXXV

IF at any time, Atilius, our acquaintance Paulus is unwell, he practises abstinence, not on himself but on his guests. You are suffering no doubt, Paulus, from a sudden—and fictitious—illness: all the same my dinner has turned up its toes.[2]

LXXXVI

BECAUSE Silius, the twofold master of the Latin tongue,[3] was lamenting the early death of his Severus,[4] I complained sadly to the Pierian band and to Phoebus. "I, too," said Apollo, "wept for my Linus." And he looked back to Calliope his sister, who stood next her brother, and said; "You, too,[5]

---

[3] *i.e.* as orator and poet : *cf.* VII. lxiii.

[4] S.'s younger son, for whom M. solicited the consulship (VIII. lxvi.), which, however, he never attained : Plin. *Ep.* III. vii. 2.

[5] Calliope was the mother of Orpheus. So, too, Jupiter had lost Sarpedon, and Domitian a son ; *cf.* IV. iii.

aspice Tarpeium Palatinumque Tonantem :
   ausa nefas Lachesis laesit utrumque Iovem.
numina cum videas duris obnoxia fatis,
   invidia possis exonerare deos."   10

LXXXVII

SEPTEM post calices Opimiani
denso cum iaceam triente blaesus,
adfers nescio quas mihi tabellas
et dicis " Modo liberum esse iussi
Nastam (servolus est mihi paternus) :   5
signa."   cras melius, Luperce, fiet :
nunc signat meus anulus lagonam.

LXXXVIII

CUM me captares, mittebas munera nobis :
   postquam cepisti, das mihi, Rufe, nihil.
ut captum teneas, capto quoque munera mitte,
   de cavea fugiat ne male pastus aper.

LXXXIX

LEGE nimis dura convivam scribere versus
   cogis, Stella ?   " Licet scribere nempe malos."

XC

SIC in gramine florido reclinis,
qua gemmantibus hinc et inde rivis

---

[1] *i.e.* as a witness. But M. hints that Lupercus wishes
him to sign a document which he would not sign when sober.

have your wound. Mark the Thunderer of the Tarpeian and him of the Palatine : Lachesis, daring a
crime, has hurt either Jove. Forasmuch as you see
that deities are subject to the inflexible Fates, of
jealousy you may acquit the gods."

LXXXVII

WHEN, after seven cups of Opimian, I lie lisping
amid my frequent potations, you bring me some
document or other and say : "I have just bade
Nasta to go free—he was my father's slave—put
your seal."[1] Better to-morrow, Lupercus : just now
my ring only seals up[2] flagons.

LXXXVIII

WHEN you were trying to catch me you used to
send me presents : after you have caught me, you,
Rufus, give me nothing. To hold your catch, send
presents to him also when caught, that the boar,
being badly fed, may not escape from its pen.

LXXXIX

Do you by too hard a regulation compel your guest
to write verses, Stella ? "Well, you are allowed to
write bad ones."

XC

So, on flower-spangled sward reclining, where in
the runnels sparkling here and there the pebble is

[2] To prevent theft : Plin. *N.H.* xxxiii. 6 ; Juv. xiv.
132.

curva calculus excitatur unda,
exclusis procul omnibus molestis,
pertundas[1] glaciem triente nigro,   5
frontem sutilibus ruber coronis;
sic uni tibi sit puer cinaedus
et castissima pruriat puella:
infamem nimio calore Cypron
observes moneo precorque, Flacce,   10
messes area cum teret crepantis
et fervens iuba saeviet leonis.
at tu, diva Paphi, remitte, nostris
inlaesum iuvenem remitte votis,
sic Martis tibi serviant Kalendae   15
et cum ture meroque victimaque
libetur tibi candidas ad aras
secta plurima quadra de placenta.

XCI

AD cenam si me diversa vocaret in astra
  hinc invitator Caesaris, inde Iovis,
astra licet propius, Palatia longius essent,
  responsa ad superos haec referenda darem:
"Quaerite qui malit fieri conviva Tonantis: 5
  me meus in terris Iuppiter ecce tenet."

XCII

QUAE mala sint domini, quae servi commoda, nescis,
  Condyle, qui servum te gemis esse diu.

                    [1] *perfundas* γ.

---

[1] Wine was strained through ice or snow: *cf.* v. lxiv. 2;
XIV. cxvii.

tumbled by the rippling wave, with all your frets banished afar, may you with measures of dark wine break through the ice[1] while your brow blushes with rose-stitched chaplets; so for you alone may a fair boy-slave and a mistress most pure be eager, if, as I warn and pray you, Flaccus, you beware of Cyprus of evil name in summer's height, when the threshing-floor shall bray the rustling harvests, and the Lion's mane[2] be hot with rage. But do thou, goddess of Paphos, send back to our prayers, send back the youth unscathed; so may March's kalends[3] be in fealty to thee, and with incense, and new wine, and victim, there be offered to thee at thy fair altars many a quarter of parcelled cake.

XCI

WERE I invited to diverse heavens to feast, on this side by Caesar's summoner, on that by Jove's, though the stars were nearer, the Palace more far, this answer would I give to be returned to the High Gods: "Seek ye one who would choose to be the Thunderer's guest; me on earth, mark ye, my Jupiter detains!"

XCII

WHAT are a master's ills, what a slave's blessings you do not know, Condylus, who groan that

[2] The constellation Leo.
[3] At the festival of the Matronalia men sent presents to their mistresses: cf. v. lxxxiv. 11.

dat tibi securos vilis tegeticula somnos,
  pervigil in pluma Gaius ecce iacet.
Gaius a prima tremebundus luce salutat   5
  tot dominos, at tu, Condyle, nec dominum.
"Quod debes, Gai, redde" inquit Phoebus et illinc
  Cinnamus : hoc dicit, Condyle, nemo tibi.
tortorem metuis ? podagra cheragraque secatur
  Gaius et mallet verbera mille pati.   10
quod nec mane vomis nec cunnum, Condyle, lingis,
  non mavis quam ter Gaius esse tuus ?

XCIII

ADDERE quid cessas, puer, inmortale Falernum ?
  quadrantem duplica de seniore cado.
nunc mihi dic, quis erit cui te, Calacisse, deorum
  sex iubeo cyathos fundere ?   "Caesar erit."
sutilis aptetur deciens rosa crinibus, ut sit   5
  qui posuit sacrae nobile gentis opus.
nunc bis quina mihi da basia, fiat ut illud
  nomen ab Odrysio quod deus orbe tulit.

XCIV

SARDONICA medicata dedit mihi pocula virga,
  os hominis! mulsum me rogat Hippocrates.

---

[1] *i.e.* to extort confession of some offence : Juv. xiv. 21.
[2] Domitian, who founded the temple of the *Gens Flavia* :
cf. IX. i. 8 ; IX. iii. 12.
[3] The six and the two tens represent respectively the
names Caesar, Domitianus, and Germanicus.   For this practice, *cf.* I. lxxi.; XI. xxxvi. 7.

you are so long a slave. Your common rush-mat
affords you sleep untroubled; wakeful all night
on down, see, Gaius lies! Gaius from early morn
salutes trembling many masters; but you, Condylus,
not even your master. "What you owe, Gaius, pay,"
says Phoebus, and after him Cinnamus: this no one,
Condylus, says to you. Do you dread the torturer?[1]
By gout in foot and hand Gaius is stabbed, and would
choose instead to endure a thousand blows. You do
not vomit in the morning, nor are you given to filthy
vice, Condylus: do you not prefer this to being your
Gaius three times over?

XCIII

WHY linger, boy, to pour in the undying Falernian?
Double three measures from the older jar. Now tell
me who shall it be of the Gods to whom I bid thee,
Calocissus, pour six measures? "Caesar it shall
be." Let the stitched rose be ten times fitted to
our locks, that he be shown who laid the noble
temple of his hallowed race.[2] Now give me twice
five kisses to shape the name he brought from the
Thracian world.[3]

XCIV

HIPPOCRATES[4] gave me—such is his impudence!—
a draught drugged with Sardinian root,[5] and asks me

[4] H. of Cos was the founder of medicine. The name is
here put for a doctor.
[5] The herbs of Sardinia were bitter, and affected honey:
Verg. *Ecl.* vii. 41. Yet H. expects in return ordinary
mulsum (wine and honey mixed).

tam stupidus numquam nec tu, puto, Glauce, fuisti,
    χάλκεα donanti χρύσεα qui dederas.
dulce aliquis munus pro munere poscit amaro?   5
    accipiat, sed si potat in elleboro.

XCV

ALPHIUS ante fuit, coepit nunc Olphius esse,
    uxorem postquam duxit Athenagoras.

XCV B

NOMEN Athenagorae quaeris, Callistrate, verum.
    si scio, dispeream, qui sit Athenagoras.
sed puta me verum, Callistrate, dicere nomen: 5
    non ego sed vester peccat Athenagoras.

XCVI

CLINICUS Herodes trullam subduxerat aegro:
    deprensus dixit "Stulte, quid ergo bibis?"

XCVII

RUMPITUR invidia quidam, carissime Iuli,
    quod me Roma legit, rumpitur invidia.

---

[1] The Trojan, who exchanged armour with Diomede the
Greek, χρύσεα χαλκείων, ἑκατόμβοι' ἐννεαβοίων : Hom. *Il.* vi.
234. Homer remarks, Κρονίδης φρένας ἐξέλετο (deprived him
of sense).

for mead wine. So great a fool even you, Glaucus,[1] never were, I fancy, who gave gold to him who gave you bronze. Does any man ask a gift of sweets for a gift of bitters? He may have it, but only if he drinks it with hellebore.[2]

XCV

ATHENAGORAS was Alphius before, now he becomes Olphius after that he has married a wife.[3]

XCV B

"Is the name 'Athenagoras' a real one," you ask, Callistratus. May I be hanged if I know who Athenagoras is! But imagine, Callistratus, I mentioned a real name: not I, but your friend Athenagoras is at fault.[4]

XCVI

DOCTOR Herodes had stolen a drinking-ladle from a sick patient. When detected he said: "You fool, why then do you drink?"[5]

XCVII

A CERTAIN fellow, dearest Julius, is bursting with envy; because Rome reads me, he is bursting with

---

[2] A supposed cure for madness: Hor. *Sat.* II. iii. 82, 166.
[3] The point of this epigram is unknown.
[4] *i.e.* that he has this name.
[5] He professes care for his patient's health by removing the article.

rumpitur invidia quod turba semper in omni
    monstramur digito, rumpitur invidia.
rumpitur invidia tribuit quod Caesar uterque   5
    ius mihi natorum, rumpitur invidia.
rumpitur invidia quod rus mihi dulce sub urbe est
    parvaque in urbe domus, rumpitur invidia.
rumpitur invidia quod sum iucundus amicis,
    quod conviva frequens, rumpitur invidia.   10
rumpitur invidia quod amamur quodque probamur.
    rumpatur quisquis rumpitur invidia.

XCVIII

VINDEMIARUM non ubique proventus
    cessavit, Ovidi ; pluvia profuit grandis.
    centum Coranus amphoras aquae fecit.

XCIX

MARCUS amat nostras Antonius, Attice, Musas,
    charta salutatrix si modo vera refert,
Marcus Palladiae non infitianda Tolosae
    gloria, quem [1] genuit Pacis alumna Quies.
tu qui longa potes dispendia ferre viarum,   5
    i, liber, absentis pignus amicitiae.
vilis eras, fateor, si te nunc mitteret emptor :
    grande tui pretium muneris auctor erit.
multum, crede mihi, refert a fonte bibatur
    quae fluit an pigro quae stupet unda lacu.   10

[1] *quam* (Friedländer).

[1] *cf.* II. xcii.; III. xcv. 6.

envy. He is bursting with envy because in every throng I am always pointed out with the finger, he is bursting with envy. He is bursting with envy because each Caesar gave me the right of a father of three sons,[1] he is bursting with envy. He is bursting with envy because I have a suburban farm and a small house in town, he is bursting with envy. He is bursting with envy because I am delightful to my friends, because I am often a guest, he is bursting with envy. He is bursting with envy because I am loved and my works are approved. Let anyone, whoever he is, who is bursting with envy, burst![2]

XCVIII

THE crop of the vineyards has not everywhere failed, Ovidius: heavy rains have been profitable. Coranus has made a hundred jars—of water.[3]

XCIX

MARCUS ANTONIUS loves my Muse, Atticus, if only his letter of greeting says true—Marcus, cultured Tolosa's indisputable glory, whom Quietude, the nursling of Peace, begot. Do you, who can put up with long journeys, go, my book, pledge of an absent friendship. A poor gift you would be, I own, if a purchaser were sending you now; the author's giving will lend you goodly value. Great is the difference, believe me, whether water is drunk from the fountain as it flows, or as it stagnates in a sluggish pool.

---

[2] *i.e.* be d——d. *Rumpatur* = διαρραγείη. The point of the epigram seems to lie in the two senses of *rumpi*.
[3] *i.e.* to mix with his wine. Coranus is probably a fraudulent vintner: *cf.* I. lvi.

C

Denaris tribus invitas et mane togatum
  observare iubes atria, Basse, tua,
deinde haerere tuo lateri, praecedere sellam,
  ad viduas tecum plus minus ire decem.
trita quidem nobis togula est vilisque vetusque : 5
  denaris tamen hanc non emo, Basse, tribus.

CI

Appia, quam simili venerandus in Hercule Caesar
  consecrat, Ausoniae maxima fama viae,
si cupis Alcidae cognoscere facta prioris,
  disce : Libyn domuit, aurea poma tulit,
peltatam Scythico discinxit Amazona nodo, 5
  addidit Arcadio terga leonis apro,
aeripedem silvis cervum, Stymphalidas astris
  abstulit, a Stygia cum cane venit aqua,
fecundam vetuit reparari mortibus hydram,
  Hesperias Tusco lavit in amne boves. 10
haec minor Alcides : maior quae gesserit audi,
  sextus ab Albana quem colit arce lapis.
adseruit possessa malis Palatia regnis,
  prima suo gessit pro Iove bella puer ;
solus Iuleas cum iam retineret habenas, 15
  tradidit inque suo tertius orbe fuit ;

---

¹ About two shillings, or double the usual dole (*cf.* III.
vii. 1) of *centum quadrantes*. Large doles were sometimes
given : *cf.* IV. xxvi. 3 ; X. xxvii. 3.

C

For three denarii[1] you invite me, and bid me don my toga in the morning and wait in your hall, Bassus; then closely to attend you, to walk before your chair, with you to call upon ten widows more or less. Worn indeed is my poor toga, and cheap and old—yet for three denarii I cannot buy it, Bassus.

CI

Thou Appian Way, which revered Caesar in the guise of Hercules[2] hallows, chiefest glory of Ausonian ways, if thou desirest to know the deeds of the ancient Alcides, learn them. The Libyan he subdued, the golden apples he won; he ungirt the Amazonian targeteer of her Scythian girdle; he crowned the spoil of the lion's skin with Arcadia's boar; he freed the woods from the brazen-hoofed hind, the sky from the Stymphalian birds; from the Stygian flood he returned with its hound; the teeming hydra he let no more grow stronger by death; he laved in the Tuscan stream Hesperian oxen. These things wrought the lesser Alcides; hear what that greater[3] did, whom men worship at the sixth stone from Alba's height. He redeemed the Palatine held by an evil power;[4] his first wars he waged, a boy, for his own Jove;[5] albeit alone he already held the reins of Julian power, he gave them up, and in a world that had been his own

---

[2] cf. IX. lxiv.   [3] Domitian.
[4] By the party of Vitellius after the death of that emperor.
[5] He was besieged in the Temple of Jupiter Capitolinus by the Vitellians.

cornua Sarmatici ter perfida contudit Histri,
   sudantem Getica ter nive lavit equum;
saepe recusatos parcus duxisse triumphos
   victor Hyperboreo nomen ab orbe tulit;   20
templa deis, mores populis dedit, otia ferro,
   astra suis, caelo sidera, serta Iovi.
Herculeum tantis numen non sufficit actis:
   Tarpeio deus hic commodet ora patri.

CII

QUADRINGENTORUM reddis mihi, Phoebe, tabellas:
   centum da potius mutua, Phoebe, mihi.
quaere alium cui te tam vano munere iactes:
   quod tibi non possum solvere, Phoebe, meum est.

CIII

QUAE nova tam similis genuit tibi Leda ministros?
   quae capta est alio nuda Lacaena cycno?
dat faciem Pollux Hiero, dat Castor Asylo,
   atque in utroque nitet Tyndaris ore soror.
ista Therapnaeis si forma fuisset Amyclis,   5
   cum vicere duas dona minora deas,
mansisses, Helene, Phrygiamque redisset in Iden
   Dardanius gemino cum Ganymede Paris.

---

¹ Though he had been proclaimed Caesar, and was in
possession of Rome, he resigned the empire to his father
Vespasian and his brother Titus in precedence to himself,
boasting, however, *patri se et fratri imperium dedisse, illos
sibi reddidisse*: Suet. *Dom.* xiii.
² In his three campaigns against the tribes on the Danube
As to the shattering of the horn, *cf.* x. vii. 6.

remained but the third;[1] thrice he shattered the treacherous horns of Sarmatian Hister;[2] his sweating steed thrice he bathed in Getic snow; loth to lead on triumphs oft resigned,[3] he won a victor's name from the Hyperborean world; temples he gave the Gods, morals to the people, rest to the sword, immortality to his own kin, to heaven stars, wreaths to Jove. The Deity of Hercules sufficed not for deeds so great: let him, our God, lend his features to the Tarpeian [4] Sire!

CII

You return me, Phoebus, my bond for four hundred thousand sesterces; rather give me on loan, Phoebus, a hundred thousand. Look out for some one else to whom you may boast of so empty a gift; what I can't pay you, Phoebus, is my own.[5]

CIII

What new Leda[6] bore you attendants so like? What nude Spartan maid was ravished by another swan? Pollux gives his features to Hierus, Castor gives his to Asylus, and in either face their sister Tyndaris shines clear. Had such beauty existed at Spartan Amyclae [7] when a lesser gift o'erweighed the goddesses twain,[8] thou, Helen, wouldst have stayed at home, and Dardan Paris have returned to Phrygian Ida with twin Ganymedes!

[3] cf. VIII. xv. 5. [4] Jup. Capitolinus.
[5] cf. for a similar idea VIII. xxxvii.
[6] The mother of Castor and Pollux, and of Helen of Troy (Tyndaris).
[7] Both Therapnae and Amyclae were associated with Castor and Pollux, but the use of *Therapnaeis* is hard to explain.
[8] When Venus' promise to Paris of Helen overweighed the promises of Hera (Juno) and Pallas in the contest of beauty.

BOOK X

LIBER DECIMUS

I

Si nimius videor seraque coronide longus
    esse liber, legito pauca : libellus ero.
terque quaterque mihi finitur carmine parvo
    pagina : fac tibi me quam cupis ipse brevem.

II

Festinata prior, decimi mihi cura libelli
    elapsum manibus nunc revocavit opus.
nota leges quaedam sed lima rasa recenti ;
    pars nova maior erit : lector, utrique fave,
lector, opes nostrae : quem cum mihi Roma dedisset,
    " Nil tibi quod demus maius habemus" ait.   6
" pigra per hunc fugies ingratae flumina Lethes
    et meliore tui parte superstes eris.
marmora Messallae findit caprificus et audax
    dimidios Crispi mulio ridet equos :   10
at chartis nec furta nocent et saecula prosunt,
    solaque non norunt haec monumenta mori."

---

[1] *i.e.* by reading only the short epigrams.
[2] This book is not the first edition, which may have been
published in 95, but an enlarged edition published in 98
after Book XI. M. afterwards issued a selection from
Books X. and XI.: *cf.* XII. v. 1-2.

BOOK X

I

If I seem too big a book and long, with my colophon delayed, read a few epigrams: I shall be a little book. Often a page of mine ends with a small poem: make me as short for yourself as you like.[1]

II

Too hurried before, the composition of my tenth book has made me now recall the work that had slipt from my hands.[2] You will read some things you know, but polished lately by the file; the greater part will be new; reader, be kind to both, reader, who are my wealth; for when Rome had given you to me, she said: "We have nothing greater to give you. By him will you escape unthankful Lethe's sluggish stream, and will in your better part survive. Messalla's marble the wild-fig sunders, and boldly the mule-driver laughs at Crispus' steeds broken in two.[3] But writings thefts do not injure, and time befriends them, and alone these monuments know not death."

[3] M. is M. Val. Messalla Corvinus, the patron of the poet Tibullus: *cf.* VIII. iii. 5. The Crispus is probably C. Passienus Crispus of the time of Claudius, and stepfather of Nero.

III

VERNACULORUM dicta, sordidum dentem,
et foeda linguae probra circulatricis,
quae sulpurato nolit empta ramento
Vatiniorum proxeneta fractorum,
poeta quidam clancularius spargit   5
et volt videri nostra. credis hoc, Prisce?
voce ut loquatur psittacus coturnicis
et concupiscat esse Canus ascaules?
procul a libellis nigra sit meis fama,
quos rumor alba gemmeus vehit pinna: 10
cur ego laborem notus esse tam prave,
constare gratis cum silentium possit?

IV

QUI legis Oedipoden caligantemque Thyesten,
   Colchidas et Scyllas, quid nisi monstra legis?
quid tibi raptus Hylas, quid Parthenopaeus et Attis,
   quid tibi dormitor proderit Endymion?
exutusve puer pinnis labentibus? aut qui   5
   odit amatrices Hermaphroditus aquas?
quid te vana iuvant miserae ludibria chartae?
   hoc lege, quod possit dicere vita "Meum est."
non hic Centauros, non Gorgonas Harpyiasque
   invenies: hominem pagina nostra sapit.   10
sed non vis, Mamurra, tuos cognoscere mores
   nec te scire: legas Aetia Callimachi.

---

[1] Beakers with four nozzles, said to be in imitation of the nose of Vatinius, a Beneventan cobbler in Nero's time: cf. XIV. xcvi.; Juv. v. 46. As to the sale of broken glass, cf. I. xli. 3–5.

III

THE scurrilities of home-born slaves, low railing, and the foul insults of a hawker's tongue, which the broker of shattered Vatinian glasses[1] would reject as the price of a sulphur match, a certain skulking poet scatters abroad, and would have them appear as mine. Do you believe this, Priscus? that a parrot speaks with the voice of a quail, and Canus[2] longs to be a bagpipe-player? Far from poems of mine be black repute, poems which lustrous fame uplifts on pinions white. Why should I toil to be known so evilly when stillness can cost me nothing?

IV

You, who read of Oedipus and Thyestes neath a darkened sun, of Colchian witches and Scyllas—of what do you read but monsters? What will the rape of Hylas avail you, what Parthenopaeus and Attis, what the sleeper Endymion? or the boy stript of his gliding wings? or Hermaphroditus who hates the amorous waters? Why does the vain twaddle of a wretched sheet attract you? Read this of which Life can say: " 'Tis my own." Not here will you find Centaurs, not Gorgons and Harpies : 'tis of man my page smacks. But you do not wish, Mamurra, to recognize your own manners, or to know yourself. Read the *Origins* of Callimachus.[3]

---

[2] A famous flute-player : cf. IV. v. 8.
[3] An Alexandrine grammarian and poet of the third century B.C. who wrote an epic on the origins (Αἴτια) of mythological stories

V

Quisquis stolaeve purpuraeve contemptor
quos colere debet laesit impio versu,
erret per urbem pontis exul et clivi,
interque raucos ultimus rogatores
oret caninas panis inprobi buccas.   5
illi December longus et madens bruma
clususque fornix triste frigus extendat:
vocet beatos clamitetque felices
Orciniana qui feruntur in sponda.
at cum supremae fila venerint horae   10
diesque tardus, sentiat canum litem
abigatque moto noxias aves panno.
nec finiantur morte supplicis poenae,
sed modo severi sectus Aeaci loris,
nunc inquieti monte Sisyphi pressus,   15
nunc inter undas garruli senis siccus
delasset omnis fabulas poetarum ;
et cum fateri Furia iusserit verum,
prodente clamet conscientia "Scripsi."

VI

Felices, quibus urna dedit spectare coruscum
   solibus Arctois sideribusque ducem.
quando erit ille dies quo campus et arbor et omnis
   lucebit Latia culta fenestra nuru ?

---

[1] *i.e.* of noble ladies, or of magistrates and senators.
[2] Resorts of beggars: *cf.* II. xix. 3 ; XII. xxxii. 10, 25.
[3] Where he took refuge.
[4] *i.e.* the pauper's bier (*sandapila*): *cf.* II. lxxxi.; VIII.
lxxv.   [5] Ready to eat him.

V

Whoe'er he be who, scorner of either stole or purple,[1] has wounded with his wicked verse those he should respect, let him wander through the city, exile from bridge and hill,[2] and, last amid the hoarse-throated beggars, pray for dogs' morsels of vile bread. To him may December be long and winter wet, and the shutting of the archway[3] prolong his miserable chill; let him call those blest, and acclaim those fortunate, who are carried on the litter of Orcus.[4] But when the threads of his last hour have been spun, and his lingering day has come, let him feel the wrangling of dogs,[5] and flap away noxious birds with waving rags. Nor let his punishment, despite his prayers, be closed by death; but now scored by the scourge of stern Aeacus,[6] now o'erwhelmed by the mountainous stone of restless Sisyphus, now parching amid the waters of the blabbing old man,[7] may he weary out all the fabled torments of the poets; and when the Fury shall bid him confess the truth, may he shriek, his conscience betraying him: "I wrote it."[8]

VI

Happy are they to whom Fortune's urn has given to see our Captain ablaze with northern suns and stars![9] When shall that day be whereon plain and tree shall be radiant, and every casement dight with

[6] One of the three Judges of the Shades.
[7] Tantalus, who was doomed to thirst in Tartarus for revealing the secrets of the gods.
[8] M. follows in this ep., often closely, the *Ibis* of Ovid.
[9] This ep. was written when the new emperor, Trajan, was expected from the Rhine in A.D. 98.

quando morae dulces longusque a Caesare pulvis   5
  totaque Flaminia Roma videnda via?
quando eques et picti tunica Nilotide Mauri
  ibitis et populi vox erit una "Venit?"?

VII

NYMPHARUM pater amniumque, Rhene,
quicumque Odrysias bibunt pruinas,
sic semper liquidis fruaris undis
nec te barbara contumeliosi
calcatum rota conterat bubulci;   5
sic et cornibus aureis receptis
et Romanus eas utraque ripa:
Traianum populis suis et urbi,
Thybris te dominus rogat, remittas.

VIII

NUBERE Paula cupit nobis, ego ducere Paulam
  nolo: anus est.   vellem, si magis esset anus.

IX

UNDENIS pedibusque syllabisque
et multo sale nec tamen protervo
notus gentibus ille Martialis
et notus populis (quid invidetis?)
non sum Andraemone notior caballo.   5

X

CUM tu, laurigeris annum qui fascibus intras,
  mane salutator limina mille teras,

---

[1] Previously shattered by defeat: *cf.* VII. vii. 3; IX. ci. 17.
[2] Elegiacs and hendecasyllables.

Latin dames? When shall be hope's sweet delays,
and the long trail of dust behind Caesar, and all
Rome visible on the Flaminian Way? When will ye
come, ye knights, and ye painted Moors in your
tunics of Nile, and one voice of the people go up,
" Does he come ? " ?

VII

FATHER, O Rhine, of Nymphs and of all rivers
that drink the Thracian frosts, so mayst thou alway
joy in limpid waters, and no insolent ox-driver's bar-
barous wain trample roughly on thy head ; so mayst
thou, with thy golden horns regained,[1] and a Roman
stream on either bank, flow on—send Trajan back to
his peoples and to his city : so doth thy Lord Tiber
entreat thee.

VIII

PAULA wishes to marry me : I decline to take
Paula to wife ; she is an old woman. I might be
willing if she were older.

IX

WITH my eleven-footed and eleven-syllabled verse,[2]
and flowing, yet not froward wit, I, that Martial,
who am known to the nations and to Rome's peoples
(why do you envy me ?) am not known better than
the horse Andraemon.

X

WHEN you, who usher in the year with laurelled
axes,[3] tread a thousand thresholds at morning levees,

[3] As consul, and the first of the year. Men of position
often did not scruple to add to their income by taking the
sportula: *cf.* Juv. i. 99. Juv. (i. 117) also alludes to the
grievances in consequence of poor clients.

hic ego quid faciam? quid nobis, Paule, relinquis,
  qui de plebe Numae densaque turba sumus?
qui me respiciet dominum regemque vocabo?   5
  hoc tu (sed quanto blandius!) ipse facis.
lecticam sellamve sequar? nec ferre recusas,
  per medium pugnas et prior isse lutum.
saepius adsurgam recitanti carmina? tu stas
  et pariter geminas tendis in ora manus.   10
quid faciet pauper cui non licet esse clienti?
  dimisit nostras purpura vestra togas.

XI

Nil aliud loqueris quam Thesea Pirithoumque
  teque putas Pyladi, Calliodore, parem.
dispeream, si tu Pyladi praestare matellam
  dignus es aut porcos pascere Pirithoi.
"Donavi tamen" inquis "amico milia quinque   5
  et lotam, ut multum, terve quaterve¹ togam."
quid quod nil umquam Pyladi donavit Orestes?
  qui donat quamvis plurima, plura negat.

XII

Aemiliae gentes et Apollineas Vercellas
  et Phaethontei qui petis arva Padi,
ne vivam, nisi te, Domiti, dimitto libenter,
  grata licet sine te sit mihi nulla dies:
sed desiderium tanti est ut messe vel una   5
  urbano releves colla perusta iugo.

---

¹ *terve quaterve* Haupt, *terque quaterque* codd.

---

¹ A method of applauding: *cf.* Juv. iii. 106. Or perhaps
the allusion is to throwing kisses: *cf.* I. iii. 7.

what can I do here? What do you leave to us, Paulus, us who are of the herd of Numa and a teeming crowd? Shall I greet as Lord and King him who but gives me a glance? This, and how much more blandly! you also do. Shall I follow a litter or chair? You don't refuse even to shoulder one, and to struggle to pass first through the middle of the mud. Shall I repeatedly rise when a man recites poems? You are already standing, and put to your lips both hands at once.[1] What shall a poor man do, debarred from being a client? Your purple has ousted our togas.

XI

You talk of nothing but Theseus and Pirithous, and think yourself, Calliodorus, the peer of Pylades. May I be hanged if you are fit to hand Pylades a chamber-pot, or to feed Pirithous' swine. "Yet," you say, "I gave a friend five thousand, and a toga only three or four times washed,[2] a considerable gift." And what if Pylades never gave anything to Orestes?[3] He who gives—however many gifts he makes—denies more.

XII

You are going to the peoples on the Aemilian Way, and to Apollo's Vercellae, and the fields by the Po where Phaethon died. May I perish, but I let you go willingly, Domitius, although without you no day is pleasant to me; but I can pay the price of regret that, even for a single summer, you may ease your neck galled by the city's yoke. Go, I pray, and

[2] *i.e.* nearly new. The phrase was apparently common : Petr. 30.

[3] P. and O. already shared in common.

i precor et totos avida cute conbibe soles:
    o quam formosus, dum peregrinus eris!
et venies albis non adgnoscendus amicis
    livebitque tuis pallida turba genis.   10
sed via quem dederit rapiet cito Roma colorem,
    Niliaco redeas tu licet ore niger.

XIII

Cum cathedralicios portet tibi raeda ministros
    et Libys in longo pulvere sudet eques,
strataque non unas cingant triclinia Baias
    et Thetis unguento palleat uncta tuo,
candida Setini rumpant crystalla trientes,   5
    dormiat in pluma nec meliore Venus:
ad nocturna iaces fastosae limina moechae
    et madet heu! lacrimis ianua surda tuis,
urere nec miserum cessant suspiria pectus.
    vis dicam male sit cur tibi, Cotta? bene est.   10

XIV

Cedere de nostris nulli te dicis amicis.
    sed, sit ut hoc verum, quid, rogo, Crispe, facis?
mutua cum peterem sestertia quinque, negasti,
    non caperet nummos cum gravis arca tuos.
quando fabae modium nobis farrisve dedisti,   5
    cum tua Niliacus rura colonus aret?

drink into your greedy pores the fullness of the sun-
shine—oh, how comely you will be while you are
abroad! And you will return not to be recognized
by your white-faced friends, and a pallid crowd will
envy your cheeks. But Rome will quickly efface
the tan your tour will have given you, though you
came home swarthy with an Egyptian's face.

XIII

ALTHOUGH a travelling-coach carries your lolling
minions, and a Libyan outrider sweats in a long
trail of dust, and your cushioned couches surround
more than one warm bath, and your sea-bath is pale
with the tinge of your perfumes; although draughts
of Setine fill to bursting your transparent crystal,
and in fairer down Venus herself does not repose;
by night you lie on the threshold of a capricious
mistress, and her deaf door is wet, alas! with your
tears, and sighs do not cease to scorch your unhappy
breast. Do you wish me to say why it is ill with
you, Cotta? Because it is well.[1]

XIV

You say that you yield to none of my friends in
love. Yet to make this true, what, I ask, Crispus,
do you do? When I was asking you for a loan of
five thousand sesterces you refused it, although your
heavy coffer could not hold your moneys. When
did you give me a peck of beans, or of spelt, although a tenant by the Nile tills fields of yours?

---

[1] C. is so well off he has to invent miseries.

quando brevis gelidae missa est toga tempore brumae?
   argenti venit quando selibra mihi?
nil aliud video quo te credamus amicum
   quam quod me coram pedere, Crispe, soles.   10

XV

DOTATAE uxori cor harundine fixit acuta,
   sed dum ludit, Aper.   ludere novit Aper.

XVI

SI donare vocas promittere nec dare, Gai,
   vincam te donis muneribusque meis.
accipe Callaicis quidquid fodit Astur in arvis,
   aurea quidquid habet divitis unda Tagi,
quidquid Erythraea niger invenit Indus in alga,   5
   quidquid et in nidis unica servat avis,
quidquid Agenoreo Tyros inproba cogit aheno:
   quidquid habent omnes, accipe, quomodo das.

XVII

SATURNALICIO Macrum fraudare tributo
   frustra, Musa, cupis: non licet: ipse petit;
sollemnesque iocos nec tristia carmina poscit
   et queritur nugas obticuisse meas.
mensorum longis sed nunc vacat ille libellis   5
   Appia, quid facies, si legit ista Macer?

---

[1] Pearls: *cf.* v. xxxvii. 4.
[2] The phoenix: *cf.* vi. lv. 2.
[3] The purple of Tyre.

When was a short toga sent me in chill winter's season? When did a half-pound of silver plate come to me? I see no other reason why I should believe you friend, than that you are wont, Crispus, to break wind in my presence.

XV

His well-dowered wife's heart Aper transfixed with a sharp arrow, but it was in sport. Aper is a clever sportsman.

XVI

If you call it bounty to promise and not to give, Gaius, I will surpass you by my bounties and offerings. Receive all wealth the Asturian mines in Gallician fields, all wealth rich Tagus' golden wave possesses, all the swarthy Indian discovers in Eastern seaweed,[1] and all the solitary bird[2] treasures in its nest, all Agenor's city, cheating Tyre, stores in her caldron.[3] All wealth of all men receive—in your fashion of giving!

XVII

You wish in vain, Muse, to defraud Macer of his Saturnalian tribute: it can't be; he himself asks for it, and he claims the customary jokes and no melancholy poems, and complains that my flippancies have become dumb. But at present he has time to look at the long reports of his surveyors. Appian Way,[4] what will you do if Macer reads these poems?[5]

[4] Of which Macer was curator.

[5] *i.e.* you will be neglected if M. devotes his leisure, not to reports, but to poetry.

XVIII

Nec vocat ad cenam Marius, nec munera mittit,
    nec spondet, nec volt credere, sed nec habet.
turba tamen non dest sterilem quae curet amicum.
    eheu! quam fatuae sunt tibi, Roma, togae!

XIX

Nec doctum satis et parum severum,
sed non rusticulum tamen libellum
facundo mea Plinio Thalia
i perfer: brevis est labor peractae
altum vincere tramitem Suburae.   5
illic Orphea protinus videbis
udi vertice lubricum theatri
mirantisque feras avemque regis,
raptum quae Phryga pertulit Tonanti;
illic parva tui domus Pedonis   10
caelata est aquilae minore pinna.
sed ne tempore non tuo disertam
pulses ebria ianuam videto:
totos dat tetricae dies Minervae,
dum centum studet auribus virorum   15
hoc quod saecula posterique possint
Arpinis quoque conparare chartis.
seras tutior ibis ad lucernas:
haec hora est tua, cum furit Lyaeus,
cum regnat rosa, cum madent capilli: 20
tunc me vel rigidi legant Catones.

---

[1] Pliny the younger, advocate and letter-writer. M. mentions him also in v. lxxx. 13, and vii. lxxxiv. 1.

[2] i.e. the ascent up the Esquiline from the Subura. Somewhere on this path was the *Lacus Orphei*, one of the reservoirs of Rome, where was a statue of Orpheus surrounded by beasts listening to his song.

XVIII

MARIUS invites no one to dinner, and sends no presents, and is surety for no one, and is unwilling to lend—in fact he has nothing. Yet a crowd is at hand to court so unprofitable a friend. Alas! what dolts, O Rome, your clients are!

XIX

THIS little book, not learned enough, nor very strict in tone, yet not all unrefined, go, my Thalia, and carry to eloquent Pliny :[1] short is your labour, when you have crossed the Subura, in breasting the steep path.[2] There you will at once notice Orpheus, spray-sprinkled, crowning his drenched audience,[3] and the wild beasts marvelling at his song, and the Monarch's bird [4] that bore to the Thunderer the ravished Phrygian ; there stands the modest dwelling of your own Pedo,[5] its frieze graven with eagle of lesser wing. But take heed you give no drunken knock on Eloquence's door at a time that is not yours ; all the day he devotes to serious study, while he prepares for the ears of the Hundred Court [6] that which time and posterity may compare even with Arpinum's pages.[7] Safer will you go at the time of the late-kindled lamps ; that hour is yours when Lyaeus is in revel, when the rose is queen, when locks are drenched. Then let even unbending Catos read me.

[3] Friedländer, however, explains *theatrum* " semicircular pool with steps." For *theatrum*=audience, *cf.* (as Housman does) Ov. *Met.* xi. 25.

[4] Jupiter's eagle that carried off· Ganymede : *cf.* I. vi.

[5] P. Albinovanus, an epic poet and epigrammatist of the Augustan age.

[6] *cf.* VI. xxxviii. 5.   [7] Cicero's.

XX

Ducit ad auriferas quod me Salo Celtiber oras,
    pendula quod patriae visere tecta libet,
tu mihi simplicibus, Mani, dilectus ab annis
    et praetextata cultus amicitia,
tu facis; in terris quo non est alter Hiberis   5
    dulcior et vero dignus amore magis.
tecum ego vel sicci Gaetula mapalia Poeni
    et poteram Scythicas hospes amare casas.
si tibi mens eadem, si nostri mutua cura est,
    in quocumque loco Roma duobus erit.   10

XXI

Scribere te quae vix intellegat ipse Modestus
    et vix Claranus quid rogo, Sexte, iuvat?
non lectore tuis opus est sed Apolline libris:
    iudice te maior Cinna Marone fuit.
sic tua laudentur sane : mea carmina, Sexte,   5
    grammaticis placeant, ut sine grammaticis.

XXII

Cur spleniato saepe prodeam mento
albave pictus sana labra cerussa,
Philaeni, quaeris?   basiare te nolo.

---

[1] Learned commentators.
[2] *i.e.* an interpreter.

XX

THAT Celtiberian Salo draws me to gold-bearing shores, that I fain would see on the hillside the roofs of my native land, you are the cause, Manius, dear to me from my ingenuous years, and wooed with boyhood's friendship; than whom none else in Hiberia's land is more sweet to me, and of genuine love more worthy. At your side could I have welcomed the sun-parched Carthaginian's Gaetulian huts and the hospitality of Scythian steads. If your heart be as mine, if you have a mutual love for me, then, in whatever place, for us twain it will be Rome.

XXI

WHY, I ask, do you, Sextus, like writing what hardly Modestus himself, and hardly Claranus,[1] could understand? Your books do not require a reader, but an Apollo;[2] in your judgment Cinna[3] was greater than Maro. On these terms let your books be praised by all means; let my poems, Sextus, please commentators—so as to do without commentators.

XXII

"WHY do I often go abroad with a plastered chin, and my healthy lips painted with white lead?" Do you ask, Philaenis? I don't want to kiss you.

[3] A friend of Catullus, who wrote a long and obscure epic called *Zmyrna*: *cf.* Cat. xciv. He is probably "Cinna the poet" of Shak. *Jul. Caes.* III. iii. 32.

XXIII

Iam numerat placido felix Antonius aevo
    quindecies actas Primus Olympiadas
praeteritosque dies et totos respicit annos
    nec metuit Lethes iam propioris aquas.
nulla recordanti lux est ingrata gravisque;   5
    nulla fuit cuius non meminisse velit.
ampliat aetatis spatium sibi vir bonus: hoc est
    vivere bis, vita posse priore frui.

XXIV

Natales mihi Martiae Kalendae,
lux formosior omnibus Kalendis,
qua mittunt mihi munus et puellae,
quinquagensima liba septimamque
vestris addimus hanc focis acerram.   5
his vos, si tamen expedit roganti,
annos addite bis precor novenos,
ut nondum nimia piger senecta
sed vitae tribus areis[1] peractis
lucos Elysiae petam puellae.   10
post hunc Nestora nec diem rogabo.[2]

XXV

In matutina nuper spectatus harena
    Mucius, inposuit qui sua membra focis,

---

[1] *areis* Ald., *aureis* codd., *auribus* L., *arcubus* Housman.
[2] *post hoc* Friedl., *Nestora* Heins., *nec hora* vel *nethora* codd.

---

[1] *i.e.* seventy-five years: *cf.* VII. xl. 6.
[2] Tacitus draws a very different picture: *cf.* the Index under "Primus."
[3] Who ordinarily received gifts on that day: *cf.* v. lxxxiv. 11.

XXIII

Now in his placid age happy Antonius Primus reckons fifteen Olympiads gone,[1] and he looks back upon past days and the vista of his years, and fears not Lethe's wave now drawing nigh. No day, as he reviews it, is unwelcome and distressing to him, none has there been he would not wish to recall. A good man [2] widens for himself his age's span; he lives twice who can find delight in life bygone.

XXIV

My natal kalends of March, day fairer to me than all the kalends, on which girls, too, send [3] me a gift, for the fifty-seventh time cakes and this censer of incense I lay on your altars. To these years—but so that it be expedient on my asking—add, I pray, twice nine years, that I, not as yet dull with too protracted age, but when life's three courses [4] are run, may reach the groves of the Elysian dame.[5] Beyond this Nestor's span I will not crave even a day more.

XXV

If Mucius,[6] whom of late you saw one morning in the arena, when he laid his hand upon the fire,

[4] Boyhood, manhood, old age. Housman's conjecture is *arcubus* = arcs, *i.e.* the four segments into which the full circle of life (100 years) is divided: *cf.* Manil. ii. 844–55. M., being fifty-seven, would in eighteen years have completed three arcs, and not have reached the last arc of too protracted age.   [5] Proserpine.

[6] *cf.* I. xxi.; VIII. xxx. In this ep. M. takes a different view of the event, saying that the criminal representing Mucius chooses the lesser evil of losing only a limb.

si patiens durusque tibi fortisque videtur,
    Abderitanae pectora plebis habes.
nam cum dicatur tunica praesente molesta   5
    " Ure manum," plus est dicere " Non facio.'

XXVI

VARE, Paraetonias Latia modo vite per urbes
    nobilis et centum dux memorande viris,
at nunc, Ausonio frustra promisse Quirino,
    hospita Lagei litoris umbra iaces.
spargere non licuit frigentia fletibus ora,   5
    pinguia nec maestis addere tura rogis.
sed datur aeterno victurum carmine nomen :
    numquid et hoc, fallax Nile, negare potes ?

XXVII

NATALI, Diodore, tuo conviva senatus
    accubat et rarus non adhibetur eques,
et tua tricenos largitur sportula nummos.
    nemo tamen natum te, Diodore, putat.

XXVIII

ANNORUM nitidique sator pulcherrime mundi,
    publica quem primum vota precesque vocant,

---

[1] The people of Abdera in Thrace were, like the Boeotians,
notorious for their stupidity : *cf.* Juv. x. 50.
[2] The *tunica molesta*: *cf.* IV. lxxxvi. 8.
[3] With which a centurion kept discipline among his
soldiers.
[4] *i.e.* whose return to Rome we were expecting.

seem to you enduring, and unflinching, and strong, you have the intelligence of Abdera's [1] rabble. For, when it is said to you, while the torturing tunic [2] is by you, " Burn your hand," it is the bolder thing to say " I refuse."

XXVI

Notable but lately with Latin vine-rod [3] mid Egypt's cities, and a captain of renown to thy hundred soldiers, yet now, O thou who wert promised in vain to Ausonian Quirinus, [4] thou liest, an alien ghost, on the Lagaean shore. 'Twas not allowed me to sprinkle thy chill cheek with my tears, nor to shed rich incense on thy lamented pyre. But there is given thee a name that shall live in deathless song: nay, treacherous Nile, canst thou refuse that too? [5]

XXVII

On your birthday, Diodorus, the Senate is your guest at dinner, and few are the knights not invited, and your dole lavishes thirty sesterces on each guest. [6] Yet no one, Diodorus, imagines you had a father. [7]

XXVIII

Father, most fair, of the years and of the bright universe, whom first of all Gods public vows and

[5] *i.e.* as well as his body?

[6] About double the usual dole. A larger than the usual dole was sometimes given (*sportula major*): *cf.* VIII. xlii. 1; IX. c. 1.

[7] *Non natus*, a phrase expressing insignificance: *cf.* VIII. lxiv. 18.

pervius [1] exiguos habitabas ante penates,
   plurima qua medium Roma terebat iter:
nunc tua Caesareis cinguntur limina donis   5
   et fora tot numeras, Iane, quot ora geris.
at tu, sancte pater, tanto pro munere gratus,
   ferrea perpetua claustra tuere sera.

XXIX

Quam mihi mittebas Saturni tempore lancem,
   misisti dominae, Sextiliane, tuae;
et quam donabas dictis a Marte Kalendis,
   de nostra prasina est synthesis empta toga.
iam constare tibi gratis coepere puellae: 5
   muneribus futuis, Sextiliane, meis.

XXX

O temperatae dulce Formiae litus,
vos, cum severi fugit oppidum Martis
et inquietas fessus exuit curas,
Apollinaris omnibus locis praefert.
non ille sanctae dulce Tibur uxoris,   5
nec Tusculanos Algidosve secessus,
Praeneste nec sic Antiumque miratur;
non blanda Circe Dardanisve Caieta
desiderantur, nec Marica nec Liris,
nec in Lucrina lota Salmacis vena.   10

       [1] *pervius* ς, *praevius* codd.

---

[1] The old temple of Janus was near the Roman Forum,
and represented Janus with two faces (Janus Geminus).
Domitian built a new temple, giving Janus four faces (*quadri-
frons*), in the Forum Transitorium: *cf.* VIII. ii. The other
three forums were the F. Romanum, F. Julii, and F. Augusti.

prayers implore, thou, pervious once, didst aforetime inhabit a petty house, wherethrough populous
Rome wore her thoroughfare. Now is thy threshold
encircled with Caesarean offerings, and as many
forums thou numberest, Janus, as the faces thou
bearest.[1] But do thou, hallowed sire, thankful
for a gift so great, guard thy iron portals with a bolt
ever undrawn.[2]

XXIX

THE dish you used to send me at Saturn's season
you have sent to your mistress, Sextilianus, and, at
the cost of the toga you used to give me on the
kalends named after Mars, has been bought a green
dinner dress. Now your girls begin to cost you
nothing: it is out of my presents, Sextilianus, you
carry on your amours.

XXX

O TEMPERATE Formiae, darling shore! When he
flies from stern Mars' town, and weariedly puts
off distracting cares, 'tis you Apollinaris prefers to
every spot. Not so does he admire his blameless
wife's darling Tibur, nor the retreats of Tusculum
or Algidus, not so does he admire Praeneste and
Antium; Circe's witching headland or Dardan
Caieta[3] are not longed for, nor Marica[4] nor Liris,
nor Salmacis[5] bathed in the Lucrine's waters. Here

[2] When the gate of the temple was shut, it was a sign
that Rome was not at war.
[3] Circeii and Caieta: *cf.* v. i. 5.
[4] A Latin nymph, who had a temple and grove at Minturnae at the mouth of the Liris in Campania.
[5] Probably a spring that fell into the Lucrine lake, and
bearing the same name as the spring in Caria associated
with the legend of Hermaphroditus: *cf.* VI. lxviii. 10. It is
here alluded to under the name of the nymph S.

hic summa leni stringitur Thetis vento;
nec languet aequor, viva sed quies ponti
pictam phaselon adiuvante fert aura.
sicut puellae non amantis aestatem
mota salubre purpura venit frigus.   15
nec saeta longo quaerit in mari praedam,
sed a cubili lectuloque iactatam
spectatus alte lineam trahit piscis.
si quando Nereus sentit Aeoli regnum,
ridet procellas tuta de suo mensa: 20
piscina rhombum pascit et lupos vernas,
natat ad magistrum delicata muraena,
nomenculator mugilem citat notum
et adesse iussi prodeunt senes mulli.
frui sed istis quando, Roma, permittis?   25
quot Formianos inputat dies annus
negotiosis rebus urbis haerenti?
o ianitores vilicique felices!
dominis parantur ista, serviunt vobis.

XXXI

ADDIXTI servum nummis here mille ducentis,
    ut bene cenares, Calliodore, semel.
nec bene cenasti: mullus tibi quattuor emptus
    librarum cenae pompa caputque fuit.
exclamare libet: "Non est hic, inprobe, non est   5
    piscis: homo est; hominem, Calliodore, comes."

XXXII

HAEC mihi quae colitur violis pictura rosisque,
    quos referat voltus, Caediciane, rogas?

---

[1] Nereus was a sea-god, and Aeolus the god of the winds.

Ocean's surface is ruffled by a gentle breeze; yet is not the sea-floor still, but a slumberous swell bears on the gaudy shallop with the assisting air, as from the fluttering of a girl's purple fan, when she shuns the heat, there comes refreshing cool. The line seeks not its prey in the distant sea, but the fish, descried from above, draws down the cord cast from bed or couch. If ever Nereus feel the power of Aeolus,[1] the table, safe-supplied from its own store, laughs at the storm; the fishpond feeds turbot and home-reared bass; to its master's call swims the dainty lamprey; the usher summons a favourite gurnard, and, bidden to appear, aged mullets put forth their heads. But when dost thou, Rome, permit to enjoy those delights? How many days of Formiae does the year put to the credit of one tied to city business? O happy porters and bailiffs! Those delights are procured for your masters, they belong to you!

XXXI

You sold a slave yesterday for twelve hundred sesterces, Calliodorus, that you might dine well once. You have not dined well:[2] a four-pound mullet which you bought was the ornament and chief dish of your dinner. A man may cry, "This is not a fish, not a fish, you profligate: 'tis a man; a man, Calliodorus, is what you eat."

XXXII

This picture which is honoured by me with violets and roses—ask you, Caedicianus, whose features it

[2] M. plays on the meaning of *bene*, "sumptuously," or "well" in a moral sense.

talis erat Marcus mediis Antonius annis
    Primus : in hoc iuvenem se videt ore senex.
ars utinam mores animumque effingere posset !   5
    pulchrior in terris nulla tabella foret.

XXXIII

SIMPLICIOR priscis, Munati Galle, Sabinis,
    Cecropium superas qui bonitate senem,
sic tibi consoceri claros retinere penates
    perpetua natae det face casta Venus,
ut tu, si viridi tinctos aerugine versus   5
    forte malus livor dixerit esse meos,
ut facis, a nobis abigas, nec scribere quemquam
    talia contendas carmina qui legitur.
hunc servare modum nostri novere libelli,
    parcere personis, dicere de vitiis.   10

XXXIV

DI tibi dent quidquid, Caesar Traiane, mereris
    et rata perpetuo quae tribuere velint :
qui sua restituis spoliato iura patrono
    (libertis exul non erit ille suis),
dignus es ut possis tutum [1] servare clientem :   5
    ut (liceat tantum vera probare) potes.

          [1] *tutum* ς, *totum* codd.

---

    [1] Referred to also in x. xxiii.
    [2] Epicurus (*cf.* VII. lxix. 3) or Socrates.

presents? Such was Marcus Antonius Primus[1] in manhood's years: in this face the old man sees himself in youth. Would that art could limn his character and mind! More beautiful in all the world would no painting be!

XXXIII

SIMPLER than the Sabines of old, Munatius Gallus, who surpass the old Athenian[2] in goodness, so may chaste Venus grant you, by your daughter's unsevered marriage tie, to keep your alliance with her father-in-law's illustrious house, if you, when perchance malicious envy shall call mine verses steeped in poisonous gall, thrust that envy from me, as you do, and urge that no man writes such poems who is read. This measure my books learn to keep, to spare the person, to denounce the vice.

XXXIV

MAY the gods grant you, Caesar Trajanus, what-e'er you deserve, and be willing to confirm for all time what they have bestowed. You, who give back to the plundered patron his rights (no more will he be his own freedman's exile),[3] are worthy of power to keep the client safe, power which—may you only be allowed to prove it true!—you have.

[3] Trajan had forbidden clients and freedmen to bring accusations against their patrons: Plin. *Pan.* 42. M. now pleads for the client.

XXXV

Omnes Sulpiciam legant puellae
uni quae cupiunt viro placere ;
omnes Sulpiciam legant mariti
uni qui cupiunt placere nuptae.
non haec Colchidos adserit furorem,   5
diri prandia nec refert Thyestae ;
Scyllam, Byblida nec fuisse credit :
sed castos docet et probos amores,
lusus delicias facetiasque.
cuius carmina qui bene aestimarit,   10
nullam dixerit esse nequiorem,
nullam dixerit esse sanctiorem.
tales Egeriae iocos fuisse
udo crediderim Numae sub antro.
hac condiscipula vel hac magistra   15
esses doctior et pudica, Sappho :
sed tecum pariter simulque visam
durus Sulpiciam Phaon amaret.
frustra : namque ea nec Tonantis uxor
nec Bacchi nec Apollinis puella   20
erepto sibi viveret Caleno.

XXXVI

Inproba Massiliae quidquid fumaria cogunt,
  accipit aetatem quisquis ab igne cadus,
a te, Munna, venit : miseris tu mittis amicis
  per freta, per longas toxica saeva vias ;

---

[1] Medea.   [2] *cf.* III. xlv. 1.
[3] One of the native Italian Camenae, or Muses, said to
have been the wife of Numa, an early king of Rome : *cf.* VI.
xlvii. 3.   The grot was at the *Porta Capena*, or at Aricia.
[4] *cf.* X. xxxviii.

XXXV

LET all young wives read Sulpicia, who wish to please their lords alone; let all husbands read Sulpicia, who wish to please their brides alone. She claims not as her theme the frenzy of the Colchian dame,[1] nor does she recount Thyestes' dreadful feast;[2] Scylla and Byblis she does not believe ever were; but she describes pure and honest love, toyings, endearments, and raillery. He who shall weigh well her poems will say no maid was so roguish, will say no maid was so modest. Such—I would believe — were Egeria's[3] pleasantries in Numa's dripping grot. With her as your school-mate, or with her as your teacher, you would have been more learned, Sappho, and have been chaste; but coy Phaon, had he seen her with Sappho and by her side, would have loved Sulpicia. In vain; for neither as the Thunderer's spouse, nor as Bacchus' or Apollo's mistress, were her Calenus taken from her, would she live.[4]

XXXVI

WHATEVER Massilia's vile smoke-rooms store,[5] whatever jar acquires its age from the fire, comes from you, Munna; to your wretched friends you consign over the sea, over long roads, deadly poison, and not

---

[5] Wine was matured by being kept over the heat of the furnace, but at Massilia the process appears to have been overdone, and a taste of smoke clung to the wine: *cf.* III. lxxxii. 23; XIII. cxxiii.

nec facili pretio sed quo contenta Falerni   5
  testa sit aut cellis Setia cara suis.
non venias quare tam longo tempore Romam,
  haec puto causa tibi est, ne tua vina bibas.

XXXVII

Iuris et aequarum cultor sanctissime legum,
  veridico Latium qui regis ore forum,
municipi, Materne, tuo veterique sodali
  Callaicum mandas si quid ad Oceanum—.
an Laurentino turpis in litore ranas   5
  et satius tenues ducere credis acus,
ad sua captivum quam saxa remittere mullum,
  visus erit libris qui minor esse tribus?
et fatuam summa cenare pelorida mensa
  quosque tegit levi cortice concha brevis   10
ostrea Baianis quam non liventia testis,
  quae domino pueri non prohibente vorent?
hic olidam clamosus ages in retia volpem
  mordebitque tuos sordida praeda canes:
illic piscoso modo vix educta profundo   15
  inpedient lepores umida lina meos.
dum loquor ecce redit sporta piscator inani,
  venator capta maele superbus adest:
omnis ab urbano venit ad mare cena macello.
  Callaicum mandas si quid ad Oceanum—.   20

---

[1] M. proceeds to compare, with regard to advantages,
Laurentum with Spain, whither he is now returning. He is

at an easy price, but at one which would satisfy a crock of Falernian or Setine, dear to its own cellars. Why you do not come to Rome after such an interval this is, I think, your reason : you shun drinking your own wines.

XXXVII

MOST conscientious student of law and of just statutes, who with your truthful tongue rule the Latin forum, if you have any commission, Maternus, to the Spanish ocean for your townsman and old comrade—or [1] do you think it better on Laurentum's shore to pull up ugly frogs and thin needle-fish,[2] than to return to its own rocks the captive mullet which shall seem to you of less than three pounds? and to dine on a tasteless Sicilian lobster set at the top of the table, and on fish which with a smooth coating a small shell covers,[3] than on oysters that do not envy the shell-fish of Baiae, and which slaves devour, unforbid by their master? Here with shouts you will drive into your toils a stinking vixen, and the foul quarry will bite your hounds; there the net, scarce drawn just now from the deep that teems with fish, will, all dripping, enmesh my own hares. While I speak, see, your fisherman comes home with empty creel, your huntsman is at hand, exulting in a badger caught! all your dinner by the sea comes from the city market. If you have any commission to the Spanish ocean—

supposed to be at Laurentum paying a farewell visit to Maternus.
[2] From the marshes of Laurentum.
[3] Probably mussels (*mituli*): *cf.* III. lx. 4.

XXXVIII

O MOLLES tibi quindecim, Calene,
quos cum Sulpicia tua iugales
indulsit deus et peregit annos!
o nox omnis et hora, quae notata est
caris litoris Indici lapillis !   5
o quae proelia, quas utrimque pugnas
felix lectulus et lucerna vidit
nimbis ebria Nicerotianis !
vixisti tribus, o Calene, lustris:
aetas haec tibi tota conputatur   10
et solos numeras dies mariti.
ex illis tibi si diu rogatam
lucem redderet Atropos vel unam,
malles quam Pyliam quater senectam.

XXXIX

CONSULE te Bruto quod iuras, Lesbia, natam,
    mentiris.   nata es, Lesbia, rege Numa ?
sic quoque mentiris. namque, ut tua saecula narrant,
    ficta Prometheo diceris esse luto.

XL

SEMPER cum mihi diceretur esse
secreto mea Polla cum cinaedo,
inrupi, Lupe.   non erat cinaedus.

XLI

MENSE novo Iani veterem, Proculeia, maritum
    deseris atque iubes res sibi habere suas.

---

¹ *cf.* VI. lv. 3.   ² Fifteen years.
³ One of the Fates.   ⁴ *i.e.* the age of Nestor.

XXXVIII

Oh, those fifteen years, rapturous to you, Calenus, those wedded years which, along with your Sulpicia, the god accorded and accomplished! O nights and hours, each marked with the precious pebbles of India's shore! Oh, what conflicts of endearments, what rivalry of love between you did your happy couch witness, and the lamp o'ersated with showers of Nicerotian [1] perfume! You have lived, O Calenus, three lustres: [2] this is all the life you sum, and you count your married days alone. Of them should Atropos [3] restore you even one long asked for, you would choose it rather than four spans of Pylian [4] old age.

XXXIX

You swear, Lesbia, you were born when Brutus was consul: you lie. Were you born, Lesbia, when Numa was king? There, too, you lie; for—as your generations declare—you are said to be fashioned of Promethean clay. [5]

XL

Since my Polla was always being reported to me as consorting in secret with a ——, I broke in upon them, Lupus. He was not a —— [6]

XLI

In Janus' opening month you abandon your old husband, Proculeia, and bid him keep his own

---

[5] *i.e.* incredibly old. P. fashioned the human race out of clay: *cf.* IX. xlv. 8.

[6] *i.e.* but much worse.

quid, rogo, quid factum est? subiti quae causa doloris,
    nil mihi respondes? dicam ego, praetor erat:
constatura fuit Megalensis purpura centum   5
    milibus, ut nimium munera parca dares,
et populare sacrum bis milia dena tulisset.
    discidium non est hoc, Proculeia: lucrum est.

XLII

TAM dubia est lanugo tibi, tam mollis ut illam
    halitus et soles et levis aura terat.
celantur simili ventura Cydonea lana,
    pollice virgineo quae spoliata nitent.
fortius inpressi quotiens tibi basia quinque,   5
    barbatus labris, Dindyme, fio tuis.

XLIII

SEPTIMA iam, Phileros, tibi conditur uxor in agro.
    plus nulli, Phileros, quam tibi reddit ager.

XLIV

QUINTE Caledonios Ovidi visure Britannos
    et viridem Tethyn Oceanumque patrem,
ergo Numae colles et Nomentana relinquis
    otia, nec retinet rusque focusque senem?

---

[1] *Tuas res tibi habeto* was the legal formula of divorce.
[2] In honour of Cybele, the Great Mother of the Gods. It was scenic, and held in April.

186

property.[1] What, I ask, what is the matter? What is the reason of this sudden resentment? Do you answer me nothing? I will tell you : he was praetor. The purple robe of the Megalensian[2] festival was likely to cost a hundred thousand sesterces, should you give even a too thrifty show, and the Plebeian festival[3] would have run off with twenty thousand. This is not divorce, Proculeia : it is good business.

XLII

So shadowy is the down on thy cheeks, so soft that a breath, or the sun, or a soft breeze, rubs it away. With such a fleecy film are veiled ripening quinces, that gleam brightly when plucked by maiden fingers. Whenever I have too strongly impressed upon thy cheek five kisses, I become, Dindymus, bearded from thy lips.

XLIII

ALREADY, Phileros, your seventh wife is being buried on your land. Better return than yours, Phileros, land makes to no man.[4]

XLIV

QUINTUS OVIDIUS, purposing to visit the Caledonian Britons, and green Tethys, and father Ocean, can it be you desert the hills of Numa and Nomentan ease, and do not your fields and fireside hold you

[3] The *Ludi Plebeii*, held in November in the Flaminian Circus.

[4] *i.e.* he succeeds to their estates : *cf.* II. lxv. 4 ; v. xxxvii. 24.

gaudia tu differs : at non et stamina differt   5
  Atropos atque omnis scribitur hora tibi.
praestiteris caro (quis non hoc laudet ?) amico
  ut potior vita sit tibi sancta fides ;
sed reddare tuis tandem mansure Sabinis
  teque tuas numeres inter amicitias.   10

XLV

Si quid lene mei dicunt et dulce libelli,
  si quid honorificum pagina blanda sonat,
hoc tu pingue putas et costam rodere mavis,
  ilia Laurentis cum tibi demus apri.
Vaticana bibas, si delectaris aceto :   5
  non facit ad stomachum nostra lagona tuum.

XLVI

Omnia vis belle, Matho, dicere. dic aliquando
  et bene ; dic neutrum ; dic aliquando male.

XLVII

Vitam quae faciunt beatiorem,
  iucundissime Martialis, haec sunt :
res non parta labore sed relicta ;
non ingratus ager, focus perennis ;
lis numquam, toga rara, mens quieta ;   5
vires ingenuae, salubre corpus ;
prudens simplicitas, pares amici,
convictus facilis, sine arte mensa ;

---

[1] One of the Fates.
[2] *i.e.* whom you promised to accompany.
[3] Consider yourself as well as your friends.
[4] This person requires (like Baeticus in III. cxxvii.) his
edibles to be full-flavoured. Pliny (*N.H.* xv. 32 and 33) con-

back in your old age? Enjoyment *you* put off, but Atropos[1] does not also put off her spinning, and every hour is scored against you. You will have shown to your dear friend[2]—who would not praise this?—that your sacred word is more to you than life; yet return to your Sabine farm, and there at length abide, and count yourself one of your own friends.[3]

XLV

IF my little books contain anything delicate and toothsome, if my flattering page has any ring of eulogy, this you call tasteless[4] and prefer to gnaw a rib, although I offer you the loin of a Laurentine boar. You may drink Vatican if you are pleased with vinegar: my wine-jar does not suit your stomach.

XLVI

You want all you say to be smart, Matho. Say sometimes what also is good; say what is middling; say sometimes what is bad.

XLVII

THE things that make life happier, most genial Martial, are these: means not acquired by labour, but bequeathed; fields not unkindly, an ever blazing hearth; no lawsuit, the toga seldom worn, a quiet mind; a free man's strength,[5] a healthy body; frankness with tact, congenial friends, good-natured guests, a board plainly spread; nights not spent

trasts the *pinguis sapor* of olives, bay-leaves, walnuts, and almonds with (*inter alia*) the sweetness of figs and the softness (*lenitas*) of milk.

[5] *i.e.* the natural strength of a gentleman, not the coarse strength of a labourer: *cf.* III. xlvi. 6; VI. xi. 6.

nox non ebria sed soluta curis,
    non tristis torus et tamen pudicus;   10
    somnus qui faciat breves tenebras:
    quod sis esse velis nihilque malis;
    summum nec metuas diem nec optes.

XLVIII

Nuntiat octavam Phariae sua turba iuvencae,
    et pilata redit †iamque subitque† cohors.[1]
temperat haec thermas, nimios prior hora vapores
    halat, et inmodico sexta Nerone calet.
Stella, Nepos, Cani, Cerialis, Flacce, venitis?   5
    septem sigma capit, sex sumus, adde Lupum.
exoneraturas ventrem mihi vilica malvas
    adtulit et varias quas habet hortus opes.
in quibus est lactuca sedens et tonsile porrum,
    nec dest ructatrix mentha nec herba salax;   10
secta coronabunt rutatos ova lacertos
    et madidum thynni de sale sumen erit.
gustus in his; una ponetur cenula mensa,
    haedus inhumani raptus ab ore lupi,
et quae non egeant ferro structoris ofellae   15
    et faba fabrorum prototomique rudes;

[1] *redît iam subiîtque cohors* Paley.

---

[1] The goddess Isis, whose temple was closed at the eighth hour : *cf.* Boissier, *Rel. Rom.* vol. ii. ch. 2 (3).

[2] Leeks were of two kinds (*cf.* III. xlvii. 8), *capitatum*, where the bulbs were allowed to grow on the top of the

in wine, but freed from cares, a wife not prudish
and yet pure; sleep such as makes the darkness
brief: be content with what you are, and wish
no change; nor dread your last day, nor long
for it.

XLVIII

HER crowd of priests announces to the Egyptian
heifer[1] the eighth hour, and the praetorian guard
now returns to camp and another takes its place.
This hour tempers the warm baths, the hour before
breathes heat too great, and the sixth is hot with
the excessive heat of Nero's baths. Stella, Nepos,
Canius, Cerialis, Flaccus, do you come? My crescent
couch takes seven: we are six, add Lupus. My
bailiff's wife has brought me mallows that will un-
load the stomach, and the various wealth the garden
bears; amongst which is squat lettuce and clipped
leek,[2] and flatulent mint is not wanting nor the sa-
lacious herb;[3] sliced eggs shall garnish lizard-fish[4]
served with rue, and there shall be a paunch dripping from the tunny's brine. Herein is your whet:
the modest dinner shall be served in a single course
—a kid rescued from the jaws of a savage wolf,[5]
and meat-balls to require no carver's knife, and
beans, the food of artisans, and tender young sprouts;

stalk, and *sectile, tonsile,* or *sectivum,* where the stalks were
cut young: cf. XI. lii. 6; see Mayor on Juv. iii. 293.
   [3] *Eruca,* or rocket: cf. III. lxxv. 3.
   [4] A poor fish: cf. VII. lxxviii. 1.
   [5] *i.e.* damaged, and thus cheaper. But the flesh of an
animal that had been mangled by a wolf or other savage
beast was supposed to be more tender: cf. III. xlvii. 11;
Plut. *Symp.* ii., *quaest.* 9.

pullus ad haec cenisque tribus iam perna superstes
    addetur.   saturis mitia poma dabo,
de Nomentana vinum sine faece lagona,
    quae bis Frontino consule trima[1] fuit.   20
accedent sine felle ioci nec mane timenda
    libertas et nil quod tacuisse velis:
de prasino conviva meus venetoque loquatur,
    nec faciunt[2] quemquam pocula nostra reum.

XLIX

    Cum potes amethystinos trientes
    et nigro madeas Opimiano,
    propinas modo conditum Sabinum
    et dicis mihi, Cotta, "Vis in auro?"
    quisquam plumbea vina volt in auro?   5

L

Frangat Idumaeas tristis Victoria palmas,
    plange, Favor, saeva pectora nuda manu;
mutet Honor cultus, et iniquis munera flammis
    mitte coronatas, Gloria maesta, comas.
heu facinus! prima fraudatus, Scorpe, iuventa   5
    occidis et nigros tam cito iungis equos.
curribus illa tuis semper properata brevisque
    cur fuit et vitae tam prope meta tuae?

---

    [1] *trima* Heins, *prima* codd.   [2] *facient* β.

---

    [1] Friedländer (Int. p. 65) states that Frontinus was made
"consul for the second time along with Trajan on Feb. 20,
98." But can *bis=iterum*? Housman takes it with *trima*,
and Athenaeus, i. 27 B, says that the wine was "fit for
drinking after five years." To read *prima* would make
M. offer an undrinkable wine: *cf*. I. cv.

to these a chicken, and a ham that has already sur-
vived three dinners, shall be added. When you have
had your fill I will give you ripe apples, wine without
lees from a Nomentan flagon, which was three years
old in Frontinus' second consulship.[1] To crown
these shall be jests without gall, and a freedom not
to be dreaded the next morning, and no word you
would wish unsaid; let my guest converse of the
Green and the Blue;[2] my cups do not make any
man a defendant.

XLIX

ALTHOUGH you drink from cups of amethyst and
are drenched with dark Opimian, you give me to
drink Sabine[3] just laid down, and say to me, Cotta:
"Will you drink in gold?" Does any man wish to
drink leaden wines[4] in gold?

L

LET Victory sadly break her Idumaean[5] palms;
beat, Favour, with cruel hand thy naked breast;
let Honour change her garb; and do thou, sorrowful
Glory, cast on the cruel flames the offering of thy
crowned locks. Ah, crime of fate! Robbed, Scorpus,[6]
of thy first youth, art thou fallen, and so soon dost
yoke Death's dusky steeds! That goal, whereto
thy car sped ever in brief course, and swiftly won,
why to thy life also was it so nigh?

[2] Factions of the charioteers in the circus.
[3] A cheap wine: cf. Hor. Od. I. xx. 1. Opimian was a
celebrated vintage of Caecuban: cf I. xxvi. 7; III. xxvi. 3.
[4] i.e. worthless ones: cf. I. xcix. 15 (bad coin).
[5] Idume was S. of Judaea, and was celebrated for its
palms. [6] cf. x. liii.

LI

Sidera iam Tyrius Phrixei respicit Agni
    Taurus et alternum Castora fugit hiemps;
ridet ager, vestitur humus, vestitur et arbor,
    Ismarium paelex Attica plorat Ityn.
quos, Faustine, dies, quales tibi Roma †Ravennae† [1] 5
    abstulit! o soles, o tunicata quies!
o nemus, o fontes solidumque madentis harenae
    litus et aequoreis splendidus Anxur aquis,
et non unius spectator lectulus undae,
    qui videt hinc puppes fluminis, inde maris!   10
sed nec Marcelli Pompeianumque, nec illic
    sunt triplices thermae nec fora iuncta quater,
nec Capitolini summum penetrale Tonantis
    quaeque nitent caelo proxima templa suo.
dicere te lassum quotiens ego credo Quirino: 15
    "Quae tua sunt, tibi habe: quae mea, redde mihi

LII

    Thelyn viderat in toga spadonem,
    damnatam Numa dixit esse moecham.

LIII

Ille ego sum Scorpus, clamosi gloria Circi,
    plausus, Roma, tui deliciaeque breves,

      [1] *recessvs* Friedl.

---

    [1] The Sun is in Gemini, having passed through Aries and
Taurus. May has begun.
    [2] Philomela (the nightingale) laments Itys, whom her
sister Procne (the swallow) slew.

LI

Now looks the Tyrian bull back on the star of Phryxus' ram, and winter has fled from Castor in Pollux' place;[1] smiling is the field, earth is putting on her garb, the tree too its garb, the Attic adulteress mourns for Thracian Itys.[2] What days, Faustinus, what fair days of Ravenna[3] has Rome robbed you of; O sunny hours, O rest in tunic clad! O thou grove, O ye founts, and thou shore of firm moist sand, and Anxur gleaming in the ocean waves, and the couch that views more waters than one, that marks on this side the river's[4] ships, on that the sea's! Aye, and no theatres of Marcellus and of Pompey are there, nor there are the three warm baths,[5] nor the four forums joined, nor the august shrine of the Capitoline Thunderer, and the temples that gleam nigh their own heaven.[6] How often do I fancy you in your weariness saying to Quirinus: "What is yours keep to yourself; what is mine restore to me."

LII

Numa saw the eunuch Thelys in a toga, and said he was a convicted adulteress.[7]

LIII

That Scorpus am I, the glory of the clamorous Circus, thy applause, O Rome, and thy short-lived

---

[3] Perhaps the name of his villa (Paley). But the text is corrupt.
[4] The canal following the course of the Appian Way: *cf.* x. lviii. 4.   [5] Agrippa's, Nero's, and Titus'.
[6] The temple of the *Gens Flavia*: *cf.* IX. i. 8.
[7] *cf.* II. xxxix. 2.

invida quem Lachesis raptum trieteride nona,
  dum numerat palmas, credidit esse senem.

LIV

MENSAS, Ole, bonas ponis, sed ponis opertas.
  ridiculum est: possum sic ego habere bonas.

LV

ARRECTUM quotiens Marulla penem
pensavit digitis diuque mensa est,
libras scripula sextulasque dicit;
idem post opus et suas palaestras
loro cum similis iacet remisso,   5
quanto sit levior Marulla dicit.
non ergo est manus ista, sed statera.

LVI

TOTIS, Galle, iubes tibi me servire diebus
  et per Aventinum ter quater ire tuum.
eximit aut reficit dentem Cascellius aegrum;
  infestos oculis uris, Hygine, pilos;
non secat et tollit stillantem Fannius uvam;   5
  tristia servorum stigmata delet Eros;
enterocelarum fertur Podalirius Hermes:
  qui sanet ruptos dic mihi, Galle, quis est?

---

¹ One of the Fates.

darling. Me, snatched away in my ninth three
years' span, jealous Lachesis,[1] counting my victories,
deemed old in years.

LIV

You lay out, Olus, handsome tables, but you lay
them out covered. Absurd! I can possess in this
fashion handsome tables.

LV

Ogni volta che Marulla ha pesato colle dita l'eretto
membro, e lungo tempo lo misurato, ne dice le libre,
gli scrupoli ed i grani. Parimenti dopo l'opera e
le sue giostre, quando giace simile ad un rilasciato
cuojo, Marulla dice di quanto sia più leggiero.
Questa dunque non è una mano ma una stadera.

LVI

All day, Gallus, you bid me serve you, and thrice,
four times to mount your Aventine. Cascellius draws
or stops the decayed tooth; the hairs that wound
the eyes you, Hyginus, sear; without cutting Fannius heals a suppurating uvula; the degrading brands
on slaves Eros obliterates; of hernia Hermes is held
a very Podalirius.[2] Who is there, Gallus, to mend
the ruptured?[3]

[2] The physician of the Greek camp before Troy.
[3] *i.e.* those broken down (*cf.* IX. lvii. 4) by fatigue. There
is a play on *ruptos.*

LVII

Argenti libram mittebas ; facta selibra est,
    sed piperis.   tanti non emo, Sexte, piper.

LVIII

Anxuris aequorei placidos, Frontine, recessus
    et propius Baias litoreamque domum,
et quod inhumanae Cancro fervente cicadae
    non novere nemus, flumineosque lacus
dum colui, doctas tecum celebrare vacabat   5
    Pieridas ; nunc nos maxima Roma terit.
hic mihi quando dies meus est ?   iactamur in alto
    urbis, et in sterili vita labore perit,
dura suburbani dum iugera pascimus agri
    vicinosque tibi, sancte Quirine, lares.   10
sed non solus amat qui nocte dieque frequentat
    limina nec vatem talia damna decent.
per veneranda mihi Musarum sacra, per omnes
    iuro deos, et non officiosus amo.

LIX

Consumpta est uno si lemmate pagina, transis,
    et breviora tibi, non meliora, placent.
dives et ex omni posita est instructa macello
    cena tibi, sed te mattea sola iuvat.
non opus est nobis nimium lectore guloso ;   5
    hunc volo, non fiat qui sine pane satur.

---

[1] M. ironically assumes that the pepper must be as valuable as the plate formerly sent.

LVII

A POUND of silver plate you used to send me; it has become half a pound, and of pepper too! I don't buy pepper so dear,[1] Sextus.

LVIII

THE calm retreat, Faustinus, of Anxur by the sea, and a nearer Baiae, and a house by the shore, and the wood which the troublesome[2] cicadas have not discovered when Cancer flames, and the fresh-water canal—while I frequented these I had leisure along with you for allegiance to the learned Muses; now mightiest Rome wears us out. Here when is a day my own? I am tossed on the deep ocean of the city, and life is wasted in sterile toil while I maintain[3] stubborn acres of suburban land and a house near to you, holy Quirinus. But he is not alone a lover who day and night haunts thresholds, and such loss of time ill befits a poet. By the Muses' rites, to be hallowed by me, by all the gods I swear: careless client as I am, I love you yet.

LIX

IF a column is taken up by a single subject, you skip it, and the shorter epigrams please you, not the better. A meal, rich and furnished from every market, has been placed before you, but only a dainty attracts you. I have no need of a reader too nice: I want him who is not satisfied without bread.

[2] An English traveller compares the chirping of the cicada in Italy to the "scream of the corn-craik."

[3] *i.e.* spend more on it than it brings in: *cf.* x. xcvi. 7; or, "live on the produce of": *cf.* IX. lxxx. 2.

LX

[URA trium petiit a Caesare discipulorum
  adsuetus semper Munna docere duos.

LXI

HIC festinata requiescit Erotion umbra,
  crimine quam fati sexta peremit hiemps.
quisquis eris nostri post me regnator agelli,
  manibus exiguis annua iusta dato:
sic lare perpetuo, sic turba sospite solus   5
  flebilis in terra sit lapis iste tua.

LXII

LUDI magister, parce simplici turbae:
  sic te frequentes audiant capillati
et delicatae diligat chorus mensae,
  nec calculator nec notarius velox
maiore quisquam circulo coronetur.   5
  albae Leone flammeo calent luces
tostamque fervens Iulius coquit messem.
  cirrata loris horridis Scythae pellis,
qua vapulavit Marsyas Celaenaeus,
  ferulaeque tristes, sceptra paedagogorum,   10
cessent et Idus dormiant in Octobres:
  aestate pueri si valent, satis discunt.

LXIII ·

MARMORA parva quidem sed non cessura, viator,
  Mausoli saxis pyramidumque legis.

---

[1] M. parodies the *jus trium liberorum*: cf. II. xci. 6; IX
xcvii. 6.
  [2] *cf.* on the same subject v. xxxiv. and xxxvii.

LX

MUNNA, who was accustomed always to teach two, begged of Caesar the rights attached to three— pupils.[1]

LXI

HERE in too early gloom rests Erotion whom, by crime of Fate, her sixth winter laid low. Whoe'er thou shalt be, the lord after me of my little field, to her tiny ghost pay thou year by year thy rites. So may thy roof-tree continue, so thy household live unscathed, and in thy fields this gravestone alone call forth a tear![2]

LXII

SCHOOLMASTER, spare your simple flock; so in crowds may curly-headed boys listen to you, and a dainty bevy round your table be fond of you, and no arithmetic master or rapid shorthand teacher be ringed with a larger circle. The glaring days glow beneath flaming Leo, and blazing July ripens the parched grain. Let the Scythian's hide, thonged with bristling lashes, with which Marsyas[3] of Celaenae was scourged, and the alarming ferules, sceptres of pedagogues, rest and sleep till October's Ides. In summer if boys are well, they learn enough.

LXIII

A MARBLE, O traveller, you read small in truth, but one that shall not give place to the stones of

[3] A famous piper who challenged Apollo to a musical contest on the terms that the loser should be dealt with as the winner chose. His statue stood in the Forum: cf. II. lxiv. 8.

bis mea Romano spectata est vita Tarento
 et nihil extremos perdidit ante rogos:
quinque dedit pueros, totidem mihi Iuno puellas,   5
 cluserunt omnes lumina nostra manus.
contigit et thalami mihi gloria rara fuitque
 una pudicitiae mentula nota meae.

LXIV

CONTIGERIS regina meos si Polla libellos,
 non tetrica nostros excipe fronte iocos.
ille tuus vates, Heliconis gloria nostri,
 Pieria caneret cum fera bella tuba,
non tamen erubuit lascivo dicere versu   5
 "Si nec pedicor, Cotta, quid hic facio?"

LXV

CUM te municipem Corinthiorum
iactes, Charmenion, negante nullo,
cur frater tibi dicor, ex Hiberis
et Celtis genitus Tagique civis?
an voltu similes videmur esse?   5
tu flexa nitidus coma vagaris,
Hispanis ego contumax capillis;
levis dropace tu cotidiano,
hirsutis ego cruribus genisque;
os blaesum tibi debilisque lingua est,   10
nobis ilia fortius loquentur:[1]

---

[1] *ilia f. loquentur* Haupt, *filia f. loquetur* β; Friedländer
suggests *loquuntur.*

[1] *cf. Lib. Spect.* i. 5.

Mausolus[1] and of the Pyramids. Twice was my life approved at Roman Tarentos,[2] and ere my pyre at last was lit it forfeited no virtue. Five sons, as many daughters Juno gave me; the hands of all closed my eyes. And rare honour fell to my wedded lot: one spouse alone was all that my pure life knew.

LXIV

POLLA,[3] queen of women, if you shall handle my little volumes, with no frowning look greet my jests. He, your own bard, the glory of our Helicon, although on Pierian trump he made resound wild wars, yet did not blush to write in playful verse: "If I am not a Ganymede, Cotta, what do I here?"[4]

LXV

SEEING that you boast yourself a townsman of the Corinthians, Charmenion—and no one denies it— why am I called "brother" by you, I, who was born of the Iberians and Celts, and am a citizen of Tagus? Is it in face we look alike? You stroll about sleek with curled hair, my locks are Spanish and stiff; you are smoothed with depilatory daily, I am one with bristly shanks and cheeks; your tongue lisps, and your utterance is feeble; my guts will speak in

[2] A spot in the Campus Martius, where was an altar of Dis (Pluto): *cf.* IV. i. 8. The *Ludi Saeculares* were celebrated here, and had been held by Claudius in A.D. 47, and by Domitian in 88. Noble ladies (γυναῖκες ἐπίσημοι: Zos. II. v.) took part, and possibly they were bound to be of acknowledged character and virtue.

[3] The wife of Lucan the poet: *cf.* VII. xxi.

[4] This line does not appear in Lucan's extant works.

tam dispar aquilae columba non est
nec dorcas rigido fugax leoni.
quare desine me vocare fratrem,
ne te, Charmenion, vocem sororem.   15

LXVI

Quis, rogo, tam durus, quis tam fuit ille superbus
   qui iussit fieri te, Theopompe, cocum?
hanc aliquis faciem nigra violare culina
   sustinet, has uncto polluit igne comas?
quis potius cyathos aut quis crystalla tenebit?   5
   qua sapient melius mixta Falerna manu?
si tam sidereos manet exitus iste ministros,
   Iuppiter utatur iam Ganymede coco.

LXVII

Pyrrhae filia, Nestoris noverca,
quam vidit Niobe puella canam,
Laertes aviam senex vocavit,
nutricem Priamus, socrum Thyestes,
iam cornicibus omnibus superstes,   5
hoc tandem sita prurit in sepulchro
calvo Plotia cum Melanthione.

LXVIII

Cum tibi non Ephesos nec sit Rhodos aut Mitylene,
   sed domus in vico, Laelia, patricio,

---

[1] "Brother" and "sister" were often used in a disreputable sense: cf. II. iv. 3; Tib. III. i. 26.

stronger tone : a dove is not so unlike an eagle, nor a timid doe a savage lion. Wherefore cease to call me "brother" lest I call you, Charmenion, "sister" ! [1]

LXVI

WHO was he, I ask, so harsh, who was he so insolent that bade you, Theopompus, become a cook ? Is this a face any man endures to mar with black kitchen-soot, these the locks he pollutes with greasy flame ? Who in your stead will hold the ladles, or who the crystal cups ? From whose hand shall the blended Falernian take sweeter savour ? If such an end as that await attendants so heavenly-bright, let Jupiter now employ his Ganymede as cook.

LXVII

PYRRHA's daughter, Nestor's step-mother, one whom Niobe, when a girl, saw as an old crone, old Laertes called his grandmother, Priam his nurse, Thyestes his mother-in-law, Plotia, having now outlived all the crows,[2] is laid in this tomb at last, and by the side of bald Melanthion—itches with lust.

LXVIII

ALTHOUGH your home is not Ephesus, nor Rhodes, nor Mitylene, but a house, Laelia, in Patrician street,[3]

[2] Crows were said to outlive nine (Hes. *apud* Plut. *De Def. Or.* xi.), or at least five (Arist. *Av.* 609) generations of men.
[3] Under the Esquiline in the middle of Rome : *cf.* VII. lxxiii. 2.

deque coloratis numquam lita mater Etruscis,
    durus Aricina de regione pater,
κύριέ μου, μέλι μου, ψυχή μου congeris usque,   5
    pro pudor ! Hersiliae civis et Egeriae.
lectulus has voces, nec lectulus audiat omnis,
    sed quem lascivo stravit amica viro.
scire cupis quo casta modo matrona loquaris ?
    numquid, cum crisas, blandior esse potes ?   10
tu licet ediscas totam referasque Corinthon
    non tamen omnino, Laelia, Lais eris.

LXIX

Custodes das, Polla, viro, non accipis ipsa.
    hoc est uxorem ducere, Polla, virum.

LXX

Quod mihi vix unus toto liber exeat anno
    desidiae tibi sum, docte Potite, reus.
iustius at quanto mirere quod exeat unus,
    labantur toti cum mihi saepe dies.
non resalutantis video nocturnus amicos,   5
    gratulor et multis ; nemo, Potite, mihi.
nunc ad luciferam signat mea gemma Dianam,
    nunc me prima sibi, nunc sibi quinta rapit.

---

[1] *i.e.* Roman, not Greek. H. was the wife of Romulus,
E. of Numa, kings of Rome.

[2] Juvenal (vi. 192–5) seems to have copied the last two
sentences.

[3] A celebrated Corinthian courtesan.

and though your mother was one of the sunburnt Etruscans, and never rouged, your sturdy father one from the district of Aricia, you are continually heaping on me in Greek "my lord," "my honey," "my soul"—shameful! although you are a fellow-citizen of Hersilia and Egeria.[1] Let a couch hear such phrases, nor even every couch, but only that which his mistress has laid out for an amorous paramour.[2] You want to know how you are to speak as a chaste matron? Can you be more alluring when your gestures are lewd? You may learn by heart and reproduce all the ways of Corinth, yet nohow, Laelia, will you be a Lais.[3]

LXIX

You set watchers over your husband, Polla, but do not receive them yourself. This, Polla, is to take your husband to wife.[4]

LXX

BECAUSE scarcely one book of mine is published in a whole year, I am by you, learned Potitus, accused of laziness. But how much more justly should you wonder that one is published at all, when often whole days of mine slip away. Before daybreak I call on friends who do not return my call, and I offer congratulations to many: no one, Potitus, offers them to me. Now my signet-ring seals a document at the temple of Diana the Light-bringer;[5] now the first hour, now the fifth hurries me off. Now consul

---

[4] Husbands often set watchers over their wives: cf. Tac. Ann. xi. 35. To return the compliment, says M., is to convert a husband into a wife: cf. VIII. xii.

[5] On the Aventine (cf. VI. lxiv. 13), far from M.'s house on the Esquiline.

nunc consul praetorve tenet reducesque choreae ;
 auditur toto saepe poeta die.   10
sed nec causidico possis inpune negare,
 nec si te rhetor grammaticusve rogent.
balnea post decumam lasso centumque petuntur
 quadrantes. fiet quando, Potite, liber ?

LXXI

QUISQUIS laeta tuis et sera parentibus optas
 fata, brevem titulum marmoris huius ama.
condidit hac caras tellure Rabirius umbras ;
 nulli sorte iacent candidiore senes :
bis sex lustra tori nox mitis et ultima clusit,   5
 arserunt uno funera bina rogo.
hos tamen ut primis raptos sibi quaerit in annis.
 inprobius nihil his fletibus esse potest.

LXXII

FRUSTRA, Blanditiae, venitis ad me
adtritis miserabiles labellis :
dicturus dominum deumque non sum.
iam non est locus hac in urbe vobis ;
ad Parthos procul ite pilleatos   5
et turpes humilesque supplicesque
pictorum sola basiate regum.
non est hic dominus sed imperator,
sed iustissimus omnium senator,

or praetor detains me, and his escorting band;[1] often a poet is listened to a whole day long. Then also you cannot with impunity refuse a pleader, nor if a rhetorician or grammarian were to ask you. After the tenth hour, fagged out, I make for the baths and my hundred farthings.[2] When, Potitus, shall a book be written?

LXXI

WHOE'ER thou art who for thy parents prayest for a happy and a late death, regard with love this marble's brief inscription. In this earth Rabirius has hidden dearly-loved shades: with fairer lot none of the old lie in death. Twice six lustres of wedded life one night, kindly and their latest, closed; on one pyre two bodies burned. Yet he looks for them as if they had been snatched away from him in early years: naught more unwarranted can be than such a lament.

LXXII

IN vain, O ye Flatteries, ye come to me, wretched creatures with your shameless lips; I think not to address any man as Master and God.[3] No longer in this city is there place for you; fly far off to the turbaned Parthians, and kiss—base, crawling and suppliant as ye are—the soles of bedizened kings. No master is here, but a commander, aye, a senator most just of all,[4] by whose means rustic Truth with

[1] *i.e.* escorting a magistrate home from some function; *cf.* II. lxxiv. 2; XI. xxiv. 1.
[2] *cf.* III. vii. 3.
[3] A title assumed by Domitian, now dead.   [4] Trajan.

per quem de Stygia domo reducta est   10
siccis rustica Veritas capillis.
hoc sub principe, si sapis, caveto
verbis, Roma, prioribus loquaris.

LXXIII

Littera facundi gratum mihi pignus amici
  pertulit, Ausoniae dona †severa†[1] togae,
qua non Fabricius, sed vellet Apicius uti,
  vellet Maecenas Caesarianus eques.
vilior haec nobis alio mittente fuisset;   5
  non quacumque manu victima caesa litat:
a te missa venit: possem nisi munus amare,
  Marce, tuum, poteram nomen amare meum.
munere sed plus est et nomine gratius ipso
  officium docti iudiciumque viri.   10

LXXIV

Iam parce lasso, Roma, gratulatori,
lasso clienti.   quamdiu salutator
anteambulones et togatulos inter
centum merebor plumbeos die toto,
cum Scorpus una quindecim graves hora   5
ferventis auri victor auferat saccos?
non ego meorum praemium libellorum
(quid enim merentur?) Apulos velim campos;
non Hybla, non me spicifer capit Nilus,
nec quae paludes delicata Pomptinas   10

---

[1] F. is a type of early simplicity; A. and M. of modern
luxury.

her unperfumed locks has been brought home from
her abode by Styx. Under such a prince, if thou
art wise, beware, O Rome, to speak the words thou
didst before.

LXXIII

THE letter of my eloquent friend has brought me
a welcome pledge of love, the staid gift of an Italian
toga, which not Fabricius,[1] but Apicius would have
been glad to wear, glad too Maecenas, Caesar's
knight. Less prized would it have been if another
sent it: 'tis not the victim slain by every hand that
wins favour. By you 'tis sent and comes; if I could
not love your gift, Marcus, I could love at least my
own name.[2] But more than the gift, and more
welcome than the name itself, is the attention and
judgment of a learned man.

LXXIV

AT length spare, O Rome, the weary congratu-
lator, the weary client! How long, at levees, among
the escort and the full-dressed throng, shall I earn a
hundred worthless farthings[3] in a whole day, whereas
in a single hour, Scorpus, a winner of the race, bears
off fifteen bags of gleaming gold? I would not as
reward for my little books—for what do they deserve?—wish for Apulian plains;[4] nor does Hybla
or corn-bearing Nile allure me, nor the dainty Setine

[2] M.'s name was perhaps embroidered on the toga. Or
M. may mean, "I value the gift as coming from another
Marcus."
[3] The usual client's dole.
[4] Celebrated for wool: *cf.* II. xlvi. 6; VIII. xxviii. 3.

ex arce clivi spectat uva Setini.
quid concupiscam quaeris ergo ?   dormire.

LXXV

MILIA viginti quondam me Galla poposcit
   et, fateor, magno non erat illa nimis.
annus abit : " Bis quina dabis sestertia," dixit.
   poscere plus visa est quam prius illa mihi.
iam duo poscenti post sextum milia mensem   5
   mille dabam nummos.   noluit accipere.
transierant binae forsan trinaeve Kalendae,
   aureolos ultro quattuor ipsa petit.
non dedimus.   centum iussit me mittere nummos ;
   sed visa est nobis haec quoque summa gravis.   10
sportula nos iunxit quadrantibus arida centum ;
   hanc voluit : puero diximus esse datam.
inferius numquid potuit descendere ?   fecit.
   dat gratis, ultro dat mihi Galla : nego.

LXXVI

Hoc, Fortuna, tibi videtur aequum ?
civis non Syriaeve Parthiaeve,
nec de Cappadocis eques catastis,
sed de plebe Remi Numaeque verna,
iucundus probus innocens amicus,   5
lingua doctus utraque, cuius unum est
sed magnum vitium quod est poeta,
pullo Maevius alget in cucullo :
cocco mulio fulget Incitatus.

---

[1] The noises of Rome are described in XII. lvii.

grape which from the hill's crest looks on the Pomptine marshes.   Do you ask, then, what I long for?
To sleep.[1]

LXXV

GALLA formerly demanded of me twenty thousand
sesterces, and I allow she was not too dear.   A year
goes by: "You will give ten thousand?" she said;
she appeared to me to be demanding more than
before.   Then after six months, when she demanded
two thousand, I offered a thousand: she would not
accept them.   Two, or perhaps three kalends had
passed, and voluntarily she herself asked for four
gold pieces:[2]   I did not give them.   She bade me
send her a hundred sesterces, but this sum, too,
seemed to me stiff.   A starveling allowance of a
hundred farthings allied me with a patron: this she
wanted; I said I had given them to my slave.   Could
she come down to lower depths?   She achieved this.
Galla offers me her favours for nothing, offers of her
own accord: I decline.

LXXVI

DOES this, Fortune, seem to you to be fair?   Here
is a citizen, not of Syria or Parthia, no knight from
Cappadocian slave-stands, but home-born, one of the
crowd of Remus and of Numa, a friend pleasant,
honest, blameless, learned in either tongue, whose
one fault—and that a great one—is that he is a
poet: 'tis Maevius,[3] who shivers in a black cowl.
Incitatus, the mule-driver, shines in scarlet.

[2] The *aureolus* was a gold coin worth 25 denarii, intrin-
sically about a pound of British money.   Four, in terms of
sesterces, would be 400.
[3] Perhaps Martial means himself.

LXXVII

Nequius a Caro nihil umquam, Maxime, factum est
  quam quod febre perit: fecit et illa nefas.
saeva nocens febris saltem quartana fuisset:[1]
  servari medico debuit illa[2] suo.

LXXVIII

Ibis litoreas, Macer, Salonas;
ibit rara fides amorque recti
et quae, cum comitem trahit pudorem,
semper pauperior redit potestas.
felix auriferae colone terrae,   5
rectorem vacuo sinu remittes
optabisque moras, et exeuntem
udo, Dalmata, gaudio sequeris.
nos Celtas, Macer, et truces Hiberos
cum desiderio tui petemus.   10
sed quaecumque tamen feretur illinc
piscosi calamo Tagi notata,
Macrum pagina nostra nominabit:
sic inter veteres legar poetas,
nec multos mihi praeferas priores,   15
uno sed tibi sim minor Catullo.

LXXIX

Ad lapidem Torquatus habet praetoria quartum;
  ad quartum breve rus emit Otacilius.

----

[1] *fuisses* β.   [2] *illa* ⌐, *ille* codd.

----

[1] C. was a specialist in quartan fever, and should have
been allowed to die by his own particular disease. With the

LXXVII

NOTHING more scandalous, Maximus, was ever done by Carus than his dying of fever, and it too committed an outrage. The cruel, fatal fever should have been at least a quartan! That malady should have been reserved for its own doctor.[1]

LXXVIII

You will go, Macer, to Salonae[2] by the sea; with you will go rare loyalty and love of right, and power, which, with moderation in its train, ever returns the poorer. Happy dweller in that gold-bearing land, you will send home your Governor with empty pouch, and will beg him to linger, and as he goes you, Dalmatian, will speed him with a tearful joy. I, Macer, will seek the Celts and fierce Hiberians, longing the while for you. Yet, whatever page of mine shall be wafted from thence, scored with a reed-pen from fish-teeming Tagus, it shall speak of Macer's name. So may I be read among the old poets, and you prefer not many to me, but may I be to you less than Catullus alone!

LXXIX

AT the fourth milestone Torquatus possesses a palace: at the fourth Otacilius bought a narrow

reading *ille* in l. 4 the meaning is that the disease should have taken the mild form of a quartan (*cf.* Juv. iv. 57), and the patient been left for his own doctor to kill.

[2] The capital of Dalmatia, where M. was going as governor. He had been (*cf.* x. xvii.) curator of the Appian Way.

Torquatus nitidas vario de marmore thermas
    extruxit ; cucumam fecit Otacilius.
disposuit daphnona suo Torquatus in agro ;   5
    castaneas centum sevit Otacilius.
consule Torquato vici fuit ille magister,
    non minor in tanto visus honore sibi.
grandis ut exiguam bos ranam ruperat olim,
    sic, puto, Torquatus rumpet Otacilium.   10

LXXX

PLORAT Eros, quotiens maculosae pocula murrae
    inspicit aut pueros nobiliusve citrum,
et gemitus imo ducit de pectore quod non
    tota miser coemat Saepta feratque domum.
quam multi faciunt quod Eros ! sed lumine sicco   5
    pars maior lacrimas ridet et intus habet.

LXXXI

CUM duo venissent ad Phyllida mane fututum
    et nudam cuperet sumere uterque prior,
promisit pariter se Phyllis utrique daturam,
    et dedit : ille pedem sustulit, hic tunicam.

LXXXII

SI quid nostra tuis adicit vexatio rebus,
    mane vel a media nocte togatus ero

---

[1] *Cucuma*, literally, is a large seething pot.
[2] Augustus divided Rome into regions and districts (Suet.

field. Torquatus built warm baths bright with variegated marble: Otacilius set up a geyser.[1] On his land Torquatus laid out a laurel-grove: Otacilius planted a hundred chestnuts. When Torquatus was consul the other was a vestryman,[2] in such a dignity deeming himself no lesser man. Just as the huge ox in the fable caused the frog to burst himself, so, I think, Torquatus will burst Otacilius.

LXXX

EROS weeps whenever he inspects cups of spotted[3] murrine, or slaves, or a citrus-wood table finer than usual, and heaves groans from the bottom of his chest because he—wretched man—cannot buy all the whole Saepta[4] and carry it home. How many act like Eros! But with dry eyes the greater part laugh at his tears—and have them in their hearts.

LXXXI

DUI essendo venuti da Fillide di mattina per immembrarla, e l'uno e l'altro desiderando goderla nuda il primo, Fillide promise darsi in una volta a tutti e due, e si diede. Quello sollevò il piede, questo la tunica.

LXXXII

IF my discomfort bring any advantage to your affairs, at daybreak, or after midnight I will don my

Aug. 30), each of the latter being put under four *vici magistri* chosen from the vicinity.

[3] Transparency or paleness was a defect: *cf.* IV. lxxxv. 2.
[4] *cf.* II. xiv. 5.

stridentesque feram flatus Aquilonis iniqui
  et patiar nimbos excipiamque nives.
sed si non fias quadrante beatior uno   5
  per gemitus nostros ingenuasque cruces,
parce, precor, fesso vanosque remitte labores
  qui tibi non prosunt et mihi, Galle, nocent.

LXXXIII

RAROS colligis hinc et hinc capillos
  et latum nitidae, Marine, calvae
campum temporibus tegis comatis;
  sed moti redeunt iubente vento
reddunturque sibi caputque nudum   5
  cirris grandibus hinc et inde cingunt.
inter Spendophorum Telesphorumque
  Cydae stare putabis Hermerotem.
vis tu simplicius senem fateri,
  ut tandem videaris unus esse?   10
calvo turpius est nihil comato.

LXXXIV

MIRARIS, quare dormitum non eat Afer?
  accumbat cum qua, Caediciane, vides.

LXXXV

IAM senior Ladon Tiberinae nauta carinae
  proxima dilectis rura paravit aquis.

---

    [1] S. and T. are beautiful boys referred to in IX. lvi.; XI.
218

toga, and bear the whistling blasts of the harsh
North wind, and endure the storm-clouds and welcome the snow. But if you don't become richer by
a single farthing through my groans and the servile
tortures of a free man, be merciful, I pray, to my
weariness, and remit these useless labours that don't
help you, Gallus, and hurt me.

LXXXIII

From the one side and the other you gather up
your scanty locks and you cover, Marinus, the wide
expanse of your shining bald scalp with the hair from
both sides of your head. But blown about, they
come back at the bidding of the wind, and return
to themselves, and gird your bare poll with big
curls on this side and on that. You would think
the Hermeros of Cydas is standing between Spendophorus and Telesphorus.[1] Will you, please, in simpler
fashion confess yourself old, so as after all to appear
a single person? Nothing is more unsightly than
a bald man covered with hair.[2]

LXXXIV

Do you wonder why Afer does not go to bed?
You see, Caedicianus, the lady with whom he reclines
at table.

LXXXV

Now grown old, Ladon, the master of a boat on
Tiber, bought some land near his beloved stream.

xxvi. Hermeros is unknown, and may be someone so called
on account of his ugliness and baldness.
  [2] cf. v. xlix. on a similar subject.

quae cum saepe vagus premeret torrentibus undis
    Thybris et hiberno rumperet arva lacu,
emeritam puppim, ripa quae stabat in alta,   5
    inplevit saxis opposuitque vadis.
sic nimias avertit aquas.   quis credere posset?
    auxilium domino mersa carina tulit.

LXXXVI

Nemo nova caluit sic inflammatus amica,
    flagravit quanto Laurus amore pilae.
sed qui primus erat lusor dum floruit aetas,
    nunc postquam desit ludere, prima pila est.

LXXXVII

Octobres age sentiat Kalendas
facundi pia Roma Restituti:
linguis omnibus et favete votis;
natalem colimus, tacete lites.
absit cereus aridi clientis,   5
et vani triplices brevesque mappae
expectent gelidi iocos Decembris.
certent muneribus beatiores:
Agrippae tumidus negotiator
Cadmi municipes ferat lacernas;   10
pugnorum reus ebriaeque noctis
cenatoria mittat advocato;

---

[1] *cf.* II. xliii. 6. L. is now good for nothing. Or perhaps
the allusion may be to his dilapidated appearance through
poverty.

As Tiber often o'erflowing was drowning it with rushing waters, and with a winter flood usurping the tilled fields, he filled with stones his boat, now past service, that stood on the high bank, and opposed it as a barrier to the waters. So he averted the deluge. Who could believe it? The sinking of his ship brought succour to its owner!

LXXXVI

No man has been so inflamed with ardour for a new mistress as Laurus has been fired with the delight of playing at ball. But he, who was a prime player while life was in its bloom, now he has ceased to play is a prime dummy.[1]

LXXXVII

COME, let duteous Rome recognise October's kalends, the birthday of eloquent Restitutus[2]: with all your tongues, and in all your prayers, utter well-omened words; we keep a birthday, be still, ye law-suits! Away with the needy client's wax taper! and let useless three-leaved tablets and curt napkins wait for the jollity of cold December.[3] Let richer men vie in gifts: let Agrippa's[4] pompous tradesman bring mantles, the fellow-citizens of Cadmus[5]; let the defendant in a charge of assault and drunkenness at night send his counsel dinner-suits. Has a slandered

---

[2] An advocate, perhaps the Claudius R. spoken of by Pliny (*Ep.* III. ix. 16) as "*vir exercitatus et vigilans, et quamlibet subitis paratus.*"

[3] "Away with rubbishy gifts: let every one send his best!"

[4] In the Saepta where were fashionable shops: *cf.* II. xiv. 5; IX. lix. 1.   [5] *i.e.* Tyrian.

> infamata virum puella vicit?
> veros sardonychas, sed ipsa tradat;
> mirator veterum senex avorum   15
> donet Phidiaci toreuma caeli;
> venator leporem, colonus haedum,
> piscator ferat aequorum rapinas.
> si mittit sua quisque, quid poetam
> missurum tibi, Restitute, credis?   20

LXXXVIII

OMNES persequeris praetorum, Cotta, libellos;
  accipis et ceras.   officiosus homo es.

LXXXIX

IUNO labor, Polyclite, tuus et gloria felix,
  Phidiacae cuperent quam meruisse manus,
ore nitet tanto quanto superasset in Ide
  iudice convictas non dubitante deas.
Iunonem, Polyclite, suam nisi frater amaret,   5
  Iunonem poterat frater amare tuam.

XC

QUID vellis vetulum, Ligeia, cunnum?
  quid busti cineres tui lacessis?
tales munditiae decent puellas
  (nam tu iam nec anus potes videri);
istud, crede mihi, Ligeia, belle   5
  non mater facit Hectoris, sed uxor.

---

[1] *cf.* IV. xxxix. 4.
[2] This ep. is unintelligible (Friedländer). It depends on
the meaning of *libellos*.

young wife defeated her husband? Let her bestow, and with her own hands, genuine sardonyxes. Let the old admirer of ancient days give chased plate of Phidias' chisel,[1] the hunter a hare, the farmer a kid, the fisher bring the spoil of the sea. If every man send his own peculiar gift, what do you think, Restitutus, a poet will send you?

LXXXVIII

You run after all the announcements of trials before the Praetor, Cotta, and you accept note books. You are an attentive person![2]

LXXXIX

Juno, thy work, Polyclitus, bringing thee proud glory, such as the hands of Phidias might be eager to have won, shines in beauty such as on Ida would have o'ercome the goddesses condemned by no hesitating judge.[3] Did not her brother[4] love his own Juno, Polyclitus, that brother might well have loved this Juno of thine!

XC

Why, Ligeia, do you depilate your aged charms? Why do you stir the ashes of your dead self? Such trickings befit young girls (for you cannot now seem to be even an old crone); that which you do, Ligeia, believe me, is not pretty in Hector's mother, only

[3] Paris, who adjudged Venus to be more beautiful than Juno or Minerva.
[4] Jupiter.

erras si tibi cunnus hic videtur,
ad quem mentula pertinere desit.
quare si pudor est, Ligeia, noli
barbam vellere mortuo leoni.   10

XCI

OMNES eunuchos habet Almo nec arrigit ipse:
et queritur pariat quod sua Polla nihil.

XCII

MARI, quietae cultor et comes vitae,
quo cive prisca gloriatur Atina,
has tibi gemellas barbari decus luci
conmendo pinus ilicesque Faunorum
et semidocta vilici manu structas   5
Tonantis aras horridique Silvani,
quas pinxit agni saepe sanguis aut haedi,
dominamque sancti virginem deam templi,
et quem sororis hospitem vides castae
Martem mearum principem Kalendarum,   10
et delicatae laureum nemus Florae,
in quod Priapo persequente confugit.
hoc omne agelli mite parvuli numen
seu tu cruore sive ture placabis,
"Ubicumque vester Martialis est," dices   15
"hac ecce mecum dextera litat vobis
absens sacerdos; vos putate praesentem
et date duobus quidquid alter optabit."

---

[1] *i.e.* do not seek to stir passion now dead.

in his wife. You are mistaken if you think those are charms, when gallantry has ceased to concern itself with them. So, if you have any shame, Ligeia, forbear to pluck the beard of a dead lion.[1]

XCI

ALMO has eunuchs all about him, and he himself is inefficient, and yet he complains that his Polla produces nothing.

XCII

MARIUS, votary of that quiet life you shared with me, citizen in whom ancient Atina makes her boast, these twin pines, the ornament of an untrimmed wood, I commend to you,[2] and the holm-oaks of the Fawns, and the altars, built by my bailiff's unpractised hand, of the Thunderer and of shaggy Silvanus, that oft the blood of lamb or goat has stained; and the virgin goddess,[3] queen of her hallowed shrine, and him whom you see, his pure sister's guest, Mars, who rules my birthday kalends; and the laurel grove of dainty Flora, whereinto she fled when Priapus pursued. To all these gentle deities of my small field, whoe'er they be, whom you propitiate, whether with blood or incense, you shall say: "Wherever your Martial is, behold, by this right hand with me he sacrifices to you, an absent priest. Deem ye that he is here, and grant to both whatever either shall pray for!"

---

[2] Martial, being about to return to Spain, commends to M. the Nomentan farm, and the duty of keeping up its sacred rites.   [3] Diana.

XCIII

Sı prior Euganeas, Clemens, Helicaonis oras
    pictaque pampineis videris arva iugis,
perfer Atestinae nondum vulgata Sabinae
    carmina, purpurea sed modo culta toga.
ut rosa delectat metitur quae pollice primo,   5
    sic nova nec mento sordida charta iuvat.

XCIV

Non mea Massylus servat pomaria serpens,
    regius Alcinoi nec mihi servit ager,
sed Nomentana securus germinat hortus
    arbore, nec furem plumbea mala timent.
haec igitur media quae sunt modo nata Subura   5
    mittimus autumni cerea poma mei.

XCV

Infantem tibi vir, tibi, Galla, remisit adulter.
    hi, puto, non dubie se futuisse negant.

XCVI

Saepe loquar nimium gentes quod, Avite, remotas
    miraris, Latia factus in urbe senex,
auriferumque Tagum sitiam patriumque Salonem
    et repetam saturae sordida rura casae.

---

[1] Euganei was the old name of the inhabitants of Venetia.
Helicaon was the son of Antenor who founded Patavium
(Padua).
    [2] iugum is regularly used by Columella of the trellis to
which the vine shoots were fastened.   [3] *cf.* I. lxvi. 8.

XCIII

IF before me, Clemens, you shall behold Helicaon's
Euganean shores,[1] and the fields decked with vine-
clad trellises,[2] carry to Sabina of Atesta poems, un-
published as yet, and that too newly arrayed in
purple wrapper. As the rose delights us that is first
plucked by the finger, so a sheet pleases when 'tis
new and unsoiled by the chin.[3]

XCIV

No Massylian serpent[4] guards my orchard, nor does
the royal plantation of Alcinous[5] serve my wants, but
my garden burgeons in security with its Nomentan
fruit-trees, and my poor fruits dread no thief. So
I send you these yellow apples of my autumn crop,
freshly grown—in the midst of the Subura.[6]

XCV

YOUR husband, Galla, has sent you back the babe,
your lover has sent it back. They, I think, in no
doubtful fashion deny connection.

XCVI

You often wonder, Avitus,[7] why I speak overmuch
of nations very far off, though I have grown old in
Latium's city, and long for gold-bearing Tagus and
my native Salo, and look back to the rough fields of

---

[4] That guarded the golden apples of the Hesperides: *cf.*
XIII. xxxvii.   [5] *cf.* VII. xlii. 6.
[6] *i.e.* bought there by M., as his own farm at Nomentum
produced nothing worth sending: *cf.* VII. xxxi. 12.
[7] *cf.* IX. i. *Ep.*

illa placet tellus in qua res parva beatum 5
   me facit et tenues luxuriantur opes :
pascitur hic, ibi pascit ager ; tepet igne maligno
   hic focus, ingenti lumine lucet ibi ;
hic pretiosa fames conturbatorque macellus,
   mensa ibi divitiis ruris operta sui ; 10
quattuor hic aestate togae pluresve teruntur,
   autumnis ibi me quattuor una tegit.
i, cole nunc reges, quidquid non praestat amicus
   cum praestare tibi possit, Avite, locus.

XCVII

Dum levis arsura struitur Libitina papyro,
   dum murram et casias flebilis uxor emit,
iam scrobe, iam lecto, iam pollinctore parato,
   heredem scripsit me Numa : convaluit.

XCVIII

Addat cum mihi Caecubum minister
Idaeo resolutior cinaedo,
quo nec filia cultior nec uxor
nec mater tua nec soror recumbit,
vis spectem potius tuas lucernas 5
aut citrum vetus Indicosque dentes ?
suspectus tibi ne tamen recumbam,
praesta de grege sordidaque villa
tonsos horridulos rudes pusillos
hircosi mihi filios subulci. 10
perdet te dolor hic : habere, Publi,
mores non potes hos et hos ministros.

a fruitful country-house. That land is dear to me
wherein small means make me rich, and a slender
store is luxury. The soil is maintained[1] here, there
it maintains you; here your hearth is scarcely warm
with its grudging fire, with a mighty blaze it shines
there. Here hunger is dear and the market makes
you bankrupt, there stands a table covered with its
own country's wealth. Here four togas or more
grow threadbare in a summer, there during four
autumns one covers me. Go to, now! and pay
court to great men, when a place can afford you,
Avitus, whatever a friend does not afford[1]

XCVII

WHILE the lightly-heaped pyre was being laid with
papyrus for the flame,[2] while his weeping wife was
buying myrrh and casia, when now the grave, when
now the bier, when now the anointer was ready,
Numa wrote me down his heir, and—got well!

XCVIII

WHEN an attendant more voluptuous than the
cupbearer of Ida[3] pours out my Caecuban, one than
whom your daughter or wife, or mother or sister, is
no smarter as she reclines at table, do you wish me
instead to look at your lamps, or at your antique
table of citrus-wood and its ivory legs? Nevertheless, that I may not be suspected by you at your table,
produce for me from the throng in your rough farm-
stead some short-haired, unkempt, clownish, puny fellows, sons of a malodorous swineherd. This jealousy
of yours will betray you! You cannot, Publius,
possess such morals and such servants at once.

[1] cf. x. lviii. 9.   [2] cf. VIII. xliv. 14.   [3] Ganymede.

XCIX

Si Romana forent haec Socratis ora, fuissent
Iulius in Saturis qualia Rufus habet.

C

Quid, stulte, nostris versibus tuos misces?
cum litigante quid tibi, miser, libro?
quid congregare cum leonibus volpes
aquilisque similes facere noctuas quaeris?
habeas licebit alterum pedem Ladae,   5
inepte, frustra crure ligneo curris.

CI

Elysio redeat si forte remissus ab agro
ille suo felix Caesare Gabba vetus,
qui Capitolinum pariter Gabbamque iocantes
audierit, dicet "Rustice Gabba, tace."

CII

Qua factus ratione sit requiris,
qui numquam futuit, pater Philinus?
Gaditanus, Avite, dicat istud,
qui scribit nihil et tamen poeta est.

CIII

Municipes, Augusta mihi quos Bilbilis acri
monte creat, rapidis quem Salo cingit aquis,

---

¹ Possibly on a portrait of R. as a frontispiece to his
Satires. The portrait is as ugly as Socrates. Others,
however, suggest *in Satyris* "amid a group of satyrs."

XCIX

IF this face of Socrates had been a Roman's, it would have been just what Julius Rufus presents in his Satires.[1]

C

WHY, you fool, do you mix your verses with mine? What have you, wretched fellow, to do with a book that is at odds with you?[2] Why do you try to herd foxes with lions, and to make owls like eagles? You may possess one foot as swift as Ladas,[3] yet, you stupid, you run in vain with a leg of wood.

CI

IF, by chance sent back from the Elysian fields, the old Gabba,[4] fortunate in his master, Caesar, were to return, he who hears Capitolinus[5] and Gabba in a jesting match will say: "Boorish Gabba, hold your tongue!"

CII

Do you ask how it comes that Philinus, who never sleeps with his wife, is yet a father? Gaditanus must answer that, Avitus: he writes nothing, and yet he is "a poet."

CIII

FELLOW-TOWNSMEN, the children of Augustan Bilbilis on its keen hillside, which Salo girds with

---

[2] cf. I. liii. 3.
[3] A celebrated Spartan runner, and winner at Olympia: cf. II. lxxxvi. 8.
[4] The jester of the Emperor Augustus: cf. I xli. 16.
[5] Trajan's jester.

ecquid laeta iuvat vestri vos gloria vatis?
  nam decus et nomen famaque vestra sumus,
nec sua plus debet tenui Verona Catullo   5
  meque velit dici non minus illa suum.
quattuor accessit tricesima messibus aestas,
  ut sine me Cereri rustica liba datis,
moenia dum colimus dominae pulcherrima Romae:
  mutavere meas Itala regna comas.   10
excipitis placida reducem si mente, venimus;
  aspera si geritis corda, redire licet.

CIV

I nostro comes, i, libelle, Flavo
  longum per mare, sed faventis undae,
et cursu facili tuisque ventis
  Hispanae pete Tarraconis arces:
illinc te rota tollet et citatus   5
  altam Bilbilin et tuum Salonem
quinto forsitan essedo videbis.
  quid mandem tibi quaeris? ut sodales
paucos, sed veteres et ante brumas
  triginta mihi quattuorque visos   10
ipsa protinus a via salutes
  et nostrum admoneas subinde Flavum
iucundos mihi nec laboriosos
  secessus pretio paret salubri,
qui pigrum faciant tuum parentem.   15
  haec sunt. iam tumidus vocat magister
castigatque moras, et aura portum
  laxavit melior: vale, libelle:
navem, scis, puto, non moratur unus.

hurrying waters, does the glad renown of your bard delight you? For I am your glory and repute, and your fame, and his own Verona owes no more to elegant Catullus, and would wish me to be called no less her own son. A thirtieth summer has been added to four harvests since without me you offered to Ceres rustic cakes, while I have sojourned within the fair walls of mistress Rome; the realm of Italy has grizzled my locks. If you greet me with gentle will on my return, I come to you; if you carry churlish hearts, I can go back.[1]

CIV

Go, fellow wayfarer of my Flavus; go, little book, over the wide sea—but when the wave befriends you—and, on easy course and with breezes all your own, seek the heights of Spanish Tarraco. From there the wheel will carry you, and, rapidly borne, you will perchance at the fifth stage see high-set Bilbilis and your Salo. Ask you what is my charge to you? That you greet, even as you are on the way, my comrades—few are they, but old ones, and last seen by me now thirty and four winters back—and now and then remind my Flavus that he procure for me at a wholesome price some retreat, pleasant and not hard to keep up, which may make a lazy man of your begetter. This is my charge. Already the skipper calls in blustering tones, and is blaming the delay, and a fairer wind has opened the harbour. Farewell, little book: you know, I think, one passenger does not delay a vessel.

[1] M. appears to anticipate jealousy: *cf.* xii. *Ep.*

BOOK XI

LIBER UNDECIMUS

I

Quo tu, quo, liber otiose, tendis
cultus Sidone [1] non cotidiana?
numquid Parthenium videre? certe:
vadas et redeas inevolutus.
libros non legit ille sed libellos;   5
nec Musis vacat, aut suis vacaret.
ecquid te satis aestimas beatum,
contingunt tibi si manus minores?
vicini pete porticum Quirini:
turbam non habet otiosiorem   10
Pompeius vel Agenoris puella,
vel primae dominus levis carinae.
sunt illic duo tresve qui revolvant
nostrarum tineas ineptiarum,
sed cum sponsio fabulaeque lassae   15
de Scorpo fuerint et Incitato.

II

Triste supercilium durique severa Catonis
frons et aratoris filia Fabricii

---

[1] He probably read these on behalf of the Emperor.
[2] The Temple of Quirinus near M.'s house; *cf.* x. lviii 10.
[3] The references are respectively to the *Porticus Pompeii*
(*cf.* II. xiv. 10); the *Porticus Europae* (*cf.* II. xiv. 15); and

BOOK XI

I

Where, where are you going, idle book, smart in purple not of every day? Can it be to see Parthenius? No doubt: go and return unopened; publications he does not read, only petitions,[1] nor has he leisure for the Muses, or he would have leisure for his own. Do you not think yourself fortunate enough if lesser hands may await you? Make for Quirinus' Colonnade[2] hard by; a crowd more idle not Pompey contains, nor Agenor's daughter, nor the inconstant captain of the first ship.[3] There are two or three there who may unroll my twaddle, fit only for worms, but only when the bet and languid tales about Scorpus and Incitatus[4] are done with.

II

Forbidding frowns, and rigid Cato's brow austere, and the daughter of Fabricius[5] the ploughman, and

the *Porticus Argonautarum* (*cf.* II. xiv. 6). Jason is called *levis* because of his conduct to Medea.

[4] Charioteers: *cf.* x. l. and x. lxxvi. 9.

[5] Fabricius, a type of the old Roman simplicity of life. On account of their poverty, his daughters were dowered by the Senate.

et personati fastus et regula morum,
    quidquid et in tenebris non sumus, ite foras.
clamant ecce mei " Io Saturnalia " versus :   5
    et licet et sub te praeside, Nerva, libet.
lectores tetrici salebrosum ediscite Santram :
    nil mihi vobiscum est : iste liber meus est.

III

Non urbana mea tantum Pimpleide gaudent
    otia, nec vacuis auribus ista damus,
sed meus in Geticis ad Martia signa pruinis
    a rigido teritur centurione liber,
dicitur et nostros cantare Britannia versus.   5
    quid prodest? nescit sacculus ista meus.
at quam victuras poteramus pangere chartas
    quantaque Pieria proelia flare tuba,
cum pia reddiderint Augustum numina terris,
    et Maecenatem si tibi, Roma, darent !¹   10

IV

Sacra laresque Phrygum, quos Troiae maluit heres
    quam rapere arsuras Laomedontis opes,
scriptus et aeterno nunc primum Iuppiter auro
    et soror et summi filia tota patris,

         ¹ *darent* Heins., *daret* codd.

---

¹ Who succeeded to the Empire in Oct. 96 A.D., this book
being published at the Saturnalia in December.
² A Roman grammarian in the time of Julius Caesar. He
wrote a treatise on famous men, and a grammatical work,
De verborum antiquitate. He is mentioned by later writers,
including Jerome.

masked Conceit, and Propriety, and all things
which in our private lives we are not, get ye gone!
See, my verses cry "Ho for the Saturnalia!" 'tis
allowed, and under you, Nerva,[1] our Governor, 'tis
our joy as well. Ye strait-laced readers, learn by
heart rugged Santra[2] : I have nothing to do with
you : this book is mine!

III

'Tis not city idleness alone that delights in my
Muse, nor do I give these epigrams to vacant ears,
but my book, amid Getic frosts, beside martial stand-
ards, is thumbed by the hardy centurion, and Britain
is said to hum my verses. What profit is it? My
money-bag knows nothing of that. But what immortal pages could I frame, and of wars how mighty
could I blow my Pierian trump, if the kindly deities,
now they have restored Augustus[3] to earth, were
also, Rome, to give you a Maecenas!

IV

Ye sacred symbols and native gods of Phrygia,
whom Troy's heir[4] chose to rescue rather than Laomedon's wealth doomed to the fire, and thou, Jupiter,
now for the first time depicted in everlasting gold,[5]
and thou, sister and daughter—all his own[6]—of the

---

[3] *i.e.* the Emperor Nerva.

[4] Aeneas at the burning of Troy.

[5] Some representation of Jupiter placed by Nerva in the
Temple on the Capitol. *Aeterno* = never again to be destroyed
by fire.

[6] Juno and Minerva, the latter being "all his own," as
having sprung from his head.

239

et qui purpureis iam tertia nomina fastis,   5
    Iane, refers Nervae, vos precor ore pio:
hunc omnes servate ducem, servate senatum;
    moribus hic vivat principis, ille suis.

V

Tanta tibi est recti reverentia, Caesar, at aequi
    quanta Numae fuerat: sed Numa pauper erat.
ardua res haec est, opibus non tradere mores
    et, cum tot Croesos viceris, esse Numam.
si redeant veteres, ingentia nomina, patres,   5
    Elysium liceat si vacuare nemus,
te colet invictus pro libertate Camillus,
    aurum Fabricius te tribuente volet;
te duce gaudebit Brutus, tibi Sulla cruentus
    imperium tradet, cum positurus erit;   10
et te privato cum Caesare Magnus amabit,
    donabit totas et tibi Crassus opes.
ipse quoque infernis revocatus Ditis ab umbris
    si Cato reddatur, Caesarianus erit.

VI

Unctis falciferi senis diebus,
regnator quibus inperat fritillus,
versu ludere non laborioso

---

[1] Nerva being consul for the third time. The consular records were kept in the Temple of Janus: *cf.* VIII. lxvi. 11.

[2] The legendary second king of Rome.

[3] The conqueror of Veii, and rescuer of Rome from the Gauls.

[4] Who refused the presents of Pyrrhus, king of Epirus.

[5] M. credits S. with patriotism. As a fact S. abdicated the dictatorship in B.C. 79 at the height of his power, as he

Almighty Sire, and thou, Janus, who for the third time now addest Nerva's name to the annals of the purple,[1] 'tis to you I pray with pious utterance. This our Chief preserve ye all, preserve ye the Senate; by its Prince's pattern may it live, he by his own!

V

As great is thy reverence for right and justice, Caesar, as was Numa's, but Numa[2] was poor. 'Tis a hard task this, not to sacrifice manners to wealth, and, though thou hast surpassed many a Croesus, to be a Numa. Were our sires of old, mighty names, to return, were it allowed to empty the Elysian grove, to thee Camillus,[3] liberty's unconquered champion, will pay his court, gold at thy giving will Fabricius[4] accept, in thee as captain will Brutus be glad, to thee bloody Sulla will resign his power when he shall seek to lay it down;[5] and thee the Great Captain, allied with Caesar, only a private citizen, will love, and Crassus[6] will bestow on thee all his wealth. Cato,[7] too, himself, were he called back to return from the nether shades of Dis, will be Caesar's partizan.

VI

On the old Scythe-bearer's[8] feastful days, whereof the dice-box[9] is king and lord, you, cap-

had exterminated all his opponents and superstitiously fearing to trespass further on the kindness of Fortune, whose child he regarded himself.

[6] A member of the first Triumvirate (Pompey, Crassus and Caesar) and one of the richest Romans.

[7] Who committed suicide rather than submit to Julius Caesar.

[8] Saturn, who gave his name to the Saturnalia.

[9] Gambling was allowed at the Saturnalia: *cf.* v. lxxxiv. 5.

permittis, puto, pilleata Roma.
risisti; licet ergo, non vetamur.   5
pallentes procul hinc abite curae;
quidquid venerit obvium loquamur
morosa sine cogitatione.
misce dimidios, puer, trientes,
quales Pythagoras dabat Neroni,   10
misce, Dindyme, sed frequentiores:
possum nil ego sobrius; bibenti
succurrent mihi quindecim poetae.
da nunc basia, sed Catulliana:
quae si tot fuerint quot ille dixit,   15
donabo tibi Passerem Catulli.

VII

Iam certe stupido non dices, Paula, marito,
    ad moechum quotiens longius ire voles,
"Caesar in Albanum iussit me mane venire,
    Caesar Circeios." iam stropha talis abit.
Penelopae licet esse tibi sub principe Nerva: 5
    sed prohibet scabies ingeniumque vetus.
infelix, quid ages? aegram simulabis amicam?
    haerebit dominae vir comes ipse suae,
ibit et ad fratrem tecum matremque patremque.
    quas igitur fraudes ingeniosa pares?   10
diceret hystericam se forsitan altera moecha
    in Sinuessano velle sedere lacu.
quanto tu melius, quotiens placet ire fututum,
    quae verum mavis dicere, Paula, viro!

---

[1] The *pilleum*, or cap of liberty worn by manumitted
slaves (*cf.* II. lxviii. 4) was also generally worn at the
Saturnalia. It was a symbol of licence. Thus, on the death
of Nero, the common people assumed it, and ran about the
whole city: Suet. *Nero* lvii.

clad[1] Rome, allow me, I wot, to trifle in verse un-
toilsome. You have smiled: I may then, I am not
forbidden. Ye pallid cares, far hence away! whatever comes to my mind let me speak without
wrinkled meditation. Blend, boy, cups half and
half, such as Pythagoras[2] offered Nero; blend them,
thou, Dindymus,[3] and that more oft; nothing sober
can I do: as I drink a fifteen-poets power will bear
me up. Give me kisses now, and by Catullus's
measure; if they be as many as he said, I will give
thee a Sparrow of Catullus.[4]

VII

Now at least you will not say, Paula, to your dolt
of a husband, every time you want to go to a lover
at a distance, " Caesar bade me come in the morning
to his Alban villa, Caesar bade me come to Circeii."
Now such a manœuvre is off. 'Tis lawful for you
to be a Penelope under Nerva as chief, but your
itch and inveterate bent forbid you. Unfortunate
woman, what will you do? Will you pretend the
sickness of a friend? Your husband in person will
cling to his dame's skirts, and will go with you to
brother and mother and father. What fraud then
would your ingenuity devise? Another wanton
would perhaps say she is hysterical, and wished to
sit in Sinuessa's baths. How much better is your
practice whenever you have a mind to stray! You,
Paula, prefer to tell your husband the truth!

[2] Nero's cupbearer, with whom he went through the form
of marriage: cf. Suet. *Nero* xxix.; Tac. *Ann.* xv. 37.

[3] M.'s attendant: cf. x. xlii.

[4] C. asked Lesbia for thousands of kisses (Cat. v. 7–9); he
also wrote a poem (Cat. iii.) on the death of her sparrow.

VIII

LASSA quod nesterni spirant opobalsama dracti,[1]
  ultima quod curvo quae cadit aura croco ;
poma quod hiberna maturescentia capsa,
  arbore quod verna luxuriosus ager ;
de Palatinis dominae quod Serica prelis,   5
  sucina virginea quod regelata manu ;
amphora quod nigri, sed longe, fracta Falerni,
  quod qui Sicanias detinet hortus apes ;
quod Cosmi redolent alabastra focique deorum,
  quod modo divitibus lapsa corona comis :   10
singula quid dicam ?   non sunt satis ; omnia misce :
  hoc fragrant pueri basia mane mei.
scire cupis nomen ?   si propter basia, dicam.
  iurasti.   nimium scire, Sabine, cupis.

IX

CLARUS fronde Iovis, Romani fama coturni,
  spirat Apellea redditus arte Memor.

X

CONTULIT ad saturas ingentia pectora Turnus.
  cur non ad Memoris carmina ?   frater erat.

XI

TOLLE, puer, calices tepidique toreumata Nili
  et mihi secura pocula trade manu

---

¹ *dracti* Housman for *drauci*; δρακτός, a vase: see new
edition of Liddell and Scott.

---

[1] Which was sprinkled about the theatre or amphitheatre:
cf. v. xxv. 8; VIII. xxxii. 4.

[2] He swears too eagerly, and M. withholds the name.

VIII

BREATH of balm from phials of yesterday, of the last effluence that falls from a curving jet of saffron; [1] perfume of apples ripening in their winter chest, of the field lavish with the leafage of spring; of Augusta's silken robes from Palatine presses, of amber warmed by a maiden's hand; of a jar of dark Falernian shattered, but far off, of a garden that stays therein Sicilian bees; the scent of Cosmus' alabaster boxes, and of the altars of the gods; of a chaplet fallen but now from a rich man's locks— why should I speak of each? Not enough are they: mix them all; such is the fragrance of my boy's kisses at morn. Would you learn his name? If the kisses only make you ask, I will tell you. You have sworn. You want to know too much, Sabinus! [2]

IX

ILLUSTRIOUS in Jove' [3] leafage, [3] Memor, the glory of the Roman buskin, breathes here, rendered by Apelles' art.

X

TURNUS [4] brought to Satire a mighty intellect, why not to Memor's song? He was his brother.

XI

AWAY, boy, with chalices and embossed glasses from the warm Nile, and offer me with fearless hand the

[3] *cf.* IV. i. 6. Memor was a tragic poet, and brother of Turnus in the next epigram.
[4] *cf.* VII. xcvii. 8. As to Memor see preceding epigram. Turnus would not compete with his own brother.

trita patrum labris et tonso pura ministro;
   anticus mensis restituatur honor.
te potare decet gemma qui Mentora frangis   5
   in scaphium moechae, Sardanapalle, tuae.

XII

Ius tibi natorum vel septem, Zoile, detur,
   dum matrem nemo det tibi, nemo patrem.

XIII

Quisquis Flaminiam teris, viator,
noli nobile praeterire marmor.
urbis deliciae salesque Nili,
ars et gratia, lusus et voluptas,
Romani decus et dolor theatri   5
atque omnes Veneres Cupidinesque
hoc sunt condita, quo Paris, sepulchro.

XIV

Heredes, nolite brevem sepelire colonum:
   nam terra est illi quantulacumque gravis.

XV

Sunt chartae mihi quas Catonis uxor
et quas horribiles legant Sabinae:

---

¹ Not by the ringleted minion of the day.
² cf. IV. xxxix. 5 ; IX. lix. 16.
³ cf. II. xci. 6.
⁴ He is a mere *terrae filius*, a *homo non natus*, *i.e.* of no
account : cf. VIII. lxiv. 18.

cups worn by our father's lips and cleansed by a short-haired attendant:[1] let its old-world honour be given back to the board. It becomes you to drink from a jewelled cup, who break up Mentor's[2] handiwork to shape, Sardanapallus, an utensil for your mistress.

XII

LET the rights of a father of sons,[3] even of seven, be granted you, Zoilus—provided no man assign you a mother, no man a father.[4]

XIII

WHOE'ER thou art, traveller, that treadest the Flaminian Way, give heed not to pass by a noble monument. The delight of the city and the wit of Nile, incarnate art and grace, frolic and joy, the fame and the affliction of Rome's theatre, and all the Venuses and Cupids,[5] are buried in this tomb where Paris[6] lies.

XIV

YE heirs, do not bury the dwarf farmer; for any earth would be heavy upon him.[7]

XV

I HAVE writings that Cato's wife and that grim Sabine dames might read; I wish this little book

---

[5] An echo of Catullus, iii. 1.

[6] A famous actor of mimes, put to death by Domitian because of an intrigue with Domitia, the Empress : *cf.* Suet. *Dom.* iii.

[7] A common wish was "*sit tibi terra levis*": *cf.* v. xxxiv. 9; IX. xxix. 11.

hic totus volo rideat libellus
et sit nequior omnibus libellis.
qui vino madeat nec erubescat   5
pingui sordidus esse Cosmiano,
ludat cum pueris, amet puellas,
nec per circuitus loquatur illam,
ex qua nascimur, omnium parentem,
quam sanctus Numa mentulam vocabat.   10
versus hos tamen esse tu memento
Saturnalicios, Apollinaris:
mores non habet hic meos libellus.

XVI

Qui gravis es nimium, potes hinc iam, lector, abire
  quo libet: urbanae scripsimus ista togae;
iam [1] mea Lampsacio lascivit pagina versu
  et Tartesiaca concrepat aera manu.
o quotiens rigida pulsabis pallia vena,   5
  sis gravior Curio Fabricioque licet!
tu quoque nequitias nostri lususque libelli
  uda, puella, leges, sis Patavina licet.
erubuit posuitque meum Lucretia librum,
  sed coram Bruto; Brute, recede: leget.   10

XVII

Non omnis nostri nocturna est pagina libri:
  invenies et quod mane, Sabine, legas.

[1] *nam* γ.

---

[1] *cf.* III. lv. 1.   [2] The second legendary king of Rome.
[3] The same caution is found in I. iv. 8.
[4] *i.e.* Priapean, L. being a town on the Hellespont where
Priapus was worshipped.

to laugh from end to end, and be naughtier than all my little books. Let it be drenched in wine and not ashamed to be stained with rich Cosmian[1] unguents; let it play with the boys, love the girls, and in no roundabout phrase speak of that wherefrom we are born, the parent of all, which hallowed Numa[2] called by its own name. Yet remember that these verses are of the Saturnalia, Apollinaris: this little book does not express[3] my own morals.

XVI

You, reader, who are too strait-laced, can now go away from here whither you will: I wrote these verses for the citizen of wit; now my page wantons in verse of Lampsacus,[4] and beats the timbrel with the hand of a figurante of Tartessus.[5] Oh, how often will you with your ardour disarrange your garb,[6] though you may be more strait-laced than Curius and Fabricius! You also, O girl, may, when in your cups, read the naughtiness and sportive sallies of my little book, though you may be from Patavium.[7] Lucretia[8] blushed and laid down my volume; but Brutus was present. Brutus, go away: she will read it.

XVII

Not every page of my book is for reading at night; you will find, too, what you may read in the morning,[9] Sabinus.

[5] *i.e.* of a female dancer from Gades: *cf.* v. lxxviii. 26.
[6] For the idea *cf.* Catullus, xxxii. 11.
[7] Where the women had the reputation of chastity: *cf.* vi. xlii. 4. [8] Put here as symbolical of chastity.
[9] *i.e.* when you are sober.

XVIII

DONASTI, Lupe, rus sub urbe nobis;
sed rus est mihi maius in fenestra.
rus hoc dicere, rus potes vocare?
in quo ruta facit nemus Dianae,
argutae tegit ala quod cicadae,   5
quod formica die comedit uno,
clusae cui folium rosae corona est;
in quo non magis invenitur herba
quam Cosmi folium piperve crudum;
in quo nec cucumis iacere rectus   10
nec serpens habitare tota possit.
urucam male pascit hortus unam,
consumpto moritur culix salicto,
et talpa est mihi fossor atque arator.
non boletus hiare, non mariscae   15
ridere aut violae patere possunt.
finis mus populatur et colono
tamquam sus Calydonius timetur,
et sublata volantis ungue Procnes
in nido seges est hirundinino;   20
et cum stet sine falce mentulaque,
non est dimidio locus Priapo.
vix implet cocleam peracta messis,
et mustum nuce condimus picata.
errasti, Lupe, littera sed una: 25
nam quo tempore praedium dedisti,
mallem tu mihi prandium dedisses.

---

[1] "A leaf of rue" seems to have been proverbial for a
narrow space: Petr. 37, 58; *cf.* also XI. xxxi. 17.
[2] The swallow.

XVIII

You have given me, Lupus, a suburban farm, but I have a bigger farm in my window. A farm can you call this, style this a farm, wherein a plant of rue [1] forms a grove of Diana, which the wing of a shrill cicala covers, which an ant eats up in a single day; for which a shut rose's petal would be a canopy; wherein grass is no more found than a leaf for Cosmus' perfumes or green pepper; wherein a cucumber cannot lie straight, nor a snake harbour its whole length? The garden gives short commons to a single caterpillar; a gnat, when it has consumed the willow, expires, and a mole is my ditcher and ploughman. No mushroom can swell, no figs can split, or violets expand. My borders a mouse ravages, and is feared by the tenant as much as a Calydonian boar, and my crop, lifted by the claws of flying Procne,[2] lies in a swallow's nest; and, though he stands shorn of his sickle and his appurtenances, there is no room by half for Priapus. My harvest, when gathered, hardly fills a snail-shell, and we store the must in a pitch-sealed nut. You have made a mistake, Lupus, but only by one letter; for when you gave me a fee I would you had given me a feed.[3]

[3] Lupus gave a *praedium* (land), and M. wanted a *prandium* (lunch), the difference being the letter n. "Fee" in law means an estate in land that descends to the holder's heir; here used in the sense of landed property.

XIX

QUAERIS cur nolim te ducere, Galla ? diserta es.
　　saepe soloecismum mentula nostra facit.

XX

CAESARIS Augusti lascivos, livide, versus
　　sex lege, qui tristis verba Latina legis :
"Quod futuit Glaphyran Antonius, hanc mihi poenam
　　Fulvia constituit, se quoque uti futuam.
Fulviam ego ut futuam ? quod si me Manius oret　　5
　　pedicem, faciam ? non puto, si sapiam.
' Aut futue, aut pugnemus ' ait. quid quod mihi vita
　　carior est ipsa mentula ? signa canant ! "
absolvis lepidos nimirum, Auguste, libellos,
　　qui scis Romana simplicitate loqui.　　　　　　　　10

XXI

LYDIA tam laxa est equitis quam culus aeni,
　　quam celer arguto qui sonat aere trochus,

---

[1] cf. Juv. vi. 456, soloecismum liceat fecisse marito, of the
husband of a learned wife. But here M. adds an obscene
sense.

[2] A beautiful hetaera, whose charms procured her son
Archelaus at the hands of Antony the kingdom of Cappadocia.

[3] These lines are historically interesting as giving the
explanation attributed to Octavius of the origin of the civil
war between him and Antony, namely, pique on the part of
Fulvia, Antony's wife, at the rejection by Octavius of her
advances. Montaigne (iii. 12) refers to them as showing for
how small causes great emperors will go to war.

The scene between Fulvia and Octavius was depicted on a

XIX

Do you ask why I am loth to marry you, Galla?
You are a blue-stocking. My manhood often commits a solecism.[1]

XX

READ six wanton verses of Caesar Augustus, you
spiteful fellow, who with a sour face read words of
Latin:

" Because Antony handles Glaphyra,[2] Fulvia has appointed this penalty for me, that I, too, should handle
her. I to handle Fulvia? What if Manius were to
implore me to treat him as a Ganymede? Am I to
do it? I trow not, if I be wise. ' Either handle me
or let us fight,' she says. And what that my person
is dearer to me than my very life? Let the trumpets
sound." [3]

You justify for certain my sprightly little books,
Augustus, who know how to speak with Roman
bluntness.[4]

XXI

LYDIA is as widely developed as the rump of a
bronze equestrian statue, as the swift hoop that resounds with its tinkling rings,[5] as the wheel so often

cameo by Arellius, probably the painter mentioned by Pliny,
N.H. xxxv. 37, as having outraged his art by depicting
prostitutes. Fulvia is represented as sitting nude upon a
bed, and holding Octavius by the arm. He is in full armour,
and is beckoning to two soldiers in the rear. The cameo has
been reproduced in a rare book published at the Vatican
Press in 1786, and entitled "Monumens de la vie privée des
douze Césars d'après une suite de pierres gravées sur leur
règne."

[4] As to Augustus's plain speech, *cf.* Suet. *Aug.* lxix.
[5] *cf.* XIV. clxviii.

quam rota transmisso totiens inpacta petauro,
  quam vetus a crassa calceus udus aqua,
quam quae rara vagos expectant retia turdos,   5
  quam Pompeiano vela negata Noto,
quam quae de pthisico lapsa est armilla cinaedo,
  culcita Leuconico quam viduata suo,
quam veteres bracae Brittonis pauperis, et quam
  turpe Ravennatis guttur onocrotali.   10
hanc in piscina dicor futuisse marina.
  nescio ; piscinam me futuisse puto.

XXII

MOLLIA quod nivei duro teris ore Galaesi
  basia, quod nudo cum Ganymede iaces,
(quis negat ?) hoc nimiumst. sed sit satis ; inguina saltem
  parce fututrici sollicitare manu.
levibus in pueris plus haec quam mentula peccat   5
  et faciunt digiti praecipitantque virum :
inde tragus celeresque pili mirandaque matri
  barba, nec in clara balnea luce placent.
divisit natura marem : pars una puellis,
  una viris genita est. utere parte tua.   10

---

¹ A very obscure line, which may mean "so often struck by the acrobat in his flight." The nature of the *petaurum* has never been clearly known ; sometimes it seems to be a kind of springboard or seesaw, sometimes a wheel suspended in the air : *cf.* II. lxxxvi. 7. The performance was dangerous : Fest. xiv. *s.v. Petaurista*, quoting Arist. *Fr.* 234.

struck from the extended springboard,[1] as a worn-
out shoe drenched by muddy water, as the wide-
meshed net that lies in wait for wandering fieldfares,
as an awning that does not belly to the wind [2] in
Pompey's theatre, as a bracelet that has slipped
from the arm of a consumptive catamite, as a pillow
widowed of its Leuconian stuffing,[3] as the aged
breeches of a pauper Briton, and as the foul throat
of a pelican [4] of Ravenna. This woman I am said
to have embraced in a marine fishpond : I don't
know ; I think I embraced the fishpond itself.

XXII

THAT with your hard mouth you rub the soft
lips of white-cheeked Galaesus, that you consort
with a naked Ganymede, 'tis too much—who denies
it ?—but let that be enough ; at least refrain from
waking passions with lascivious hand. Towards
beardless boys this is a greater sinner than your
yard, and your fingers create and hasten manhood.
Thence comes a goatish odour, and quick-springing
hair, and a beard, a wonder to mothers, and baths
in broad day are displeasing. Nature has separated
the male : one part has been produced for girls, one
for men. Use your own part.

---

[2] cf. IX. xxxviii. 6.   [3] cf. XIV. clix.
[4] Described by Pliny, *N.H.* x. 66. By "throat" M.
means the large pouch under the mandibles (the *alterius uteri
genus* of Pliny's description), where the pelican stores its
catch of fish previously to consumption.

XXIII

Nubere Sila mihi nulla non lege parata est;
  sed Silam nulla ducere lege volo.
cum tamen instaret, " Deciens mihi dotis in auro
  sponsa dabis " dixi ; " quid minus esse potest ?
nec futuam quamvis prima te nocte maritus,   5
  communis tecum nec mihi lectus erit ;
complectarque meam, nec tu prohibebis, amicam,
  ancillam mittes et mihi iussa tuam.
te spectante dabit nobis lasciva minister
  basia, sive meus sive erit ille tuus.   10
ad cenam venies, sed sic divisa recumbes
  ut non tangantur pallia nostra tuis.
oscula rara dabis nobis et non dabis ultro,
  nec quasi nupta dabis sed quasi mater anus.
si potes ista pati, si nil perferre recusas,   15
  invenies qui te ducere, Sila, velit."

XXIV

Dum te prosequor et domum reduco,
  aurem dum tibi praesto garrienti,
  et quidquid loqueris facisque laudo,
  quot versus poterant, Labulle, nasci !
  hoc damnum tibi non videtur esse,   5
  si quod Roma legit, requirit hospes,
  non deridet eques, tenet senator,
  laudat causidicus, poeta carpit,
  propter te perit ? hoc, Labulle, verum est ?
  hoc quisquam ferat ? ut tibi tuorum   10
  sit maior numerus togatulorum,
  librorum mihi sit minor meorum ?

XXIII

Sila is ready to marry me on any terms, but on no terms am I willing to take Sila to wife. Yet, when she urged me: "You shall bring me, as bride's dower, in gold a million sesterces," I said: "What can be smaller than that? And I will have no marital relations with you even on the wedding-night, nor shall my bed be the same as yours; and I will embrace my mistress, and you shall not forbid me, and, if bidden, you shall send me your own maid. Before your eyes an attendant shall give me wanton kisses, whether he is my own or yours. You shall dine with me, but you shall recline so apart from me that my robe is not touched by yours. Kisses you shall give me but rarely, and you shall not give them uninvited; and you shall not give them like a bride, but like an aged mother. If you can suffer that, if there be nothing you refuse to endure—you will find a man, Sila, who is willing to marry you!"

XXIV

While I escort you and bring you home, while I lend my ear to your babbling, and praise whatever you say and do, how many verses, Labullus, might have seen the light! Does not this seem to you an injury if, what Rome reads, the stranger asks for, the knight does not laugh at, the senator knows by heart, the pleader praises, the poet carps at—this because of you is lost? Is this fair, Labullus? Is this what any man would endure? That the number of your wretched clients should increase, of my books the number decrease? 'Tis now almost thirty

triginta prope iam diebus una est
nobis pagina vix peracta.   sic fit
cum cenare domi poeta non vult.   15

XXV

ILLA salax nimium nec paucis nota puellis
stare Lino desit mentula.   lingua, cave.

XXVI

O MIHI grata quies, o blanda, Telesphore, cura,
qualis in amplexu non fuit ante meo,
basia da nobis vetulo, puer, uda Falerno,
pocula da labris facta minora tuis.
addideris super haec Veneris si gaudia vera,   5
esse negem melius cum Ganymede Iovi.

XXVII

FERREUS es, si stare potest tibi mentula, Flacce,
cum te sex cyathos orat amica gari,
vel duo frusta rogat cybii tenuemve lacertum
nec dignam toto se botryone putat ;
cui portat gaudens ancilla paropside rubra   5
allecem, sed quam protinus illa voret ;
aut cum perfricuit frontem posuitque pudorem,
sucida palliolo vellera quinque petit.
at mea me libram foliati poscat amica
aut virides gemmas sardonychasve pares,   10
nec nisi prima velit de Tusco Serica vico
aut centum aureolos sic velut aera roget.
nunc tu velle putas haec me donare puellae ?
nolo, sed his ut sit digna puella volo.

---

¹ The *foliatum* or *nardinum* was a choice compound of
nard, myrrh, and other aromatic herbs: *cf.* Plin. *N.H.* xiii. 2.

days, and scarce a single page has been finished.
This is the result when a poet does not wish to dine
at home!

XXV

QUELLA troppo salace mentola, nè nota a poche
ragazze, cessa stare a Lino: guardati, O lingua.

XXVI

O THOU, my pleasant solace, O thou, Telesphorus,
my soothing care, whose peer has never yet lain in
my embrace, give me kisses, boy, dewy with aged
Falernian, give me the cup that has minished beneath
thy lips. If, to crown these, thou shalt add love's
true joys, then should I say Jove's lot with Ganymede
is not more blest.

XXVII

You are a man of iron if you can show any amorous
power, Flaccus, when your mistress prays you for
six helpings of fish-pickle, or asks for two slices of
tunny, or a skinny lizard-fish, and does not think herself worth a whole bunch of grapes—a woman to
whom her maid delightedly carries anchovy sauce in
a dark earthenware platter, to be immediately gulped
down; or, who, when she has hardened her brow
and laid aside all shame, solicits five greasy skins to
make a small mantle. But let my mistress demand
of me a pound of nard,[1] or emeralds, or a pair of
sardonyxes, and not look at any but prime silk from
the Tuscan street, or let her beg a hundred gold
coins just as if they were pence. Now do you
imagine I am willing to give these things to a girl?
I am not; but that a girl should be worthy of these
things, I do wish.

XXVIII

INVASIT medici Nasica phreneticus Eucti
  et percidit Hylan. hic, puto, sanus erat.

XXIX

LANGUIDA cum vetula tractare virilia dextra
  coepisti, iugulor pollice, Phylli, tuo :
nam cum me murem, cum me tua lumina dicis,
  horis me refici vix puto posse decem.
blanditias nescis : " Dabo " dic " tibi milia centum   5
  et dabo Setini iugera culta soli ;
accipe vina domum pueros chrysendeta mensas."
  nil opus est digitis : sic mihi, Phylli, frica.

XXX

OS male causidicis et dicis olere poetis.
  sed fellatori, Zoile, peius olet.

XXXI

ATREUS Caecilius cucurbitarum
  sic illas quasi filios Thyestae
in partes lacerat secatque mille.
  gustu protinus has edes in ipso,
has prima feret alterave cena,   5
  has cena tibi tertia reponet,
ninc seras epidipnidas parabit.
  hinc pistor fatuas facit placentas,

XXVIII

NASICA, "a madman," attacked Doctor Euctus's Hylas and outraged him. This fellow was, I imagine, sane !

XXIX

WHEN you begin to paw my apathetic person with your antediluvian hands, I am murdered by that finger of yours, Phyllis ; for when you call me "mouse," when you call me "light of your eyes," I can scarcely, I think, get over it in ten hours. Blandishments you know nothing of : say, " I will give you a hundred thousand sesterces," and " I will give you well-tilled acres of Setine land ; accept wines, a town house, slaves, enamelled dishes, tables." I don't require your thumbing : scratch me in this way, Phyllis.

XXX

VILELY smells, you say, the breath of lawyers, and of poets.[1] But that of a ——, Zoilus, smells worse !

XXXI

CAECILIUS is a very Atreus to gourds : he so mangles them and cuts them into a thousand pieces, just as if they were the sons of Thyestes.[2] Gourds you will eat at once even among the *hors d'œuvre*, gourds he will bring you in the first or second course, these in the third course he will set again before you, out of these he will furnish later on your dessert. Out of these the baker makes insipid cakes, and out of

---

[1] From anxiety as to their cases or poems, like the *rei* of IV. iv. 8 ? 　　[2] See note to III. xlv. 1.

hinc et multiplices struit tabellas
et notas caryotidas theatris.   10
hinc exit varium coco minutal,
ut lentem positam fabamque credas;
boletos imitatur et botellos,
et caudam cybii brevesque maenas.
hinc cellarius experitur artes,   15
ut condat vario vafer sapore
in rutae folium Capelliana.
sic inplet gabatas paropsidesque
et leves scutulas cavasque lances.
hoc lautum vocat, hoc putat venustum,   20
unum ponere ferculis tot assem.

XXXII

Nec toga nec focus est nec tritus cimice lectus
    nec tibi de bibula sarta palude teges,
nec puer aut senior, nulla est ancilla nec infans,
    nec sera nec clavis nec canis atque calix.
tu tamen adfectas, Nestor, dici atque videri   5
    pauper, et in populo quaeris habere locum.
mentiris vanoque tibi blandiris honore.
    non est paupertas, Nestor, habere nihil.

XXXIII

Saepius ad palmam prasinus post fata Neronis
    pervenit et victor praemia plura refert.
i nunc, livor edax, dic te cessisse Neroni:
    vicit nimirum non Nero, sed prasinus.

---

[1] Possibly rare sweetmeats named after a famous maker;
cf. *Cosmianum* in XI. xv. 6 and XII. lv. 7. The *cellarius*, by
the use of various flavours, makes bits of gourd taste like the
famous *Capelliana*.

[2] A play on the two meanings of *ponere*, to serve up and to
spend.

these he constructs sweets of all shapes, and dates such as the theatres know well. From these are turned out the cook's various mincemeats, so that you believe lentils and beans are set before you ; he imitates mushrooms and black-puddings, and tunny's tail, and tiny sprats. On these the store-keeper tries his art, with various flavours wrapping up—cunning man!—Capellian sweetmeats[1] in a leaf of rue. So he fills his platters, and side-dishes, and polished saucers, and hollow plates. This he calls sumptuous, this he fancies elegant—in so many courses to lay out[2] one penny!

XXXII

You have neither toga, nor fire, nor bug-haunted bed, nor have you a mat stitched of thirsty rushes, nor boy, nor older slave; you have no maid, nor infant, nor door-bolt, nor key, nor dog, nor cup.[3] Yet you aim, Nestor, at being called, and seeming a poor man, and look to having a place among the people. You are a fraud, and flatter yourself with an empty honour. It is not poverty, Nestor, to have nothing at all.[4]

XXXIII

Oftener after Nero's[5] death the green charioteer reaches the goal, and as winner bears off more prizes. Go to now, grudging envy,[6] say you yielded to Nero! 'Twas not Nero, I wot, who won, but the Green.

[3] Imitated from Cat. xxiii. 1–2.   [4] But sheer beggary.
[5] *i.e.* Domitian, the *calvus Nero* of Juv. iv. 38. He favoured the green faction of the charioteers.
[6] *i.e.* of a rival charioteer.

XXXIV

Aedes emit Aper sed quas nec noctua vellet
  esse suas; adeo nigra vetusque casa est.
vicinos illi nitidus Maro possidet hortos.
  cenabit belle, non habitabit Aper.

XXXV

Ignotos mihi cum voces trecentos,
  quare non veniam vocatus ad te
  miraris quererisque litigasque.
solus ceno, Fabulle, non libenter.

XXXVI

Gaius hanc lucem gemma mihi Iulius alba
  signat, io, votis redditus ecce meis:
desperasse iuvat veluti iam rupta sororum
  fila; minus gaudent qui timuere nihil.
Hypne, quid expectas, piger? inmortale Falernum 5
  funde, senem poscunt talia vota cadum:
quincunces et sex cyathos bessemque bibamus,
  Gaius ut fiat Iulius et Proculus.

XXXVII

Zoile, quid tota gemmam praecingere libra
  te iuvat et miserum perdere sardonycha?
anulus iste tuis fuerat modo cruribus aptus:
  non eadem digitis pondera conveniunt.

---

[1] The numbers represent the letters in the three names
respectively. *cf.* note to IX. xciii. 8.

XXXIV

APER bought a house, but one that not even an owl would wish its own, so dark and tumbledown is the cottage. Next door to him fashionable Maro owns gardens. Aper will dine but not lodge nicely.

XXXV

ALTHOUGH you invite three hundred guests unknown to me, you wonder why, when invited, I don't come to you, and you complain and quarrel with me. 'Tis no pleasure to me, Fabullus, to dine alone.

XXXVI

GAIUS JULIUS marks this day for me with a white stone: ho! see he comes, given back to my vows! Glad am I that I despaired, as though the Sisters' threads were already snapped: they rejoice less who have known no fear. Hypnus, why linger, you laggard? Pour the immortal Falernian: such vows as mine call for an olden jar. Measures five and six and eight let us drink, that the name "Gaius Julius Proculus" be summed up.[1]

XXXVII

ZOILUS, why do you like to set your jewel in a whole pound of gold, and to overwhelm your unhappy sardonyx? That ring of yours was lately suited to your shanks;[2] the same weight does not suit fingers.

[2] Z. had been a slave, and is now a knight: *cf.* III. xxix.

XXXVIII

Mulio viginti venit modo milibus, Aule.
    miraris pretium tam grave ? surdus erat.

XXXIX

Cunarum fueras motor, Charideme, mearum
    et pueri custos adsiduusque comes.
iam mihi nigrescunt tonsa sudaria barba
    et queritur labris puncta puella meis;
sed tibi non crevi[1] : te noster vilicus horret,   5
    te dispensator, te domus ipsa pavet.
ludere nec nobis nec tu permittis amare ;
    nil mihi vis et vis cuncta licere tibi.
corripis, observas, quereris, suspiria ducis,
    et vix a ferulis temperat ira tua.   10
si Tyrios sumpsi cultus unxive capillos,
    exclamas "Numquam fecerat ista pater" ;
et numeras nostros adstricta fronte trientes,
    tamquam de cella sit cadus ille tua.
desine ; non possum libertum ferre Catonem.   15
    esse virum iam me dicet amica tibi.

XL

Formosam Glyceran amat Lupercus
et solus tenet imperatque solus.
quam toto sibi mense non fututam
cum tristis quereretur et roganti
causam reddere vellet Aeliano,   5
respondit Glycerae dolere dentes.

---

[1] *crevit* TβV.

XXXVIII

A MULE-DRIVER was lately sold, Aulus, for twenty thousand sesterces. Do you wonder at so heavy a price? He was deaf [1]

XXXIX

You were the rocker of my cradle, Charidemus, and guardian of my boyhood, and my constant companion. By now the napkin grows black from the shavings of my beard, and my mistress complains of being pricked by my lips. But to you I have not grown: from you my steward shrinks, at you my treasurer, at you my very house is in a panic! You don't allow me to frolic, nor do you allow me to woo: you wish me to have no liberty, and wish to have all liberty yourself. You take me up, watch me, grumble, heave sighs, and your wrath scarce keeps your hand off the ferule. If I have put on a purple dress or anointed my hair, you cry out: "Never did your father do that"; and with knitted brow you count my cups, as if the jar they came from were one from your own cellar. Desist: I cannot stand a freedman Cato. That I am now a man my mistress will inform you.

XL

LUPERCUS loves the beautiful Glycera, and he is her sole possessor and her sole commander. When he was sadly regretting that for a whole month he had not enjoyed her favours, and wished to give the reason to Aelianus who asked him, he replied that Glycera had the toothache. [2]

[1] And so could not hear the talk of those in the carriage: cf. XII. xxiv. 8.
[2] There appears to be an obscene inference here.

XLI

INDULGET pecori nimium dum pastor Amyntas
  et gaudet fama luxuriaque gregis,
cedentis oneri ramos silvamque fluentem
  vicit, concussas ipse secutus opes.
triste nemus dirae vetuit superesse ruinae[1]   5
  damnavitque rogis noxia ligna pater.
pingues, Lygde, sues habeat vicinus Iollas :
  te satis est nobis adnumerare pecus.

XLII

VIVIDA cum poscas epigrammata, mortua ponis
  lemmata.   qui fieri, Caeciliane, potest ?
mella iubes Hyblaea tibi vel Hymettia nasci,
  et thyma Cecropiae Corsica ponis api !

XLIII

DEPRENSUM in puero tetricis me vocibus, uxor,
  corripis et culum te quoque habere refers.
dixit idem quotiens lascivo Iuno Tonanti !
  ille tamen grandi cum Ganymede iacet.
incurvabat Hylan posito Tirynthius arcu :   5
  tu Megaran credis non habuisse natis ?
torquebat Phoebum Daphne fugitiva : sed illas
  Oebalius flammas iussit abire puer.

----

¹ *ruinae* de Rooy, *rapinae* codd.

----

¹ The acorns.

XLI

Too eager to indulge his charge, and proud of the fame and fatness of his herd, their keeper Amyntas broke the boughs that yielded to his weight, and the down-streaming foliage, himself following the spoil[1] he shook to earth. His sire forbade the ill-omened tree survive such dread ruin, and condemned the fatal timber to the funeral pyre.

Lygdus,[2] let neighbour Iollas have his swine fat: 'tis enough for me that you keep well the reckoning of my herd.

XLII

ALTHOUGH you call for lively epigrams you set lifeless themes. How is that possible, Caecilianus? You bid Hyblan or Hymettian honey be made for you, and serve up to the Cecropian bee Corsican thyme[3]!

XLIII

Tu, moglie, con arrabiate parole rimbrotti me sorpreso con ragazzo, ed adduci che anche tu hai il culo. Quante volte Giunone non disse lo stesso a Giove Tonante! con tutto ciò esso giace col grande Ganimede. Tirinzio, deposto l'arco, incurvava Ila; credi tu che Megara non avesse natiche? Dafne fuggitiva tormentava Febo; ma il ragazzo Oebalio fece partire quelle fiamme. Quantunque Briseide

[2] The swineherd of the writer, who is warned not to be venturesome like A., but to be content with not losing the swine. M. means that L.'s life is too precious to be risked.

[3] Which produced the inferior honey of Corsica: cf. IX. xxvi. 4.

Briseis multum quamvis aversa iaceret,
    Aeacidae propior levis amicus erat.   10
parce tuis igitur dare mascula nomina rebus
    teque puta cunnos, uxor, habere duos.

XLIV

Orbus es et locuples et Bruto consule natus:
    esse tibi veras credis amicitias?
sunt verae, sed quas iuvenis, quas pauper habebas.
    qui novus est, mortem diligit ille tuam.

XLV

Intrasti quotiens inscriptae limina cellae,
    seu puer adrisit sive puella tibi,
contentus non es foribus veloque seraque,
    secretumque iubes grandius esse tibi:
oblinitur minimae si qua est suspicio rimae   5
    punctaque lasciva quae terebrantur acu.
nemo est tam teneri tam sollicitique pudoris
    qui vel pedicat, Canthare, vel futuit.

XLVI

Iam nisi per somnum non arrigis et tibi, Maevi,
    incipit in medios meiere verpa pedes,
truditur et digitis pannucea mentula lassis
    nec levat extinctum sollicitata caput.
quid miseros frustra cunnos culosque lacessis?   5
    summa petas: illic mentula vivit anus.

---

[1] *i.e.* you are incredibly old : *cf.* x. xxxix. 1.

giacesse molto aversa, l'imberbe amico era più con-
tiguo ad Eacide.   Contieniti dunque di dar nomi
mascolini alle cose tue, ed immaginati, O moglie,
d'aver due c—ni!

XLIV

You are childless and rich and were born in the
consulship of Brutus:[1] do you imagine you have
true friendships?   True friendships there are, but
those you possessed when young, those when poor.
The new friend is one who has an affection for
your death.

XLV

WHENEVER you have passed the threshold of a
placarded cubicle, whether it be a boy or a girl who
has smiled on you, you are not satisfied with a door
and a curtain and a bolt, and you require that
greater secrecy should be provided for you.   It
there be any suspicion of the smallest chink it is
plastered up, as also the eyelets that are bored by
a mischievous needle.   No one is of a modesty so
tender and so anxious, Cantharus, who is either
a —— or a ——.[2]

XLVI

DI gia non arrigi che in sogno, ed il tuo pene, O
Mevio, incommincia pisciarti fra i piedi, e la corrugata
mentola è provocata dalle stanche dita, ne sollicitata
rizza l' estinto capo.   A che inutilmente importuni i
poveri c—ni e culi?   Va in alto: colà una vecchia
mentola vive.

[2] *i.e.* whose tastes are not abnormal.

XLVII

OMNIA femineis quare dilecta catervis
　　balnea devitat Lattara? ne futuat.
cur nec Pompeia lentus spatiatur in umbra
　　nec petit Inachidos limina? ne futuat.
cur Lacedaemonio luteum ceromate corpus　　5
　　perfundit gelida Virgine? ne futuat.
cum sic feminei generis contagia vitet,
　　cur lingit cunnum Lattara? ne futuat.

XLVIII

SILIUS haec magni celebrat monimenta Maronis,
　　iugera facundi qui Ciceronis habet.
heredem dominumque sui tumulive larisve
　　non alium mallet nec Maro nec Cicero.

XLIX

IAM prope desertos cineres et sancta Maronis
　　nomina qui coleret, pauper et unus erat.
[1] †Silius optatae† succurrere censuit umbrae,
　　Silius et [2] vatem, non minor ipse, colit.

---

[1] *illius*, Lindsay.　*orbatae* Ribbeck, *ut patriae* Postgate,
o pietas Lindsay, *en tantae* Gilbert.　*censuit umbrae* Heins.,
cenis ut cliabrae (vel *diabrae*) γ.

[2] *filius ut* Ribbeck.　*minor ipse colit* Heins., *minus ipse
tulit* γ.

---

[1] cf. II. xiv. 10; XI. i. 11.
[2] *i.e.* of Isis; *cf.* II. xiv. 7. This temple is called by Juv.

XLVII

WHY does Lattara avoid all the baths affected by crowds of women? that he may not be tempted. Why does he not idly stroll in the shade of Pompey's Porch,[1] nor resort to the threshold of the daughter of Inachus?[2] that he may not be tempted. Why does he plunge in the cold Virgin water his body yellow with Lacedaemonian ointment?[3] that he may not be tempted. Seeing that he so avoids the contagion of the generation of women, why is Lattara a woman's —— ? That he may not be tempted.

XLVIII

SILIUS, who possesses the land which was eloquent Cicero's, honours this monument of great Maro.[4] As heir and owner of his tomb or dwelling no other would either Maro or Cicero choose.

XLIX

To honour the ashes, now well-nigh abandoned, and the sacred name of Maro was there but one,[5] and he was poor. Silius resolved to rescue the regretted dead: and Silius—no less himself a poet—honours the bard.

(vi. 489) "*Isiacae sacraria lenae*," as being the resort of prostitutes.   [3] *cf.* VII. xxxii. 9.
[4] Silius the poet, who was a rich man and possessed one of Cicero's villas, had bought the ground on which Vergil's tomb stood. Pliny says (*Ep.* iii. 7) that he kept Vergil's birthday more religiously than his own, and regarded his tomb in the light of a temple.
[5] *i.e.* the owner of the ground before Silius bought it.

L

NULLA est hora tibi qua non me, Phylli, furentem
    despolies : tanta calliditate rapis.
nunc plorat speculo fallax ancilla relicto,
    gemma vel a digito vel cadit aure lapis ;
nunc furtiva lucri fieri bombycina possunt,   5
    profertur Cosmi nunc mihi siccus onyx ;
amphora nunc petitur nigri cariosa Falerni,
    expiet ut somnos garrula saga tuos ;
nunc ut emam grandemve lupum mullumve bilibrem,
    indixit cenam dives amica tibi.   10
sit pudor et tandem veri respectus et aequi :
    nil tibi, Phylli, nego ; nil mihi, Phylli, nega.

LI

TANTA est quae Titio columna pendet
    quantam Lampsaciae colunt puellae.
    hic nullo comitante nec molesto
    thermis grandibus et suis lavatur.
    anguste Titius tamen lavatur.   5

LII

CENABIS belle, Iuli Cerialis, apud me ;
    condicio est melior si tibi nulla, veni.
octavam poteris servare ; lavabimur una :
    scis quam sint Stephani balnea iuncta mihi.

---

[1] cf. VII. liv. 4.
[2] See note to XI. xvi. 3.

L

THERE is not an hour comes amiss to you, Phyllis, for plundering me in my infatuation : with such cunning do you rob me. Now your lying maid laments because a mirror has been left behind, or a jewel drops from your finger, or a stone from your ear ; at one time silks lost by theft may be a means of profit, at another there is shown to me an empty casket of Cosmus' perfume ; now a crumbling jar of dark Falernian is asked for that a chattering wise-woman may exorcise your dreams ;[1] now, to induce me to buy, either a huge bass or a two-pound mullet, a rich woman friend has proposed a dinner at your house. Let there be some moderation and at length some regard for fairness and justice. I deny nothing to you, Phyllis : deny nothing, Phyllis, to me.

LI

SI grande è la colonna che pende a Tizio quanto quella che le zitelle Lampsiache[2] venerano. Costui senza compagno nè molestato si lava in ampie terme e nelle sue : con tutto ciò angustamente Tizio si lava.

LII

You will dine nicely, Julius Cerialis, at my house ; if you have no better engagement, come. You will be able to observe the eighth hour ;[3] we will bathe together : you know how near Stephanus' baths are

---

[3] The usual hour for dining in summer, the bath being taken before : cf. x. xlviii. 1. There were sundials at the baths.

prima tibi dabitur ventri lactuca movendo   5
    utilis, et porris fila resecta suis,
mox vetus et tenui maior cordyla lacerto,
    sed quam cum rutae frondibus ova tegant ;
altera non derunt tenui versata favilla,
    et Velabrensi massa coacta foco,   10
et quae Picenum senserunt frigus olivae.
    haec satis in gustu.   cetera nosse cupis ?
mentiar, ut venias : pisces, conchylia, sumen,
    et chortis saturas atque paludis aves,
quae nec Stella solet rara nisi ponere cena.   15
    plus ego polliceor : nil recitabo tibi,
ipse tuos nobis relegas licet usque Gigantas,
    rura vel aeterno proxima Vergilio.

LIII

CLAUDIA caeruleis cum sit Rufina Britannis
    edita, quam Latiae pectora gentis habet !
quale decus formae !   Romanam credere matres
    Italides possunt, Atthides esse suam.
di bene quod sancto peperit fecunda marito,   5
    quod sperat generos quodque puella nurus.
sic placeat superis ut coniuge gaudeat uno
    et semper natis gaudeat illa tribus.

LIV

UNGUENTA et casias et olentem funera murram
    turaque de medio semicremata rogo

---

  [1] *Porrum sectivum* : *cf.* X. xlviii. 9.   [2] *cf.* XIII. xxxii.

to me. First, there will be given you lettuce useful
for relaxing the bowels, and shoots cut from their
parent leeks;[1] then tunny salted and bigger than a
small lizard-fish, and one too which eggs will garnish
in leaves of rue. Other eggs will not be wanting,
roasted in embers of moderate heat, and a lump of
cheese ripened over a Velabran hearth,[2] and olives
that have felt the Picenian frost. These are enough
for a whet: do you want to know the rest? I will
deceive you to make you come: fish, mussels, sow's
paps, and fat birds of the poultry-yard and the marsh,
which even Stella is not used to serve except at a
special dinner. More I promise you: I will recite
nothing to you, even although you yourself read
again your "Giants" straight through, or your
"Pastorals" that rank next to immortal Virgil.

LIII

THOUGH Claudia Rufina[3] has sprung from the woad-
stained Britons, how she possesses the feelings of
the Latin race! What grace of form has she!
Mothers of Italy may deem her Roman, those of
Attica their own. May the Gods bless her in that
she, a fertile wife, has borne children to her constant
spouse, in that she hopes, though youthful still, for
sons- and daughters-in-law. So may it please the
Gods above she should joy in one mate alone, and
joy ever in three sons!

LIV

THE unguents and casia, and myrrh that smells of
funerals, and the frankincense half-burned snatched

[3] Probably the Claudia Peregrina of IV. xiii.

et quae de Stygio rapuisti cinnama lecto,
    inprobe, de turpi, Zoile, redde sinu.
a pedibus didicere manus peccare protervae.   5
    non miror furem, qui fugitivus eras.

LV

Hortatur fieri quod e Lupus, Urbice, patrem,
    ne credas ; nihil est quod minus ille velit.
ars est captandi quod nolis velle videri ;
    ne facias optat quod rogat ut facias.
dicat praegnantem tua se Cosconia tantum :   5
    pallidior fiet iam pariente Lupus.
at tu consilio videaris ut usus amici,
    sic morere ut factum te putet esse patrem.

LVI

Quod nimium mortem, Chaeremon Stoice, laudas,
    vis animum mirer suspiciamque tuum ?
hanc tibi virtutem fracta facit urceus ansa,
    et tristis nullo qui tepet igne focus,
et teges et cimex et nudi sponda grabati,   5
    et brevis atque eadem nocte dieque toga.
o quam magnus homo es qui faece rubentis aceti
    et stipula et nigro pane carere potes !
Leuconicis agedum tumeat tibi culcita lanis
    constringatque tuos purpura pexa toros,   10
dormiat et tecum modo qui dum Caecuba miscet
    convivas roseo torserat ore puer :

278

from the midst of the pyre, and the cinnamon you
have snatched from the bier of death—these, rascally
Zoilus, surrender out of your foul pocket. 'Tis from
your feet your froward hands have learned mis-
doings: I don't wonder you are a thief who were
a runaway slave.

LV

Lupus urges you, Urbicus, to become a father:
don't believe him; there is nothing he wishes less.
The art of the legacy-hunter is to seem to wish what
one does not wish: he prays you will not do what he
asks you to do. Let your Cosconia only say she is
pregnant, Lupus will become paler than a lady
already in labour. But do you, by way of seeming
to adopt your friend's counsel, die in such a way[1]
that he may think you have become a father.

LVI

Because you, Stoic Chaeremon, so much praise
death, do you want me to admire and look up to
your mind? 'Tis a jug with a broken handle that
creates this virtue of yours, and a melancholy hearth
chill with no fire, and a beggar's rug, and bugs and
the framework of a bare truckle-bed, and a short toga,
your one covering night and day alike. Oh, what a
great man you are, who can do without dregs of red
vinegar and straw and black bread! Come, imagine
your pillow swells with Leuconian wool,[2] and that
close-napped purple binds your couches, and a boy
waits upon you who, while he mixed the Caecuban
yesterday, distracted your guests with his rosy lips!

---

[1] *i.e.* leave him nothing.   [2] *cf.* XIV. clix.

o quam tu cupies ter vivere Nestoris annos
    et nihil ex ulla perdere luce voles!
rebus in angustis facile est contemnere vitam :   15
    fortiter ille facit qui miser esse potest.

LVII

Miraris docto quod carmina mitto Severo,
    ad cenam cum te, docte Severe, vocem?
Iuppiter ambrosia satur est et nectare vivit;
    nos tamen exta Iovi cruda merumque damus.
omnia cum tibi sint dono concessa deorum,   5
    si quod habes non vis, ergo quid accipies?

LVIII

Cum me velle vides tentumque, Telesphore, sentis,
    magna rogas : puta me velle negare : licet?
et nisi iuratus dixi "Dabo," subtrahis illas,
    permittunt in me quae tibi multa, natis.
quid si me tonsor, cum stricta novacula supra est,   5
    tunc libertatem divitiasque roget?
promittam; neque enim rogat illo tempore tonsor,
    latro rogat; res est inperiosa timor :
sed fuerit curva cum tuta novacula theca,
    frangam tonsori crura manusque simul.   10
at tibi nil faciam, sed lota mentula laeva
    λαικάζειν cupidae dicet avaritiae.

---

    [1] cf. II. liii.   [2] In its regular sense of "poetic."
    [3] cf. XI. lxxiii. 4; IX. xlii. 1.

Oh, how you will long to live Nestor's years thrice over, and wish to lose no moment of any day! In narrow means 'tis easy to despise life: he acts the strong man who is wretched and can endure.[1]

LVII

Do you wonder I send learned[2] Severus verse when I ask you, learned Severus, to dinner? Jupiter is cloyed with ambrosia and he lives on nectar, yet we offer to Jupiter raw entrails and new wine. As by the gift of the Gods all things have been granted to you, if you do not wish to receive what you possess, what then will you accept?

LVIII

WHEN you see that I am desirous, and perceive that I am on the stretch, Telesphorus, you ask a big price. Imagine I wish to refuse it: can I? And unless I swear when I say " I will give it," you withdraw those charms that give you much licence with me. What if a barber, when his drawn razor is over my head, should then ask me for his liberty and for wealth? I will promise it; for it is not a barber who asks on that occasion, a highwayman asks; a thing imperious is fear: but when his razor is safe in its crooked case, I will break the barber's shanks and his hands to boot. To you, however, I will do nothing; but, when it is otherwise sated,[3] my ardour will bid your grasping avarice to go hang.[4]

---

[4] The word λαικάζειν is possibly only a coarse imprecation, and is not to be taken literally.

LIX

SENOS Charinus omnibus digitis gerit
  nec nocte ponit anulos
nec cum lavatur. causa quae sit quaeritis?
  dactyliothecam non habet.

LX

SIT Phlogis an Chione Veneri magis apta requiris?
  pulchrior est Chione; sed Phlogis ulcus habet,
ulcus habet Priami quod tendere possit alutam
  quodque senem Pelian non sinat esse senem;
ulcus habet quod habere suam vult quisque puellam, 5
  quod sanare Criton, non quod Hygia potest.
at Chione non sentit opus nec vocibus ullis
  adiuvat, absentem marmoreamve putes.
exorare, dei, si vos tam magna liceret
  et bona velletis tam pretiosa dare, 10
hoc quod habet Chione corpus faceretis haberet
  ut Phlogis, et Chione quod Phlogis ulcus habet.

LXI

LINGUA maritus, moechus ore Nanneius,
  Summemmianis inquinatior buccis;
quem cum fenestra vidit a Suburana [1]
  obscena nudum Leda, fornicem cludit
mediumque mavult basiare quam summum; 5

  [1] *Suburana* ς, *suburbana* codd.

---

  [1] *i.e.* he has merely hired them. The reason given is a
surprise.

LIX

Six rings Charinus wears on each of his fingers, and he does not take them off at night nor when he bathes. Do you ask the reason? He has not got a ring-case.[1]

LX

Is Phlogis or Chione the more fitted for dalliance, do you ask? More beautiful is Chione, but Phlogis has an itch; she has an itch that would rejuvenate Priam's powers and would not permit the aged Pylian[2] to be aged; she has an itch that every man wishes his own mistress to have, one Criton can cure, not Hygeia.[3] But Chione is impassive, nor does she encourage you by any wooing word: you would fancy she were away from you, or were a marble statue. Ye Gods, were it permitted to prevail on you to bestow so great a gift, and were ye willing to give a blessing so precious, you would make Phlogis to have this body that Chione has and Chione the itch that Phlogis has!

LXI

Nanejo è marito colla lingua, adultero colla bocca, più sporco delle bocche Summemiane: il quale quando l'oscena Leda vede nudo dalla Suburana finestra ella chiude il lupanario, ed ama meglio baciare al mezzo che all' alto; il quale poco fà entrava per

[2] Nestor, the typical old man.
[3] *i.e.* to be cured by male, not by female doctors : *cf.* XI. lxxi. 9. Criton was a doctor of M.'s time; Hygeia, the Goddess of Health, the daughter of Aesculapius, is here put for female doctors generally.

modo qui per omnes viscerum tubos ibat
et voce certa consciaque dicebat
puer an puella matris esset in ventre,
(gaudete cunni; vestra namque res acta est)
arrigere linguam non potest fututricem.   10
nam dum tumenti mersus haeret in volva
et vagientes intus audit infantes,
partem gulosam solvit indecens morbus.
nec purus esse nunc potest nec inpurus.

LXII

Lesbia se iurat gratis numquam esse fututam.
   verum est.   cum futui vult, numerare solet.

LXIII

Spectas nos, Philomuse, cum lavamur,
et quare mihi tam mutuniati
sint leves pueri subinde quaeris.
dicam simpliciter tibi roganti:
pedicant, Philomuse, curiosos.   5

LXIV

Nescio tam multis quid scribas, Fauste, puellis:
   hoc scio, quod scribit nulla puella tibi.

LXV

Sescenti cenant a te, Iustine, vocati
   lucis ad officium quae tibi prima fuit.

tutti i tubi delle viscere, e con certa e consapevole
asserzione diceva se era un maschio o una femina nel
ventre della madre (rallegratevi, c—ni, perchè le
vostre faccende sono finite); non puo erigere l'
immembratice lingua. Imperocchè, mentre che sta
immerso nella tumente volva, e dentro sente i vagi-
enti bambini, un' indecente morbo[1] struge la parte
golosa : nè ora può esser puro nè impuro.

LXII

Lesbia swears she has never granted her favours
without a price. That is true : on those occasions she
is wont herself to pay it.

LXIII

You eye me, Philomusus, when I bathe, and continually enquire why I have with me smooth-cheeked
boys so well developed. I will answer your question
in plain terms : Philomusus, they assault meddlers.

LXIV

I don't know what you write, Faustus, to so many
girls : this I know, what[2] no girl writes to you.

LXV

A crowd of guests dine at your invitation, Justinus,
to celebrate the day of your birth. Among them,

---

[1] cf. XI. lxxxv. 1.　　[2] i.e. "Come."

ınter quos, memini, non ultimus esse solebam;
  nec locus hic nobis invidiosus erat.
postera sed festae reddis sollemnia mensae :   5
  sescentis hodie, cras mihi natus eris.

LXVI

Et delator es et calumniator,
et fraudator es et negotiator,
et fellator es et lanista. miror
quare non habeas, Vacerra, nummos.

LXVII

Nil mihi das vivus; dicis post fata daturum.
  si non es stultus, scis, Maro, quid cupiam.

LXVIII

Parva rogas magnos; sed non dant haec quoque
      magni.
  ut pudeat levius te, Matho, magna roga.

LXIX

Amphitheatrales inter nutrita magistros
  venatrix, silvis aspera, blanda domi,
Lydia dicebar, domino fidissima Dextro,
  qui non Erigones mallet habere canem,

---

¹ M. has been invited on the morrow to the remnants of
to-day's birthday feast to J.'s fine friends. "To-morrow," he
says, "it will be my turn to find out that you are a gentleman." For this sense of *natus*, *cf.* iv. lxxxiii. 3 ; viii. lx iv.
18 ; and x. xxvii. 4.

I recollect, I used not to be the last, and this place
was not begrudged me. But to-morrow you repeat
the festive ceremony : for the crowd you are born
to-day, to-morrow you shall be born for me.[1]

LXVI

You are an informer and a backbiter, and you are
a cheat and a pimp, and you are a foul rascal and a
master of gladiators. I wonder why you are not
rich, Vacerra.[2]

LXVII

NOTHING you give me while you are living : you
say you will give after your death. If you are not
a fool you know, Maro, what I desire.[3]

LXVIII

FOR small gifts you solicit great men, but not even
these do your great men give. That you may be
the less ashamed, Matho, solicit great gifts.

LXIX

REARED among the trainers of the amphitheatre,
a hunter, savage in the woods, gentle at home, I was
called Lydia, most faithful to my master Dexter,
who would not have prized Erigone's hound[4] more

---

[2] See further as to this person, XI. lxxvii. and XII. xxxii.
[3] *cf.* VIII. xxvii.
[4] Maera, the dog that showed to Erigone where her
murdered father Icarius lay. Erigone became the constellation Virgo and Maera Procyon.

nec qui Dictaea Cephalum de gente secutus   5
    luciferae pariter venit ad astra deae.
non me longa dies nec inutilis abstulit aetas,
    qualia Dulichio fata fuere cani :
fulmineo spumantis apri sum dente perempta,
    quantus erat, Calydon, aut, Erymanthe, tuus.   10
nec queror infernas quamvis cito rapta sub umbras.
    non potui fato nobiliore mori.

LXX

VENDERE, Tucca, potes centenis milibus emptos?
    plorantis dominos vendere, Tucca, potes?
nec te blanditiae, nec verba rudesve querellae,
    nec te dente tuo saucia colla movent?
a facinus! tunica patet inguen utrimque levata,   5
    inspiciturque tua mentula facta manu.
si te delectat numerata pecunia, vende
    argentum mensas murrina rura domum ;
vende senes servos, ignoscent, vende paternos ;
    ne pueros vendas omnia vende miser.   10
luxuria est emere hos (quis enim dubitatve negatve?)
    sed multo maior vendere luxuria est.

LXXI

HYSTERICAM vetulo se dixerat esse marito
    et queritur futui Leda necesse sibi ;

---

[1] Laelaps, given to Procris by Diana and by her to her husband Cephalus. When Cephalus was added to the stars by Aurora, his hound followed him.

than me, nor the one of Dicte's breed that
followed Cephalus,[1] and with him passed to the
heaven of the goddess, the Bringer of Light. Not
length of days nor fruitless age carried me off, as
was the fate of the Dulichian hound:[2] I was slain
by the lightning tusk of a foaming boar, huge as was
thine, Calydon, or, Erymanthus, thine. Yet I murmur
not, albeit swiftly hurried to the Nether Shades: I
could not die by nobler death.

LXX

CAN you endure to sell, Tucca, those you bought
for a hundred thousand sesterces? Can you endure,
Tucca, to sell your weeping masters?[3] Do not their
caresses, or their prattle or artless plaints, or the
necks wounded by your tooth, move you? Ah,
shame! Lift up the tunic of either, and his nakedness is seen, and there is revealed the manhood,
fashioned[4] by your hand. If money paid down is
your attraction, sell silver plate, tables, porcelain
cups, land, town-house; sell aged slaves—they will
pardon—sell paternal slaves: to avoid selling your
boys, sell, wretched man, everything. 'Twas extravagance to buy these boys—for who either doubts or
denies it?—but much greater extravagance is it to
sell them.

LXXI

LYDIA told her aged husband that she was
hysterical, and regrets that intercourse is necessary

---

[2] Argus, the hound of Ulysses, that recognised him after
twenty years, and died: Hom. *Od.* xvii. 291–327.

[3] This word has an indecent sense: *cf.* XII. lxvi. 8.

[4] This word is probably explained by XI. xxii. 6.

sed flens atque gemens tanti negat esse salutem
 seque refert potius proposuisse mori.
vir rogat ut vivat, virides nec deserat annos,   5
 et fieri quod iam non facit ipse sinit.
protinus accedunt medici medicaeque recedunt,
 tollunturque pedes. o medicina gravis!

LXXII

 Drauci Natta sui vocat pipinnam,
 conlatus cui Gallus est Priapus.

LXXIII

Venturum iuras semper mihi, Lygde, roganti
 constituisque horam constituisque locum.
cum frustra iacui longa prurigine tentus,
 succurrit pro te saepe sinistra mihi.
quid precer, o fallax, meritis et moribus istis? 5
 umbellam luscae, Lygde, feras dominae.

LXXIV

Curandum penem commisit Baccara Raetus[1]
 rivali medico. Baccara Gallus erit.

LXXV

 Theca tectus ahenea lavatur
 tecum, Caelia, servus; ut quid, oro,

   [1] *Raetus* Schneid., *graecus* β, *vetus* γ.

for her; yet with tears and groans she says her
health is not worth the sacrifice, and declares she
would rather choose to die. Her lord bids her
live, and not desert the bloom of her years, and
he permits to be done what he cannot do himself.
Immediately men doctors come in, and lady doctors
depart, and her feet are hoisted. Oh, what stringent
treatment!

LXXII

Natta chiama pipinna quella del suo drauco, alla
quale Priapo[1] confrontato è un Gallo.[2]

LXXIII

You always swear, Lygdus, you will come to me
when I ask you, and you appoint the hour and you
appoint the place. When I have lain fruitlessly
racked with lingering desire, a substitute has often
come to my rescue. What should be my curse, false
boy, one fitted to deserts and habits like yours?
May you carry, Lygdus, the sunshade of a one-eyed
mistress!

LXXIV

Baccara, a Rhaetian, entrusted the care of his
person to a doctor, his rival in love: Baccara will
now be a Gaul.[2]

LXXV

Your slave bathes with you, Caelia, covered with
a sheath of brass; to what end, I pray, seeing he is

[1] cf. VI. xlix. 2.
[2] i.e. a eunuch : see notes to I. xxxv. 15 and III. xxiv. 13.

non sit cum citharoedus aut choraules?
non vis, ut puto, mentulam videre.
quare cum populo lavaris ergo?   5
omnes an tibi nos sumus spadones?
ergo, ne videaris invidere,
servo, Caelia, fibulam remitte.

LXXVI

SOLVERE, Paete, decem tibi me sestertia cogis,
    perdiderit quoniam Bucco ducenta tibi.
ne noceant, oro, mihi non mea crimina: tu qui
    bis centena potes perdere, perde decem.

LXXVII

IN omnibus Vacerra quod conclavibus
    consumit horas et die toto sedet,
cenaturit Vacerra, non cacaturit.

LXXVIII

UTERE femineis conplexibus, utere, Victor,
    ignotumque sibi mentula discat opus.
flammea texuntur sponsae, iam virgo paratur,
    tondebit pueros iam nova nupta tuos.
pedicare semel cupido dabit illa marito,   5
    dum metuit teli vulnera prima novi:
saepius hoc fieri nutrix materque vetabunt
    et dicent: "Uxor, non puer, ista tibi est."
heu quantos aestus, quantos patiere labores,
    si fuerit cunnus res peregrina tibi!   10
ergo Suburanae tironem trade magistrae.
    illa virum faciet; non bene virgo docet.

---

[1] *cf.* VII. lxxxii. 1; XIV. ccxv.

no harper or flutist in the chorus?[1] You don't wish,
as I suppose, to see his nakedness. Why, then, do
you bathe with the crowd? Are all of us eunuchs
to you? Therefore, that you may not appear to be
jealous, undo, Caelia, your slave's fibula.

LXXVI

You compel me, Paetus, to pay you ten thousand
sesterces because Bucco has lost you your two hundred thousand. Don't let offences not mine injure
me, I pray: do you, who can endure to lose two
hundred, lose ten.

LXXVII

VACERRA dallies for hours, and sits a whole day in
all the closets. Vacerra wishes to dine, not to dis-
embogue.[2]

LXXVIII

FA uso, fa uso dei feminei amplessi, O Vittore, e
la mentola impari l'opra ad essa ignota. Il velo è
tessuto per la sposa, di già la vergine è preparata, di
già la nuova maritata toserà[3] i tuoi ragazzi. Essa
darà una volta da pedicare all' avido marito mentre
teme le prime ferite della nuova lancia; la nutrice
e la madre vieteranno che ciò si facia troppo sovente,
e diranno "questa ti è moglie, non ragazzo." Oh,
quanti furori e quanti stenti se il c—no sarà a te
cosa insolita! Dunque consegnati qual novizio ad
una Suburana maestra. Quella ti farà uomo; una
vergine insegna ciò malamente.

[2] He hopes to meet some acquaintance and to get an
invitation.   [3] Youths of that character wore long hair.

LXXIX

Ad primum decuma lapidem quod venimus hora,
  arguimur lentae crimine pigritiae.
non est ista viae, non est mea, sed tua culpa est,
  misisti mulas qui mihi, Paete, tuas.

LXXX

Litus beatae Veneris aureum Baias,
Baias superbae blanda dona Naturae,
ut mille laudem, Flacce, versibus Baias,
laudabo digne non satis tamen Baias.
sed Martialem malo, Flacce, quam Baias.   5
optare utrumque pariter inprobi votum est.
quod si deorum munere hoc tibi [1] detur,
quid gaudiorum est Martialis et Baiae!

LXXXI

Cum sene communem vexat spado Dindymus Aeglen
  et iacet in medio sicca puella toro.
viribus hic, operi non est hic utilis annis:
  ergo sine effectu prurit utrique labor.
supplex illa rogat pro se miserisque duobus,   5
  hunc iuvenem facias, hunc, Cytherea, virum.

LXXXII

A Sinuessanis conviva Philostratus undis
  conductum repetens nocte iubente larem

[1] *tibi.   tamen* Munro.

---

[1] M. has arrived an hour late for dinner : *cf.* IV. viii. 6.
[2] Under this view *tibi* can have no meaning, so I have

LXXIX

BECAUSE I have reached the first milestone at the tenth hour I am convicted on a charge of tardiness and sloth.[1] It is not the fault of the road ; it is not mine, but yours, who sent me your mules, Paetus.

LXXX

BAIAE, the golden shore of blessed Venus; Baiae, the witching gift of proud Nature !—though in a thousand verses, Flaccus, I were to laud Baiae, yet I shall not laud Baiae as it deserves. But I prefer Martial, Flaccus, to Baiae : to ask for both at once were a presumptuous prayer. Yet if by heaven's bounty this could still be granted, what wealth of joy —Martial and Baiae too ![2]

LXXXI

L'EUNUCO Dindimo vessa Egle in comune con un vecchio, e la giovane giace asciutta in mezzo al letto. Quello non ha vigore all' opra, questo è inutili per gli anni ; perciò gli sforzi dell' uno e dell' altro incitano senza effetto. Essa supplichevole prega per se e per i due sfortunati che tu, O Citerea, renda questo giovane, e quello uomo.

LXXXII

PHILOSTRATUS, returning from a party at the baths of Sinuessa to his hired house at the bidding of

rendered Munro's *tamen.* Some, however, take "Martialis" as meaning the poet, in which case " tibi" means Flaccus, and the last lines of the epigram are self-depreciatory.

paene imitatus obit saevis Elpenora fatis,
    praeceps per longos dum ruit usque gradus.
non esset, Nymphae, tam magna pericula passus   5
    si potius vestras ille bibisset aquas.

LXXXIII

Nemo habitat gratis nisi dives et orbus apud te.
    nemo domum pluris, Sosibiane, locat.

LXXXIV

Qui nondum Stygias descendere quaerit ad umbras
    tonsorem fugiat, si sapit, Antiochum.
alba minus saevis lacerantur bracchia cultris,
    cum furit ad Phrygios enthea turba modos;
mitior inplicitas Alcon secat enterocelas   5
    fractaque fabrili dedolat ossa manu.
tondeat hic inopes Cynicos et Stoica menta
    collaque pulverea nudet equina iuba.
hic miserum Scythica sub rupe Promethea radat,
    carnificem duro pectore poscet avem;   10
ad matrem fugiet Pentheus, ad Maenadas Orpheus,
    Antiochi tantum barbara tela sonent.
haec quaecumque meo numeratis stigmata mento,
    in vetuli pyctae qualia fronte sedent,

---

[1] The companion of Ulysses, who, awaking suddenly from
a drunken sleep in the house of Circe, fell from the roof:
Hom. *Od.* x. 552 *seqq.*
[2] And not wine. Moreover, the waters of Sinuessa were
medicinal: *cf.* xi. vii. 12.
[3] The votaries of Cybele.

night, nearly copied Elpenor,[1] and died by a cruel death while he was hurrying headlong down a long flight of steps. He would not have incurred such great danger, ye Nymphs, if he had drunk your waters instead.[2]

LXXXIII

NOBODY lives scot-free with you, unless he be rich and childless. Nobody, Sosibianus, lets his house on better terms.

LXXXIV

HE who desires not yet to go down to Stygian shades, let him, if he be wise, avoid barber Antiochus. White arms are mangled with knives less cruel when the frenzied throng[3] raves to Phrygian strains; with gentler touch Alcon[4] cuts the knotted hernia, and lops away broken bones with a workman's hand. Shearer let this man be of starveling Cynics and of Stoic chins, and let him bare the necks of steeds of their dusty manes. Let this man but rasp hapless Prometheus neath the Scythian crag, with bared breast will he summon the bird his torturer;[5] to his mother will Pentheus fly; to the Maenads Orpheus,[6] at the mere clash of Antiochus' savage steel. These scars, whate'er they are thou numberest on my chin, scars such as are fixed on some time-worn

[4] A surgeon of the day : cf. VI. lxx. 6.
[5] The eagle preyed upon his liver, which was always renewed.
[6] Pentheus, king of Thebes, for his hostility to the rites of Bacchus, was torn to pieces by his mother and other Maenads; and Orpheus was similarly treated by the Thracian women because he slighted them.

non iracundis fecit gravis unguibus uxor :   15
   Antiochi ferrum est et scelerata manus.
unus de cunctis animalibus hircus habet cor :
   barbatus vivit ne ferat Antiochum.

LXXXV

SIDERE percussa est subito tibi, Zoile, lingua,
   dum lingis.   certe, Zoile, nunc futues.

LXXXVI

LENIAT ut fauces medicus, quas aspera vexat
   adsidue tussis, Parthenopaee, tibi,
mella dari nucleosque iubet dulcesque placentas
   et quidquid pueros non sinit esse truces.
at tu non cessas totis tussire diebus.   5
   non est haec tussis, Parthenopaee, gula est.

LXXXVII

DIVES eras quondam : sed tunc pedico fuisti
   et tibi nulla diu femina nota fuit.
nunc sectaris anus.   o quantum cogit egestas !
   illa fututorem te, Charideme, facit.

LXXXVIII

MULTIS iam, Lupe, posse se diebus
   pedicare negat Charisianus.
causam cum modo quaererent sodales,
   ventrem dixit habere se solutum.

boxer's face—these a wife, formidable with wrathful talons, wrought not: 'tis Antiochus' steel and hand accursed. Alone among all beasts the he-goat has sense: bearded he lives to escape Antiochus.

LXXXV

IMPROVISAMENTE, O Zoilo, t'è da un contagio[1] percossa la lingua mentre lingi il c—no. Almeno ora, O Zoilo, immembrerai.

LXXXVI

To soothe your throat, which a racking cough incessantly afflicts, Parthenopaeus, your doctor prescribes honey, and nuts, and sweet cakes, and whatever thing stops the fractiousness of boys. Yet all and every day you don't cease coughing. This is no cough, Parthenopaeus: it is gluttony.[2]

LXXXVII

YOU were once rich, but then young men were your favourites, and for long no woman was known to you. Now you run after old crones. Oh, how compelling is poverty! It turns you, Charidemus, into a gallant.

LXXXVIII

CARISIANO dice, O Lupo, di non poter pedicare da molti giorni. Dimandandogliene poco fà i compagni la cagione, disse che aveva la diarrea.[3]

---

[1] *i.e.* planet-struck. This was called *sideratio* : Plin. *N. H.* ii. 41 ; Petr. 2. *cf.* VII. xcii. 9.   [2] *cf.* II. xl.

[3] Thus betraying the fact that he was a pathic.

LXXXIX

INTACTAS quare mittis mihi, Polla, coronas?
    vexatas a te malo tenere rosas.

XC

CARMINA nulla probas molli quae limite currunt,
    sed quae per salebras altaque saxa cadunt,
et tibi Maeonio quoque carmine maius habetur,
    " Lucili columella hic situ' Metrophanes";
attonitusque legis "terrai frugiferai,"   5
    Accius et quidquid Pacuviusque vomunt.
vis imiter veteres, Chrestille, tuosque poetas?
    dispeream ni scis mentula quid sapiat.

XCI

AEOLIDOS Canace iacet hoc tumulata sepulchro,
    ultima cui parvae septima venit hiemps.
a scelus, a facinus! properas qui flere, viator,
    non licet hic vitae de brevitate queri:
tristius est leto leti genus: horrida vultus   5
    apstulit et tenero sedit in ore lues,
ipsaque crudeles ederunt oscula morbi
    nec data sunt nigris tota labella rogis.

---

[1] " Tenfold the length of this terrene."—MILTON. *Terrai
filius* is found in Ennius.

LXXXIX

WHY dost thou send me, Polla, chaplets thou hast not fingered? Liefer would I handle roses tumbled by thee.

XC

No poems win your favour that speed on a gentle path, only those that fall over rough places and high cliffs, and this appears to you finer even than Homer's song:

"Pillar of Lucilius' house, here lieth Metrophanes."

And in amazed wonder you read of the "frugiferous terrene," [1] and whatever phrase Accius and Pacuvius spew.[2] Do you want *me*, Chrestillus, to copy the old poets, your poets? May I die, but you appreciate the flavour of virility![3]

XCI

AEOLIS' child, Canace, lies buried in this tomb, little Canace, whose seventh winter came her last. Ah! for the guilt, the crime! Thou, wayfarer, who art quick to weep, here mayst thou not lament the shortness of life: sadder than death is death's guise; a dire canker wasted her face, and settled on her tender mouth, and her very kisses the cruel scourge consumed; not whole were her lips surrendered to

[2] Old Roman tragic poets. L. Accius died B.C. 180, M. Pacuvius about 131. Only fragments of their works remain. As to the preference for ancient poets in Horace's time: cf. *Ep.* II. i. 49 *seq.*

[3] *i.e.* (acc. to Housman) a virile style; or (in another sense) "*fellator es.*"

si tam praecipiti fuerant ventura volatu,
    debuerant alia fata venire via.   10
sed mors vocis iter properavit cludere blandae,
    ne posset duras flectere lingua deas.

XCII

MENTITUR qui te vitiosum, Zoile, dicit.
    non vitiosus homo es, Zoile, sed vitium.

XCIII

PIERIOS vatis Theodori flamma penates
    abstulit.   hoc Musis et tibi, Phoebe, placet ?
o scelus, o magnum facinus crimenque deorum,
    non arsit pariter quod domus et dominus !

XCIV

QUOD nimium lives nostris et ubique libellis
    detrahis, ignosco : verpe poeta, sapis.
hoc quoque non curo, quod cum mea carmina carpas,
    conpilas : et sic, verpe poeta, sapis.
illud me cruciat, Solymis quod natus in ipsis   5
    pedicas puerum, verpe poeta, meum.
ecce negas iurasque mihi per templa Tonantis.
    non credo : iura, verpe, per Anchialum.

---

[1] Supposed to represent the ejaculation " as the Lord
liveth " in Hebrew, and mistaken by Romans for the name
of a deity.   Another explanation (out of many) is that

the smoky pyre. If it had to come with so mistimed a flight, fate should have come by other path. But death hasted to close the channel of her winsome speech, lest her tongue might have power to bend the hard goddesses.

XCII

HE lies who says you are vicious, Zoilus: you are not a vicious man, Zoilus, but vice.

XCIII

THE poetic abode of bard Theodorus a fire has destroyed. Does this please you, ye Muses, and you, Phoebus? Oh, what guilt, oh, what a huge crime and scandal of the gods is here! House and master did not burn together!

XCIV

YOUR overflowing malice, and your detraction everywhere of my books, I pardon: circumcised poet, you are wise! This, too, I disregard, that when you carp at my poems you plunder them: so, too, circumcised poet, you are wise! What tortures me is this, that you, circumcised poet, although born in the very midst of Solyma, outrage my boy. There! you deny it, and swear to me by the Thunderer's Temple. I don't believe you: swear, circumcised one, by Anchialus.[1]

Anchialus is the name of M.'s boy, and the name is common in inscriptions of slaves and freedmen. Friedländer considers it the name of some Rothschild of Jerusalem.

XCV

INCIDERIS quotiens in basia fellatorum,
  in solium puta te mergere, Flacce, caput.

XCVI

MARCIA, non Rhenus, salit hic, Germane: quid
    obstas
  et puerum prohibes divitis imbre lacus?
barbare, non debet, summoto cive, ministro
  captivam victrix unda levare sitim.

XCVII

UNA nocte quater possum : sed quattuor annis
  si possum, peream, te, Telesilla, semel.

XCVIII

EFFUGERE non est, Flacce, basiatores.
instant, morantur, persecuntur, occurrunt
et hinc et illinc, usquequaque, quacumque.
non ulcus acre pusulaeve lucentes,
nec triste mentum sordidique lichenes,   5
nec labra pingui delibuta cerato,
nec congelati gutta proderit nasi.
et aestuantem basiant et algentem,

---

[1] Made foul by bathers of impure habits : *cf.* II. xlii.;
vi. lxxxi.
[2] A German slave had prevented a freeborn Roman boy
from drinking of a reservoir fed by the aqua Marcia.

XCV

WHENEVER you run across the kisses of some rascals think you are plunging your head, Flaccus, into a bath-tub.[1]

XCVI

'Tis Marcia, not Rhine, that jets here, German; why withstand and elbow the boy from the gush of the precious pool? Barbarian, 'tis not meet that a citizen be thrust aside, and the victor's fountain slake a captive's thirst.[2]

XCVII

I CAN dally with four women in a single night, but may I die if I could in four years dally with you, Thelesilla, once!

XCVIII

'Tis impossible, Flaccus, to get free from kissers;[3] they press on you, stay you, follow you up, meet you, and from this side and from that, no matter when, wherever. No malignant ulcer or inflamed pustules, nor diseased chin[4] and dirty scabs, nor lips smeared with oily salve, nor icicle on a frozen nose, will protect you. They kiss you both when you are hot and when you are cold, and when

---

[3] See on the same subject VII. xcv. and XII. lix.
[4] An allusion to the *mentagra*, a skin disease attacking first the chin, and propagated by kissing: *cf.* Pliny, *N.H.* xxvi. 2, 3. It was brought to Rome from Asia in Tiberius' reign. Pliny says that women, and slaves, and the *plebs* were immune.

et nuptiale basium reservantem.
non te cucullis adseret caput tectum,   10
lectica nec te tuta pelle veloque,
nec vindicabit sella saepius clusa :
rimas per omnis basiator intrabit.
non consulatus ipse, non tribunatus
senive fasces nec superba clamosi   15
lictoris abiget virga basiatorem :
sedeas in alto tu licet tribunali
et e curuli iura gentibus reddas,
ascendet illa basiator atque illa.
febricitantem basiabit et flentem,   20
dabit oscitanti basium natantique,
dabit cacanti.   remedium mali solum est,
facias amicum basiare quem nolis.

XCIX

De cathedra quotiens surgis (iam saepe notavi),
    pedicant miserae, Lesbia, te tunicae.
quas cum conata es dextra, conata sinistra
    vellere, cum lacrimis eximis et gemitu :
sic constringuntur magni Symplegade culi   5
    et nimias intrant Cyaneasque natis.
emendare cupis vitium deforme ? docebo :
    Lesbia, nec surgas censeo nec sedeas.

---

¹ The praetor was preceded by a lictor, or beadle, and by
six attendants carrying bundles of rods surrounding an axe
(*fasces*).

you are keeping a kiss for your bride. A head shrouded in a cowl will not free you, nor a litter defended with head and curtain; nor will a sedan, though oftener closed, protect you: through any chink the kisser will enter. Not even the very consul's office, not the tribunate, nor the six fasces, nor the lordly rod of the clamorous lictor,[1] will drive off the kisser: you may be sitting on a high tribunal, and from curule chair be declaring the laws to the nations, the kisser will climb up to that place and to that. When you are fevered he will kiss you, and when you are in tears; he will give a kiss to you when you are yawning, and when you are swimming; he will give it when you are in the jakes Remedy for the evil is this alone: make a friend of a man you don't want to kiss.[2]

XCIX

WHENEVER you get up from your chair—I have often noticed it ere now—your unhappy garments, Lesbia, treat you indecently. When you attempt with your right hand, attempt with your left, to pluck them away, you wrench them out with tears and groans; they are so gripped by the straits of your mighty rump, and enter a pass difficult and Cyanean.[3] Do you wish to cure this ugly defect? I will instruct you: Lesbia, I advise you neither to get up nor to sit down!

[2] *i.e.* who, if he be really your friend, will respect your wish not to be kissed.

[3] The *Symplegades*, or *Cyaneae rupes*, were two rocks at the entrance of the Bosphorus that were said to clash together and crush ships: *cf.* VII. xix. 3.

C

Habere amicam nolo, Flacce, subtilem,
  cuius lacertos anuli mei cingant,
  quae clune nudo radat et genu pungat,
  cui serra lumbis, cuspis eminet culo.
  sed idem amicam nolo mille librarum.   5
  carnarius sum, pinguarius non sum.

CI

Thaida tam tenuem potuisti, Flacce, videre?
  tu, puto, quod non est, Flacce, videre potes.

CII

Non est mentitus qui te mihi dixit habere
  formosam carnem, Lydia, non faciem.
est ita, si taceas et si tam muta recumbas
  quam silet in cera vultus et in tabula.
sed quotiens loqueris, carnem quoque, Lydia, perdis   5
  et sua plus nulli quam tibi lingua nocet.
audiat aedilis ne te videatque caveto:
  portentum est, quotiens coepit imago loqui.

CIII

Tanta tibi est animi probitas orisque, Safroni,
  ut mirer fieri te potuisse patrem.

---

¹ It was the duty of the aedile to note and report all
prodigies, such as a talking statue. M. means that Lydia is

C

I DON'T wish, Flaccus, to have a mistress who is thin, whose arms my rings can go round, who rasps me with her skinny haunch and pricks me with her knee, from whose spine protrudes a saw, from whose latter-end a spear. But all the same I reject a mistress a thousand pounds' weight : I am an admirer of flesh—of tallow, no!

CI

COULD you see Thais who is so thin, Flaccus? You, I think, are able, Flaccus, to see what does not exist.

CII

HE was not wrong who told me that you had a beautiful complexion, Lydia, but no expression. 'Tis so, should you not speak, and should you recline as mute as a silent face depicted in wax and in a picture. But as often as you talk you ruin, Lydia, even your complexion, and her tongue spoils no woman more than you. Take care the aedile does not hear and see you![1] It is a portent whenever an image begins to speak.

CIII

SUCH is your modesty in mind and aspect, Safronius, that I wonder you have managed to become a father.

only a beautiful image. A similar idea is found in a Greek epigram : *Pal. Anth.* xi. 420.

CIV

Uxor, vade foras aut moribus utere nostris :
  non sum ego nec Curius nec Numa nec Tatius.
me iucunda iuvant tractae per pocula noctes :
  tu properas pota surgere tristis aqua.
tu tenebris gaudes : me ludere teste lucerna   5
  et iuvat admissa rumpere luce latus.
fascia te tunicaeque obscuraque pallia celant :
  at mihi nulla satis nuda puella iacet.
basia me capiunt blandas imitata columbas :
  tu mihi das aviae qualia mane soles.   10
nec motu dignaris opus nec voce iuvare
  nec digitis, tamquam tura merumque pares :
masturbabantur Phrygii post ostia servi,
  Hectoreo quotiens sederat uxor equo,
et quamvis Ithaco stertente pudica solebat   15
  illic Penelope semper habere manum.
pedicare negas : dabat hoc Cornelia Graccho,
  Iulia Pompeio, Porcia, Brute, tibi ;
dulcia Dardanio nondum miscente ministro
  pocula, Iuno fuit pro Ganymede Iovi.   20
si te delectat gravitas, Lucretia toto
  sis licet usque die ; Laida nocte volo.

CV

Mittebas libram, quadrantem, Garrice, mittis.
  saltem semissem, Garrice, solve mihi.

---

¹ Types of ancient Roman manners.
² *i.e.* for purposes of a vow, or of purification in a temple.
Chastity on the previous night (sometimes for ten days :
Prop. III. xxii. 62) was essential according to the rites of

CIV

WIFE, out of my house, or conform to my ways;
no Curius am I, or Numa, or Tatius.[1] Nights drawn
out by cheerful cups are my pleasure: you with a
sad air haste to get up after drinking water. You
delight in darkness: it pleases me to revel, with
the lamp my witness, and to strain my flanks
though I have admitted daylight. A breast-band,
and a tunic, and opaque robes conceal you; but
for me no girl lies naked enough. Kisses that are
like those of caressing doves attract me; you give
me such as you are wont in the morning to give
your grandmother. Nor by gesture, nor by words,
speech, or fingers, do you deign to accommodate me,
just as if you were getting ready incense and wine.[2]
I Frigii servi masturbavano dietro le porte ogni volta
che la moglie sedeva su l'Ettoreo cavallo, e Itaco
quantunque russante, la pudica Penelope suoleva aver
sempre colà la mano. Tu ricusi pedicare: Cornelia
accordava ciò a Gracco, Giulia a Pompeo, e Porzia a
te, Bruto; il Dardanio ministro quando non mischiava
i dolci bicchieri, Giunone era a Giove in vece di
Ganymede. If austerity please you, you may be
Lucretia all through the day: Lais I wish for at
night.

CV

You used to send me a pound's weight; a quarter,
Garricus, you now send. At least pay me half,
Garricus.[3]

Ceres (Ov. *Am.* III. x. 2) or of Isis: Ov. *Am.* I. viii. 74;
Tib. I. iii. 25.
[3] *cf.* x. lvii. M. humorously treats the present as a debt.
Moreover payment should be reduced gradually: *cf.* VIII.
lxxi.

CVI

Vibi Maxime, si vacas havere,
hoc tantum lege : namque et occupatus
et non es nimium laboriosus.
transis hos quoque quattuor? sapisti.

CVII

Explicitum nobis usque ad sua cornua librum
et quasi perlectum, Septiciane, refers.
omnia legisti.   credo, scio, gaudeo, verum est.
perlegi libros sic ego quinque tuos.

CVIII

Quamvis tam longo possis satur esse libello,
lector, adhuc a me disticha pauca petis.
sed Lupus usuram puerique diaria poscunt.
lector, solve.   taces dissimulasque ? vale.

---

[1] The *cornua* were the knobs at the end of the roller
(*umbilicus*) round which the parchment or papyrus was
wrapped.   The text means "unrolled to the very end."

CVI

VIBIUS MAXIMUS, if you have time for a greeting, read this only; for you are both engaged and not over-industrious. Do you skip even these four lines? You are wise.

CVII

You return me my book unrolled to its very horns,[1] and as if, Septicianus, you had read it through. " You have read it all." I believe it, I know it, I am glad, what you say is true. I have read through your five books in the same way.[2]

CVIII

ALTHOUGH with so long a book you may well be sated, reader, you still ask for a few distichs from me. But Lupus[3] requires his interest, and my slaves their rations. Reader, pay me. Do you say nothing, and pretend you don't understand? Good bye!

[2] *i.e.* not read it at all.
[3] A moneylender

BOOK XII

LIBER DUODECIMUS

Valerius Martialis Prisco suo Salutem

Scio me patrocinium debere contumacissimae
trienni desidiae ; quo absolvenda non esset inter illas
quoque urbicas occupationes, quibus facilius con-
sequimur ut molesti potius quam ut officiosi esse
videamur ; nedum in hac provinciali solitudine, ubi
nisi etiam intemperanter studemus, et sine solacio et
sine excusatione secessimus. accipe ergo rationem.
in qua hoc maximum et primum est, quod civitatis
aures quibus adsueveram quaero, et videor mihi in
alieno foro litigare ; si quid est enim quod in libellis
meis placeat, dictavit auditor : illam iudiciorum sub-
tilitatem, illud materiarum ingenium, bibliothecas
theatra convictus, in quibus studere se voluptates
non sentiunt, ad summam omnium illa quae delicati
reliquimus desideramus quasi destituti. accedit his
municipalium robigo dentium et iudici loco livor, et
unus aut alter mali, in pusillo loco multi ; adversus
quod difficile est habere cotidie bonum stomachum :

BOOK XII

I know that I ought to offer some plea in defence of a most obstinate three-years' indolence; yet no such plea could have secured an acquittal even amid those City pursuits in which we more easily succeed in appearing troublesome than dutiful;[1] much less in this provincial solitude, where, unless we study even immoderately, retirement is at once without solace and without excuse. Hear, then, my reasons. Of these this is the most important and first of all: I miss that audience of my fellow-citizens to which I had grown accustomed, and seem to myself a pleader in a strange court; for whatever is popular in my small books my hearer inspired. That subtlety of judgment, that inspiration of the subject, the libraries, theatres, meeting-places, where pleasure is a student without knowing it—to sum up all, those things which fastidiously I deserted I regret, like one desolate. Added to this is the back-biting of my fellow-townsmen, and envy ousting judgment, and one or other evilly disposed persons—a host in a tiny place—a circumstance against which it is

---

[1] The allusion is to the so-called "duties" of a client which in reality bored the patron.

ne mireris igitur abiecta ab indignante quae a gestiente fieri solebant. ne quid tamen et advenienti tibi ab urbe et exigenti negarem (cui non refero gratiam, si tantum ea praesto quae possum), inperavi mihi quod indulgere consueram, et studui paucissimis diebus, ut familiarissimas mihi aures tuas exciperem adventoria sua. tu velim ista, quae tantum apud te non periclitantur, diligenter aestimare et excutere non graveris ; et, quod tibi difficillimum est, de nugis nostris iudices candore [1] seposito ne Romam, si ita decreveris, non Hispaniensem librum mittamus sed Hispanum.

I

Retia dum cessant latratoresque Molossi
   et non invento silva quiescit apro,
otia, Prisce, brevi poteris donare libello.
   hora nec aestiva est nec tibi tota perit.

---

[1] *candore* Housman, *nidore β, nitore γ, nimio favore* Munro.

---

[1] The *cena adventoria* was a dinner given to one arriving from abroad. The phrase here represents a book of epigrams which was handed to Terentius Priscus on his arrival in Spain in the winter of 101, and immediately forwarded to Rome. This book, having been written *paucissimis diebus,* is probably the *brevis libellus* of XII. i. 3, and not Book XII. as we have it, which was probably an enlarged edition, perhaps compiled even after Martial's death, and which

difficult every day to keep a good stomach; do not wonder therefore that occupations have been cast aside in repugnance which I used to follow with ardour. Yet, not to deny you anything on your arriving from the City and claiming it—and I am not shewing you any fitting thanks if I do only what I can—I have enjoined on myself a task that I used to allow myself as a pleasure, and have devoted a very few days to study that I might greet your ears, my most friendly hearer, with their due feast of welcome.[1] I would wish you not to think it a trouble to weigh with care and to scrutinise those efforts that in your hands alone are in no danger, and—what is most difficult for you—to judge my trifling effusions with especial impartiality, so that, if you decide it should go, I may not transmit to Rome a book, not merely written in Spain, but Spanish.

I

WHILE the nets are idle, and your barking Molossian hounds, and the wood is at rest, now you have found no boar, you will be able, Priscus, to bestow your leisure on my small volume.[2] The hour is neither summer's nor is it lost to you wholly.[3]

[1] certainly contains epigrams written earlier than 101, *e.g.* vi., viii., xi., and xv. So Friedländer.

[2] Studious men used to read or write in the intervals of the chase: Plin. *Ep.* i. 6; v. 18.

[3] "It will take you less time to read, and the time will be well spent." A Roman hour, being a twelfth of the time between sunrise and sunset, was shorter in winter.

II

Quae modo litoreos ibatis carmina Pyrgos,
    ite Sacra, iam non pulverulenta, via.

III

Ad populos mitti qui nuper ab urbe solebas,
    ibis io Romam nunc peregrine liber
auriferi de gente Tagi tetricique Salonis,
    dat patrios amnes [1] quos mihi terra potens.
non tamen hospes eris nec iam potes advena dici   5
    cuius habet fratres tot domus alta Remi.
iure tuo veneranda novi pete limina templi,
    reddita Pierio sunt ubi templa choro.
vel si malueris, prima gradiere Subura ;
    atria sunt illic consulis alta mei :   10
laurigeros habitat facundus Stella penatis,
    clarus Iantheae Stella sititor aquae ;
fons ibi Castalius vitreo torrente superbit,
    unde novem dominas saepe bibisse ferunt :
ille dabit populo patribusque equitique legendum 15
    nec nimium siccis perleget ipse genis.
quid titulum poscis ? versus duo tresve legantur,
    clamabunt omnes te, liber, esse meum.

---

[1] *amnes quos* Housman, *manes quod* γ, *manes quae* β. *tibi* β.

---

[1] The book went by sea to Pyrgi, an ancient town in
Etruria on the Via Aurelia, about 26 English miles N.W. of
Rome, and was to enter Rome by the *Via Sacra*, which in
December would not be dusty. The distich seems to be a
fragment.

II

YE poems of mine that went of late to Pyrgi on the coast, go thence by the Sacred Way: it is not dusty now.[1]

III

You that lately used to be sent from the City to the provinces, ho! you will now go to Rome, O foreign book, from the people of gold-bearing Tagus and of rugged Salo, native streams that a great land makes mine. Yet you will not be a stranger, nor can you now be called a visitor, whose many brothers the lofty house of Remus holds. Of your own right make for the reverend threshold of the new temple where a fane has been restored to the Pierian choir.[2] Or, if you prefer, you will walk through the entrance to the Subura; there stands the high hall of my consul; eloquent Stella inhabits a house crowned with bay[3]— illustrious Stella, who thirsts for the stream of his Ianthis;[4] a fount of Castaly there proudly wells with its glassy torrent, whereof the Nine Dames oft, they say, have drunk. He will give you to people and senate and knight to be read, nor with eyes over-tearless will he himself read you through. Why do you require a title? Let two or three verses be read: all will cry that you, O book, are mine.

[2] Either the Temple of Apollo on the Palatine, rebuilt by Augustus (cf. Hor. Od. I. xxxi), with a portico attached and library of Greek and Latin books : Suet. Aug. xxix. ; or the Temple of Augustus, to which was added a library dedicated to the Muses, which Domitian removed and Trajan restored.

[3] Stella was consul A.D. 101.

[4] Stella had called a spring in his house after his wife Ianthis : cf. VII. xv. 1.

IV

Quod Flacco Varioque fuit summoque Maroni
    Maecenas, atavis regibus ortus eques,
gentibus et populis hoc te mihi, Prisce Terenti,
    fama fuisse loquax chartaque dicet anus.
tu facis ingenium, tu, si quid posse videmur ;   5
    tu das ingenuae ius mihi pigritiae.

V

Longior undecimi nobis decimique libelli
    artatus labor est et breve rasit opus.
plura legant vacui, quibus otia tuta dedisti :
    haec lege tu, Caesar ; forsan et illa leges.

VI

Contigit Ausoniae procerum mitissimus aulae
    Nerva : licet toto [1] nunc Helicone frui :
recta Fides, hilaris Clementia, cauta Potestas
    iam redeunt ; longi terga dedere Metus.
hoc populi gentesque tuae, pia Roma, precantur :   5
    dux tibi sit semper talis, et iste diu.
macte animi, quem rarus habes, morumque tuorum,
    quos Numa, quos hilaris possit habere Cato.
largiri, praestare, breves extendere census
    et dare quae faciles vix tribuere dei,   10

            [1] *tuto* Friedl.

---

[1] A quotation from Hor. *Od.* I. i. 1.
[2] Horace, Varius, and Virgil.

IV

WHAT Maecenas, a knight sprung from ancestral kings,[1] was to Flaccus and Varius and illustrious Maro,[2] this chattering fame and antique records shall tell the nations and provinces, Priscus Terentius, that you were to me. You create my genius, you create whatever power I seem to show ; you give me the free man's right of idleness.

V

THE too lengthy labour of my eleventh and tenth books has been shortened, and has filed down my work to a brief compass. Let idle men, to whom you have given protected leisure, read a fuller number ; do you, Caesar, read these : perhaps you will read those too ![3]

VI

MILDEST of princes, Nerva [4] has attained the Ausonian hall : we may enjoy now full draughts of Helicon. Steadfast Honour, cheerful Clemency, chastened Power now return ; long lasting Terrors have turned to flight. This prayer thy peoples and nations make, duteous Rome—may thy Chief be ever such as he, and he abide long ! Blessings on thy heart—the heart of few—and on thy manners, such as a Numa, such as a Cato in cheerful mood might possess ! To be bounteous, to lend protection, to enlarge narrow incomes, and to bestow gifts which even the gracious gods have scarce given, is now

[3] M. had published a selection from Bks. X. and XI. He hopes Caesar will read the fuller work.
[4] He became Emperor A.D. 96.

nunc licet et fas est.   sed tu sub principe duro
temporibusque malis ausus es esse bonus.

VII

Toto vertice quot gerit capillos
annos si tot habet Ligeia, trima est.

VIII

Terrarum dea gentiumque Roma,
cui par est nihil et nihil secundum,
Traiani modo laeta cum futuros
tot per saecula conputaret annos,
et fortem iuvenemque Martiumque   5
in tanto duce militem videret,
dixit praeside gloriosa tali :
" Parthorum proceres ducesque Serum,
Thraces, Sauromatae, Getae, Britanni,
possum ostendere Caesarem ; venite."   10

IX

Palma regit nostros, mitissime Caesar, Hiberos,
et placido fruitur Pax peregrina iugo.
ergo agimus laeti tanto pro munere grates:
misisti mores in loca nostra tuos.

X

Habet Africanus miliens, tamen captat.
Fortuna multis dat nimis, satis nulli.

---

¹ Under Domitian.
² Nerva's successor, A.D. 98, in January.
³ Trajan was born A.D. 52 at Italica, near Seville.

permitted and is right; but thou, under a hard prince and in evil times,[1] didst have courage to be good.

VII

IF Ligeia has as many years as the number of hairs she carries on the whole of her head, she is three years old.

VIII

WHAT time Rome, Goddess of Earth and of the nations, that has no peer and no second, was of late joyfully counting Trajan's[2] future years through so many generations, and saw a soldier strong, young, and warlike in so great a chief, glorying in such a governor, she said: " Ye rulers of the Parthians and chiefs of the Seres, Thracians, Sauromatians, Getians, Britons, I can show you a Caesar: come."

IX

PALMA governs our[3] native Iberians, most gentle Caesar, and Peace beyond the sea enjoys his placid sway. Gladly therefore we pay thee thanks for a boon so great: thou hast sent into our land the manners that are thine.

X

AFRICANUS possesses a hundred millions, yet he angles[4] for more. Fortune to many gives too much, enough to none.

[4] As a *captator* or fortune-hunter: *cf.* IX. lxxx. viii.; XI. lv.

XI

PARTHENIO dic, Musa, tuo nostroque salutem :
   nam quis ab Aonio largius amne bibit ?
cuius Pimpleo lyra clarior exit ab antro ?
   quem plus Pierio de grege Phoebus amat ?
et si forte (sed hoc vix est sperare) vacabit,   5
   tradat ut ipse duci carmina nostra roga,
quattuor et tantum timidumque brevemque libellum
   commendet verbis " Hunc tua Roma legit."

XII

OMNIA promittis cum tota nocte bibisti :
   mane nihil praestas. Pollio, mane bibe.

XIII

   GENUS, Aucte, lucri divites habent iram :
   odisse quam donare vilius constat.

XIV

PARCIUS utaris moneo rapiente veredo,
   Prisce, nec in lepores tam violentus eas.
saepe satisfecit praedae venator et acri
   decidit excussus nec rediturus equo.
insidias et campus habet : nec fossa nec agger   5
   nec sint saxa licet, fallere plana solent.
non derit qui tanta tibi spectacula praestet [1]
   invidia fati sed leviore cadat.[2]

      [1] *deerunt—praestent* βγ.   [2] *cadant* β.

---

[1] The Emperor's secretary : *cf.* v. vi. 2 ; XI. i. He was
murdered by the Praetorian guard in A.D. 97.

XI

BEAR greeting, Muse, to your Parthenius[1] and mine; for who more fully drinks of the Aonian stream? Whose lyre with clearer tone sounds forth from Pimpla's grot? Whom of the Pierian band loves Phoebus more? And if by chance—yet can I scarce so hope—he shall be at leisure, bid him offer with his own hand my verses to our Chief, and in four words only let him commend my shrinking and brief little[2] book: "This thy Rome reads."

XII

You promise everything when you have drunk all night: in the morning you make good no promise. Pollio, drink in the morning!

XIII

RICH men, Auctus, regard anger as a kind of profit; to hate is cheaper than to give![3]

XIV

USE more sparingly, I warn you, Priscus, your tearing hunter, nor rush so violently after hares. Often has the huntsman atoned to his prey, and, flung from his mettled horse, fallen to mount no more. Snares even a plain has: though there be no ditch, nor mound, nor stones, level ground can oft deceive. Never will you lack some one to offer you such a sight, but let it be one whose fall brings lighter

---

[2] Possibly the selection alluded to in XII. v.

[3] Picking quarrels with clients saves you giving them presents: *cf.* III. xxxvii.

si te delectant animosa pericula, Tuscis
    (tutior est virtus) insidiemur apris.   10
quid te frena iuvant temeraria? saepius illis,
    Prisce, datum est equitem rumpere quam leporem.

XV

Quidquid Parrhasia nitebat aula
donatum est oculis deisque nostris.
miratur Scythicas virentis auri
flammas Iuppiter et stupet superbi
regis delicias gravesque luxus: 5
haec sunt pocula quae decent Tonantem,
haec sunt quae Phrygium decent ministrum.
omnes cum Iove nunc sumus beati;
at nuper (pudet, a pudet fateri)
omnes cum Iove pauperes eramus.   10

XVI

Addixti, Labiene, tres agellos;
emisti, Labiene, tres cinaedos.
pedicas, Labiene, tres agellos.

XVII

Quare tam multis a te, Laetine, diebus
    non abeat febris quaeris et usque gemis.
gestatur tecum pariter tecumque lavatur;
    cenat boletos, ostrea, sumen, aprum;

---

¹ The Palatine is called Parrhasian because Evander, who
settled on the P., came from Parrhasia, a district of Arcadia:
cf. vii. lvi. 2 and xcix. 3.

reproach of fate. If perilous hardihood delight you, let us then—safer is such courage—lay snares for Tuscan boars. Why does rash riding please you? More often its issue, Priscus, is to break up the rider rather than the hare.

XV

ALL that glittered in the Palatine [1] hall has been given to our view and to our gods.[2] Jupiter wonders at the flashing of gold set with Scythian emeralds, and is amazed at the toys and grievous luxury of a haughty king[3]; here are cups that befit the Thunderer, here are such as befit his Phrygian cupbearer;[4] we all, together with Jove, are now rich; but of late —'tis shame, ah, 'tis shame to confess it!—we all, together with Jove, were poor.

XVI

You have sold, Labienus, three small fields; you have bought, Labienus, three favourites. You defile, Labienus, your three small fields.

XVII

You ask, Laetinus, why, after so many days, your fever doesn't leave you, and you are incessantly groaning. It rides in your litter with you, and with you it bathes; it dines on mushrooms, oysters,

---

[2] Trajan dedicated the Imperial jewels to Jupiter Capitolinus and other gods.
[3] *i.e.* Domitian. M. chooses in "king" the term most offensive to a Roman ear.   [4] Ganymede.

ebria Setino fit saepe et saepe Falerno   5
  nec nisi per niveam Caecuba potat aquam;
circumfusa rosis et nigra recumbit amomo,
  dormit et in pluma purpureoque toro.
cum sit ei pulchre, cum tam bene vivat apud te,
  ad Damam potius vis tua febris eat?   10

XVIII

Dum tu forsitan inquietus erras
clamosa, Iuvenalis, in Subura
aut collem dominae teris Dianae;
dum per limina te potentiorum
sudatrix toga ventilat vagumque   5
maior Caelius et minor fatigant:
me multos repetita post Decembres
accepit mea rusticumque fecit
auro Bilbilis et superba ferro.
hic pigri colimus labore dulci   10
Boterdum Plateamque (Celtiberis
haec sunt nomina crassiora terris):
ingenti fruor inproboque somno
quem nec tertia saepe rumpit hora,
et totum mihi nunc repono quidquid   15
ter denos vigilaveram per annos.
ignota est toga, sed datur petenti
rupta proxima vestis a cathedra.
surgentem focus excipit superba
vicini strue cultus iliceti,   20
multa vilica quem coronat olla.
venator sequitur, sed ille quem tu

sow's paps, boar; it often gets drunk on Setine, and often on Falernian, and drinks Caecuban only when strained through snow-water; wreathed with roses and dark with balsam it lies at board, and it sleeps in down and on a purple bed. Seeing it is so well-off, seeing it lives so comfortably with you, do you wish your fever to migrate in preference to Dama?[1]

XVIII

WHILE perchance you are restlessly wandering, Juvenal, in the noisy Subura, or treading the hill of Queen Diana; while, amid the thresholds of great men, your sweaty toga fans you, and, as you stray, the greater Caelian and the less[2] wearies you, me my Bilbilis, sought once more after many Decembers, has received and made a countryman, Bilbilis, proud of its gold and iron. Here indolently, with pleasant toil, I frequent Boterdus and Platea (such in Celtiberian lands are the uncouth names!); I enjoy a huge unconscionable sleep which often not even the third hour breaks, and I pay myself now in full for all my sleeplessness for thrice ten years. Unknown is the toga; rather, when I ask for it, the first covering at hand is given to me from a broken chair. When I get up, a fire, served with a lordly heap of logs from the neighbouring oak-wood, welcomes me, and my bailiff's wife crowns it with many a pot. Next comes my huntsman, and he too a

[1] A slave (cf. Hor. *Sat.* II. v. 18), or a beggar. A Greek epigram (*Pal. Anth.* xi. 403), which M. may have remembered, has the same idea as the last line of this epigram.

[2] The *Mons Caelius* properly consisted of the *Caelius* and the *Caeliolus*, a lesser height.

secreta cupias habere silva :
dispensat pueris rogatque longos
levis ponere vilicus capillos.   25
sic me vivere, sic iuvat perire.

XIX

IN thermis sumit lactucas, ova, lacertum,
et cenare domi se negat Aemilius.

XX

QUARE non habeat, Fabulle, quaeris
uxorem Themison ? habet sororem.

XXI

MUNICIPEM rigidi quis te, Marcella, Salonis
et genitam nostris quis putet esse locis ?
tam rarum, tam dulce sapis.   Palatia dicent,
audierint si te vel semel, esse suam ;
nulla nec in media certabit nata Subura   5
nec Capitolini collis alumna tibi ;
nec cito ridebit[1] peregrini gloria partus,
Romanam deceat quam magis esse nurum.
tu desiderium dominae mihi mitius urbis
esse iubes : Romam tu mihi sola facis.   10

XXII

QUAM sit lusca Philaenis indecenter
vis dicam breviter tibi, Fabulle ?
esset caeca decentior Philaenis.

[1] *ridebit.   parebit* Munro.

---

[1] *cf.* v. xlvii. What he takes at the baths is all he will get.

youth whom you would desire to consort with in some secret grove. The unbearded bailiff gives my slaves their rations, and asks permission to crop his long hair. So I love to live, so I love to die.

XIX

AT the warm baths Aemilius takes lettuce, eggs, lizard-fish, and says that he is not dining at home![1]

XX

Do you ask, Fabullus, why Themison has not got a wife? He has[2] a sister.

XXI

WHO would think, Marcella,[3] that you were a burgess of iron-tempering[4] Salo, who, that you were born in my native land? So rare, so sweet is your quality! The Palatine will declare, should it but hear you once, that you are its own; nor will a daughter of mid Subura, nor a nursling of the Capitoline hill, vie with you; nor soon shall the fairest of foreign birth laugh at one whom it would more befit to be a Roman bride. You bid my longing for the Queen City be allayed: you by yourself make a Rome for me!

XXII

WOULD you have me say shortly how uncomely one-eyed Philaenis is, Fabullus? If she were blind Philaenis would be comelier.

---

[2] Used ambiguously in two senses. As to one sense : *cf.* *Quis heri Chrysidem habuit?* Ter. *And.* 85 ; and line 23 of Ep. xviii. of this Book. So ἔχειν in Grk.: Thuc. vi. 54.

[3] *cf.* Intr. to vol. i. p. xi., and XII. xxxi. [4] *cf.* I. xlix. 12.

XXIII

DENTIBUS atque comis (nec te pudet) uteris emptis.
quid facies oculo, Laelia? non emitur.

XXIV

O IUCUNDA, covinne, solitudo,
carruca magis essedoque gratum
facundi mihi munus Aeliani!
hic mecum licet, hic, Iubate,[1] quidquid
in buccam tibi venerit loquaris.   5
non rector Libyci niger caballi
succinctus neque cursor antecedit;
nusquam est mulio: mannuli tacebunt.
o si conscius esset hic Avitus,
aurem non ego tertiam timerem.   10
totus quam bene sic dies abiret!

XXV

CUM rogo te nummos sine pignore, 'Non habeo'
     inquis;
  idem, si pro me spondet agellus, habes.
quod mihi non credis veteri, Telesine, sodali,
  credis coliculis arboribusque meis?
ecce reum Carus te detulit: adsit agellus.
  exilii comitem quaeris: agellus eat.   5

        [1] *Iubate* Postgate, *iuvate* codd.

---

[1] *cf. Pal. Anth.* xi. 310.
[2] Stertinius Avitus, who had placed a bust of M. in his
library: *cf.* IX. *Intr. Ep.*

XXIII

You use, and you are not ashamed, teeth and hair that you have bought. What will you do for an eye, Laelia? That cannot be bought.[1]

XXIV

O thou chaise, that affordest pleasant solitude, the gift to me of eloquent Aelianus, more grateful than travelling-coach and curricle! Here at my side, here may you, Jubatus, say whatever rises to your lips. No black driver of Libyan steed, nor runner with upgirt loins goes before; nowhere is any muleteer; the nags will be silent. Oh, if Avitus[2] were here to share our secrets, I should dread no third ear! How well thus would a whole day pass!

XXV

When I ask you for money without security, "I haven't any," you say; all the same, if my little farm pledge itself on my behalf, you have. The credit you will not give me, your old comrade, Telesinus, do you give my cabbages and trees? See, Carus[3] has informed against you: let my little farm appear for you; you ask for a companion in exile:[4] let my little farm go with you.

[3] Mettius Carus, a favourite dwarf of Nero's and an informer: Juv. i. 36. The name is here put generally for an informer.

[4] To follow a friend into exile was the highest proof of friendship: cf. vii. xliv. and xlv.

XXVI

Sexagena teras cum limina mane senator,
  esse tibi videor desidiosus eques,
quod non a prima discurram luce per urbem
  et referam lassus basia mille domum.
sed tu, purpureis ut des nova nomina fastis   5
  aut Nomadum gentes Cappadocumve regas :
at mihi, quem cogis medios abrumpere somnos
  et matutinum ferre patique lutum,
quid petitur ? rupta cum pes vagus exit aluta
  et subitus crassae decidit imber aquae   10
nec venit ablatis clamatus verna lacernis,
  accedit gelidam servus ad auriculam,
et ' Rogat ut secum cenes Laetorius ' inquit.
  viginti nummis ? non ego : malo famem
quam sit cena mihi, tibi sit provincia merces,   15
  et faciamus idem nec mereamur idem.

XXVII

A latronibus esse te fututam
dicis, Saenia : sed negant latrones.

XXVIII

Poto ego sextantes, tu potas, Cinna, deunces :
  et quereris quod non, Cinna, bibamus idem ?

---

[1] *i.e.* become a consul. Consul's names were entered in
the Fasti in the Temple of Janus : *cf.* VIII. lxvi. 12 ; XI. iv. 5.
[2] " Negant te impulsam ab iis ; vel negant hoc, aiuntque
te inhonestius quippiam passam esse ": *cf.* XII. xxxv.

XXVI

INASMUCH as you, though a senator, tread innumerable thresholds in the morning, I, a knight, appear to you slothful because I do not scour the city from early dawn, and wearily bring home with me a thousand kisses. But you do this that you may add a new name to the purple records,[1] or be sent to govern Numidian or Cappadocian tribes. But I, whom you compel to break off my slumber in the middle, and to bear and endure the morning mud, what do I look for? When my protruding foot gapes out of a broken shoe, and a sudden downpour of heavy rain falls, and my home-born slave, who has taken away my cloak, does not appear when I bawl for him, a slave approaches my frozen ear and " Laetorius asks you to dine with him," he says. For twenty sesterces a head? Not I: I prefer starvation to getting a dinner as reward, while you get a province, and to our performing the same services and not earning the same recompense.

XXVII

You say, Saenia, you were raped by footpads; but the footpads deny it.[2]

XXVIII

I DRINK cups containing two measures; you, Cinna, drink cups holding eleven. And do you then complain, Cinna, that we don't drink the same wine?[3]

---

[3] It was a vulgar habit of some hosts to give their guests inferior food or wine to what the host and his particular friends ate or drank: *cf.* VI. xi. 2 ; Plin. *Ep.* II. vi. 2. See on the subject generally Juv. v. In the epigram in the text the host excuses himself : "You cannot expect the best wine if you drink so much."

XXIX

Hermogenes tantus mapparum, Pontice, fur est
   quantus nummorum vix, puto, Massa fuit ;
tu licet observes dextram teneasque sinistram,
   inveniet mappam qua ratione trahat :
cervinus gelidum sorbet sic halitus anguem ;   5
   casuras alte sic rapit Iris aquas.
nuper cum Myrino peteretur missio laeso,
   subduxit mappas quattuor Hermogenes ;
cretatam praetor cum vellet mittere mappam,
   praetori mappam surpuit Hermogenes.   10
attulerat mappam nemo dum furta timentur ;
   mantele a mensa surpuit Hermogenes.
hoc quoque si derit, medios discingere lectos
   mensarumque pedes non timet Hermogenes.
quamvis non modico caleant spectacula sole,   15
   vela reducuntur cum venit Hermogenes.
festinant trepidi substringere carbasa nautae,
   ad portum quotiens paruit Hermogenes.
linigeri fugiunt calvi sistrataque turba,
   inter adorantes cum stetit Hermogenes.   20
ad cenam Hermogenes mappam non attulit umquam,
   a cena semper rettulit Hermogenes.

---

[1] Hermes was the thief among the gods : *cf.* Hor. *Od.* i. x. 7;
accordingly M. invents the name "Sprung of Hermes."

[2] Stealing napkins was common, and was satirised by
Catullus (Cat. xii.).

[3] Probably Baebius Massa, a mountebank of Nero's : Schol.
on Juv. i. 35. He was, on the accusation of the younger
Pliny, condemned A.D. 93 for embezzlement when proconsul
of Hispania Baetica.

[4] The left was the thievish hand (Cat. xlvii. 1 ; Ov. *Met.*
xiii. 110 (*natasque ad furta sinistras*)) ; hence M.'s distinction
between watching and holding.

XXIX

HERMOGENES[1] is as great a thief, Ponticus, of napkins[2] as I hardly imagine even Massa[3] was of money. You may watch his right hand and hold his left,[4] he will discover some method of withdrawing a napkin. So a stag's breath sucks up a clammy snake,[5] so Iris[6] plucks up the waters that will afterwards fall from on high. Of late when a discharge was sought for wounded Myrinus, Hermogenes filched four napkins ;[7] when the praetor wanted to throw his white napkin,[8] Hermogenes pilfered his napkin from the praetor. When no one had brought a napkin, in fear of theft, Hermogenes pilfered the table-cloth from off the table. If this, too, is not to be found, Hermogenes is not afraid to strip the valance from round the couches and the feet of the tables. Although the arena is burning under an immoderate sun, the awning is drawn back when Hermogenes arrives. Sailors in a panic hurry to brail up their canvas whenever Hermogenes has appeared at the port. Linen-clad, bald priests and the company with the timbrels[9] fly when Hermogenes has taken his stand among the worshippers. To a dinner Hermogenes has never brought a napkin : from a dinner Hermogenes has always carried a napkin home.

[5] According to Pliny (*N. H.* viii. 50) stags with their breath drew serpents out of their holes : *cf.* also Lucr. vi. 765.

[6] The rainbow.

[7] Handkerchiefs were waved when a discharge or quarter was wished by the spectators for a gladiator : *cf. Lib. Spect.* xxix. 3.

[8] As a signal for the starting of the races in the circus. The praetor presided.

[9] The priests and worshippers of Isis. The priests and initiates wore linen, and their heads were shaved : Juv. vi. 533.

XXX

Siccus, sobrius est Aper; quid ad me?
servum sic ego laudo, non amicum.

XXXI

Hoc nemus, hi fontes, haec textilis umbra supini
    palmitis, hoc riguae ductile flumen aquae,
prataque, nec bifero cessura rosaria Paesto,
    quodque viret Iani mense nec alget holus,
quaeque natat clusis anguilla domestica lymphis,   5
    quaeque gerit similes candida turris aves,
munera sunt dominae: post septima lustra reverso
    has Marcella domos parvaque regna dedit.
si mihi Nausicaa patrios concederet hortos,
    Alcinoo possem dicere "Malo meos."   10

XXXII

O Iuliarum dedecus Kalendarum,
vidi, Vacerra, sarcinas tuas, vidi;
quas non retentas pensione pro bima
portabat uxor rufa crinibus septem
et cum sorore cana mater ingenti.   5
Furias putavi nocte Ditis emersas.
has tu priores frigore et fame siccus
et non recenti pallidus magis buxo
Irus tuorum temporum sequebaris.
migrare clivom crederes Aricinum.   10

---

[1] Paestum in Campania was celebrated for roses: *cf.* VI.
lxxx. 6. "Twice-bearing" was a common epithet: Verg.
G. iv. 119.

[2] A Spanish lady to whom he also addresses XII. xxi.

XXX

APER is abstemious, sober : what is that to me ?
A slave I praise so, not a friend.

XXXI

THIS grove, these founts, this matted shade of
arching vine, this conduit of refreshing water, and
the meadows, and the beds of rose that will not
yield to twice-bearing Paestum,[1] and the pot-herb
in January green, nor seared by frost ; and the tame
eel that swims in its shut tank, and the white dove-
cote that harbours birds as white—these are my
lady's gifts : to me returned after seven lustres has
Marcella[2] given this house and tiny realm. If Nausicaa were to yield me her sire's gardens, I could say
to Alcinous[3] "I prefer my own."

XXXII

O you disgrace of July's kalends,[4] I have séen
your traps, Vacerra, I have seen them, the lot that
was not distrained upon for two years' rent, and
which your wife carried, red-headed with her seven
curls, and your white-headed mother, together with
your hulking sister. Furies were they, methought,
emerged from the night of Dis ! These two ladies
in front, you, parched with cold and hunger, and
paler than faded boxwood, the Irus[5] of your day,
followed : you would have thought Aricia's hill[6] was

---

[3] "The gardens of Alcinous," king of Phaeacia, was proverbial.   [4] Quarter-day.
[5] The beggar in the *Odyssey* who was beaten by Ulysses.
[6] Where beggars took their stand : *cf.* II. xix. 3.

ibat tripes grabatus et bipes mensa
et cum lucerna corneoque cratere
matella curto rupta latere meiebat ;
foco virenti suberat amphorae cervix ;
fuisse gerres aut inutiles maenas   15
odor inpudicus urcei fatebatur,
qualis marinae vix sit aura piscinae.
nec quadra derat casei Telosatis,
quadrima nigri nec corona pulei
calvaeque restes alioque caepisque,   20
nec plena turpi matris olla resina
Summemmianae qua pilantur uxores.
quid quaeris aedes vilicosque derides,
habitare gratis, o Vacerra, cum possis ?
haec sarcinarum pompa convenit ponti.   25

XXXIII

Ut pueros emeret Labienus vendidit hortos.
nil nisi ficetum nunc Labienus habet.

XXXIV

Triginta mihi quattuorque messes
tecum, si memini, fuere, Iuli.
quarum dulcia mixta sunt amaris
sed iucunda tamen fuere plura ;
et si calculus omnis huc et illuc   5
diversus bicolorque digeratur,
vincet candida turba nigriorem.
si vitare voles acerba quaedam
et tristis animi cavere morsus,
nulli te facias nimis sodalem :   10
gaudebis minus et minus dolebis.

shifting! There went along a three-legged truckle bed and a two-legged table, and, alongside a lantern and bowl of cornel, a cracked chamberpot was making water through its broken side; the neck of a flagon was lying under a brazier green with verdigris; that there were salted gudgeons, too, or worthless sprats, the obscene stench of a jug confessed—such a stench as a whiff of a marine fish-pond would scarcely equal. Nor was there wanting a section of Tolosan cheese, nor a four-year-old chaplet of black pennyroyal, and ropes shorn of their garlic and onions, nor your mother's pot full of foul resin, the depilatory of dames under the walls. Why do you look for a house and scoff at rent-collectors when you can lodge for nothing, O Vacerra? This procession of your traps befits Beggars' bridge.

XXXIII

To purchase slaves, Labienus sold gardens. Now Labienus has nothing but a clump of figs.[1]

XXXIV

THIRTY summers and four there were which, if I mind me, I spent, Julius,[2] with you. Thereof the sweets were blended with the bitters, but yet were the pleasant things the more; and if all the pebbles were sorted, on this side and on that, into two heaps of diverse colour, the white heap will outnumber that more dark. If you wish to shun some bitternesses and to beware of sorrows that gnaw the heart, to no man make yourself too much a comrade: your joy will be less and less will be your grief.

[1] A play on the two meanings of *ficus*: *cf.* i. lxv.; iv. lii.
[2] His friend and namesake Julius Martialis.

XXXV

Tamquam simpliciter mecum, Callistrate, vivas,
　dicere percisum te mihi saepe soles.
non es tam simplex quam vis, Callistrate, credi.
　nam quisquis narrat talia plura tacet.

XXXVI

Libras quattuor aut duas amico
algentemque togam brevemque laenam,
interdum aureolos manu crepantis,
possint ducere qui duas Kalendas,
quod nemo nisi tu, Labulle, donas, 5
non es, crede mihi, bonus.　quid ergo?
ut verum loquar, optimus malorum es.
Pisones Senecasque Memmiosque
et Crispos mihi redde, sed priores:
fies protinus ultimus bonorum. 10
vis cursu pedibusque gloriari?
Tigrim vince levemque Passerinum:
nulla est gloria praeterire asellos.

XXXVII

Nasutus nimium cupis videri.
nasutum volo, nolo polyposum.

XXXVIII

Hunc qui femineis noctesque diesque cathedris
　incedit tota notus in urbe nimis,

---

[1] cf. IV. xlviii. 1.
[2] Racehorses: cf. VII. vii. 10.

XXXV

As if you lived with me on the frankest terms, Callistratus, you are used often to tell me you have been debauched.[1] You are not so frank as you would have it believed, Callistratus; for a man who blabs of such things, conceals more.

XXXVI

Four pounds of plate, or two, to a friend, and a shivering toga and short cloak, sometimes sovereigns that chink in your hand, sufficient to last over two kalends—because no one but you, Labullus, makes such presents, you are not, believe me, good at giving. What then? To say the truth, you are the best of a bad lot. Give me back the Pisos, and the Senecas, and the Memmiuses, and the Crispuses—but those of former days—you will at once become the worst of a good lot. Would you pride yourself on your running and speed of foot? Beat Tigris and nimble Passarinus:[2] there is no glory in outstripping donkeys.

XXXVII

You are over-anxious to appear a man with a nose.[3] I approve of a man with a nose: I object to one with a polypus.

XXXVIII

Here is a fellow who day and night parades in women's chairs[4]—one notorious through the whole

---

[3] *i.e.* a fine critic: *cf.* I. iii. 6 ; XIII. ii. 1. "Don't overdo it," says M.; "your critical faculty has become a disease."

[4] Effeminate men often used the woman's chair as a sedan: *cf.* X. xiii. 1 ; Juv. i. 65.

crine nitens, niger unguento, perlucidus ostro,
    ore tener, latus pectore, crure glaber,
uxori qui saepe tuae comes inprobus haeret,   5
    non est quod timeas, Candide : non futuit.

XXXIX

    Odi te quia bellus es, Sabelle.
    res est putida, bellus et Sabellus ;
    bellum denique malo quam Sabellum.
    tabescas utinam, Sabelle, belle !

XL

Mentiris, credo : recitas mala carmina, laudo :
    cantas, canto : bibis, Pontiliane, bibo :
pedis, dissimulo : gemma vis ludere, vincor :
    res una est sine me quam facis, et taceo.
nil tamen omnino praestas mihi. "Mortuus" inquis   5
    "accipiam bene te."   nil volo : sed morere.

XLI

    Non est, Tucca, satis quod es gulosus :
    et dici cupis et cupis videri.

XLII

Barbatus rigido nupsit Callistratus Afro
    hac qua lege viro nubere virgo solet.

---

city—sleek of hair, dark with unguent, bright with purple, languishing of eye, broad of breast, smooth of shank, who often clings to your wife as an officious attendant. You need not be alarmed, Candidus: he is no practitioner.

XXXIX

I detest you because you are a pretty fellow, Sabellus. 'Tis a disgusting object, and so is pretty Sabellus. In a word, I prefer a pretty fellow[1] to Sabellus. May you go off into a pretty decline, Sabellus.[2]

XL

You tell fibs, I believe you; you recite poor poems, I praise them; you sing, I sing; you drink, Pontilianus, I drink; you break wind, I pretend not to hear; you want to play at draughts, I am beaten; there is one thing you do without my privity, and I hold my tongue. Yet you guarantee me nothing at all. "When I am dead," you say, "I will treat you well." I want nothing—nevertheless die!

XLI

It is not enough, Tucca, that you are a glutton: you want to be called one, and you want to appear one.

XLII

Bearded Callistratus as a bride wedded the brawny Afer in the usual form as when a virgin weds a

---

[2] The ep. is untranslatable in English so as to keep up the puns on the syllable "bell."

praeluxere faces, velarunt flammea vultus,
    nec tua defuerunt verba, Talasse, tibi.
dos etiam dicta est.   nondum tibi, Roma, videtur   5
    hoc satis? expectas numquid ut et pariat?

XLIII

FACUNDOS mihi de libidinosis
legisti nimium, Sabelle, versus,
quales nec Didymi sciunt puellae
nec molles Elephantidos libelli.
sunt illic Veneris novae figurae,   5
quales perditus audeat fututor,
praestent et taceant quid exoleti,
quo symplegmate quinque copulentur,
qua plures teneantur a catena,
extinctam liceat quid ad lucernam.   10
tanti non erat esse te disertum.

XLIV

UNICE, cognato iunctum mihi sanguine nomen
    qui geris et studio corda propinqua meis;
carmina cum facias soli cedentia fratri,
    pectore non minor es sed pietate prior.
Lesbia cum lepido te posset amare Catullo,   5
    te post Nasonem blanda Corinna sequi.
nec derant Zephyri si te dare vela iuvaret;
    sed tu litus amas.   hoc quoque fratris habes.

---

    [1] *cf.* the nuptials of Nero and Pythagoras described by
Tac. *Ann.* xv. 37.
    [2] Unknown.

husband. The torches shone before him, a wedding-
veil disguised his face, nor were the words of thy
song, God of Marriage, unheard. A dower even was
arranged. Do you not yet think, O Rome, this is
enough? Are you waiting also for an accouchement?[1]

XLIII

Tu m'hai letto, O Sabello, dei versi troppo facondi
di cose libidinose, che nè le ragazze di Didimo[2]
sanno, nè gli effeminati Elefantidi[3] libri. Qui vi
sono nuove figure di venere, che il più scellerato
immembratore avventurebbe; che i vecchi libertini
fanno e tacciono; con qual accoppiamento cinque
sono legati; da qual catena parecchi sono tenuti,
qual cosa è permessa, estinta la lucerna. La materia
non era si sublime per comparire eloquente.

XLIV

Unicus,[4] that bearest a name knit to mine by kin-
dred blood, and a heart close allied to my studies,
though thou shapest lays that yield the palm to thy
brother alone, yet in genius art thou not less than
he, albeit in mutual devotion greater. Lesbia might
have loved thee as well as witty Catullus; to thee,
after Naso, might winsome Corinna have clung.
Winds failed not didst thou wish to spread thy sails;
but thou lovest the shore: herein, too, art thou like
thy brother.

[3] Elephantis was a Greek poetess of the period who wrote
lascivious poems. The Emperor Tiberius had these at his
villa at Capreae as guidebooks to his lusts: Suet. *Tib.* xliii.
[4] "Possibly a Valerius Unicus, only mentioned here."

XLV

Haedina tibi pelle contegenti
nudae tempora verticemque calvae
festive tibi, Phoebe, dixit ille
qui dixit caput esse calceatum.

XLVI

Vendunt carmina Gallus et Lupercus.
sanos, Classice, nunc nega poetas.

XLVII

Difficilis facilis, iucundus acerbus es idem :
nec tecum possum vivere nec sine te.

XLVIII

Boletos et aprum si tamquam vilia ponis
et non esse putas haec mea vota, volo :
si fortunatum fieri me credis et heres
vis scribi propter quinque Lucrina, vale.
lauta tamen cena est : fateor, lautissima, sed cras   5
nil erit, immo hodie, protinus immo nihil,
quod sciat infelix damnatae spongea virgae
vel quicumque canis iunctaque testa viae :
mullorum leporumque et suminis exitus hic est.
sulpureusque color carnificesque pedes.   10

---

¹ As to such a covering *cf.* xiv. l.
² The last line is borrowed from Ovid, *Am.* iii. xi. 39.
³ Used for sanitary purposes. Seneca (*Ep.* 70) tells the story of a *bestiarius* who asked leave to retire to the latrine and choked himself with the sponge.

XLV

As you cover with a kid's skin [1] your temples and the crown of your bald pate, he made a happy remark to you, Phoebus, who told you your head was well shod.

XLVI

GALLUS and Lupercus sell their poems: now, Classicus, tell us poets are not sane!

XLVII

DIFFICULT and easy-going, pleasant and churlish, you are at the same time: I can neither live with you nor without you.[2]

XLVIII

IF you serve me mushrooms and boar as your usual fare, and don't imagine that these are what I pray for, I am willing to come; if you believe I am becoming wealthy, and you want to be written down my heir in return for five Lucrine oysters, goodbye! Yet your dinner is sumptuous: I confess, most sumptuous, but to-morrow 'twill be nought, nay to-day, nay a moment hence, nought that the luckless sponge at the end of a degraded mop-stick [3] would discover, or any dog,[4] or crock by the highway.[5] Of mullets, and hares, and sow's paps, this is the result—a bilious complexion and torturing feet. No

---

[4] *Qui ad vomitum accurrit*—Schrev.
[5] Set by the roadside as a urinal: *cf.* VI. xciii. 2.

non Albana mihi sit comissatio tanti
  nec Capitolinae pontificumque dapes;
inputet ipse deus nectar mihi, fiet acetum
  et Vaticani perfida vappa cadi.
convivas alios cenarum quaere magister   15
  quos capiant mensae regna superba tuae:
me meus ad subitas invitet amicus ofellas:
  haec mihi quam possum reddere cena placet.

XLIX

CRINITAE Line paedagoge turbae,
rerum quem dominum vocat suarum
et credit cui Postumilla dives
gemmas, aurea, vina, concubinos,
sic te perpetua fide probatum   5
nulli non tua praeferat patrona:
succurras misero, precor, furori
et serves aliquando neglegenter
illos qui male cor meum perurunt,
quos et noctibus et diebus opto   10
in nostro cupidus sinu videre,
formosos niveos pares gemellos
grandes, non pueros, sed uniones.

L

DAPHNONAS, platanonas et aerios pityonas
  et non unius balnea solus habes,
et tibi centenis stat porticus alta columnis
  calcatusque tuo sub pede lucet onyx,

---

[1] Such as Domitian gave at his Alban villa.
[2] Banquets by the Epulones to Jupiter Capitolinus, or
those given by the College of Pontiffs: as to the latter *cf.*

Alban revel [1] would be worth it to me, or Capitoline and Pontifical feasts; [2] should the God himself account me his debtor for nectar, it will become vinegar and the deceptive vapidity of a Vatican [3] jar. Look out, as lord of the banquet, for other guests whom the royal magnificence of your table may attract: as for me, let my friend invite me to hasty collops. The dinner I like is the dinner I can return.

XLIX

LINUS, guardian of a long-haired troop, whom rich Postumilla calls the master of her fortune, and to whom she entrusts gems, gold plate, wines, paramours; so may your patroness prefer none other to you who are proved by constant fidelity; come, I pray you, to the aid of my wretched frenzy, and sometimes guard negligently those that sadly consume my heart, those that night and day I long in eagerness to see in my bosom, beautiful, snowy-white, a pair, twins, big—I mean not boys, but pearls.

L

LAUREL-groves, plane-groves, and acry pine-groves, and a bath not made for one, you keep to yourself, and your colonnade stands high on a hundred columns, and trodden under your foot gleams the alabaster;

Hor. *Od.* II. xiv. 28. Macrobius (*Sat.* iii. 13) describes the courses of a pontifical feast given by Cecilius Metellus, who was pontiff before Julius Caesar.　　　[3] *cf.* VI. xcii. 2.

pulvereumque fugax hippodromon ungula plaudit   5
    et pereuntis aquae fluctus ubique sonat;
atria longa patent.   sed nec cenantibus usquam
    nec somno locus est.   quam bene non habitas!

LI

Tam saepe nostrum decipi Fabullinum
  miraris, Aule? semper homo bonus tiro est.

LII

Tempora Pieria solitus redimire corona
  nec minus attonitis vox celebrata reis,
hic situs est, hic ille tuus, Sempronia, Rufus,
  cuius et ipse tui flagrat amore cinis.
dulcis in Elysio narraris fabula campo   5
  et stupet ad raptus Tyndaris ipsa tuos:
tu melior quae deserto raptore redisti,
  illa virum voluit nec repetita sequi.
audit[1] et Iliacos ridet Menelaus amores:
  absolvit Phrygium vestra rapina Parim.   10
accipient olim cum te loca laeta piorum,
  non erit in Stygia notior umbra domo:
non aliena videt sed amat Proserpina raptas:
  iste tibi dominam conciliabit amor.

---

[1] *audet—ridet* Stephenson, *ridet—audit* codd., *ridet ut*
Postgate.

and the flying hoof makes ring your dusty drive, and on every side babbles the water of a stream crossing your ground; your halls lie open without end. But nowhere is there a place for dining or for sleep. How well you are—not housed!

LI

Do you wonder, Aulus, that our friend Fabullinus is so often taken in? A good man is always a greenhorn.

LII

HE who was wont to bind his temples with the Muses' crown, whose eloquence was no less famed among dismayed defendants, here, here he lies, Sempronia, who was once thy own Rufus, whose very ashes glow with love for thee. Sweetly mid Elysian fields is thy story told, and dazed is even Tyndarus' daughter [1] at thy ravishment; thy fame is the happier, for, quitting thy ravisher, thou didst return; she, even when sought again, would not join her spouse. Menelaus [2] listens to a Trojan love-tale and smiles: the story of your rape makes Phrygian Paris guiltless. When the joyous abodes of pious souls shall some day receive thee, no shade more famed will dwell in the house of Styx; Proserpina looks not strangely on the ravished, [3] but loves them: that love thou hast shown shall win thy Queen's good-will.

[1] Helen of Troy.
[2] King of Sparta, and husband of Helen. The meaning seems to be that the charm of the story of these two would make even M. pardon Paris.
[3] For she was herself carried off by Pluto.

LIII

Nummi cum tibi sint opesque tantae
quantas civis habet, Paterne, rarus
largiris nihil incubasque gazae
ut magnus draco quem canunt poetae
custodem Scythici fuisse luci.　　　　　　　5
sed causa, ut memoras et ipse iactas,
dirae filius est rapacitatis.
ecquid tu fatuos rudesque quaeris
inludas quibus auferasque mentem?
huic semper vitio pater fuisti.　　　　　　10

LIV

Crine ruber, niger ore, brevis pede, lumine laesus,
rem magnam praestas, Zoile, si bonus es.

LV

Gratis qui dare vos iubet, puellae,
insulsissimus inprobissimusque est.
gratis ne date, basiate gratis.
hoc Aegle negat, hoc avara vendit
(sed vendat: bene basiare quantum est!)　　5
hoc vendit quoque nec levi rapina:[1]
aut libram petit illa Cosmiani
aut binos quater a nova moneta,
ne sint basia muta, ne maligna,
ne clusis aditum neget labellis.　　　　　　10
humane tamen hoc facit: recusat[2]
gratis quae dare basium, sed unum,
gratis lingere non recusat Aegle.

[1] 5, 6 om. β, post 8 transp. Friedl.
[2] *recusat* Housman, *sed unum* codd.

LIII

THOUGH you have moneys and wealth such as only a citizen here and there owns, you bestow nothing, Paternus, and brood over your treasure like the great dragon that poets sing of as guardian once of the Scythian grove.[1] But the reason, as you report, and yourself repeat, is a son of dreadful rapaciousness. Are you looking, then, for simpletons and ignoramuses to delude and rob of sense? To this vice you have always been father.

LIV

OF hair red, swarthy of face, short of foot, of eye blear, you show yourself to be a portent, Zoilus, if you are virtuous.[2]

LV

HE who bids you, girls, give your favours for nothing, is a most foolish and impudent fellow. Do not give them for nothing, kiss for nothing. This Aegle refuses, this in her greed she sells. But let her sell it: how precious is a good kiss! This she sells, I say, and for no small plunder too; she asks for either a pound of Cosmian unguent, or four times two gold coins of the new mintage, that her kisses may not be silent ones or grudgingly given, that she may not with shut lips deny their approach. Yet this one thing she does graciously; Aegle, who refuses to give a kiss, a single kiss, for nothing, does not refuse to —— for nothing.

---

[1] Guarding the golden fleece.
[2] *i.e.* Heaven has marked you as one to be avoided.

357

LVI

Aegrotas uno decies aut saepius anno,
   nec tibi sed nobis hoc, Polycharme, nocet:
nam quotiens surgis, soteria poscis amicos.
   sit pudor: aegrota iam, Polycharme, semel.

LVII

Cur saepe sicci parva rura Nomenti
laremque villae sordidum petam, quaeris?
nec cogitandi, Sparse, nec quiescendi
in urbe locus est pauperi.   negant vitam
ludi magistri mane, nocte pistores,   5
aerariorum marculi die toto;
hinc otiosus sordidam quatit mensam
Neroniana nummularius massa,
illinc palucis[1] malleator Hispanae
tritum nitenti fuste verberat saxum;   10
nec turba cessat entheata Bellonae,
nec fasciato naufragus loquax trunco,
a matre doctus nec rogare Iudaeus,
nec sulpuratae lippus institor mercis.
numerare pigri damna qui potest somni,   15
dicet quot aera verberent manus urbis,
cum secta Colcho Luna vapulat rhombo.
tu, Sparse, nescis ista nec potes scire,

---

[1] *palucis* Friedl., *balucis* Turnebus, *paludis* βγ, *pollicent* T.

---

[1] *i.e.* either coins of light weight introduced by Nero, who debased the coinage, or small coins bearing the head of the emperor stamped in a particular way to distinguish them. The *nummularius* had a heap (*massa*) of these.

[2] *Palux* is the smaller gold found by washing in Spain, not large enough to constitute a nugget: Plin. *N.H.* xxxiii. 21.

LVI

You are ill in a single year ten times, or oftener, and this does not hurt you, but it hurts us, Polycharmus; for every time you rise from your bed you claim congratulatory gifts from your friends. Be moderate: now be ill, Polycharmus, once for all.

LVII

Do you ask why I often resort to my small fields in arid Nomentum, and the unkempt household of my villa? Neither for thought, Sparsus, nor for quiet is there any place in the city for a poor man. Schoolmasters in the morning do not let you live; before daybreak, bakers; the hammers of the coppersmiths all day. On this side the money-changer idly rattles on his dirty table Nero's coins,[1] on that the hammerer of Spanish gold-dust[2] beats his well-worn stone with burnished mallet; and Bellona's raving throng does not rest, nor the canting shipwrecked seaman with his swathed body,[3] nor the Jew taught by his mother to beg, nor the blear-eyed huckster of sulphur wares. He who can count the losses lazy sleep must bear will say how many brass pots and pans city hands clash when the eclipsed moon is being assailed by the Colchian magic-wheel.[4] You, Sparsus, know nothing of these things, and cannot know, luxurious as you are in your

---

[3] So pretending he had lost a limb. Some however understand *fasciato trunco* as a fragment of the wrecked vessel, or a picture of the ship, perhaps painted on a plank, swathed in a covering: *cf.* Pers. i. 88; Juv. xiv. 302.

[4] An eclipse was attributed to witches, and the clashing of brass vessels was in order to drive away evil demons: *cf.* Theocr. ii. 36; Tac. *Ann.* i. 28.

Petilianis delicatus in regnis,
cui plana summos despicit domus montis,   20
et rus in urbe est vinitorque Romanus
(nec in Falerno colle maior autumnus)
intraque limen latus essedo cursus,
et in profundo somnus et quies nullis
offensa linguis, nec dies nisi admissus.   25
nos transeuntis risus excitat turbae,
et ad cubile est Roma.   taedio fessis
dormire quotiens libuit, imus ad villam.

LVIII

Ancillariolum tua te vocat uxor, et ipsa
lecticariola est.   estis, Alauda, pares.

LIX

Tantum dat tibi Roma basiorum
post annos modo quindecim reverso
quantum Lesbia non dedit Catullo.
te vicinia tota, te pilosus
hircoso premit osculo colonus;   5
hinc instat tibi textor, inde fullo,
hinc sutor modo pelle basiata,
hinc menti dominus periculosi,
hinc †dexiocholus†,[1] inde lippus
fellatorque recensque cunnilingus.   10
iam tanti tibi non fuit redire.

---

[1] *dexiocholus et* β, *dexiocolus* E, *dexioculus* A, *istinc dexio-*
cholus Lindsay, *nec deest hinc oculis et* Heins.

---

[1] *i.e.* a palace that had once belonged to Petilius, perhaps
the P. Cerealis who had been in A.D. 71 the governor of
Britain.

Petilian [1] domain whose ground floor looks down on the hill tops, and where you have country in the town, and a Roman for your vine-dresser—not on Falernian hills is there a greater crop—and within your boundary a broad drive for your curricle, and unfathomed depths of slumber, and a stillness broken by no tongues, and no daylight unless you let it in. As for me, the laughter of the passing throng wakes me, and Rome is at my bed's head. Whenever, worn out with worry, I wish to sleep, I go to my villa.

LVIII

Your wife calls you an admirer of servant maids,[2] and she herself is an admirer of litter-bearers. You are a pair, Alauda.

LIX

Rome gives you as many kisses, when after fifteen years you have just returned, as Lesbia never gave Catullus.[3] Upon you all the neighbourhood presses, upon you the bristly farmer with a kiss like a he-goat's; on this side the weaver crowds you, on that the fuller, on this the cobbler who has just been kissing his hide, on this the owner of a perilous chin;[4] on this side the one-eyed and on that the blear-eyed, and many a rascal with foulest lips. By now you find it was not worth while to return.

---

[2] This seems to have been, among Roman matrons, a term of reproach of those who kept mistresses of low degree : *cf.* Sen. *De Ben.* i. 9.

[3] *cf.* Cat. v.

[4] *i.e.* suffering from *mentagra* ; *cf.* IV. xxxvi. 2; XI. xcviii. 5.

LX

Martis alumne dies, roseam quo lampada primum
    magnaque siderei vidimus ora dei,
si te rure coli viridisque pudebit ad aras,
    qui fueras Latia cultus in urbe mihi:
da veniam, servire meis quod nolo Kalendis   5
    et qua sum genitus vivere luce volo.
natali pallere suo, ne calda Sabello   [LXᵇ
    desit; et ut liquidum potet Alauda merum,
turbida sollicito transmittere Caecuba sacco;
    atque inter mensas ire redire suas;   10
excipere hos illos et tota surgere cena
    marmora calcantem frigidiora gelu:
quae ratio est haec sponte sua perferre patique
    quae te si iubeat rex dominusque, neges?

LXI

Versus et breve vividumque carmen
in te ne faciam times, Ligurra,
et dignus cupis hoc metu videri.
sed frustra metuis cupisque frustra.
in tauros Libyci ruunt leones,   5
non sunt papilionibus molesti.
quaeras censeo, si legi laboras,
nigri fornicis ebrium poetam,
qui carbone rudi putrique creta
scribit carmina quae legunt cacantes.   10
frons haec stigmate non meo notanda est.

---

¹ M. is in Spain celebrating his birthday, the First of March,
a day sacred to Mars. He contrasts the simplicity of his
celebration with a birthday feast at Rome.

² The Sun. The epithet is an allusion to the statue of the
Sun in front of the Colosseum: *cf. Spect.* ii. 1.

LX

THOU day, nursling of Mars,[1] whereon I first saw
the rosy light and the mighty visage of the star-
encircled god,[2] if it shall shame thee to be worshipped
in the country and at green altars, who wert worshipped by me in the Latian city, grant thy pardon
in that I refuse to be a slave on my kalends, but
wish to *live*[3] on the day I was born.   To grow pale
on one's birthday lest Sabellus lack warm water ; and,
that Alauda may drink his wine strained, anxiously
to pass the turbid Caecuban through the bag ; and
to go to and fro among one's tables ; to receive these
and those guests, and all through the dinner to be
getting up, treading on marble colder than ice [4]—
what reason is there why one should suffer and
endure these things of one's own accord, which, if
your lord and master [5] bade you, you would refuse ?

LXI

You are afraid, Ligurra, I should write verses on
you, and some short and lively poem, and you long
to be thought a man that justifies such fear.   But
vain is your fear, and your longing is vain.   Against
bulls Libyan lions rage, they are not hostile to but-
terflies.   Look out, I advise you, if you are anxious
to be read of, for some dark cellar's sottish poet, one
who with coarse charcoal or crumbling chalk scrawls
poems which people read in the jakes.   Your brow
is not one to be marked by my brand.

[3] M. constantly harps upon this idea : *cf.* II. xc. 3 ; v.
xxi. 11.
[4] M. would be barefooted, as the shoes were not worn
during dinner.
[5] Your patron.

LXII

Antiqui rex magne poli mundique prioris,
   sub quo pigra quies nec labor ullus erat,
nec regale nimis fulmen nec fulmine digni,
   scissa nec ad Manes sed sibi dives humus:
laetus ad haec facilisque veni sollemnia Prisci   5
   gaudia: cum sacris te decet esse tuis.
tu reducem patriae sexta, pater optime, bruma
   pacifici Latia reddis ab urbe Numae.
cernis ut Ausonio similis tibi pompa macello
   pendeat et quantus luxurietur honos?   10
quam non parca manus largaeque nomismata mensae,
   quae, Saturne, tibi pernumerentur opes?
utque sit his pretium meritis et gratia maior,
   et pater et frugi sic tua sacra colit.
at tu sancte (tuo sic semper amere Decembri)   15
   hos illi iubeas saepe redire dies.

LXIII

Uncto Corduba laetior Venafro,
Histra nec minus absoluta testa,
albi quae superas oves Galaesi
nullo murice nec cruore mendax,
sed tinctis gregibus colore vivo: 5
dic vestro, rogo, sit pudor poetae

---

[1] When there was no mining for precious metals.
[2] Priscus' father is giving a feast to celebrate his son's return to Spain: *cf.* xii. *Epist.*
[3] Rome: *cf.* VIII. viii. 5.
[4] Representing prizes to be taken away by guests. The fourteenth Book is wholly concerned with such prizes.

LXII

GREAT king of the ancient heaven and of a bygone world, under whose reign was lazy rest and no toil, nor over-tyrannous thunderbolt, nor men that deserved the bolt, when earth was not cleft to its nether deeps but kept her riches for herself,[1] gladly and graciously come thou to Priscus'[2] festival of joy: it befits thee to attend thy own rites. Thou in the sixth winter, Father most good, bringest him back to his fatherland from peaceful Numa's Latin city.[3] Seest thou how, as in a Roman market, hangs cheer, to honour thee, how full is festive luxury? how unsparing the hand? and the tokens[4] on the loaded board? what rich gifts, Saturnus, are measured out to thee? And, to give value and greater praise to such worth, 'tis a father and a frugal man who so celebrates thy rites. And do thou, hallowed Sire (so mayst thou be ever loved thus in thy own December), bid days like these return upon him oft.

LXIII

CORDUBA, more prolific than oil-bearing Venafrum,[5] nor less perfect than the jars of Istria,[6] thou that dost outvie the sheep of white Galaesus,[7] not by the aid of any cheating shell-fish or blood, but by flocks coloured in native hues,[8] tell your poet, I beg you,

[5] A town on the borders of Latium celebrated for the excellence of its olives : cf. Hor. Od. II. vi. 16.

[6] A district on the N. of the Adriatic, celebrated for its oil.

[7] A river flowing into the gulf of Tarentum, on the banks of which sheep fed, celebrated for the whiteness of their wool, which was protected by skins : cf. Hor. Od. II. vi. 10.

[8] The fleeces of the sheep fed by the Baetis were not artificially dyed, but had a natural golden hue : cf. VIII. xxviii. 6.

nec gratis recitet meos libellos.
ferrem, si faceret bonus poeta,
cui possem dare mutuos dolores.
corrumpit sine talione caeleps ;　　　　　10
caecus perdere non potest quod aufert.
nil est deterius latrone nudo :
nil securius est malo poeta.

LXIV

VINCENTEM roseos facieque comaque ministros
　　Cinna cocum fecit.　　Cinna, gulosus homo es.

LXV

FORMOSA Phyllis nocte cum mihi tota
se praestitisset omnibus modis largam,
et cogitarem mane quod darem munus,
utrumne Cosmi, Nicerotis an libram,
an Baeticarum pondus acre lanarum,　　　　5
an de moneta Caesaris decem flavos,
amplexa collum basioque tam longo
blandita quam sunt nuptiae columbarum,
rogare coepit Phyllis amphoram vini.

LXVI

BIS quinquagenis domus est tibi milibus empta,
　　vendere quam summa vel breviore cupis.
arte sed emptorem vafra corrumpis, Amoene,
　　et casa divitiis ambitiosa latet.
gemmantes prima fulgent testudine lecti　　　　5
　　et Maurusiaci pondera rara citri ;

---

¹ His sight.
² Because his poems are not worth stealing.

to have some shame, and not to recite my poems
scot-free. I could bear it if a good bard did this,
one I could visit with pain in his turn. A bachelor
debauches without reprisal, a blind man cannot lose
that [1] whereof he robs you. Nothing is worse than
a naked robber, nothing more safe than a bad poet.[2]

LXIV

A slave surpassing with his face and locks the
rosy-cheeked attendants Cinna has made his cook.
Cinna, you are a lickerish fellow!

LXV

When lovely Phyllis had all the evening yielded
herself bounteously to me in every way, and I was
considering next morning what present to give her,
whether a pound of unguent of Cosmus' or Niceros'[3]
make, or full weight of Baetic wool, or ten yellow
boys of Caesar's mintage, Phyllis, embracing my
neck, and wheedling me with a kiss as lingering as
that of wedded doves, began to ask me for a—jar
of wine!

LXVI

A town house was bought by you for twice fifty
thousand sesterces, and you long to sell it even
for a scantier sum. But you seek to seduce a purchaser with crafty art, Amoenus; and a cottage lies
disguised pretentiously in riches. Couches gleam
bright, inlaid with peerless tortoiseshell, and there
are pieces, choice and weighty, of Moorish citrus-

---

[3] Noted perfumers of the day, and often mentioned by M.

argentum atque aurum non simplex Delphica portat;
  stant pueri, dominos quos precer esse meos.
deinde ducenta sonas et ais non esse minoris.
  instructam vili vendis, Amoene, domum.   10

LXVII

MAIAE Mercurium creastis Idus,
Augustis redit Idibus Diana,
Octobres Maro consecravit Idus.
Idus saepe colas et has et illas,
qui magni celebras Maronis Idus.   5

LXVIII

MATUTINE cliens, urbis mihi causa relictae,
  atria, si sapias, ambitiosa colas.
non sum ego causidicus nec amaris litibus aptus
  sed piger et senior Pieridumque comes;
otia me somnusque iuvant, quae magna negavit   5
  Roma mihi: redeo, si vigilatur et hic.

LXIX

SIC tamquam tabulas scyphosque, Paule,
omnes archetypos habes amicos.

---

¹ This term has an indecent sense: *cf.* XI. lxx. 2.
² Amoenus disguised the poorness of the house, which was
a mere cottage (l. 4), by fine furniture, which was not to be
sold with the house. A. asks 200,000, although he had given
only half that sum, and would take less (l. 2). M. ironically
ignoring the fact that the house was not sold furnished,
pretends to agree with A. that the house was cheap.
³ May 15 was the dedication day of the Temple of Mer-

wood; an elaborate sideboard is loaded with silver and gold plate; young slaves are standing there whom I would wish my masters![1] Then you loudly prate of two hundred thousand sesterces, and say the place is not worth less. Furnished as it is, Amoenus, you are selling your town house cheap.[2]

LXVII

You, Ides of May, brought forth Mercurius; on August's Ides return Diana's feasts; Maro has hallowed the Ides of October. Oft may you keep these Ides and those, you, who celebrate great Maro's Ides![3]

LXVIII

Morning client, the cause of my leaving Rome, you would court, were you wise, the halls of greatness. No pleader am I, nor fitted for bitter lawsuits, but an indolent man and one growing old, and the comrade of the Muses. Ease and sleep attract me, and great Rome denied me these; I return if I am sleepless even here.[4]

LXIX

Just like your pictures and cups, Paulus, all the friends you possess are "genuine antiques."[5]

cury; Aug. 13 that of the Temple of Diana on the Aventine; and Oct. 15 the birthday of Virgil. The person addressed is probably Silius Italicus: cf. XI. xlix.

[4] "It is no use your calling on me in the morning," says M.; "the duties of a client drove me from Rome: I don't expect to be a client in Spain, and lose my sleep."

[5] i.e. as false as they are; or (perhaps) kept only for show (Paley). Housman, however, treats the epigram as laudatory of P.'s friends.

LXX

Lintea ferret Apro vatius cum vernula nuper
    et supra togulam lusca sederet anus
atque olei stillam daret enterocelicus unctor,
    udorum tetricus censor et asper erat:
frangendos calices effundendumque Falernum   5
    clamabat, biberet quod modo lotus eques.
a sene sed postquam patruo venere trecenta,
    sobrius a thermis nescit abire domum.
o quantum diatreta valent et quinque comati !
    tunc, cum pauper erat, non sitiebat Aper.   10

LXXI

Nil non, Lygde, mihi negas roganti .
at quondam mihi, Lygde, nil negabas.

LXXII

Iugera mercatus prope busta latentis agelli
    et male compactae culmina fulta casae,
deseris urbanas, tua praedia, Pannyche, lites
    parvaque sed tritae praemia certa togae.
frumentum, milium tisanamque fabamque solebas   5
    vendere pragmaticus, nunc emis agricola.

LXXIII

Heredem tibi me, Catulle, dicis.
non credam, nisi legero, Catulle.

---

[1] cf. XI. lxxiii.
[2] Lining the great roads leading out of Rome. It was so
small that the tombs dwarfed it.

LXX

WHEN of late a bow-legged home-born slave carried his towels for Aper, and a one-eyed old crone sat guard over his scanty toga, and a ruptured anointer offered him his drop of oil, he was a stern and harsh censor of drinkers; he used to shout that the cups ought to be smashed, and the Falernian poured away that the knight, just bathed, was drinking. But after three hundred thousand sesterces came to him from an old uncle, he doesn't know how to go home from the warm baths sober. Oh, how great is the influence of fretwork chalices and five long-haired slaves! Then, when he was poor, Aper was not thirsty!

LXXI

THERE is nothing you do not deny me, Lygdus, when I ask; but once there was nothing, Lygdus, you denied.[1]

LXXII

HAVING purchased the acres of a small farm lying hid near the tombs,[2] and an ill-built cottage with a shored-up roof, you desert the city law-suits, that were your landed estate, Pannychus, and the small but certain reward of your threadbare gown. Wheat, millet, and barley and beans you used to sell when you were an attorney: you buy them now you are a farmer.

LXXIII

You say I am your heir, Catullus. I won't believe it unless I read my name, Catullus.[3]

---

[3] *i.e.* in the will, which would be after C.'s death. A hint to him to die.

LXXIV

Dum tibi Niliacus portat crystalla cataplus,
    accipe de circo pocula Flaminio.
hi magis audaces, an sunt qui talia mittunt
    munera? sed geminus vilibus usus inest:
nullum sollicitant haec, Flacce, toreumata furem   5
    et nimium calidis non vitiantur aquis.
quid quod securo potat conviva ministro
    et casum tremulae non timuere manus?
hoc quoque non nihil est, quod propinabis in istis,
    frangendus fuerit si tibi, Flacce, calix.   10

LXXV

    Festinat Polytimus ad puellas;
    invitus puerum fatetur Hypnus;
    pastas glande natis habet Secundus;
    mollis Dindymus est sed esse non vult;
    Amphion potuit puella nasci.   5
    horum delicias superbiamque
    et fastus querulos, Avite, malo
    quam dotis mihi quinquies ducena.

LXXVI

Amphora vigesis, modius datur aere quaterno.
    ebrius et crudus nil habet agricola.

---

¹ The ninth region of Rome, N.W. of the Capitol, and
including the *Saepta*, where were shops: cf. IX. lix. 1. It
took its name from the *Circus Flaminius* on the Tiber, S. of
the *Campus Martius*.
² *Audaces calices* were cups not valuable enough to cause
anxiety as to breakage: cf. XIV. xciv. It is a "bold" thing
to send such cups to a man that imports crystal.

LXXIV

WHILE a fleet from Nile is bringing you crystal glass, accept some cups from the Flaminian Circus.[1] Are these the more "dreadnought"[2] or are they who send such presents? But in cheap vessels is a double advantage: these embossed cups attract no thief, Flaccus, and they are not cracked by water too hot. What of this, too, that the attendant is not nervous while a guest drinks, and shaky hands do not fear a slip? This, also, is something: you will drink a health in these vessels, Flaccus, if you have to break the cup afterwards.[3]

LXXV

POLYTIMUS hurries off to girls, Hypnus unwillingly confesses that he is a boy, Secundus has buttocks yard-fed,[4] Dindymus is effeminate but wishes not to seem so, Amphion might have been born a girl. The caprice of these boys, and their haughtiness, and their querulous disdain, I prefer, Avitus, to five times two hundred thousand sesterces of dower.

LXXVI

A FLAGON of wine is sold for twenty pence, a peck of corn for four. The husbandman is drunk and overfed, but has nothing.[5]

[3] As having been defiled by impure lips: *cf.* II. xv. and *Anth. Pal.* xi. 39.

[4] There is a play in the Latin on *glande*. The metaphor is taken from the feeding of hogs on acorns. As to the ambiguous meaning of "yard," *cf.* Shak. *L.L.L.* v. ii. 676

[5] Things are so cheap it does not pay to sell.

LXXVII

Multis dum precibus Iovem salutat
stans summos resupinus usque in ungues
Aethon in Capitolio, pepedit.
riserunt homines, sed ipse divom
offensus genitor trinoctiali   5
adfecit domicenio clientem.
post hoc flagitium misellus Aethon,
cum vult in Capitolium venire,
sellas ante petit Paterclianas
et pedit deciesque viciesque.   10
sed quamvis sibi caverit crepando,
compressis natibus Iovem salutat.

LXXVIII

Nil in te scripsi, Bithynice.   credere non vis
et iurare iubes?   malo satisfacere.

LXXIX

Donavi tibi multa quae rogasti;
donavi tibi plura quam rogasti:
non cessas tamen usque me rogare.
quisquis nil negat, Atticilla, fellat.

LXXX

Ne laudet dignos, laudat Callistratus omnes.
cui malus est nemo quis bonus esse potest?

---

¹ Aethon was a parasite, to whom "dining at home" was
a penalty.
² A plaintiff was entitled by Roman law to challenge the
defendant to take an oath as to the justice of his own case,
refusal being treated as tantamount to an admission of the

LXXVII

WHILE with many prayers he addressed Jupiter, standing all the time, with eyes upturned, on the tips of his toes, Aethon in the Capitol broke wind. Men laughed, but the Father of the Gods himself was offended, and amerced his client in domiciliary dinners for three nights.[1] After this outrage wretched Aethon, when he is minded to enter the Capitol, makes beforehand for Paterclius' latrines, and lets off his piece ten and twenty times. But, however much he has taken precautions by this crepitation, 'tis with constricted buttocks he addresses Jove!

LXXVIII

I WROTE nothing against you, Bithynicus. Do you refuse to believe me, and require me to swear? I prefer to pay the debt.[2]

LXXIX

I HAVE given you much you asked; I have given you more than you asked; yet you do not cease continually to ask me. He who refuses nothing, Atticilla, is capable of anything.

LXXX

To avoid praising the worthy, Callistratus praises everybody. Who can be good in his eyes to whom no man is bad?

plaintiff's claim. Hence the oath was called *jusjurandum necessarium.* Thus a debtor must deny the debt or pay it. M. being challenged by B. says that he prefers to discharge what he regards as an obligation, *i.e.* to write an offensive epigram.

LXXXI

Brumae diebus feriisque Saturni
mittebat Umber aliculam mihi pauper;
nunc mittit alicam: factus est enim dives.

LXXXII

Effugere in thermis et circa balnea non est
    Menogenen, omni tu licet arte velis.
captabit tepidum dextra laevaque trigonem,
    inputet exceptas ut tibi saepe pilas.
colligit et referet laxum de pulvere follem,   5
    et si iam lotus, iam soleatus erit.
lintea si sumes, nive candidiora loquetur,
    sint licet infantis sordidiora sinu.
exiguos secto comentem dente capillos
    dicet Achilleas disposuisse comas.   10
fumosae feret ipse tropin¹ de faece lagonae,
    frontis et umorem colligit ille tuae.
omnia laudabit, mirabitur omnia, donec
    perpessus dicas taedia mille "Veni!"

LXXXIII

Derisor Fabianus hirnearum,
omnes quem modo colei timebant

¹ *tropin* ς, *propin* codd.

---

¹ The point of the epigram is that *alicula*, the first gift, is
in form a diminutive of *alica*, the second (barley water:
cf. xiii. 6), whereas in fact *alica* is a smaller gift than *alicula*.
² *Trigon* was a game of handball played by three standing

LXXXI

In the days of winter and at the feast of Saturn,
Umber used to send me a cape: he was poor. Now
he sends me capers: for he has become rich.[1]

LXXXII

To escape Menogenes in the warm baths and about
the baths is impossible, try what artifice you will. He
will grab the warm hand-ball with right and left,
that he may be able often to score to your account
the balls he catches.[2] He picks up and will restore
to you the flaccid bladder-ball from the dust, even if
he has already bathed, is already in his dinner slippers. If you take your towels, he will speak of
them as whiter than snow, although they are dirtier
than an infant's bib. While you are arranging with
a comb your scanty hairs, he will say these are
Achilles' locks that you have ordered. He will with
his own hands bring you the dregs from the bottom
of the smoky wine-jar,[3] and he wipes the moisture
on your brow. Everything he will praise, will admire everything, until, having endured to the end a
thousand boredoms, you say "Come and dine."

LXXXIII

Fabianus, who derided hernia, whom of late all
lewd fellows dreaded,[4] when he inveighed against

in a triangle: cf. IV. xix. 7. M. scores his own catches to
Martial. But the meaning of l. 4 is very uncertain.
    [3] Perhaps to be used as an emetic before dinner: cf. Sen.
Ad Helv. x. 3; or as a detergent of the skin. The line may,
however, mean "will put up with the dregs for himself."
    [4] Possibly his rivals in amours whom he stigmatised as
diseased.

dicentem tumidas in hydrocelas
quantum nec duo dicerent Catulli,
in thermis subito Neronianis   5
vidit se miser et tacere coepit.

LXXXIV

NOLUERAM, Polytime, tuos violare capillos,
    sed iuvat hoc precibus me tribuisse tuis.
talis eras, modo tonse Pelops, positisque nitebas
    crinibus ut totum sponsa videret ebur.

LXXXV

PEDICONIBUS os olere dicis.
    hoc si, sicut ais, Fabulle, verum est,
    quid tu credis olere cunnilingis?

LXXXVI

TRIGINTA tibi sunt pueri totidemque puellae:
    una est nec surgit mentula.   quid facies?

LXXXVII

BIS Cotta soleas perdidisse se questus,
    dum neglegentem ducit ad pedes vernam,
qui solus inopi praestat et facit turbam,
    excogitavit homo sagax et astutus
ne facere posset tale saepius damnum: 5
    excalceatus ire coepit ad cenam.

---

[1] A writer of mimes: *cf.* v xxxi. 3.
[2] Now his hair is cut Polytimus' skin will be seen,

swelling ruptures in tones even two Catulluses [1] could not match, suddenly beheld himself—wretched fellow!—in Nero's warm baths, and began to hold his tongue.

LXXXIV

I was loth, Polytimus, to mar those locks of thine, but glad am I to have granted that much to thy prayers. Such wert thou, O Pelops lately shorn, and thus, when thy hair was laid aside, didst thou shine, so that thy spouse saw all the ivory of thy shoulder. [2]

LXXXV

You say that the breath of unnatural rascals smells. If this be, as you say, true, Fabullus, what do you imagine is the smell of some others?

LXXXVI

Tu hai trenta ragazzi, ed altre tante ragazze: la mentola non è che una, nè si rizza.   Che farai?

LXXXVII

Cotta, after complaining that he had twice lost his house-shoes while he brought with him a careless attendant, the only slave that serves for and makes up his staff, thought out—sagacious and acute man!—how to avoid such a loss too often. He now goes out to dine without outdoor shoes! [3]

as white as the shoulder of Pelops, which was made of ivory.

[3] *i.e.* barefoot.   He has in fact neither indoor nor outdoor shoes.

LXXXVIII

Tongilianus habet nasum, scio, non nego.[1]   sed iam
nil praeter nasum Tongilianus habet.

LXXXIX

Quod lana caput alligas, Charine,
non aures tibi sed dolent capilli.

XC

Pro sene, sed clare, votum Maro fecit amico,
  cui gravis et fervens hemitritaeos erat,
si Stygias aeger non esset missus ad umbras,
  ut caderet magno victima grata Iovi.
coeperunt certam medici spondere salutem.   5
  ne votum solvat nunc Maro vota facit.

XCI

Communis tibi cum viro, Magulla,
cum sit lectulus et sit exoletus,
quare, dic mihi, non sit et minister.
suspiras ; ratio est, times lagonam.

XCII

Saepe rogare soles qualis sim, Prisce, futurus,
  si fiam locuples simque repente potens.
quemquam posse putas mores narrare futuros ?
  dic mihi, si fias tu leo, qualis eris ?

  [1] *non nego* ⛬, *non ego* codd.

---

[1] He is all nose, *i.e.* critic and nothing else : *cf.* XIII. ii. 2.
[2] C. swathes his head really to conceal his baldness.

LXXXVIII

TONGILIANUS has a nose: I know, I don't deny it. But now Tongilianus has nothing but a nose.[1]

LXXXIX

You swathe your head in wool, Charinus; but it is not with your ears that it goes sadly, but with your hair.[2]

XC

FOR his old friend, ill of a severe and burning semi-tertian fever, Maro—and aloud [3]—made a vow that, if the sick man were not sent down to the Stygian shades, there should die a victim welcome to mighty Jove. The doctors begin to guarantee a certain recovery. Maro now makes vows not to pay his vow.

XCI

ALTHOUGH, Magulla, you have a couch, and have a concubine in common with your husband, tell me why you have not a cupbearer also. You sigh: the reason is, you fear the wine-cup.[4]

XCII

You are often wont to ask me what sort of person I should be, Priscus, if I became rich and were suddenly powerful. Do you think any man can declare his character in future? Tell me, if you became a lion, what sort of lion will you be?

---

[3] *i.e.* that it should be reported to the sick man (Maro was a *captator*) ; or perhaps this was his public vow, his real vow for the patient's death being under his breath : *cf.* Pers. ii. 8 ; Juv. xii. 98.   [4] *i.e.* poison.

XCIII

Qua moechum ratione basiaret
coram coniuge repperit Labulla.
parvum basiat usque morionem;
hunc multis rapit osculis madentem
moechus protinus et suis repletum   5
ridenti dominae statim remittit.
quanto morio maior est maritus!

XCIV

Scribebamus epos; coepisti scribere: cessi,
   aemula ne starent carmina nostra tuis.
transtulit ad tragicos se nostra Thalia cothurnos:
   aptasti longum tu quoque syrma tibi.
fila lyrae movi Calabris exculta Camenis: 5
   plectra rapis nobis, ambitiose, nova.
audemus saturas: Lucilius esse laboras.
   ludo levis elegos: tu quoque ludis idem.
quid minus esse potest? epigrammata fingere coepi:
   hinc etiam petitur iam mea palma tibi.   10
elige quid nolis (quis enim pudor omnia velle?)
   et si quid non vis, Tucca, relinque mihi.

XCV

Musaei pathicissimos libellos,
qui certant Sybariticis libellis,

---

[1] By Horace, who however was not born in Calabria: cf.
VIII. xviii. 5.
[2] The instrument with which the strings of the lyre were
struck.
[3] The father of Roman satire.

XCIII

LABULLA has discovered how to kiss her lover
in the presence of her husband. She gives repeated
kisses to her dwarf fool; this creature, slobbered
with many kisses, the lover at once pounces upon,
fills him up with his own kisses, and hands him back
to the smiling lady. How much bigger as a fool is
the husband!

XCIV

I WAS writing an epic; you began to write one:
I left off, that my poems should not stand in rivalry
with yours. My Thalia shifted to tragic buskins:
you also fitted on yourself the long train of tragedy.
I struck the strings of a lyre practised by the Calabrian Muses:[1] you, ambitious man, snatch from me
the new quill.[2] I venture satire: you strain to be
a Lucilius.[3] I sport with light elegies: you, too,
sport with the same thing. What lesser art can there
be? I begin to model epigrams: in this quarter, too,
my fame is already sought after by you. Pick out
something you do not want—for what modesty is
there in wanting everything?—and if there is anything you don't want, Tucca, leave it to me.

XCV

LEGGI, O Istantio Rufo, i paticissimi libelli di
Museo che garreggiano coi Sibaritici libelli,[4] e le

[4] By Hemitheon, "a Sybarite of the vilest character," and
the author of an obscene work, a text-book of vice, probably
called *Sybaritis*. He is called by Lucian ὁ κίναιδος (*adv. In-
doctum*, c. 23), and is probably alluded to by Ovid (*Trist.* ii.
417). If there the reading "nuper" be correct, H. flourished
not long before Ovid.

    et tinctas sale pruriente chartas
    Instanti lege Rufe; sed puella
    sit tecum tua, ne thalassionem   5
    indicas manibus libidinosis
    et fias sine femina maritus.

XCVI

Cum tibi nota tui sit vita fidesque mariti
    nec premat ulla tuos sollicitetve toros,
quid quasi paelicibus torqueris inepta ministris,
    in quibus et brevis est et fugitiva Venus?
plus tibi quam domino pueros praestare probabo: 5
    hi faciunt ut sis femina sola viro;
hi dant quod non vis uxor dare. "Do tamen" inquis
    "ne vagus a thalamis coniugis erret amor."
non eadem res est: Chiam volo, nolo mariscam:
    ne dubites quae sit Chia, marisca tua est.   10
scire suos fines matrona et femina debet:
    cede sua pueris, utere parte tua.

XCVII

    Uxor cum tibi sit puella qualem
    votis vix petat inprobus maritus,
    dives nobilis erudita casta,
    rumpis, Basse, latus, sed in comatis,
    uxoris tibi dote quos parasti.   5
    et sic ad dominam reversa languet
    multis mentula milibus redempta;
    sed nec vocibus excitata blandis,
    molli pollice nec rogata surgit.
    sit tandem pudor aut eamus in ius.   10
    non est haec tua, Basse: vendidisti.

carte asperse di sale solleticante; ma la tua ragazza sia teco, affinche tu non publici Talassione alle mani libidinose,[1] e diventi marito senza donna.

XCVI

Essendo la vita e la fedeltà del tuo marito a te nota, e veruna premendo o sollicitando il tuo talamo, a che, sciocca, ti tormenti tu dei servi come di concubine, coi quali il piacere di venere è breve e fuggitivo? Ti proverò che i ragazzi giovano più a te che al loro padrone: questi son la cagione che tu sola sii moglie al tuo marito; essi danno ciò che tu, come moglie, non vuoi dare. "Peraltro il do," di tu, "affinche l'amore non travii incostante dai talami conjugali." Non è la stessa cosa: voglio una Chia, non voglia una mariscka.[2] Affinche non dubbiti cosa sia una Chia, la tua è una Mariscka. Una matrona deve sapere i suoi limiti, ed una femina i suoi. Cedi ai ragazzi la loro parte: tu fa uso della tua.

XCVII

Ancorchè tua moglie sia una pulcella quale un' improbo marito appena dimandarebbe, ricca, nobile, erudita, casta, tu, O Basso, ti rompi i lati, ma in cincinnati, che ti procacciasti colla dote della tua moglie. E cosi la tua mentola, comparata con molti milliaja, sul ritorno alla padrona è fiacca; sì; nè eccitata con dolci parole, nè pregata con tenera mano, surge. Vergognati finalmente, o andiamo in judicio. Questa mentola non è tua, O Basso: tu l'hai venduto.[1]

[1] cf. IX. xli. [2] cf. VII. xxv. 7, 8.
[3] i.e. to your wife at the price of her dower.

XCVIII

BAETIS olivifera crinem redimite corona,
  aurea qui nitidis vellera tinguis aquis;
quem Bromius, quem Pallas amat; cui rector aquarum
  Albula navigerum per freta pandit iter:
ominibus laetis vestras Instantius oras   5
  intret, et hic populis ut prior annus eat.
non ignorat onus quod sit succedere Macro;
  qui sua metitur pondera, ferre potest.

---

[1] The Guadalquiver.   [2] cf. v. xxxvii. 7; IX. lxi. 3.
[3] Bacchus.   The province of Baetica abounds in wine and
oil.

XCVIII

BAETIS,[1] with thy hair wreathed with the olive
crown, that dippest thy golden [2] fleeces in sparkling
waters, whom Bromius,[3] whom Pallas loves, to whom
the king of waters, Albula,[4] opens a path that wafts
the ships over the seas, with glad omens may Instantius [5] first tread thy shores, and this year pass
for the peoples as the last. He is not blind to the
burthen of succeeding Macer: he that gauges his
load can bear it.

[4] An old name of the Tiber: Ov. *F.* ii. 389.
[5] Perhaps the same as is mentioned in VIII. lxxiii. 1 and
VIII. li. 21.

XCVIII

Bassa] with thy hair wreathed with the olive
crown, that dippest thy golden fleeces in sparkling
waters, whom Bromius, whom Pallas loves, to whom
the king of waters, Alburi, opens a path that walls
the ships over the seas, with glad omens may thy
sextile's flash lead thy shores, and this your pass
for the peoples as the last. He is not blind to the
burthen of succeeding Macer; he that gauges his
load can bear it.

An old name of the Tiber: Os. F. ii. 389.

whose the same as is mentioned in viii. lxviii. i and
viii. li. 5.

BOOK XIII

[LIBER TERTIUS DECIMUS]

XENIA

I

Ne toga cordylis et paenula desit olivis
  aut inopem metuat sordida blatta famem,
perdite Niliacas, Musae, mea damna, papyros:
  postulat ecce novos ebria bruma sales.
non mea magnanimo depugnat tessera telo,[1]   5
  senio nec nostrum cum cane quassat ebur:
haec mihi charta nuces, haec est mihi charta fritillus:
  alea nec damnum nec facit ista lucrum.

II

Nasutus sis usque licet, sis denique nasus,
  quantum noluerat ferre rogatus Atlans,
et possis ipsum tu deridere Latinum,
  non potes in nugas dicere plura meas
ipse ego quam dixi.   quid dentem dente iuvabit   5
  rodere?   carne opus est, si satur esse velis.

          [1] *talo βγ.*

---

[1] *i.e.* wrappers: *cf.* III. ii. 4; IV. lxxxvi. 8.
[2] Often used to gamble with, especially by boys: *cf.* V.
lxxxiv. 1.

BOOK XIII

GUEST-GIFTS

I

THAT tunny-fry may not lack a gown, and olives a capote,[1] nor the foul black beetle fear pinching hunger, destroy, ye Muses—the loss is mine—papyrus from the Nile: see tipsy winter calls for new pleasantries. No die of mine contends with dauntless weapon, nor does sice together with ace shake my ivory box: this paper is my nuts,[2] this paper is my dice-box; hazard that brings me no loss nor yet any gain.

II

ALTHOUGH you have always a critic's nose, are in a word a nose so great that Atlas[3] on request would not have consented to shoulder it, and though you can deride even Latinus[4] himself, you cannot say more against my trifling effusions than I have said myself. What pleasure is there in tooth gnawing tooth?[5] you require flesh if you want to be fat.

---

[3] Who bore the weight of heaven.
[4] A celebrated mime or comic actor: *cf.* IX. xxviii.
[5] *i.e.* something that can retort? Or (perhaps) "why gnaw something that cannot be hurt, like the viper in Aesop that gnawed a file?"

ne perdas operam, qui se mirantur, in illos
    virus habe ; nos haec novimus esse nihil.
non tamen hoc nimium nihil est, si candidus aure
    nec matutina si mihi fronte venis.   10

III

Omnis in hoc gracili xeniorum turba libello
    constabit nummis quattuor empta tibi.
quattuor est nimium ?   poterit constare duobus,
    et faciat lucrum bybliopola Tryphon.
haec licet hospitibus pro munere disticha mittas,   5
    si tibi tam rarus quam mihi nummus erit.
addita per titulos sua nomina rebus habebis :
    praetereas, si quid non facit ad stomachum.

IV.—*Tus*

Serus ut aetheriae Germanicus imperet aulae
    utque diu terris, da pia tura Iovi.

V.—*Piper*

Cerea quae patulo lucet ficedula lumbo,
    cum tibi sorte datur, si sapis, adde piper.

VI.—*Alica*

Nos alicam, poterit mulsum tibi mittere dives.
    si tibi noluerit mittere dives, emes.[1]

---

[1] *eme* γ.

---

[1] *i.e.* too sober.

Lest you should waste your time, keep your venom
for those that fancy themselves ; I know these efforts
of mine are nothing worth. And yet not altogether
nothing if you come to me with a just ear, and not
with a morning [1] aspect.

III

THE whole collection of Mottoes [2] in this slender
little volume will cost you to buy four sesterces. Is
four too much ? it can cost you two, and bookseller
Tryphon would make his profit. These distichs you
can send to your guests instead of a gift, if a coin
shall be as rare with you as with me. In addition
you will get the names of the things on the headings :
pass it by if anything is not to your stomach.

IV.—*Incense*

THAT it may be late ere Germanicus rule the
palace of Heaven, and that he may long rule earth,
give pious incense to Jove.

V.—*Pepper*

WHEN a beccafico, with its bright waxen flesh and
plump sides, falls to you by lot, if you have taste,
add pepper.

VI.—*Barley-water*

I CAN send you barley-water,[3] a rich man will be
able to send you mead. If the rich man be unwilling
to send it, you will buy.

[2] Lit. *Xenia* (gifts to guests). M. means here the headed
distichs, which were like the mottoes on Christmas crackers.
[3] A cheap drink : *cf.* XII. lxxxi. 3.

VII.—*Faba*

Si spumet rubra conchis tibi pallida testa,
  lautorum cenis saepe negare potes.

VIII.—*Far*

Inbue plebeias Clusinis pultibus ollas,
  ut satur in vacuis dulcia musta bibas.

IX.—*Lens*

Accipe Niliacam, Pelusia munera, lentem:
  vilior est alica, carior illa faba.

X.—*Simula*

Nec dotes simulae possis numerare nec usus,
  pistori totiens cum sit et apta coco.

XI.—*Hordeum*

Mulio quod non det tacituris, accipe, mulis.
  haec ego coponi, non tibi, dona dedi.

XII.—*Frumentum*

Ter centum Libyci modios de messe coloni
  sume, suburbanus ne moriatur ager.

---

[1] "You will get such a good dinner at home."
[2] Pulse was probably supposed to ripen new wine.
[3] Celebrated for its lentils: Verg. *Georg.* i. 228.

VII.—*Beans*

IF pale beans bubble for you in a red earthenware pot you can often decline the dinners of sumptuous hosts.[1]

VIII.—*Spelt*

FLAVOUR common jars with pulse from Clusium, that, after dinner, you may drink from them, when empty, new wine.[2]

IX.—*Lentils*

RECEIVE lentils of Nile, a present from Pelusium[3]; they are cheaper than spelt, dearer than beans.

X.—*Flour*

ONE cannot enumerate the properties or the uses of flour, seeing that it is so often handy for the baker and the cook.

XI.—*Barley*

RECEIVE something for your muleteer to withhold from your mules that will not blab. I have given this to the inn-keeper, not to you,[4] as a gift.

XII.—*Corn*

TAKE three hundred pecks from the harvest of the Libyan farmer, that your suburban land may not grow sterile.[5]

[4] The muleteer steals the barley and sells it to the inn-keeper.

[5] By being over-cropped, and not allowed to lie fallow. This gift of Libyan corn will maintain the farmer for a time.

XIII.—*Betae*

Ut sapiant fatuae, fabrorum prandia, betae,
 o quam saepe petet vina piperque cocus!

XIV.—*Lactucae*

Cludere quae cenas lactuca solebat avorum,
 dic mihi, cur nostras inchoat illa dapes?

XV.—*Ligna Acapna*

Si vicina tibi Nomento rura coluntur,
 ad villam moneo, rustice, ligna feras.

XVI.—*Rapa*

Haec tibi brumali gaudentia frigore rapa
 quae damus, in caelo Romulus esse solet.

XVII.—*Fascis Coliculi*

Ne tibi pallentes moveant fastidia caules,
 nitrata viridis brassica fiat aqua.

XVIII.—*Porri Sectivi*

Fila Tarentini graviter redolentia porri
 edisti quotiens, oscula clusa dato.

---

[1] *cf.* xi. lii. 5, where M. gives the reason.
[2] Situated in a marshy district, where the wood would be
wet and not smokeless. Wood was also made smokeless by
special treatment, viz. soaking in water and drying, or in
the lees of oil (Plin. *N.H.* xv. 8), or by scorching.
[3] The deified Romulus retains his simple tastes in Heaven:

XIII.—*Beet*

THAT insipid beet, the noon-meal of artizans, may acquire flavour, oh, how often will the cook ask for wine and pepper!

XIV.—*Lettuce*

TELL me, why is it that lettuce, which used to end our grandsires' dinners, ushers in[1] our banquets?

XV.—*Smokeless Wood*

IF you till fields near to me at Nomentum,[2] I remind you, rustic, to bring wood to my villa.

XVI.—*Rape*

THESE rapes, delighting in winter's cold, which I give you, in heaven Romulus is wont to eat.[3]

XVII.—*A Bundle of Cabbage Sprouts*

IN order that pale sprouts may not move your disgust, let the cabbage become green in water and soda.

XVIII.—*Cut Leeks*

As often as you have eaten the strong-smelling shoots[4] of Tarentine leeks, give kisses with shut mouth.

---

cf. Sen. *Apoc.* 9, where Hercules is of opinion that it is "to the interest of the state" that R. should have someone to "devour hot rape" with him, and therefore that the Emperor Claudius should be admitted as a God.

[4] *i.e. porrum sectivum: cf.* x. xlviii. 9. Nero ate them in oil to improve his voice: Plin. *N.H.* xix. 33.

THE EPIGRAMS OF MARTIAL

XIX.—*Porri Capitati*

MITTIT praecipuos nemoralis Aricia porros :
in niveo virides stipite cerne comas.

XX.—*Napi*

Hos Amiternus ager felicibus educat hortis :
Nursinas poteris parcius esse pilas.

XXI.—*Asparagi*

MOLLIS in aequorea quae crevit spina Ravenna
non erit incultis gratior asparagis.

XXII.—*Uvae Duracinae*

NON habilis cyathis et inutilis uva Lyaeo,
sed non potanti me tibi nectar ero.

XXIII.—*Ficus Chiae*

CHIA seni similis Baccho, quem Setia misit,
ipsa merum secum portat et ipsa salem.

---

¹ But, according to Pliny (*N.H.* xix. 33), the finest came
from Egypt, those from Ostia and Aricia ranking next.
² The navew is also called the French turnip (*Napus
brassica*), in Greek ῥάφυς or βουνιάς, and has a root elongated
like a carrot. It likes a sloping situation, and a light and
dry soil, whereas the ordinary rape thrives in the marsh :
Col. ii. 10. Amiternum was famed for them, and Nursia
came second: Plin. *N.H.* xix. 25.
³ Which often produced asparagus of three to the pound ;

XIX.—*Headed Leeks*

Woody Aricia sends the finest leeks[1]: observe on the white stem the green blades.

XX.—*Navews*

These the land of Amiternum nurtures in its fertile gardens; the round rapes of Nursia you will be able to eat at less cost.[2]

XXI.—*Asparagus*

The succulent stalk that has grown in watery Ravenna[3] will not be more palatable than wild asparagus.

XXII.—*Hard-skinned Grapes*

I am a grape unfit for the wine-cup and worthless to Lyaeus, but, if you do not drink me, I shall be nectar to you.[4]

XXIII.—*Chian Figs*

A Chian fig is like the old wine Setia has sent you; it carries in itself new wine, and in itself salt too.[5]

Pliny, *N.H.* xix. 19 (2). According to Athenaeus (ii. 62) the planted asparagus grew to a great size, but the best were not the cultivated. The wild was called *corruda* : Plin. *supra*.

[4] These grapes were kept to be eaten, and not turned into wine. They were when eaten seemingly very palatable. The temperate Augustus speaks of himself (Suet. *Aug.* lxxvi). as eating in his litter an ounce of bread and a few *duracinae*.

[5] The Chian fig was not only pungent (*cf.* VII. xxv. 8), but also juicy.

XXIV.—*Cydonea*

Si tibi Cecropio saturata Cydonea melle
  ponentur, dicas : " Haec melimela placent."

XXV.—*Nuces Pineae*

Poma sumus Cybeles : procul hinc discede, viator,
  ne cadat in miserum nostra ruina caput.

XXVI.—*Sorba*

Sorba sumus, molles nimium tendentia ventres :
  aptius haec puero quam tibi poma dabis.

XXVII.—*Petalium* [1] *Caryotarum*

Aurea porrigitur Iani caryota Kalendis ;
  sed tamen hoc munus pauperis esse solet.

XXVIII.—*Vas Cottanorum*

Haec tibi quae torta venerunt condita meta,
  si maiora forent cottana, ficus erat.

XXIX.—*Vas Damascenorum*

Pruna peregrinae carie rugosa senectae
  sume : solent duri solvere ventris onus.

---

[1] *petadium* β, *petavivum* T, *palathion* Salmasius.

---

[1] As recommended by Pliny (*N.H.* xv. 18 (2)).

[2] Because she turned her favourite Attis into a fir, which
thus became sacred to her.

[3] *i.e. cinaedo.* Pliny (*N.H.* xxiii. 73) says the dried berries
were astringent. Wine was sometimes made of them : Verg.
Georg. iii. 379.

BOOK XIII. xxiv–xxix

XXIV.—*Quinces*

IF quinces steeped in Attic honey[1] shall be put before you, you would say: "These honey-apples are delicious."

XXV.—*Pine Cones*

WE are Cybele's apples[2]; depart far hence, traveller, lest our downfall descend on your wretched head.

XXVI.—*Service Berries*

WE are service berries that astrict too relaxed bowels; you will better give these apples to your boy[3] than to yourself.

XXVII.—*A Stem with Dates*

A GILT date is offered on the kalends of January[4]; but yet this is wont to be the gift of a poor man.

XXVIII.—*A Jar of small Syrian Figs*

THESE Syrian figs, which, stored in a round conical jar, have reached you, would, if larger,[5] be figs.

XXIX.—*A Jar of Damascene Plums*

TAKE plums wrinkled by shrivelling old age abroad[6]: they are used to lighten the load of an obstinate stomach.

[4] By poor clients to their patrons: *cf.* VIII. xxxiii. 11, 12.
[5] *Cottana* were *small* figs from Syria: Plin. *N.H.* xiii. 10; *cf.* IV. lxxxviii. 6 and VII. liii. 7.
[6] *cf.* v. xviii. 8. Pliny (*N.H.* xv. 12) says that D. plums grown in Italy did not shrivel for lack of sun.

XXX.—*Caseus Lunensis*

Caseus Etruscae signatus imagine Lunae
praestabit pueris prandia mille tuis.

XXXI.—*Caseus Vestinus*

Si sine carne voles ientacula sumere frugi,
haec tibi Vestino de grege massa venit.

XXXII.—*Caseus Fumosus*

Non quemcumque focum nec fumum caseus omnem,
sed Velabrensem qui bibit, ille sapit.

XXXIII.—*Casei Trebulani*

Trebula nos genuit; commendat gratia duplex,
sive levi flamma sive domamur aqua.

XXXIV.—*Bulbi*

Cum sit anus coniunx et sint tibi mortua membra,
nil aliud bulbis quam satur esse potes.

XXXV.—*Lucanicae*

Filia Picenae venio Lucanica porcae:
pultibus hinc niveis grata corona datur.

---

¹ Cheeses were made very large at Luna: Plin. *N.H.* xi.
97, who says they were made of a thousand pounds' weight.
² Vestinian cheese was a favourite with the Romans. The
Vestini were in central Italy, between the Apennines and
the Adriatic.
³ A district of Rome on the W. slope of the Palatine.
Cheeses were smoked here to improve their flavour.
⁴ A town in the Sabine country: *cf.* v. lxxi. 1. The

XXX.—*Cheese from Luna*

CHEESE, stamped with the crest of Etruscan Luna, will afford your slaves a thousand lunches.[1]

XXXI.—*A Vestinian Cheese*

IF you wish without meat to take a frugal breakfast, this lump comes to you from a Vestinian[2] flock.

XXXII.—*Smoked Cheese*

It is not every heat, or every smoke that a cheese imbibes; but that which has imbibed Velabran[3] has flavour.

XXXIII.—*Cheese from Trebula*

TREBULA[4] gave us birth; a double excellence recommends us; we are tamed by a moderate fire or by water.

XXXIV.—*Bulbs*

SINCE your wife is an old woman, and your members are nerveless, you can do nothing but satisfy your hunger with bulbs.[5]

XXXV.—*Lucanian Sausages*

DAUGHTER of a Picenian sow,[6] here I come, a Lucanian sausage; with me you may put a toothsome garnish round white pottage.

cheese was good to eat, whether toasted, or moistened in water.

[5] Bulbs were eaten as aphrodisiacs: *cf.* III. lxxv. 3; Athen. ii. 64.

[6] *cf.* IV. xlvi. 8; v. lxxviii. 9. According to Apicius (ii. 4) the sausage was compounded of minced pork flavoured with pepper, cumin, savory, rue, parsley, and bay-leaves. It was called in Low Latin *salsicia*, whence the word sausage.

XXXVI.—*Cistella Olivarum*

HAEC quae Picenis venit subducta trapetis
inchoat atque eadem finit oliva dapes.

XXXVII.—*Mala Citrea*

AUT Corcyraei sunt haec de frondibus horti,
aut haec Massyli poma draconis erant.

XXXVIII.—*Colustrum*

SUBRIPUIT pastor quae nondum stantibus haedis
de primo matrum lacte colustra damus.

XXXIX.—*Haedus*

LASCIVUM pecus et viridi non utile Baccho
det poenas; nocuit iam tener ille deo.

XL.—*Ova*

CANDIDA si croceos circumfluit unda vitellos,
Hesperius scombri temperet ova liquor.

XLI.—*Porcellus Lactans*

LACTE mero pastum pigrae mihi matris alumnum
ponat, et Aetolo de sue dives edat.

---

[1] *cf.* I. xliii. 8.
[2] They were either from King Alcinous' garden: *cf.* x.
xciv. 2, or were golden apples of the Hesperides.
[3] The first milk given by the mother: Plin. *N. H.* xxviii. 33.

XXXVI.—*A Small Box of Olives*

THESE olives which have reached you, withdrawn from the oil presses of Picenum,[1] begin and also end our repasts.

XXXVII.—*Citrons*

THESE were either from the branches of Corcyra's garden, or they were apples, the Massylian dragon's charge.[2]

XXXVIII.—*Beestings*

BEESTINGS,[3] whereof the shepherd has robbed the kids while not yet able to stand, I give you from the first milk of the dams.

XXXIX.—*A Kid*

LET the wanton beast, and one of no service to the green vine, pay the penalty; though young, it has already injured the god.[4]

XL.—*Eggs*

IF a white liquid surround the saffron-coloured yolks, let the sauce[5] of Spanish mackerel season the eggs.

XLI.—*A Sucking Pig*

LET a rich man set before me the nursling, fed on milk alone, of a lazy mother, and let him eat of an Aetolian boar.[6]

[4] Bacchus. The kid has nibbled the vine. In *Anth. Pal.* x. 75 and 79 the wounded vine retorts. The goat was a victim sacred to Bacchus. [5] *i.e. garum*: *cf.* XIII. cii.
[6] Like that slain by Meleager: *cf.* VII. xxvii. 2.

XLII.—*Apyrina et Tubures*

Non tibi de Libycis tubures et apyrina ramis,
de Nomentanis sed damus arboribus.

XLIII.—*Idem*

Lecta suburbanis mittuntur apyrina ramis
et vernae tubures.   quid tibi cum Libycis?

XLIV.—*Sumen*

Esse putes nondum sumen; sic ubere largo
et fluit [1] et vivo lacte papilla tumet.

XLV.—*Pulli Gallinacei*

Si Libycae nobis volucres et Phasides essent,
acciperes, at nunc accipe chortis aves.

XLVI.—*Persica Praecocia* [2]

Vilia maternis fueramus Persica ramis:
nunc in adoptivis Persica cara sumus.

---

[1] *effluet* βγ.   [2] *praecocta* α, *praecoqua* γ.

---

[1] According to Pliny (*N.H.* xv. 14) a kind of African apple,
or rather berry, of two kinds, one white, the other red.   At
Verona grew a variety called *lanata* from having a down like
a peach.

[2] Pliny says (*N.H.* xv. 14) the tuber-apple was introduced
into Italy by Sextus Papinius, "*quem consulem vidimus*,"
i.e. comparatively recently.   Suetonius (*Dom.* xvi.) tells a

XLII.—*Pomegranates and Tuber-apples*

I DO not give you tuber-apples[1] and pomegranates from Libyan boughs, but from my Nomentan trees.

XLIII.—*The Same*

CULLED from suburban boughs are sent you pomegranates and home-grown tuber-apples.[2] What do you want with Libyans?

XLIV.—*Son's Paps*

YOU would think it not yet a dish of udder, so full-flowing is the dug, and so does the pap swell with living milk.[3]

XLV.—*Fowls*

IF I possessed guinea-fowls and pheasants you should receive them; but now receive the birds of the farmyard.

XLVI.—*Early Peaches*

OF little worth should we peaches have been on the branches of our mother tree; now on adoptive boughs we peaches are prized.[4]

story how Domitian on the day before his murder, being offered some tuber-apples, commanded their being kept for the morrow, " *si modo uti licuerit.*"

[3] The thing sent is apparently the udder cooked, which is so full of milk it seems alive.

[4] Friedländer explains of peaches grafted on an apricot (*malum praecox*) tree; *cf.* Calp. ii. 42, of peaches grafted on a plum tree.

XLVII.—*Panes Picentini*

PICENTINA Ceres niveo sic nectare crescit
ut levis accepta spongea turget aqua.

XLVIII.—*Boleti*

ARGENTUM atque aurum facilest laenamque togamque
mittere; boletos mittere difficilest.

XLIX.—*Ficedulae*

CUM me ficus alat, cum pascar dulcibus uvis,
cur potius nomen non dedit uva mihi?

L.—*Terrae Tubera*

RUMPIMUS altricem tenero quae vertice terram
tubera, boletis poma secunda sumus.

LI.—*Turdorum Decuria*

TEXTA rosis fortasse tibi vel divite nardo,
at mihi de turdis facta corona placet.

LII.—*Anates*

TOTA quidem ponatur anas, sed pectore tantum
et cervice sapit: cetera redde coco.

---

¹ According to Pliny (*N.H.* xviii. 27) Picenian bread was
made of spelt (*alica*), steeped for nine days, then mixed with
raisin juice, and kneaded into the shape of a spool of wool
(*in speciem tractae*), and then baked. He adds that it was
not fit to eat till it had been moistened with milk mixed with
honey (*mulsum*).

² Either because they grow only at certain seasons (Friedländer), or because they are so precious that one prefers to
eat them oneself.

XLVII.—*Picenian Loaves*

THE bread of Picenum grows big with its white nectar as a light sponge swells when it has taken in water.[1]

XLVIII.—*Mushrooms*

SILVER and gold, and a mantle, and a toga it is easy to send; to send mushrooms is difficult.[2]

XLIX.—*Beccaficos*

SEEING that figs nourish me, seeing that I am fed on sweet grapes, why did not the grape rather give me my name?[3]

L.—*Truffles*

WE truffles[4] that burst through the nurturing soil with our soft heads are of earth's apples second to mushrooms.

LI.—*A Decade of Fieldfares*

A CIRCLET woven of roses or rich spikenard perhaps pleases you, but one made of fieldfares[5] pleases me.

LII.—*Ducks*

LET a duck certainly be served up whole; but it is tasty only in the breast and neck: the rest return to the cook.

[3] "Why am I not called *uvedula*?"

[4] In Greek ὕδνα. See Athen. ii. 60 and Plin. xix. 11. They grow of their own accord, particularly in dry and sandy soil. Pliny calls them "callosities of the earth" (*terrae callum*). Juvenal (v. 115) refers to the fable (rejected by Plutarch: *Quaest. Conv.* iv. 2) that truffles were produced by thunderstorms.

[5] Fieldfares were often strung round a hoop: *cf.* III. xlvii. 10.

LIII.—*Turtures*

Cum pinguis mihi turtur erit, lactuca, valebis;
  et cocleas tibi habe.   perdere nolo famem.

LIV.—*Perna*

Cerretana mihi fiat vel missa licebit
  de Menapis : lauti de petasone vorent.

LV.—*Petaso*

Musteus est: propera, caros nec differ amicos.
  nam mihi cum vetulo sit petasone nihil.

LVI.—*Volva*

Te fortasse magis capiat de virgine porca;
  me materna gravi de sue volva capit.

LVII.—*Colocasia*

Niliacum ridebis holus lanasque sequaces,
  inproba cum morsu fila manuque trahes.

LVIII.—*Iecur Anserinum*

Aspice quam tumeat magno iecur ansere maius !
  miratus dices " Hoc, rogo, crevit ubi ? "

---

¹ By eating the lettuce and snails at the *gustatio*.
² Spanish.   The Cerritani were a people in the Pyrenees, celebrated for bacon.
³ A people on the left bank of the Rhine, near its mouth.
⁴ *cf.* vii. xx. 11.   There is a long dissertation on the subject in Ath. iii. 57 *seqq.*
⁵ *cf.* viii. xxxiii. 13. Pliny (*N.H.* xxi. 51) says it is " caule

LIII.—*Turtle-doves*

WHEN I shall have a fat turtle-dove, good-bye, lettuce; and keep the snails for yourself. I don't want to spoil my appetite.[1]

LIV.—*Gammon of Bacon*

LET me have Cerretanian[2] gammon served to me, or it may be sent from the Menapians[3]; let gourmets devour ham.

LV.—*Ham*

IT is freshly cured: make haste, and do not put off your dear friends; for let me have nothing to do with an old ham.

LVI.—*Womb*

YOU perhaps the womb of a virgin pig may allure more: the maternal womb of a pregnant sow allures me.[4]

LVII.—*Egyptian Beans*

YOU will scoff at this vegetable from Nile and its tenacious threads when with teeth and hands you draw out its stubborn fibres.[5]

LVIII.—*Goose's Liver*

SEE how the liver is swollen bigger than a big goose! In wonder you will say: "Where, I ask, did this grow?"[6]

araneoso in mandendo," *i.e.* like spider's webs. Athenaeus (iii. 2) gives a long description of it from Theophrastus.

[6] Geese were fattened on figs by gourmets: Hor. *Sat.* II. viii. 88; and their livers grew to a great size: Juv. v. 114. See generally Athen. ix. 32. The practice is recalled by the word *fegato,* Italian for liver.

THE EPIGRAMS OF MARTIAL

LIX.—*Glires*

Tota mihi dormitur hiemps et pinguior illo
 tempore sum quo me nil nisi somnus alit.

LX.—*Cuniculi*

Gaudet in effossis habitare cuniculus antris.
 monstravit tacitas hostibus ille vias.

LXI.—*Attagenae*

Inter sapores fertur alitum primus
 Ionicarum gustus attagenarum.

LXII.—*Gallinae Altiles*

Pascitur et dulci facilis gallina farina,
 pascitur et tenebris.   ingeniosa gula est.

LXIII.—*Capones*

Ne nimis exhausto macresceret inguine gallus,
 amisit testes.   nunc mihi Gallus erit.

LXIV.—*Idem*

Succumbit sterili frustra gallina marito.
 hunc matris Cybeles esse decebat avem.

---

[1] *cf.* III. lviii. 36.   Dormice were kept in pens (*gliraria*),
and, for purposes of fattening, even in casks : Varr. *R.R.* iii.
15.   They were fattened on beech-nuts : Plin. *N.H.* xvi. 7.

[2] *Cuniculus* is also a military term for a mine.

[3] So, according to Pliny, *N.H.* x. lxviii., who says the
attagen was formerly a rare bird, but in his day was found
in Gaul and Spain and in the Alps.

LIX.—*Dormice*

ALL my winter is passed in sleep, and I am fatter at that season during which nothing but sleep nourishes me.[1]

LX.—*Rabbits*

A RABBIT delights in dwelling in burrowed holes: he taught foes the art of secret paths.[2]

LXI.—*Heathcocks*

OF all flavours of fowls the most tasty is said to be that of Ionian[3] heathcocks.

LXII.—*Fatted Fowls*

THE hen is easily fattened on sweetened meal; it fattens, too, on the dark.[4] Ingenious is gluttony!

LXIII.—*Capons*

THAT the cock might not grow thin by over indulgence, he has been gelded. Now he will be to me a Gaul.[5]

LXIV.—*The Same*

IN vain the hen submits to her sterile husband. This bird it beseemed to have been the bird of Mother Cybele.[6]

[4] *Ut immotae facile pinguescant, in obscuro continentur:* Sen. *Ep.* cxxii. 4.
[5] M. plays on the meanings of *gallus*, viz. a cock, a Gaul, or a priest of Cybele. See next epigram.
[6] Whose priests were called Galli: cf. II. xlv. 2; VIII. lxxv. 16.

LXV.—*Perdices*

PONITUR Ausoniis avis haec rarissima mensis:
hanc in piscina ludere saepe soles.

LXVI.—*Columbinae*

NE violes teneras periuro dente columbas,
tradita si Gnidiae sunt tibi sacra deae.

LXVII.—*Palumbi*

INGUINA torquati tardant hebetantque palumbi:
non edat hanc volucrem qui cupit esse salax.

LXVIII.—*Galbuli*

GALBINA [1] decipitur calamis et retibus ales,
turget adhuc viridi cum rudis uva mero.

LXIX.—*Cattae*

PANNONICAS nobis numquam dedit Umbria cattas:
mavult haec domino [2] mittere dona Pudens.

LXX.—*Pavones*

MIRARIS, quotiens gemmantis explicat alas.
et potes hunc saevo tradere, dure, coco?

[1] *Galbula* γ.   [2] *dominae* β.

---

[1] No explanation of this epigram is known.
[2] Doves were sacred to Venus.
[3] The identity of the bird, here called witwall, is very
obscure. It is generally supposed to be the same as the
ἴκτερος, or *vireo*, and has been variously identified with the

LXV.—*Partridges*

THIS bird is very rarely served on Italian tables:
one often sees it playing in the fishpond.[1]

LXVI.—*Doves*

Do not violate with profane tooth tender doves,
if the rites of the goddess of Cnidos[2] have been
entrusted to you.

LXVII.—*Wood-pigeons*

RINGDOVES check and blunt the manly powers: let
not him eat this bird who wishes to be lickerish.

LXVIII.—*Witwalls*

THE green bird[3] is beguiled by canes[4] and nets at
the season when the young grape is swelling with
juice yet immature.

LXIX.—*Cattae*

UMBRIA has never supplied us with Pannonian
cattae; these are the gifts Pudens prefers to send
to his lord.[5]

LXX.—*Peacocks*

DOST thou admire it, oft as it spreads its spangled
wings, and hast the heart, unfeeling man, to deliver
this bird to a cruel cook?

golden oriole (*O. galbula*), the greenfinch, and the green
woodpecker.

[4] Limed canes: *cf.* IX. liv. 3 ; XIV. ccxviii.

[5] P., who came from Umbria, preferred to send these birds,
which he had reared in Umbria, as a present to his patron,
rather than birds of his native country. The *catta* is
unknown.

415

LXXI.—*Phoenicopteri*

Dat mihi pinna rubens nomen, sed lingua gulosis
   nostra sapit. quid si garrula lingua foret?

LXXII.—*Phasiani*

Argoa primum sum transportata carina:
   ante mihi notum nil nisi Phasis erat.

LXXIII.—*Numidicae*

Ansere Romano quamvis satur Hannibal esset,
   ipse suas numquam barbarus edit aves.

LXXIV.—*Anseres*

Haec servavit avis Tarpeia templa Tonantis.
   miraris? nondum fecerat illa deus.

LXXV.—*Grues*

Turbabis versus nec littera tota volabit,
   unam perdideris si Palamedis avem.

LXXVI.—*Rusticulae*

Rustica sim an perdix quid refert, si sapor idem est?
   carior est perdix. sic sapit illa magis.

---

[1] This may be an allusion to Aesopus, the tragic actor, who
served up a dish consisting only of singing birds: Plin. *N.H.*
x. 72. Housman, however, thinks that *garrula* = telltale,
and that the bird could say how impure the mouths were
that fed on it.

[2] A river of the Colchians from which the Argonauts are
said to have brought the pheasant (the Phasian bird).

[3] Because luxury had not at that time introduced them
into Italy. As to *Numidicae*, *cf.* iii. lviii. 15.

LXXI.—*Flamingoes*

My ruddy wing gives me a name, but my tongue
is a delicacy to gluttons. What if my tongue were
to speak ? [1]

LXXII.—*Pheasants*

I was transported first by Argo's keel; ere that
Phasis [2] was all I knew.

LXXIII.—*Guinea-fowls*

Although Hannibal ate his fill of Roman geese,
yet the barbarian never ate the birds of his own
land. [3]

LXXIV.—*Geese*

This bird saved the Thunderer's Tarpeian fane.
Do you wonder? a god had not yet built it. [4]

LXXV.—*Cranes*

You will disorder the lines, and the letter will not
fly complete if you make away with a single bird of
Palamedes. [5]

LXXVI.—*Woodcock*

Whether I am woodcock or partridge, what does
it matter if the flavour be the same? A partridge
is dearer. 'Tis thus it has better flavour. [6]

[4] The cackling of geese saved the Capitol B.C. 390 from a
night attack by the Gauls. Now it can run no risk. Domitian rebuilt the Temple of Jupiter Capitolinus, which had
been twice burnt : Suet. *Dom.* v ; IX. iii. 7.

[5] P. is said to have copied the shape of the letters he invented from the order of the flight of cranes. In IX. xiii. 7
the letter is $\Upsilon = V$. M. is probably playing on two meanings
of *versus* (line). See also Luc. v. 716, which M. had in mind.

[6] cf. *Magis illa juvant quae pluris emuntur*, Juv. xi. 16.

LXXVII.—*Cycni*

Dulcia defecta modulatur carmina lingua
cantator cycnus funeris ipse sui.

LXXVIII.—*Porphyriones*

Nomen habet magni volucris tam parva gigantis?
et nomen prasini Porphyrionis habet.

LXXIX.—*Mulli Vivi*

Spirat in advecto sed iam piger aequore mullus
languescit. vivum da mare : fortis erit.

LXXX.—*Muraenae*

Quae natat in Siculo grandis muraena profundo,
non valet exustam mergere sole cutem.

LXXXI.—*Rhombi*

Quamvis lata gerat patella rhombum,
rhombus latior est tamen patella.

---

¹ According to Aristotle (Athen. ix. 49), "εἰσὶν ᾠδικοὶ καὶ
μάλιστα περὶ τὰς τελευτάς." Plin. (*N.H.* x. 32) denies it.
² The porphyrion is unknown. It was a bird with a long
and narrow neck, and long legs. The beak and legs were
red. So Pliny, *N.H.* x. lxiii. and xi. lxxix. It is distinguished from the pelican in Arist. *Av.* 881. According to
Athen. (ix. 40) it came from Libya, and was also a domestic
bird.
³ P. one of the giants who made war on the gods : Hor.
Od. iii. iv. 54.
⁴ A charioteer of the Green faction of the Circus.

LXXVII.—*Swans*

THE swan gives forth its sweet measured song with failing tongue, itself the minstrel of its own death.[1]

LXXVIII.—*Porphyrions*

HAS so small a bird[2] the name of a great giant ? It has, too, the name of Porphyrion[3] of the Green.[4]

LXXIX.—*Live Mullets*

THE mullet breathes in the sea-water brought with him, but, already torpid, he begins to languish. Give him the fresh sea ; he will be strong.[5]

LXXX.—*Lampreys*

THE big lamprey that swims in the Sicilian deep sea has not the strength to plunge when its skin is scorched by the sun.[6]

LXXXI.—*Turbots*

HOWEVER wide is the dish that bears the turbot, yet the turbot is wider than the dish.

[5] According to Friedländer fish were brought alive to table in glass vessels and boiled before the eyes of the guests, who observed the changing hues of the dying fish : *cf.* Sen. *Quaest.* iii. 17, who observes that it sounds like a fable that the eyes were fed before the throat.

[6] According to Arist. (*H.A.* VIII. iii. 4) turtles, when their shells were scorched by the sun, were unable to sink, and so were caught ; see also Plin. *N.H.* ix. 12. M. says the same thing of the lamprey. Such animals were called πλῶται or *flutae* : Macrob. *Sat.* iii. 15. The best lampreys came from the Straits of Messena : *ibid.*

LXXXII.—*Ostrea*

EBRIA Baiano modo veni concha Lucrino:
nobile nunc sitio luxuriosa garum.

LXXXIII.—*Squillae*

CAERULEUS nos Liris amat, quem silva Maricae
protegit: hinc squillae maxima turba sumus.

LXXXIV.—*Scarus*

HIC scarus, aequoreis qui venit adesus ab undis,
visceribus bonus est, cetera vile sapit.

LXXXV.—*Coracinus*

PRINCEPS Niliaci raperis, coracine, macelli:
Pellaeae prior est gloria nulla gulae.

LXXXVI.—*Echini*

ISTE licet digitos testudine pungat acuta,
cortice deposita mollis echinus erit.

---

¹ Which produced the finest oysters: *cf.* III. lx. 3;
Macrob. *Sat.* iii. 15.   ² *Garum* : *cf.* XIV. cii.
³ A river in Campania near Minturnae. Marica was its
tutelary nymph who had a grove near it: Hor. *Od.* III.
xvii. 7.
⁴ The *scarus* is really unknown. It was a favourite fish,
brought originally, according to Pliny (*N.H.* ix. 29), by
Tiberius from the Carpathian Sea, and planted by Optatus,
praefectus classis, in the sea between Ostia and Campania.
It was preserved for the first five years. Athenaeus (vii. 113)
gives a description.

LXXXII.—*Oysters*

DRUNKEN with the water of Baiae's Lucrine,[1] have I, a shell-fish, just arrived. Now, luxurious that I am, I thirst for the noble pickle.[2]

LXXXIII.—*Prawns*

CERULEAN Liris,[3] which Marica's wood guards, is fond of us: from hence we prawns come in greatest numbers.

LXXXIV.—*Sea-bream*

OF this sea-bream,[4] which has come lean from the sea-waves, the entrails are good eating; as to the rest it has poor flavour.

LXXXV.—*Coracinus*

YOU of all fish are scrambled for, Coracinus,[5] in the markets of Nile; to Alexandria's gourmets no fish has renown surpassing yours.

LXXXVI.—*Sea-urchins*

ALTHOUGH that sea-urchin may prick your fingers with its sharp shell, yet, when it lays aside its husk, it will be soft.[6]

[5] An unknown but valued fish peculiar to the Nile: Plin. *N.H* xxxii. 19, who says it was not caught in winter except on the same few days: *N.H.* ix. 24. See also Athen. vii. 81, who says it was so called from its continually moving the pupils of its eyes (κόραι). It was regarded as in every way superior to the *mullus* : Athen. iii. 93.

[6] It was eaten with vinegar and honey sauce, parsley, and mint : Athen. iii. 41. Athenaeus (*loc. cit.*) tells the story of a Spartan who at a dinner bit a sea-urchin, shell and all, in ignorance and cursed the viand (φάγημα μιαρὸν), adding he would not be beaten by it, but would never eat another.

THE EPIGRAMS OF MARTIAL

LXXXVII.—*Murices*

Sanguine de nostro tinctas, ingrate, lacernas
induis, et non est hoc satis : esca sumus.

LXXXVIII.—*Gobii*

In Venetis sint lauta licet convivia terris,
principium cenae gobius esse solet.

LXXXIX.—*Lupus*

Laneus Euganei lupus excipit ora Timavi,
aequoreo dulces cum sale pastus aquas.

XC.—*Aurata*

Non omnis laudes pretiumque aurata meretur,
sed cui solus erit concha Lucrina cibus.

XCI.—*Acipensis*

Ad Palatinas acipensem mittite mensas :
ambrosias ornent munera rara dapes.

---

¹ *cf.* v. xxiii. 5.   Pliny (ix. 60) says that luxury had made
the fish as precious as pearls.   Travellers speak of a hill still
standing at Tarentum of the debris of the *murex*.
² *cf.* Col. viii. 16 ; Hor. *Sat.* II. iv. 32.
³ A small fish, ordinarily little esteemed, but common in
the lagoons of Venice.   Inferior to a blenny : Diog. L. ii. 67.
Juv. (xi. 37) treats the price of a *gobius* as an insignificant
sum, as compared with the price of a *mullus*.
⁴ The most prized *lupi* were called *lanati* or *lanei* from the
whiteness and softness of their flesh : Plin. *N.H.* ix. 28.
The *lupus* may have been the bass, one name of which is the
sea-wolf, from its rapaciousness (Grk. λάβραξ); *cf.* the proverb
λάβραχες Μιλήσιοι of greedy persons ; and generally Athen.
vii. 86.

LXXXVII.—*Purple Mussels*

CLOAKS dyed in our blood,[1] ingrate, you put on;
and this is not enough : we are your food.[2]

LXXXVIII.—*Gudgeons*

IN Venetian territory, however choice may be the
entertainment, the beginning of the dinner is wont
to be a gudgeon.[3]

LXXXIX.—*The Bass*

SOFT and white[4] the bass breasts the mouths of
Euganean Timavus,[5] fed on fresh water and the salt
of the sea.

XC.—*The Gilthead*

NOT every gilthead[6] deserves praise and a big
price, but the one that feeds only on Lucrine shell-
fish.

XCI.—*The Sturgeon*

SEND sturgeon to Palatine tables ; let rare offering adorn ambrosial[8] feasts.

[5] A river, now the Timavo, forming the boundary of
Istria and Venetia and falling into the Adriatic.

[6] The same as the Greek χρύσοφρυς (the zoological name of
which is *Chrysophrys aurata*), and probably not the John
Dory, the name of which is *Zeus faber*. It feeds on molluscs.

[7] According to Pliny (*N.H.* ix. 27) the fish, though rare,
was little esteemed in his time.

[8] *i.e.* of the emperor. M. anticipates the English common
law whereby " whales and sturgeons are royal fish, and
belong to the King by his prerogative " : 7 *Coke's Reports*,
16 A. Macrob. (*Sat.* iii. 16) says that, at a banquet of the
Emperor Septimius Severus, the fish was ushered in by
crowned attendants to the sound of flutes, *quasi numinis
pompa.*

XCII.—*Lepores*

INTER aves turdus, si quid me iudice certum est,
inter quadripedes mattea prima lepus.

XCIII.—*Aper*

QUI Diomedeis metuendus saetiger agris
Aetola cecidit cuspide, talis erat.

XCIV.—*Dammae*

DENTE timetur aper, defendunt cornua cervum:
inbelles dammae quid nisi praeda sumus?

XCV.—*Oryx*

MATUTINARUM non ultima praeda ferarum
saevos oryx constat quot mihi morte canum!

XCVI.—*Cervus*

HIC erat ille tuo domitus, Cyparisse, capistro.
an magis iste tuus, Silvia, cervus erat?

XCVII.—*Lalisio*

DUM tener est onager solaque lalisio matre
pascitur, hoc infans sed breve nomen habet.

---

¹ Meleager's, who slew the Calydonian boar: *cf.* IX.
xlviii. 6; XI. lxix. 10. ² *cf.* VIII. lxvii. 4.
³ A one-horned, cloven-hoofed animal, not unlike a wild
goat: Plin. *N.H.* xi. 106. It was a ferocious animal, and
came from Gaetulia: Opp. *De Ven.* ii. 445. Its flesh was
esteemed by rich epicures: Juv. xi. 140.
⁴ C., having by accident shot his favourite stag, prayed
the gods to grant him perpetual grief, and was turned into a
cypress, the symbol of mourning: Ov. *Met.* x. 109 *et seqq.*

XCII.—*Hares*

Amongst birds the fieldfare, if my judgment can aught decide, amongst quadrupeds the primest delicacy is a hare.

XCIII.—*A Boar*

The terror in the land of Diomedes, the bristly beast that fell beneath an Aetolian spear,[1] was such as this.

XCIV.—*Does*

For his tusk is the boar dreaded, his horns defend the stag; we, unwarlike does, what are we but a prey?

XCV.—*The Oryx*

Not the meanest quarry among the beasts of morning shows,[2] the savage oryx [3] costs me the death of how many dogs!

XCVI.—*The Stag*

Was this the stag tamed by your halter, Cyparissus,[4] or rather was it your stag, Silvia[5]?

XCVII.—*The Milk-foal of the Wild Ass*

While he is a young wild ass, and is fed by his mother alone, the lalisio [6] has, as a nursling, this name, but one short-lived.[7]

---

[5] Silvia was the daughter of Tyrrheus, the huntsman of King Latinus. Ascanius, the son of Aeneas, shot her favourite stag, and thus brought about the war between the Trojans and the Latins : *cf.* Verg. *Aen.* vii. 483 *et seqq.*

[6] Pliny (*N.H.* viii. 69) says that the flesh of the *lalisio* was much appreciated.

[7] When weaned it is called a wild ass.

XCVIII.—*Caprea*

PENDENTEM summa capream de rupe videbis:
casuram speres; despicit illa canes.

XCIX.—*Dorcas*

DELICIUM parvo donabis dorcada nato:
iactatis solet hanc mittere turba togis.

C.—*Onager*

PULCHER adest onager: mitti venatio debet
dentis Erythraei: iam removete sinus.

CI.—*Oleum Venaɟrum*

Hoc tibi Campani sudavit baca Venafri:
unguentum quotiens sumis, et istud olet.

CII.—*Garum Sociorum*

EXPIRANTIS adhuc scombri de sanguine primo
accipe fastosum, munera cara, garum.

CIII.—*Amphora Muriae*

ANTIPOLITANI, fateor, sum filia thynni:
essem si scombri, non tibi missa forem.

---

¹ Perhaps a reminiscence of Verg. *Ecl.* i. 76.
² *i.e.* in the Amphitheatre.
³ It is no use to supplicate for the return of the elephant
hunt.   As to this practice, *cf.* Ov. *Am.* III. ii. 74.
⁴ Which was celebrated for its olives: *cf.* XII. lxiii.; Hor.
Od. II. vi. 16.
⁵ *Garum*, made of the intestines and offal of mackerel. The

XCVIII.—*The Roe*

You will see a roe poised on the summit of a rock;[1] one can only hope she will fall; she is showing contempt of the dogs.

XCIX.—*The Gazelle*

You shall give a gazelle as a pet to your little son. The crowd loves to procure its dismissal by fluttering their togas.[2]

C.—*The Wild Ass*

A BEAUTIFUL wild ass comes; the hunt of the Indian tusk must be sent away; now shake your togas no longer.[3]

CI.—*Venafran Oil*

THIS oil the berry of Campanian Venafrum [4] has distilled for you; your unguent, as often as you use it, smells too of that oil.

CII.—*Fish Sauce of the Allies*

RECEIVE this proud sauce,[5] made of the first blood of a mackerel breathing still, an expensive gift.

CIII.—*A Jar of Tunny-fish Sauce*

DAUGHTER of the tunny of Antipolis I confess I am.[6] Were I of the mackerel, I should not have been sent to you.[7]

---

finest was called *garum sociorum*, and came from a manufactory at New Carthage in Spain : Plin. *N.H.* xxxi. 43, who says it was almost as dear as unguent, and was sold for a thousand sesterces (£8) for 2 *congii* = 12 pints.

[6] *i.e.* I am the inferior fish sauce called *muria*, made of the entrails of other fish than mackerel, principally tunny.

[7] But to a rich man.

CIV.—*Mel Atticum*

Hoc tibi Thesei populatrix misit Hymetti
Pallados a silvis nobile nectar apis.

CV.—*Favi Siculi*

Cum dederis Siculos mediae de collibus Hyblae,
Cecropios dicas tu licet esse favos.

CVI.—*Passum*

Gnosia Minoae genuit vindemia Cretae
hoc tibi, quod mulsum pauperis esse solet.

CVII.—*Picatum*

Haec de vitifera venisse picata Vienna
ne dubites, misit Romulus ipse mihi.

CVIII.—*Mulsum*

Attica nectareum turbatis mella Falernum.
misceri decet hoc a Ganymede merum.

CIX.—*Albanum*

Hoc de Caesareis mitis vindemia cellis
misit, Iuleo quae sibi monte placet.

---

¹ A hill near Athens famous for its thyme.
² Sicilian honey was inferior to Attic, though Hyblan and
Hymettian honey are constantly mentioned together : *cf.*
xi. xlii. 3. Pliny calls each *optimum* : *N.H.* xi. 13.
³ *Mulsum* was wine and honey mixed : *cf.* Ep. cviii.
Passum was made from a grape called *apiana* (? muscatel)
dried in the sun : Plin. *N.H.* xi. 11.
⁴ Vienne in *Gallia Narbonensis.* The district bore vines

CIV.—*Attic Honey*

THIS the bee, spoiler of Thesean Hymettus,[1] has sent you, noble nectar from the woods of Pallas.

CV.—*Sicilian Honeycombs*

WHEN you make a present of Sicilian combs from amid Hybla's hills[2] you may say they are Attic combs.

CVI.—*Raisin Wine*

THE vintage of Gnossos in Minoan Crete brought forth for you this, which is wont to be the poor man's mead.[3]

CVII.—*Pitch-flavoured Wine*

THAT this pitch-flavoured wine came from vine-bearing Vienna[4] do not doubt; Romulus[5] himself sent it to me.

CVIII.—*Honeyed Wine or Mead*

YOU, Attic honey, thicken the nectarous[6] Falernian. It is meet that such a drink be mixed by a Ganymede.

CIX.—*Alban Wine*

THIS wine the mild grape, proud of itself on the Julian mount,[7] sends you from Caesar's cellars.

producing wine with a natural taste of pitch : Plin. *N.H.* xiv. 3 ; xxiii. 24.

[5] Some friend at V. where Martial was known : *cf.* VII. lxxxviii. 2.

[6] To blend with honey the wine had to be old : Plin. *N.H.* xxii. 53.

[7] It was inferior only to Falernian and Setine : Plin. *N.H.* xiv. 8 (3). One variety was sweet (Athen. i. 48). Juv. (xiii. 214) speaks of its *pretiosa senectus.*

CX.—*Surrentinum*

SURRENTINA bibis? nec murrina picta nec aurum
sume: dabunt calices haec tibi vina suos.

CXI.—*Falernum*

DE Sinuessanis venerunt Massica prelis:
condita quo quaeris consule? nullus erat.

CXII.—*Setinum*

PENDULA Pomptinos quae spectat Setia campos,
exigua vetulos misit ab urbe cados.

CXIII.—*Fundanum*

HAEC Fundana tulit felix autumnus Opimi.
expressit mustum consul et ipse bibit.

CXIV.—*Trifolinum*

NON sum de primo, fateor, trifolina Lyaeo,
inter vina tamen septima vitis ero.

---

¹ Tiberius called it generous vinegar, and Claudius noble
vapidity: Plin. *N.H.* xiv. 8 (3). It was a thin wine, suitable
for invalids: *ibid.*
² *cf.* XIV. cxiii. 1.
³ Surrentine earthenware: *cf.* XIV. cii.; VIII. vi. 2.
⁴ In Campania, near which was *Mons Massicus* and *Mons Falernus.*
⁵ The wine was as old as the kings (B.C. 510). This is of
course hyperbolical.

BOOK XIII. CX–CXIV

CX.—*Surrentine Wine*

DRINK you Surrentine?[1] Take not beakers of painted murrine,[2] nor of gold: these wines will supply you with their native cups.[3]

CXI.—*Falernian Wine*

FROM presses of Sinuessa[4] has the Massic come. Stored in what consul's year do you ask? there was no consul then.[5]

CXII.—*Seline Wine*

SETIA high-poised, that looks on the Pomptine levels, has sent from a tiny city casks of aged wine.[6]

CXIII.—*Fundanian Wine*

THIS Fundanian the rich autumn of Opimius' year[7] produced. The consul squeezed out the must, and himself drank the wine.

CXIV.—*Trifoline Wine*

I AM not, I confess, of the first brand of Lyaeus; yet among wines my vintage shall be the seventh.[8]

[6] The favourite wine of the Emperor Augustus : Plin. *N.H.* xiv. 8 (1). Pliny describes it as less strong than Surrentine, less rough than Alban, and more fiery than Falernian : *N.H.* xxiii. 21.

[7] B.C. 121, a famous year : *cf.* I. xxvi. 7. Athen. (i. 48) describes it as a heady wine.

[8] The wine was called *trifolinum* because it matured *tertio foliorum exortu*, *i.e.* in three years. It had an earthy flavour : Athen. i. 48; and is called by Pliny (*N.H.* xiv. 8 (6)) *plebeium*. But it is praised by Juv. (ix. 56).

CXV.—*Caecubum*

CAECUBA Fundanis generosa cocuntur Amyclis,
vitis et in media nata palude viret.

CXVI.—*Signinum*

POTABIS liquidum Signina morantia ventrem?
ne nimium sistas, sit tibi parca sitis.

CXVII.—*Mamertinum*

AMPHORA Nestorea tibi Mamertina senecta
si detur, quodvis nomen habere potest.

CXVIII.—*Tarraconense*

TARRACO, Campano tantum cessura Lyaeo,
haec genuit Tuscis aemula vina cadis.

CXIX.—*Nomentanum*

NOMENTANA meum tibi dat vindemia Bacchum:
si te Quintus amat, commodiora bibes.

CXX.—*Spoletinum*

DE Spoletinis quae sunt cariosa lagonis
malueris quam si musta Falerna bibas.

---

[1] A stimulating and vigorous wine, to be laid down:
Athen. i. 48.

[2] Pliny says (*N.H.* xiv. 8 (3)) that it was considered a
medicine "*austeritate nimia continendae utile alvo.*" It
improved after six years: Athen. i. 48.

[3] From Messena, in Sicily. It was a sweet and light wine:
Athen. i. 48.

[4] *i.e.* it is as good as any wine.

CXV.—*Caecuban Wine*

GENEROUS Caecuban[1] is ripened at Amyclae by Fundi, and the vine grows green, born in the middle of the marsh.

CXVI.—*Signine Wine*

WILL you drink Signine that constricts relaxed bowels? That you may not check them too much, let your thirst be sparing.[2]

CXVII.—*Mamertine Wine*

IF a jar of Mamertine[3] as old as Nestor be given to you, it can bear any name you please.[4]

CXVIII.—*Tarraconian Wine*

TARRACO, that will yield only to Campanian vine-yards, begot this wine that vies with Tuscan jars.[5]

CXIX.—*Nomentan Wine*

A NOMENTAN vintage gives you this wine of my own. If Quintus loves you, you will drink better wines.[6]

CXX.—*Spoletine Wine*

CRUSTED wines from Spoletine flagons you will prefer to the drinking of Falernian must.[7]

[5] "*Nobilitantur elegantia Tarraconensia, et conferuntur Italiae primis*": Plin. *N.H.* xiv. 8 (6).
[6] Yet M. says that Nomentan, when it is old, can compare with any wine : *cf.* I. cv. 4. It ripened quickly, and was drinkable after five years : Athen. i. 48.
[7] *i.e.* F. new wine. Yet Spoletine was a poor wine : *cf.* XIV. cvi. In Athen. (i. 48) it is described as sweet and golden in colour.

CXXI.—*Paelignum*

MARSICA Paeligni mittunt turbata coloni :
  non tu, libertus sed bibat illa tuus.

CXXII.—*Acetum*

AMPHORA Niliaci non sit tibi vilis aceti :
  esset cum vinum, vilior illa fuit.

CXXIII.—*Massilitanum*

CUM tua centenos expunget [1] sportula civis,
  fumea Massiliae ponere vina potes.

CXXIV.—*Caeretanum*

CAERETANA Nepos ponat, Setina putabis.
  non ponit turbae, cum tribus illa bibit.

CXXV.—*Tarentinum*

NOBILIS et lanis et felix vitibus Aulon
  det pretiosa tibi vellera, vina mihi.

[1] *expugnet* Tβ.

---

[1] *cf.* XIV. cvi. A rough, but stomachic wine : Athen. i. 48.
[2] Egyptian vinegar was celebrated : Athen. ii. 76 ; Juv.
xiii. 85.
[3] *i.e.* when you wish to repay clients for their services.
Massilia had a bad reputation for exposing its wines too long

CXXI.—*Paelignian Wine*

PAELIGNIAN wine-growers send you turbid Marsic[1] wine. Do not drink it yourself, but let your freedman do so.

CXXII.—*Vinegar*

LET not a jar of Egyptian vinegar be mean in your eyes. When it was wine it was more mean.[2]

CXXIII.—*Massilian Wine*

WHEN your dole shall strike off the list a hundred citizens,[3] you can serve them the smoky wines of Massilia.

CXXIV.—*Caeretan Wine*

LET Nepos[4] serve Caeretan,[5] you will imagine it Setine. He does not serve it to a crowd : with three guests he drinks it.

CXXV.—*Tarentine Wine*

LET Aulon,[6] renowned for wool and blest in vines, give precious fleeces to you, wines[7] to me.

to the smoke of the furnace : *cf.* x. xxxvi. 1. But Athenaeus (i. 48) calls it a good full-bodied wine.

[4] *cf.* vi. xxvii. 1.

[5] From Caere in Etruria, now Cervetri.

[6] A valley in the region of Tarentum. M. has in mind Hor. *Od.* ii. vi. 18.

[7] T. wine was sweet and soft, with no strength : Athen. i. 48.

THE EPIGRAMS OF MARTIAL

CXXVI.—*Unguentum*

Unguentum heredi numquam nec vina relinquas.
ille habeat nummos, haec tibi tota dato.

CXXVII.—*Coronae Roseae*

Dat festinatas, Caesar, tibi bruma coronas:
quondam veris erat, nunc tua facta rosa est.

CXXVI.—*Unguent*

UNGUENT or wine never bequeath to your heir;
let him have your cash: the whole of these give to
your own self.

CXXVII.—*A Crown of Roses*

FORCED coronals winter gives thee, Caesar: erewhile the rose was Spring's: now has it become
thine.[1]

[1] *cf.* VI. lxxx.

BOOK XIV

[LIBER QUARTUS DECIMUS]

APOPHORETA

I

Synthesibus dum gaudet eques dominusque senator
  dumque decent nostrum pillea sumpta Iovem ;
nec timet aedilem moto spectare fritillo,
  cum videat gelidos tam prope verna lacus :
divitis alternas et pauperis accipe sortes :   5
  praemia convivae dent sua quisque suo.
" Sunt apinae tricaeque et si quid vilius istis."
  quis nescit ? vel quis tam manifesta negat ?
sed quid agam potius madidis, Saturne, diebus,
  quos tibi pro caelo filius ipse dedit ?   10
vis scribam Thebas Troiamve malasve Mycenas ?
  " Lude" inquis " nucibus " : perdere nolo nuces.

---

[1] Domitian : *cf.* XI. vi. 4. The wearing of the *pilleum*, or cap of liberty, was common at the Saturnalia, as being symbolical of the licence of the season.

[2] *i.e.* when he sees that the time is winter. Lucian, however, says (*Saturn.* 2) that a common Saturnalian joke was to blacken a man's face and to duck him in the water. If M. alludes to this, the rendering should be " although he sees " etc.

[3] *Apophoreta* are presents given " to be carried away " by guests, and probably distributed by lot (*sortes* i. 5 and

BOOK XIV

APOPHORETA

I

WHILE the knight and My Lord the Senator rejoice in dinner-dress, while wearing freedom's cap beseems our Jove,[1] and the home-bred slave, as he shakes the dice-box, does not fear to look the Aedile in the face, when he sees the cold tanks so near,[2] receive these lots, gifts of rich and poor alternate; let everyone give his own guest his proper prize.[3] "They are worthless and gim-cracks, or anything still meaner, if possible." Who does not know it? Or who denies what is so plain? But what else am I to do, Saturn, on the unsober days your son[4] himself gave you in exchange for Heaven? Do you wish me to write of Thebes, or Troy, or guilty Mycenae? "Play with nuts," you say. I don't want to lose my nuts.[5]

Petr. 40, 56). Martial's couplets describe such gifts, and were clearly intended to go in pairs, one couplet describing something that would be given by a rich man, and the next something similar that would be given by a poor man. But some couplets appear to have been lost or to have got out of order—*e.g.* lxvii. and lxxi. ; but the following are among some of the pairs about which there can be no doubt, viz. v. and vi. ; xliii. and xliv. ; lxxxix. and xc. ; xciii. and xciv. ; clix. and clx. ; clxi. and clxii. See Friedländer's full examination. [4] Jupiter. [5] *cf.* v. xxx. 8.

II

Quo vis cumque loco potes hunc finire libellum :
    versibus explicitumst omne duobus opus.
lemmata si quaeris cur sint adscripta, docebo,
    ut, si malueris, lemmata sola legas.

III.—*Pugillares Citrei*

Secta nisi in tenues essemus ligna tabellas,
    essemus Libyci nobile dentis onus.

IV.—*Quinquiplices*

Caede iuvencorum domini calet area felix,
    quinquiplici cera cum datur altus honos.

V.—*Pugillares Eborei*

Languida ne cristes obscurent lumina cerae,
    nigra tibi niveum littera pingat ebur.

VI.—*Triplices*

Tunc triplices nostros non vilia dona putabis,
    cum se venturam scribet amica tibi.

VII.—*Pugillares Membranei*

Esse puta ceras, licet haec membrana vocetur :
    delebis, quotiens scripta novare voles.

---

[1] Round table-tops (*orbes*) were supported on ivory legs :
cf. IX. lix. 7, 8.

[2] The sacrifice takes place when the tablets arrived by
which the emperor sent notice of promotion.

[3] But generally so considered : *cf.* VII. lxxii. 2 ; x. lxxxvii. 6.

II

You can finish this little book at whatever point you like; every subject is summed up in two verses. If you ask why headings are added, I will explain: it is that, if you prefer, you may read the headings only.

III.—*Tablets of Citrus-wood*

HAD not our wood been cut into thin plates, we should have been the noble burden of a Libyan tusk.[1]

IV.—*Five-leaved Tablets*

THE glad court of our master is warm with the slaughter of steers, when by the five-leaved waxen tablet is conferred on him high honour.[2]

V.—*Ivory Tablets*

LEST dark-coloured waxen tablets dim your failing eyesight, let black letters dye for you snow-white ivory.

VI.—*Three-leaved Tablets*

You will then deem my three-leaved tablets no mean[3] gift, when your mistress shall write to you that she will come.

VII.—*Parchment Tablets*

IMAGINE these tablets are waxen, although they are called parchment. You will rub out as often as you wish to write afresh.[4]

[4] Parchment according to Quintilian (x. 3) was used by persons of weak sight. The parchment seems therefore to have been specially prepared so as to admit of erasure, as on a wax tablet.

VIII.—*Vitelliani*

NONDUM legerit hos licet puella,
novit quid cupiant Vitelliani.

IX.—*Idem*

QUOD minimos cernis, mitti nos credis amicae.
falleris: et nummos ista tabella rogat.

X.—*Chartae Maiores*

NON est munera quod putes pusilla,
cum donat vacuas poeta chartas.

XI.—*Chartae Epistulares*

SEU leviter noto seu caro missa sodali
omnes ista solet charta vocare suos.

XII.—*Loculi Eborei*

Hos nisi de flava loculos implere moneta
non decet: argentum vilia ligna ferant.

XIII.—*Loculi Lignei*

SI quid adhuc superest in nostri faece locelli,
munus erit. nihil est? ipse locellus erit.

---

[1] Possibly of very small size and named after the maker.
They were often used for billets-doux: *cf.* II. vi. 6.
[2] *i.e.* you will not be bored by any poems.

VIII.—*Vitellian Tablets*

ALTHOUGH she may not as yet have read them, a girl knows what Vitellian [1] tablets wish for.

IX.—*The Same*

BECAUSE you see we are very small, you believe we are being sent to a mistress. You are mistaken: a tablet of that sort also duns for money.

X.—*Bigger Sheets*

THERE is no reason you should think the offering puny when a poet gives you blank sheets. [2]

XI.—*Letter-paper*

WHETHER sent to a slight acquaintance or to a dear comrade, this paper is accustomed to address everyone as its "Dear friend." [3]

XII.—*Ivory Money-boxes*

To fill these money-boxes with anything but yellow money is unfitting: let cheap wood carry silver.

XIII.—*Wooden Money-boxes*

IF anything still remain at the bottom of me, a little money-box, it shall be a gift. Is there nothing? The little box itself shall be the gift.

---

[3] *Suus* was commonly used in the heading to a letter, e.g. *C. Plinius Maximo suo S.* (*salutem*). S. is the "*felix litera*" of VII. xlv. 4.

XIV.—*Tali Eborei*

Cum steterit nullus vultu tibi talus eodem,
munera me dices magna dedisse tibi.

XV.—*Tesserae*

Non sim talorum numero par tessera, dum sit
maior quam talis alea saepe mihi.

XVI.—*Turricula*

Quae scit compositos manus inproba mittere talos,
si per me misit, nil nisi vota feret.

XVII.—*Tabula Lusoria*

Hac mihi bis seno numeratur tessera puncto;
calculus hac gemino discolor hoste perit.

XVIII.—*Nuces*

Alfa parva nuces et non damnosa videtur;
saepe tamen pueris abstulit illa natis.

---

¹ The *jactus Veneris*, or highest throw with the *tali*, was
where each of them turned up a different number. The *tali*
were three or four in number, and on four of the flat sides
were marked 1, 3, 4, and 6. The remaining two sides were
rounded and blank.
² Two, sometimes three, dice (*tesserae*) were used, but four
tali.
³ Gambling with dice was for money, and seems to have
been a more expensive mode of gambling than with the
knucklebones : *cf.* iv. lxvi. 15.

XIV.—*Ivory Knuckle-bones*

WHEN no one of the bones you throw stands with the same face as another you will say I have given you a great present.[1]

XV.—*Dice*

LET us dice be not equal in number to the knuckle-bones,[2] if only our stakes be often greater than with the knuckle-bones.[3]

XVI.—*The Little Tower Dice-box*

IF the cheating hand, that knows how to arrange and throw the bones, has thrown them through me, he will achieve nothing beyond prayers.[4]

XVII.—*A Gaming-board*

ON this side of me dice are counted by double sixes : on this other the piece of hostile colour is taken by twin foemen.[5]

XVIII.—*Nuts*

NUTS appear a small stake, and one not ruinous; yet often has that stake made prize of boys' buttocks.[6]

[4] *i.e.* his fraud does not succeed. The *turricula* appears to have been made with internal grooves to prevent cheating.

[5] The epigram is on a gaming-table suitable both for the game " of the twelve lines " (similar to backgammon) and the game of "robbers" (like chess or draughts) : *cf.* VII. lxxii. 8. In the first game the highest throw appears to have been two sixes : *cf.* (of three dice) Aesch. *Ag.* 33. In the second game a piece was taken by being hemmed in by two opposing "robbers" : *cf.* Ep. xx.

[6] When they gamble, whereas they ought to be in school : *cf.* v. lxxxiv. 1, 2. But Gronovius' comment is, " *Videtur potius turpe aliquid ac nefandum significari.*"

XIX.—*Theca Libraria*

SORTITUS thecam calamis armare memento :
cetera nos dedimus, tu leviora para.

XX.—*Calculi*

INSIDIOSORUM si ludis bella latronum,
gemmeus iste tibi miles et hostis erit.

XXI.—*Graphiarium*

HAEC tibi erunt armata suo graphiaria ferro :
si puero dones, non leve munus erit.

XXII.—*Dentiscalpium*

LENTISCUM melius : sed si tibi frondea cuspis
defuerit, dentes pinna levare potest.

XXIII.—*Auriscalpium*

SI tibi morosa prurigine verminat auris,
arma damus tantis apta libidinibus.

XXIV.—*Acus Aurea*

SPLENDIDA ne madidi violent bombycina crines,
figat acus tortas sustineatque comas.

XXV.—*Pectines*

QUID faciet nullos hic inventura capillos
multifido buxus quae tibi dente datur ?

---

[1] *Libraria* marks it as for the use of the *librarius*, containing all that he needed.   [2] *cf.* Ep. xvii.

XIX.—*A Case for Writing Materials*

HAVING won the case[1] in the raffle, remember to equip it with pens: we have given you all else, do you provide the slighter things.

XX.—*Draught Pieces*

IF you play the war-game of robbers in ambush, these glass pieces will be your soldiers and their enemies.[2]

XXI.—*A Style-case*

THIS style-case, fitted with its proper iron styles,[3] shall be for you: if you give it to your boy, it will be no slight gift.

XXII.—*A Toothpick*

MASTICK[4] is better; but if pointed wood be not forthcoming, a quill can relieve your teeth.

XXIII.—*An Earpick*

IF your ear is troubled with a persistent itching, I give you an instrument appropriate to such vagaries.

XXIV.—*A Gold Hairpin*

THAT your moistened hair may not soil your bright silks, let a pin fix and hold up your knotted locks.

XXV.—*Combs*

WHAT will be the use, when it will find here no hair, of this many-toothed piece of box which is given you?

---

[3] Pointed instruments for writing on wax.
[4] *cf.* III. lxxxii. 9.

449

XXVI.—*Crines*

CHATTICA [1] Teutonicos accendit spuma capillos :
  captivis poteris cultior esse comis.

XXVII.—*Sapo*

SI mutare paras longaevos cana capillos,
  accipe Mattiacas (quo tibi calva ?) pilas.

XXVIII.—*Umbella*

ACCIPE quae nimios vincant umbracula soles :
  sit licet et ventus, te tua vela tegent.

XXIX.—*Causea*

IN Pompeiano tecum spectabo theatro.
  mandatus [2] populo vela negare solet.

XXX.—*Venabula*

EXCIPIENT apros expectabuntque leones,
  intrabunt ursos, sit modo firma manus.

XXXI.—*Culter Venatorius*

SI deiecta gemas longo venabula rostro,
  hic brevis ingentem comminus ibit aprum.

---

[1] *Chaticas* T, *Castica* βγ.
[2] *mandatus* quid sit nondum satis liquet, *nam ventus* γ,
nam flatus Pontanus.

---

[1] Ladies wore false hair, much of which came from
Germany, or from German captives. This hair was dyed
with *sapo*, consisting of goats' fat and beechwood ashes (Plin.
N.H. xxviii. 51) in the form of balls. See next epigram, and
cf. spuma Batava in VIII. xxxiii. 20.

XXVI.—*Soap*

THE spume of the Chatti turns to flame Teutonic locks: you can be smarter with the hair of a captive slave.[1]

XXVII.—*Soap-balls from Mattiacum*

IF white-haired you are set on dyeing your aged locks, accept—why be hairless?—these balls from Mattiacum.[2]

XXVIII.—*A Sunshade*

ACCEPT a sunshade to subdue the overpowering heat; even though there be a wind,[3] your own awning will cover you.

XXIX.—*A Broad-brimmed Hat*

I WILL be a spectator with you in Pompey's theatre, for blasts of wind are apt to deny the people an awning.[4]

XXX.—*Hunting-spears*

THEY will counter boars, and will wait for the lion's rush; they will pierce bears if the hand be but firm enough.

XXXI.—*A Hunting-knife*

IF you lament that your hunting spear with its long blade has been struck down, this short weapon will closely engage a huge boar.

[2] Supposed to be Marpurg or Wiesbaden. It was a town of the Chatti.

[3] When the ordinary *vela* could not be spread, or had to be furled: *cf*. xxix. 2.

[4] Therefore the head requires a covering. The *causea* was a high-crowned and broad-brimmed hat. It came originally from Macedonia: Val. Max. v. i. 4, and was especially worn by fishermen and sailors.

XXXII.—*Parazonium*

MILITIAE decus hoc gratique erit omen honoris,
arma tribunicium cingere digna latus.

XXXIII.—*Pugio*

PUGIO, quem curva signat brevis orbita vena,
stridentem gelidis hunc Salo tinxit aquis.

XXXIV.—*Falx*

PAX me certa ducis placidos curvavit in usus.
agricolae nunc sum, militis ante fui.

XXXV.—*Securicula*

CUM fieret tristis solvendis auctio nummis,
haec quadringentis milibus empta fuit.

XXXVI.—*Ferramenta Tonsoria*

TONDENDIS haec arma tibi sunt apta capillis;
unguibus hic longis utilis, illa genis.

XXXVII.—*Scrinium*

SELECTOS nisi das mihi libellos,
admittam tineas trucesque blattas.

---

¹ The *parazonium* was a waist belt carrying a sword worn
on the left side by military tribunes, whereas the ordinary
soldier wore his sword slung on the right side by a shoulder-
strap.   ² *i.e.* of an appointment to a tribuneship.
³ *cf.* I. xlix. 12. Salo was the river of Bilbilis, M.'s birthplace.

XXXII.—*A Belt and Sword*

A SOLDIER's decoration[1] is this, and it will be a sign of a prized honour,[2] a weapon worthy to gird a tribune's side.

XXXIII.—*A Dagger*

THIS dagger, which a narrow circle marks with its rounded groove, Salo dipt[3] while it was hissing in his chilling waters.

XXXIV.—*A Sickle*

ME our Captain's assured peace has bent to serve quiet uses: the husbandman's am I now, the soldier's was I aforetime.

XXXV.—*A Small Axe*

WHEN a melancholy auction for payment of debts was held, this was bought for four hundred thousand sesterces.[4]

XXXVI.—*A Barber's Implements*

THESE instruments are suitable for the cutting of your hair; this one[5] is serviceable to long nails, that[6] to your cheeks.

XXXVII.—*A Bookcase*

UNLESS you provide me[7] with choice books I will let in moths and savage bookworms.

[4] The price is meant to be absurd. The *securicula* was a child's ornament or toy: *cf.* Plaut. *Rud.* 1159 Such things were also hung round children's necks as amulets, or as proofs of identity.   [5] *Cultellus.*   [6] *Novacula.*

[7] The *scrinium* was a circular case (Ov. *Trist.* i. i. 106) for holding books and papers.

XXXVIII.—*Fasces Calamorum*

DAT chartis habiles calamos Memphitica tellus;
texantur reliqua tecta palude tibi.

XXXIX.—*Lucerna Cubicularis*

DULCIS conscia lectuli lucerna,
quidquid vis facias licet, tacebo.

XL.—*Cicindela*

ANCILLAM tibi sors dedit lucernae,
totas quae vigil exigit tenebras.

XLI.—*Lucerna Polymyxos*

INLUSTREM cum tota meis convivia flammis
totque geram myxas, una lucerna vocor.

XLII.—*Cereus*

HIC tibi nocturnos praestabit cereus ignis:
subducta est puero namque lucerna tuo.

XLIII.—*Candelabrum Corinthium*

NOMINA candelae nobis antiqua dederunt.
non norat parcos uncta lucerna patres.

XLIV.—*Candelabrum Ligneum*

ESSE vides lignum; servas nisi lumina, fiet
de candelabro magna lucerna tibi.

---

[1] Candles were made of rope or rush dipped in wax, tallow,
or pitch: Varr. *De Ling. Lat.* v. 119; Plin. *N.H.* xvi. 70.
A candle was a poor man's light; hence it is called a
"handmaid" of the rich man's lamp: *cf.* Juv. iii. 287.

[2] Lamps with even fourteen wicks have been found at
Pompeii and Herculaneum.

XXXVIII.—*Bundles of Pens*

THE land of Memphis supplies reeds handy for writing : let your roof be thatched with the reeds from other marshes.

XXXIX.—*A Bedroom Lamp*

I AM a lamp, privy to the pleasures of your couch : you may do what you will, I shall be silent.

XL.—*A Candle* [1]

THE lot has given you the lamp's handmaid, which is awake and dispels complete darkness.

XLI.—*A Lamp with many Wicks*

ALTHOUGH I illume whole entertainments with my flames, and carry so many wicks,[2] I am called a single lamp.

XLII.—*A Taper*

THIS taper will afford you light by night, for your lamp has been stolen from your slave.

XLIII.—*A Corinthian* [3] *Candelabrum*

CANDLES gave me my name of old ; the oil-lamp had no knowledge of our thrifty sires.

XLIV.—*A Wooden Candelabrum*

You see I am wood ; unless you guard the light, a great lamp will be made of your candelabrum.[4]

---

[3] According to Pliny (*N.H.* xxxiv. 3), there were three kinds of *aes Corinthium*, one in which silver was the principal ingredient, another in which gold, and a third with equal proportions of gold and silver.

[4] The wicks will set fire to the wood.

XLV.—*Pila Paganica*

HAEC quae difficili turget paganica pluma,
   folle minus laxast et minus arta pila.

XLVI.—*Pila Trigonalis*

SI me mobilibus scis expulsare sinistris,
   sum tua. tu nescis ? rustice, redde pilam.

XLVII.—*Follis*

ITE procul, iuvenes : mitis mihi convenit aetas :
   folle decet pueros ludere, folle senes.

XLVIII.—*Harpasta*

HAEC rapit Antaei velox in pulvere draucus,
   grandia qui vano colla labore facit.

XLIX.—*Halteres*

QUID pereunt stulto fortes haltere lacerti ?
   exercet melius vinea fossa viros.

L.—*Galericulum*

NE lutet inmundum nitidos ceroma capillos,
   hac poteris madidas condere pelle comas.

---

¹ As to the balls mentioned in this and the three following
epigrams, *cf.* IV. xix. 5 *seqq.*, and VII. xxxii. 7.
   ² *cf.* VII. lxxii. 11.   ³ *i.e. cinaedus* : *cf.* IX. xxvii. 10.
   ⁴ *i.e.* on the athletic ground. A. was a Libyan wrestler
vanquished by Hercules : *cf.* IX. ci. 4. The development of
a short, muscular neck was aimed at by athletes : Juv. iii.
88 ; and see Plin. *N.H.* xiv. 28 (*pectorosa cervicis repandae*

XLV.—*A Feather-stuffed Ball*

THIS ball which swells with tightly-crammed feathers is less flaccid than the bladder-ball and less compact than a hand-ball.[1]

XLVI.—*A Ball for the Three-cornered Game*

IF you know how to bandy me with your nimble left-handers,[2] I am yours. Don't you know how? You clown, give back the ball.

XLVII.—*The Bladder-ball*

GO far off, you young men; unstrenuous age befits me: with the bladder-ball it becomes boys to play, with the bladder-ball old men.

XLVIII.—*Scrimmage-balls*

THESE the dissolute youth,[3] who with empty labour makes big his neck, swiftly catches at on the dusty ground of Antaeus.[4]

XLIX.—*Dumb-bells*

WHY is strength of arm wasted on the silly[5] dumb-bell? Trenching a vineyard better employs men.

L.—*A Small Cap*

THAT the wrestler's dirty oil may not soil your sleek locks, you may cover your moist hair with this skin cap.[6]

ostentatio). In this case, says M., the labour is vain, for it produces nothing. See the next epigram.

[5] "*Stulta est occupatio exercendi lacertos et dilatandi cervicem*": Sen. *Ep.* 15. He speaks of "*manus plumbo graves*": *Ep.* 56. Dumb-bells were also used by masculine women at the baths: Juv. vi. 421, and Mart. vii. lxvii. 6.

[6] It was a skull-cap with the fur outside.

LI.—*Strigiles*

PERGAMON has misit.   curvo destringere ferro:
non tam saepe teret lintea fullo tibi.

LII.—*Gutus Corneus*

GESTAVIT modo fronte me iuvencus:
verum rhinocerota me putabas.

LIII.—*Rhinoceros*

NUPER in Ausonia domini spectatus harena
hic erit ille tibi cui pila taurus erat.

LIV.—*Crepitacillum*

SI quis plorator collo tibi vernula pendet,
haec quatiat tenera garrula sistra manu.

LV.—*Flagellum*

PROFICIES nihil hoc, caedas licet usque, flagello,
si tibi purpureo de grege currit equus.

LVI.—*Dentifricium*

QUID mecum est tibi?   me puella sumat:
emptos non soleo polire dentes.

---

[1] *i.e.* they will not be sent to him so dirty : *cf.* x. xi. 6.
[2] The horn was so big.   Oil-flasks made of rhinoceros
horn were used at the baths by rich men : Juv. vii. 130.
[3] *cf. Spect.* ix. 4 ; x. lxxxvi. 4.
[4] The *sistrum* was originally used in the rites of Isis.

LI.—*Skin-scrapers*

PERGAMUS sent these; scrape yourself with the curved blade: the laundryman will not so often wear out your towels.[1]

LII.—*A Horn Oil-flask*

A STEER bore me lately on his forehead: you fancied me a real rhinoceros horn.[2]

LIII.—*A Rhinoceros-horn Oil-flask*

THIS shall be for you, that horn, lately seen in our Master's Italian arena, to which a bull was as a straw-dummy.[3]

LIV.—*A Small Rattle*

IF any little home-born slave shall hang on your neck in tears, let him shake this noisy rattle[4] with his infant hand.

LV.—*A Whip*

YOU will make no way with this whip though you may continually use the lash, if your courser be of the Purple[5] faction.

LVI.—*Dentifrice*

WHAT have you to do with me?[6] Let a young maid use me: I am not wont to polish purchased teeth.

[5] Which was not favoured by Domitian any more than the Blues: *cf.* VI. xlvi., although it and the Gold had been added by himself: Suet. *Dom.* vii.

[6] According to Pliny (xxx. 8) dentifrice was made of the ashes of dogs' teeth mixed with honey. Pumice was also used: xxxvi. 42.

LVII.—*Myrobalanum*

QUOD nec Vergilius nec carmine dicit Homerus,
hoc ex unguento constat et ex balano.

LVIII.—*Aphronitrum*

RUSTICUS es? nescis quid Graeco nomine dicar:
spuma vocor nitri. Graecus es? aphronitrum.

LIX.—*Opobalsama*

BALSAMA me capiunt, haec sunt unguenta virorum:
delicias Cosmi vos redolete, nurus.

LX.—*Lomentum*

GRATUM munus erit scisso nec inutile ventri,
si clara Stephani balnea luce petes.

LXI.—*Lanterna Cornea*

DUX lanterna viae clusis feror aurea flammis,
et tuta est gremio parva lucerna meo.

---

[1] The word would not go into the metre. *Myrobalanum*
is described by Pliny (*N.H.* xii. 46) as the fruit of a tree
found in the Thebais and in Arabia with a leaf like that of a
heliotrope, the fruit being of the size of a filbert. From it
was extracted an oil used in compounding unguent. The
Encyclopaedia calls the tree the horse-radish tree (*Moringa
pterygosperma*), the oil being oil of ben used by perfumers.

[2] *Spuma nitri* was prized, and prescribed by doctors in
pills or pastilles: Plin. *N.H.* xxxi. 46 (3); and balls of it
were given as presents: Stat. *Silv.* IV. ix. 37. It was found

LVII.—*Myrobalsam*

THIS, which neither Virgil nor Homer mentions in his poems,[1] is compounded of unguent and ben-nut.

LVIII.—*Saltpetre*

ARE you a countryman? You do not know what I am styled by a Greek name : I am called the froth of nitre. Are you a Greek? Aphronitrum.[2]

LIX.—*Opobalsam*

BALSAMS[3] attract me ; these are the unguents of men [4] : ye matrons, exhale the choice perfumes of Cosmus.[5]

LX.—*Bean-meal*

'TWILL be a welcome gift, and one not without use to a wrinkled belly, if in broad daylight you go to Stephanus' bath.[6]

LXI.—*A Horn Lantern*

GUIDE of your way am I carried, a lantern golden with fenced flame, and safe in my bosom is a small light.

in Asia in caves called *colycae* as a distillation from the rock, and was afterwards dried in the sun. The best was Lydian : Pliny *ibid.*

[3] The juice of the balsam-tree ; called balm of Gilead or of Mecca, and found, according to Pliny (*N.H.* xii. 54) only in Judaea. It appears to have become known in Rome in the time of Pompey, who displayed the tree in one of his triumphs. Pliny gives a detailed description.

[4] Juv. (ii. 41) seems to have been of a different opinion.

[5] *cf.* III. lv. 1 ; XI. viii. 9.   [6] *cf.* III. xlii. 1.

LXII.—*Lanterna de Vesica*

CORNEA si non sum, numquid sum fuscior? aut me
vesicam, contra qui venit, esse putat?

LXIII.—*Fistula*

QUID me conpactam ceris et harundine rides?
quae primum structa est fistula talis erat.

LXIV.—*Tibiae*

EBRIA nos madidis rumpit tibicina buccis:
saepe duas pariter, saepe monaulon habet.

LXV.—*Soleae Lanatae*

DEFUERIT si forte puer soleasque libebit
sumere, pro puero pes erit ipse sibi.

LXVI.—*Mamillare*

TAURINO poteras pectus constringere tergo:
nam pellis mammas non capit ista tuas.

LXVII.—*Muscarium Pavoninum*

LAMBERE quae turpes prohibet tua prandia muscas,
alitis eximiae cauda superba fuit.

---

[1] By the god Pan : *cf.* Verg. *Ecl.* ii. 32.
[2] Two pipes were sometimes played, and they were *pares*
or *impares*, the former being of the same length, the latter

BOOK XIV. LXII–LXVII

LXII.—*A Lantern made of Bladder*

IF I be not of horn, am I the dimmer? or does he that meets me think me a bladder?

LXIII.—*A Pipe of Reed*

WHY do you laugh at me, compact of wax and reed? The first pipe that was made[1] was such as I.

LXIV.—*Flutes*

THE drunken flautist bursts our ears with her bibulous cheeks; often she uses two pipes at once, often only one.[2]

LXV.—*Wool-lined Slippers*

IF it happens your slave is not at hand, and you want to put on your house-shoes, your foot will itself be its own slave.[3]

LXVI.—*A Bosom-band*

"WITH a bull's hide"[4] you might well have braced up your bosom; for this skin stomacher of yours is too small for your breasts.

LXVII.—*A Peacock's Feather Fly-flap*

THIS which forbids foul flies to taste your meal was the proud tail of a peerless bird.

of unequal length. The right-hand pipe was the bass or manly pipe, the left-hand one the treble or womanly pipe.

[3] *i.e.* it will slip easily into the slippers.

[4] An allusion to Verg. *Aen.* i. 368 (*Taurino quantum possent circumdare tergo*).

LXVIII.—*Copta Rhodiaca*

PECCANTIS famuli pugno ne percute dentes :
clara Rhodos coptam quam tibi misit edat.

LXIX.—*Priapus Siligineus*

SI vis esse satur, nostrum potes esse Priapum ;
ipsa licet rodas inguina, purus eris.

LXX.—*Porcus*

ISTE tibi faciet bona Saturnalia porcus,
inter spumantes ilice pastus apros.

LXXI.—*Muscarium Bubulum*

SORDIDA si flavo fuerit tibi pulvere vestis,
corrigat hoc [1] tenui verbere cauda levis.

LXXII.—*Botulus*

QUI venit botulus mediae tibi tempore brumae,
Saturni septem venerat ante dies.

LXXIII.—*Psittacus*

PSITTACUS a vobis aliorum nomina discam :
hoc didici per me dicere "Caesar have."

[1] *corrigat hoc* Postgate, coll. Iuv. xiv. 67, *colligat hunc* codd.

---

[1] The Rhodian biscuit was very hard. There may be also
a play upon the name *copta* and the Greek κόπτειν (to beat).

LXVIII.—*Rhodian Pastry*

Don't strike with your fist the teeth of your offending servant; let him eat the biscuit illustrious Rhodes has sent you.[1]

LXIX.—*A Priapus made from Flour*

If you want to satisfy your hunger you can eat my Priapus; you may gnaw his very appendage,[2] yet you will be undefiled.

LXX.—*A Pig*

This pig will make you a " Good Saturnalia " : he was fed on acorns among the foaming boars.

LXXI.—*An Ox-tail Brush*

If your dress has been soiled with yellow dust let this light ox-tail emend this with a gentle flap.

LXXII.—*A Sausage*

The sausage that has reached you at the mid-season of winter had reached me before Saturn's seven days.[3]

LXXIII.—*A Parrot*

I, a parrot, will learn of you the names of others : this I learned of my own accord to say, " Caesar, hail! "[4]

---

[2] *cf* vi. xlix. 2. The Priapus was sometimes stuffed, *e.g.* with apples and grapes : Petr. 60.

[3] Dec. 17–23. The sender had received the sausage as a present, and now passes it on to another person.

[4] *cf.* note to iii. xcv. 2.

LXXIV.—*Corvus*

CORVE salutator, quare fellator haberis?
in caput intravit mentula nulla tuum.

LXXV.—*Luscinia*

FLET Philomela nefas incesti Tereos, et quae
muta puella fuit, garrula fertur avis.

LXXVI.—*Pica*

PICA loquax certa dominum te voce saluto:
si me non videas, esse negabis avem.

LXXVII.—*Cavea Eborea*

SI tibi talis erit, qualem dilecta Catullo
Lesbia plorabat, hic habitare potest.

LXXVIII.—*Narthecium*

ARTIS ebur medicae narthecia cernis: habebis
munera quae cuperet Paccius esse sua.

LXXIX.—*Flagra*

LUDITE lascivi, sed tantum ludite, servi:
haec signata mihi quinque diebus erunt.

---

[1] Pliny (*N.H.* x. 15) says: "*Ore eos parere aut coire vulgus arbitratur* . . . *Aristoteles negat* . . . *sed illam osculationem, quae saepe cernitur, qualem in columbis, esse.*" See Arist. *De Gen. Anim.* iii. 6, who traces the vulgar opinion to Anaxagoras.

[2] T., king of Thrace, offered violence to Philomela, his sister-in-law, and cut out her tongue to prevent her revealing the crime. P. was changed into a nightingale.

LXXIV.—*A Raven*

O corvo salutatore, perchè sei tu tenuto un fellatore? Veruna mentola entrò nella tua bocca.[1]

LXXV.—*A Nightingale*

Philomela laments the crime of incestuous Tereus:[2] she who was a silent maiden is acclaimed as a bird of song.

LXXVI.—*A Magpie*

A chattering pie,[3] I with intelligible voice salute you, my master; did you not see me you will say I am no bird.

LXXVII.—*An Ivory Cage*

If you shall have such a bird[4] as Lesbia, beloved of Catullus, mourned, here it can dwell.

LXXVIII.—*A Medicine Chest*

You see a medicine chest, the ivory equipment of a doctor's art: you will have a gift which Paccius[5] would wish his own.

LXXIX.—*Whips*

Play, ye jovial slaves, but play only; I will keep these sealed up for five days.[6]

---

[3] *cf.* VII. lxxxvii. 6 ; IX. liv. 9. Petr. 28 describes a magpie in a golden cage that saluted all who entered.

[4] A sparrow : *cf.* Cat. ii. and iii.

[5] A physician. Juv. (xii. 99) mentions a Paccius, an *orbus*, who may be the same. The *narthecium* was, as its name implies, made in the shape of a joint of the giant fennel (νάρθηξ).

[6] Slaves during the Saturnalia were allowed a degree of licence.

LXXX.—*Ferulae*

Invisae nimium pueris grataeque magistris,
  clara Prometheo munere ligna sumus.

LXXXI.—*Pera*

Ne mendica ferat barbati prandia nudi,
  dormiat et tristi cum cane, pera rogat.

LXXXII.—*Scopae*

In pretio scopas testatur palma fuisse.
  otia sed scopis nunc analecta dedit.

LXXXIII.—*Scalptorium Eboreum*

Defendet manus haec scapulas mordente molesto
  pulice, vel si quid pulice sordidius.

LXXXIV.—*Manuale*

Ne toga barbatos faciat vel paenula libros,
  haec abies chartis tempora longa dabit.

LXXXV.—*Lectus Pavoninus*

Nomina dat spondae pictis pulcherrima pinnis
  nunc Iunonis avis, sed prius Argus erat.

---

¹ Prometheus, according to the myth, brought fire from
Heaven in the stem of the giant fennel (*ferula* or νάρθηξ),
and gave it to men.

² Used as a pillow. The Cynics, in imitation of beggars,
equipped themselves with a staff and wallet : *cf.* IV. liii. 3.

³ *cf.* Hor. *Sat.* II. iv. 83. As to the *analecta*, *cf.* VII. xx. 17.

⁴ It was in the shape of a hand.

LXXX.—*Ferules*

HATED much by boys and welcome to school-masters, we are the wood made famous by Prometheus' gift.[1]

LXXXI.—*A Wallet*

THAT he may not carry the mendicant scraps of a half-clad bearded philosopher, nor sleep[2] with a sour cynic, is the prayer of the wallet.

LXXXII.—*Brooms*

THE palm-tree testifies that brooms were once in demand,[3] but the crumb-collector has now given a rest to brooms.

LXXXIII.—*An Ivory Scratcher*

THIS hand[4] will protect your shoulder-blades when an irritating flea is biting you, or any insect fouler than a flea.

LXXXIV.—*A Wooden Book-holder*

To prevent your toga or cloak making your books frayed, this fir-wood will give long life to your paper.

LXXXV.—*A Couch of Peacock-veined Citrus-wood*

THE bird, most lovely with its painted plumage, gives its name to a couch;[5] it is now the bird of Juno, but once it was Argus.[6]

---

[5] Couches of *citrus* wood variegated by wavy lines, as on a peacock's tail, were valued : Plin. *N.H.* xiii. 30.

[6] Argus had a hundred eyes, of which two only slept at a time. Juno set him to watch Io, whom Jupiter had turned into a heifer. Argus was afterwards turned into a peacock with the eyes in the tail.

LXXXVI.—*Ephippium*

STRAGULA succincti venator sume veredi:
nam solet a nudo surgere ficus equo.

LXXXVII.—*Stibadia*

ACCIPE lunata scriptum testudine sigma.
octo capit; veniat quisquis amicus erit.

LXXXVIII.—*Gustatorium*

FEMINEAM nobis cherson si credis inesse,
deciperis: pelagi mascula praeda sumus.

LXXXIX.—*Mensa Citrea*

ACCIPE felices, Atlantica munera, silvas:
aurea qui dederit dona, minora dabit.

XC.—*Mensa Acerna*

NON sum crispa quidem nec silvae filia Maurae,
sed norunt lautas et mea ligna dapes.

XCI.—*Dentes Eborei*

GRANDIA taurorum portant qui corpora, quaeris
an Libycas possint sustinuisse trabes?

---

[1] The *ephippium* was soft, being more like a cushion than a saddle.

[2] In the shape of the Greek *s*, which was often written in the shape of a horse-shoe: *cf.* x. xlviii. 6.

[3] Shell from the sea-tortoise (? turtle) was held superior to that of the land-tortoise, and the male shell was superior to the female. According to Pliny (*N.H.* ix. 12) the land-tortoises were called *chersinae* and were found in African deserts, where they subsisted on dew.

LXXXVI.—*A Pad-saddle*

TAKE, hunter, the housing of a nimble steed, for from a bare-backed horse piles are wont to spring.[1]

LXXXVII.—*A Semi-circular Couch*

RECEIVE a horse-shoe couch [2] inlaid with crescent lines of tortoise-shell. It takes eight: let everyone come who shall be my friend.

LXXXVIII.—*A Buffet*

IF you think shell of a female land-tortoise is part of me, you are deceived: I am the male catch of the sea.[3]

LXXXIX.—*A Citrus-wood Table*

RECEIVE this wood of a fruitful tree, the offering of Atlas: he who shall give you golden gifts will give you less.[4]

XC.—*A Maple Table*

I AM indeed not veined, nor the daughter of a Moorish forest,[5] but even my wood knows sumptuous feasts.

XCI.—*Ivory Tusks.*

TUSKS that upbear the huge bodies of bulls [6]—do you ask whether they can uphold tables of Libyan wood ? [7]

---

[4] The *citrus* (a kind of cypress, *Thuja articulata*, the Greek θύα or θύον) came from Mauretania, in N.-W. Africa : Plin. *N.H.* xiii. 29, 30. Round table tops (*orbes*) were made of it, for which incredible sums were often paid.

[5] *i.e.* neither veined (a feature greatly valued : Plin. *N.H.* xiii. 30) nor *citrus*. Maple was second to *citrus* : Plin. *N.H.* xvi. 26 ; and one species was also peacock-veined : *ibid.*

[6] *cf. Spect.* xix.

[7] *i.e.* the *citrus* table tops mentioned in lxxxix.

XCII.—*Quinquepedal*[1]

PUNCTA notis ilex et acuta cuspide clusa
    saepe redemptoris prodere furta solet.

XCIII.—*Pocula Archetypa*

NON est ista recens nec nostri gloria caeli:
    primus in his Mentor, dum facit illa, bibit.

XCIV.—*Calices Audaces*

NOS sumus audacis plebeia toreumata vitri,
    nostra neque ardenti gemma feritur aqua.

XCV.—*Phiala Aurea Caelata*

QUAMVIS Callaico rubeam generosa metallo,
    glorior arte magis: nam Myos iste labor.

XCVI.—*Calices Vatinii*

VILIA sutoris calicem monimenta Vatini
    accipe; sed nasus longior ille fuit.

XCVII.—*Lances Chrysendetae*

GRANDIA ne viola parvo chrysendeta mullo:
    ut minimum, libras debet habere duas.

---

[1] A celebrated chaser in silver of the fourth century B.C.:
cf. III. xli. 1; IV. xxxix. 5.
[2] *cf.* XII. lxxiv. 3.
[3] *cf.* VIII. xxxiv. 1. He engraved the figures on the shield
of Athene Promachus in the Acropolis at Athens.

BOOK XIV. xcii–xcvii

XCII.—*A Five-foot Rule*

An oaken rule, marked off into lengths and ending in a sharp point, is often apt to detect a contractor's fraud.

XCIII.—*Antique Cups*

That is no recent work, nor pride of Roman chisel; Mentor [1] made these cups and first drank from them.

XCIV.—*Dreadnought Cups*

We are plebeian chased cups of dreadnought [2] glass, and our ware is not cracked by boiling water.

XCV.—*A Chased Gold Bowl*

Though I am noble and ruddy with Gallician ore, I glory more in my workmanship, for of Mys [3] was the labour you see.

XCVI.—*Vatinian Cups*

Receive a cup, a cheap memento of cobbler Vatinius,[4] but that nose was longer.

XCVII.—*Gold-inlaid Dishes*

Do not insult large gold-inlaid dishes [5] with a small mullet: at the least it ought to weigh two pounds.

---

[4] Of Beneventum, who gave his name to glassware with long spouts like noses: *cf.* x. iii. 3, 4; and Juv. v. 46. He was a buffoon and *delator* in the time of Nero.

[5] *Chrysendeta* appear to be silver dishes with gold ornaments inlaid or in relief: *cf.* ii. xliii. 11; vi. xciv. 1.

XCVIII.—*Vasa Arretina*

Arretina nimis ne spernas vasa monemus:
lautus erat Tuscis Porsena fictilibus.

XCIX.—*Bascauda*

Barbara de pictis veni bascauda Britannis,
sed me iam mavolt dicere Roma suam.

C.—*Panaca*

Si non ignota est docti tibi terra Catulli,
potasti testa Raetica vina mea.

CI.—*Boletaria*

Cum mihi boleti dederint tam nobile nomen,
prototomis (pudet heu!) servio coliculis.

CII.—*Calices Surrentini*

Accipe non vili calices de pulvere natos,
sed Surrentinae leve toreuma rotae.

CIII.—*Colum Nivarium*

Setinos, moneo, nostra nive frange trientes:
pauperiore mero tinguere lina potes.

---

¹ Earthenware: *cf.* I. liii. 6. Pliny (*N.H.* xxxv. 46) speaks
of the *nobilitas* of the red Samian ware of Arretium.

² King of Etruria, who besieged Rome in the sixth century
B.C.

³ Nothing is known of this. The Panaci seem to be a
Rhaetian people.

XCVIII.—*Arretian Vases*

WE advise you not overmuch to despise Arretian [1] vases: Tuscan earthenware was luxury to Porsena. [2]

XCIX.—*A Basket*

I HAVE come, a barbarian basket, from the woad-stained Britons; but Rome now prefers to call me her own.

C.—*A Panacian Crock* [3]

IF the country of the elegant Catullus is not unknown to you, you have drunk Rhaetian wine from my crock.

CI.—*Mushroom Boilers*

ALTHOUGH mushrooms have given me so noble a name, yet I am a slave—alas! I am ashamed to own it—to early greens.

CII.—*Surrentine Chalices*

RECEIVE chalices not sprung of common clay, but the smooth embossed work of a Surrentine potter's-wheel. [4]

CIII.—*A Strainer for Wine and Snow*

WITH the snow I contain, I warn you, subdue your cups of Setine: [5] in a poorer wine you may dip linen bags.

[4] Pliny classes Surrentine earthenware cups for excellence with those from Asta and Pollentia, and from Saguntum in Spain: *N.H.* xxxv. 46.

[5] *cf.* v. lxiv. 2. The *colum nivarium* was a metal colander in which a lump of frozen snow was placed, and the wine was strained through it into the cup or other wine vessel.

CIV.—*Saccus Nivarius*

ATTENUARE nives norunt et lintea nostra:
  frigidior colo non salit unda tuo.

CV.—*Urceoli Ministratorii*

FRIGIDA non derit, non derit calda petenti.
  sed tu morosa ludere parce siti.

CVI.—*Urceus Fictilis*

HIC tibi donatur panda ruber urceus ansa.
  Stoicus hoc gelidam Fronto petebat aquam.

CVII.—*Calathi*

Nos Satyri, nos Bacchus amat, nos ebria tigris,
  perfusos domini lambere docta pedes.

CVIII.—*Calices Saguntini*

QUAE non sollicitus teneat servetque minister
  sume Saguntino pocula facta luto.

CIX.—*Calices Gemmati*

GEMMATUM Scythicis ut luceat ignibus aurum
  aspice.   quot digitos exuit iste calix!

---

[1] According to Pliny barley meal was sometimes put into
the *saccus* to mitigate the strength of the wine: *N.H.* xxiv. 1.

[2] A *calathus* was a drinking vessel in the shape of a
woman's workbasket.

[3] Bacchus.

CIV.—*A Bag for Straining through Snow*

MY linen also knows how to liquefy snow: no colder spirts the water from your strainer.[1]

CV.—*Small Jugs for Table-service*

COLD water will not be wanting; there will not be wanting hot, if you ask for it; but do not you be dainty with a craving thirst.

CVI.—*An Earthenware Jug*

HERE is given you a red jug with a spreading handle: Stoic Fronto used to go to this for cold water.

CVII.—*Tankards* [2]

THE Satyrs love us, Bacchus loves us; us, too, the drunken tigress which has been taught to lick the wine-dabbled feet of her master.[3]

CVIII.—*Saguntine Chalices*

TAKE cups made of Saguntine clay, which without anxiety[4] your servant may handle and guard.

CIX.—*Gemmed Chalices*

SEE how the gold gleams, gemmed with the fire of Scythian emeralds! How many fingers has that chalice stripped![5]

---

[4] They are "dreadnought": *cf.* XII. lxxiv. 3, and Ep. xciv. *supra.* M. speaks poorly of Saguntine clay-ware; *cf.* VIII. vi. 2; but Pliny praises it: *N.H.* xxxv. 46.

[5] Rich men often ornamented their cups with jewels from their finger rings: *cf.* Juv. v. 42.

CX.—*Ampulla Potoria*

Hac licet in gemma, servat quae nomina Cosmi,
luxuriose, bibas, si foliata sitis.

CXI.—*Crystallina*

Frangere dum metuis, franges crystallina : peccant
securae nimium sollicitaeque manus.

CXII.—*Nimbus Vitreus*

A Iove qui veniet, miscenda ad pocula largas
fundet nimbus aquas : hic tibi vina dabit.

CXIII.—*Murrina*

Si caldum potas, ardenti murra Falerno
convenit et melior fit sapor inde mero.

CXIV.—*Patella Cumana*

Hanc tibi Cumano rubicundam pulvere testam
municipem misit casta Sibylla suam.

---

[1] *i.e.* the flask will flavour the wine.   Nard and other perfumes were however often mixed with wine : Juv. vi. 303,
464 ; and *foliata* alludes to this practice.   The *foliatum* was
the same as *nardinum*, a mixture of spikenard and other
perfumes, a list of which is given in Pliny (*N.H.* xiii. 2).

[2] A *nimbus* (lit. storm-cloud) is supposed to have been a
glass vessel with apertures for sprinkling wine, like a water-
ing-pot.   The name may have been derived from the cloud
on the glass caused by the snow-cooled wine.

[3] *Murra* was perhaps a natural earth, and may have been

CX.—*A Drinking-flask*

In this jewelled flask that bears the name of Cosmus you may drink, luxurious man, if your thirst is for perfumed wine.[1]

CXI.—*Crystal Cups*

So long as you fear to break them, you will break crystal cups: hands too careless and too anxious alike offend.

CXII.—*A Glass Sprinkler*

The storm-cloud that comes from Jove will pour you water in plenty to blend your cups: this one will give you wine.[2]

CXIII.—*Murrine Cups*

If you drink your wine warm, murrine[3] suits the burning Falernian, and better flavour comes therefrom to the wine.

CXIV.—*A Platter from Cumae*

This platter, her own townsman, ruddy with the soil of Cumae, the chaste Sibyl[4] has sent you.

spar: Plin. *N.H.* xxxvii. 8. See the authorities collected in Mayor's note to Juv. vii. 133. Murrine vases have however been regarded as porcelain, and porcelain vases agreeing with Pliny's description are said to have been found. These vases were first brought to Rome by Pompey after his victory over Mithridates in B.C. 63. Enormous sums were paid for them, Nero paying 300 talents (say £60,000) for a drinking cup.

[4] *cf.* IX. xxix. 3. The ware in question is the red Arretian: *cf.* xcviii.; which was made also at Capua and Cumae in the first century.

CXV.—*Calices Vitrei*

Aspicis ingenium Nili : quibus addere plura
dum cupit, a quotiens perdidit auctor opus !

CXVI.—*Lagona Nivaria*

Spoletina bibis vel Marsis condita cellis :
quo tibi decoctae nobile frigus aquae ?

CXVII.—*Idem*

Non potare nivem sed aquam potare recentem [1]
de nive commenta est ingeniosa sitis.

CXVIII.—*Idem*

Massiliae fumos miscere nivalibus undis
parce, puer, constet ne tibi pluris aqua.

CXIX.—*Matella Fictilis*

Dum poscor crepitu digitorum et verna moratur,
o quotiens paelex culcita facta mea est !

CXX.—*Ligula Argentea*

Quamvis me ligulam dicant equitesque patresque,
dicor ab indoctis lingula grammaticis.

[1] *rigentem* βγ.

---

[1] Excessive ornamentation. The allusion appears to be to
diatreta, which were chalices made in one piece with a net-
work ornamentation : *cf.* XII. lxx. 9.

[2] These wines were inferior : *cf.* XIII. cxx. and cxxi.

CXV.—*Glass Chalices*

You observe the ingenuity of Egypt. Ah, how often has the artist, in wishing to make additions,[1] ruined his work!

CXVI.—*A Flagon for Iced Water*

You drink Spoletine, or wine stored in Marsian[2] cellars : what is the use to you of the noble coolness of boiled water?[3]

CXVII.—*The Same*

The drinking, not of snow, but of water fresh from the snow, the ingenuity of thirst has devised.[4]

CXVIII.—*The Same*

Boy, forbear to mix Massilia's smoke[5] with iced water, that the water may not cost you more than the wine.

CXIX.—*An Earthen Chamber-utensil*

While I am called for by a snapping of the fingers,[6] and the home-born slave lingers, oh, how often has a pillow been made my rival!

CXX.—*A Silver Spoon*

However much both knights and senators may call me *ligula*, I am called by ignorant grammarians[7] *lingula*.

---

[3] *Decocta* (as to which *cf.* II. lxxxv. 1) is wasted on them.
[4] *cf.* v. lxiv. 2.   [5] *cf.* x. xxxvi. 1 ; XIII. cxxiii. 2.
[6] *cf.* III. lxxxii. 15.
[7] Who pedantically insist on the etymology from *lingua*, and disregard use.

CXXI.—*Coclearia*

Sum cocleis habilis sed nec minus utilis ovis.
numquid scis, potius cur cocleare vocer?

CXXII.—*Anuli*

Ante frequens sed nunc rarus nos donat amicus.
felix cui comes est non alienus eques.

CXXIII.—*Dactyliotheca*

Saepe gravis digitis elabitur anulus unctis;
tuta mea fiet sed tua gemma fide.

CXXIV.—*Toga*

" Romanos rerum dominos gentemque togatam "
ille facit, magno qui dedit astra patri.

CXXV.—*Idem*

Si matutinos facilest tibi perdere somnos,
attrita veniet sportula saepe toga.

---

[1] The *cocleare* was a spoon with a point at one end, and smaller (*cf.* VIII. lxxi. 9, 10) than the *ligula*. The point was used to pick snails (*cocleæ*) or shellfish out of their shells; hence the name. Petr. 33 speaks of *coclearia* of "not less than half a pound" weight used for eating eggs, but then they were Trimalchio's spoons. Pliny (*N.H.* xxviii. 4) tells us that it was a superstition to perforate empty egg-shells as a defence against evil spells.

CXXI.—*A Snail-pick*

I AM convenient for eating snails, and no less useful for eating eggs. Do you know why I am rather called a snail-pick ?[1]

CXXII.—*Rings*

FORMERLY many a friend gave us as presents, but now here and there a friend. Happy is he whose comrade is a knight he himself has made ![2]

CXXIII.—*A Ring-case*[3]

OFTEN a heavy ring slips from fingers moist with unguent; but your gem will be made safe in my faithful charge.

CXXIV.—*A Toga*

HE makes the Romans "lords of the world and the race that wears the toga,"[4] who granted his mighty sire immortality.[5]

CXXV.—*The Same*

IF it comes easily to you to lose your morning sleep, by wearing out your toga[6] a dole will often come to you.

---

[2] *i.e.* whose qualification he has supplied (*cf.* v. xix. 10), and whose gratitude he looks for. The ring was the mark of a knight : *cf.* VIII. v. 2.   [3] *cf.* XI. lix. 4.

[4] A quotation from Verg. *Aen.* i. 282.

[5] Domitian, who founded a temple to the Flavian family (*cf.* IX. i. 8), and also enjoined the use of the toga at spectacles : *cf.* IV. ii. 4.

[6] By constant attendance at levees : *cf.* IX. c. 5.

CXXVI.—*Endromis*

PAUPERIS est munus sed non est pauperis usus:
hanc tibi pro laena mittimus endromida.

CXXVII.—*Canusinae Fuscae*

HAEC tibi turbato Canusina simillima mulso
munus erit.   gaude: non cito fiet anus.

CXXVIII.—*Bardocucullus*

GALLIA Santonico vestit te bardocucullo.
cercopithecorum paenula nuper erat.

CXXIX.—*Canusinae Rufae*

ROMA magis fuscis vestitur, Gallia rufis,
et placet hic pueris militibusque color.

CXXX.—*Paenula Scortea*

INGREDIARE viam caelo licet usque sereno,
ad subitas nusquam[1] scortea desit aquas.

CXXXI.—*Lacernae Coccineae*

SI veneto prasinove faves, quid coccina sumes?
ne fias ista transfuga sorte vide.

[1] *numquam* βXV.

---

[1] The *endromis* was not a garment, but a warm wrapper
of rough texture used by richer men for warmth after gym-
nastic exercises: *cf.* IV. xix.

[2] *cf.* IX. xxii. 9.   Canusium (now Canosa) was a town in
Apulia on the high road from Rome to Brundusium: *cf.* Hor.
Sat. I. v. 91.   It was celebrated for its wool, which Pliny
(*N.H.* VIII. lxxiii.) calls *fulvus.*

[3] *cf.* I. liii. 5.   The *bardocucullus* was a hooded cloak
covering the whole body, worn principally by common

CXXVI.—*A Warm Wrapper*

'TIS a poor man's offering but not a poor man's wear.   This wrapper I send you in place of a cloak.[1]

CXXVII.—*A Brown Cloak of Canusian Wool*

THIS cloak of Canusian [2] wool, very like in colour to turbid mead, shall be your present.   Rejoice: it will not quickly become old.

CXXVIII.—*A Cowled Cloak*

GAUL clothes you in a Santonian cowled cloak.[3] Formerly it was the frock of long-tailed monkeys.

CXXIX.—*Red Cloaks of Canusian Wool*

ROME is clad more in brown, Gaul in red, and this colour pleases boys and soldiers.

CXXX.—*A Leather Surtout* [4]

ALTHOUGH you may set out on your journey when the sky is continuously serene, let a leather surtout nowhere be wanting against sudden showers.

CXXXI.—*A Scarlet Mantle*

IF you favour the Blue or the Green,[5] why will you assume scarlet?   See that by this lot [6] you do not become a deserter.

people, and bearing some resemblance to the *paenula*, as to which *cf.* cxxx.   Hence the juxtaposition here of the two names.
    [4] The *paenula* was a closed garment, fitting closely, with an opening for the head and a hood.   It was an outer garment, worn over the tunic in wet or cold weather, and was made of frieze or leather.
    [5] Factions of the charioteers in the Circus.
    [6] *cf.* XIV. i. 5.

CXXXII.—*Pilleum*

Si possem, totas cuperem misisse lacernas:
nunc tantum capiti munera mitto tuo.

CXXXIII.—*Lacernae Baeticae*

Non est lana mihi mendax nec mutor aheno.
sic placeant Tyriae: me mea tinxit ovis.

CXXXIV.—*Fascia Pectoralis*

Fascia, crescentes dominae compesce papillas,
ut sit quod capiat nostra tegatque manus.

CXXXV.—*Cenatoria*

Nec fora sunt nobis nec sunt vadimonia nota:
hoc opus est, pictis accubuisse toris.

CXXXVI.—*Laena*

Tempore brumali non multum levia prosunt:
calfaciunt villi pallia vestra mei.

CXXXVII.—*Lacernae Albae*

Amphitheatrali nos commendamus ab usu,
cum teget algentes [1] alba lacerna togas.

[1] *tegit* βγ. *albentes* β.

---

[1] The *lacerna* was a mantle fastened with a buckle, and
not closed in like the *paenula*. It often had a hood, and was
ample, so that it could be worn over the *toga* (*cf.* Juv. ix. 29)
or other garment.   [2] *cf.* XII. lxiii. 4.

[3] The *fascia*, like the *mamillare* in lxvi., was a bandage

CXXXII.—*A Cap*

If I could, I should have wished to have sent a mantle complete: now I send you a present only for your head.[1]

CXXXIII.—*A Baetic Mantle*

My wool is not deceptive, nor am I transformed in the vat. Let Tyrian mantles please you by such means: my own sheep dyed me.[2]

CXXXIV.—*A Stomacher*

Stomacher, compress the swelling breasts of my mistress that there may be something for my hand to seize and cover.[3]

CXXXV.—*Dinner Suits*

Nor courts are known to us, nor are bail bonds: this is our business—to recline on inlaid couches.

CXXXVI.—*A Warm Cloak*[4]

In the winter season smooth coverings do not much avail: my wool makes warm your outer garment.

CXXXVII.—*White Mantles*

We recommend ourselves by our use in the amphitheatre,[5] when a white mantle shall cover a chilly toga.

usually meant to restrain development of the bust. Here it is meant to give firmness and shape.

[4] The *laena* was in winter often worn over the *toga* or *pallium*: cf. XII. xxxvi. 2.

[5] It was customary to wear white at public spectacles: cf. IV. ii.

CXXXVIII.—*Mantele*

NOBILIUS villosa tegant tibi lintea citrum :
  orbibus in nostris circulus esse potest.

CXXXIX.—*Cuculli Liburnici*

IUNGERE nescisti nobis, o stulte, lacernas :
  indueras albas, exue callainas.

CXL.—*Udones Cilicii*

NON hos lana dedit sed olentis barba mariti :
  Cinyphio poterit planta latere sinu.

CXLI.—*Synthesis*

DUM toga per quinas gaudet requiescere luces,
  hos poteris cultus sumere iure tuo.

CXLII.—*Focale*

SI recitaturus dedero tibi forte libellum,
  hoc focale tuas adserat auriculas.

---

[1] Made by wet, round-footed vessels. M.'s tables were common ones, and not of *citrus*.

[2] *Callainas* = the colour of the *callais*, a stone which, according to Pliny (*N.H.* xxxvii. 56), *sapphirum imitatur, candidior, et literoso mari similis*, *i.e.* a kind of sea-green. The hood and mantle should have been of the same hue, as the green hood, wetted by rain, would be apt to stain the white mantle.

[3] *i.e.* a he-goat's : *cf.* Hor. *Od.* I. xvii. 7, *Olentis uxores mariti*.

CXXXVIII.—*A Tablecloth*

LET woollen cloths cover your nobler citrus wood: on my round tables a circular mark [1] may stand.

CXXXIX.—*A Liburnian Hood*

You have not known, O foolish fellow, how to match your mantle with me: you put it on white; take it off now green.[2]

CXL.—*Cilician Socks*

WOOL did not supply these, but the beard of the noisome husband:[3] your foot will be able to take refuge in a Cinyphian [4] nest.

CXLI.—*A Holiday Garment*

WHILE the toga gladly rests for five days, you may assume this garb as of right.[5]

CXLII.—*A Comforter*

IF, meaning to recite, I shall perhaps have sent you a note of invitation, let this comforter emancipate your ears.[6]

---

[4] *Cilicium* was a cloth made of goats' hair, and garments or other articles made of it were called *cilicia*: cf. Cic. *Verr.* iii. 38; Liv. xxxviii. 7; even where, as here, the hair came from Africa, Cinyps being the name of a river near the Syrtes: *cf.* VII. xcv. 13.

[5] The *synthesis* was worn at the Saturnalia: *cf.* XIV. i. 1. It was ordinarily a dinner dress: *cf.* v. lxxix. 2.

[6] From boredom: *cf.* IV. xli. 2. *Asserere in libertatem* was the regular phrase for setting a slave free: *cf.* I. lii. 5.

CXLIII.—*Tunicae Patavinae*

Vellera consumunt Patavinae multa trilices,
et pingues tunicas serra secare potest.

CXLIV.—*Spongea*

Haec tibi sorte datur tergendis spongea mensis
utilis, expresso cum levis imbre tumet.

CXLV.—*Paenula Gausapina*

Is mihi candor inest, villorum gratia tanta,
ut me vel media sumere messe velis.

CXLVI.—*Cervical*

Tingue caput Cosmi folio, cervical olebit:
perdidit unguentum cum coma, pluma tenet.

CXLVII.—*Cubicularia Gausapina*

Stragula purpureis lucent villosa tapetis.
quid prodest, si te congelat uxor anus?

CXLVIII.—*Lodices*

Nudo stragula ne toro paterent,
iunctae nos tibi venimus sorores.

---

¹ The *trilix* was where every weft-thread was passed over
one and then under three of the warp-threads, instead of
over one and under the next in regular succession, as in
ordinary weaving. The process is called twilling, and the
fabric would be triple-twilled. Verg. speaks of a breastplate
auro trilix: *Aen.* iii. 467; *i.e.* chain-mail.
² Frieze garments were ordinarily worn in winter: *cf.* vi.
lix. 2.

490

CXLIII.—*Patavian Tunics*

PADUAN garments of triple thread[1] use up many fleeces, and only a saw can sever the thick tunics.

CXLIV.—*A Sponge*

THIS sponge is given you by lot: it is useful for wiping tables when it lightly swells after the water has been squeezed out.

CXLV.—*A Frieze Surtout*

SUCH is my whiteness, the beauty of my wool is such, that you would choose to wear me even in the midst of harvest.[2]

CXLVI.—*A Pillow*

ANOINT your head with Cosmus' unguent, your pillow will smell of it : when your hair has lost the fragrance the feathers retain it.

CXLVII.—*Frieze Coverlets*[3]

YOUR coverlet of wool is bright with purple brocade. What is the use of it if an aged wife freeze you ?

CXLVIII.—*Blankets*

THAT the sacking on your bare bed might not show, we sisters, knit together, have come to you.[4]

---

[3] *Gausapum* was woollen cloth having, like frieze, a thick nap on one side only, as distinguished from *amphimallum*, which had a nap on both. It was introduced into Rome in the time of the Elder Pliny's father : Plin. *N.H.* viii. lxxiii.

[4] The *lodix* was a small shaggy blanket. Sometimes two were sewed together to form a coverlet. The Emperor Augustus used it as a wrap for warmth in the open air : Suet. *Aug.* lxxxiii. *Lodices* came from Verona : *cf.* Ep. clii.

CXLIX.—*Amictorium*

MAMMOSAS metuo; tenerae me trade puellae,
ut possint niveo pectore lina frui.

CL.—*Cubicularia Polymita*

HAEC tibi Memphitis tellus dat munera: victa est
pectine·Niliaco iam Babylonos acus.

CLI.—*Zona*

LONGA satis nunc sum; dulci sed pondere venter
si tumeat, fiam tunc tibi zona brevis.

CLII.—*Gausapum Quadratum*

LODICES mittet docti tibi terra Catulli:
nos Helicaonia de regione sumus.

CLIII.—*Semicinctium*

DET tunicam locuples: ego te praecingere possum.
essem si locuples, munus utrumque darem.

CLIV.—*Lanae Amethystinae*

EBRIA Sidoniae cum sim de sanguine conchae,
non video quare sobria lana vocer.

---

[1] Damask is a variety of twill (*cf.* cxliii.), and depends
upon the number of warp threads (generally four) intersected
by the weft.   [2] A weaver's reed.
[3] Babylon was celebrated for embroidery in colour; the
art of many-threaded work (*polymita*) came from Alexandria:
cf. Plin. *N.H.* viii. 74.

CXLIX.—*A Tucker*

I SHRINK from big-breasted women : hand me over to some young girl, that my linen may enjoy a bosom of snow.

CL.—*Damask* [1] *Coverlets*

THIS present the land of Memphis makes you : now has the needle of Babylon been surpassed by the sley [2] of the Nile. [3]

CLI.—*A Female Girdle*

LONG enough am I now ; but if your shape should swell under its grateful burden, then shall I become to you a narrow girdle.

CLII.—*A Square Woollen Rug*

BLANKETS the country of elegant Catullus will send you : we are from the region of Helicaon. [4]

CLIII.—*An Apron*

LET a rich man give a tunic : I can gird you in front. Were I rich, I would give both gifts.

CLIV.—*Amethyst-dyed Wool*

DRUNKEN as I am with the blood of Sidon's shell-fish, I do not see why I am called sober wool. [5]

---

[4] Paduan : *cf.* x. xciii. 1.
[5] " Amethyst " etymologically means " unintoxicated," either, as Pliny says (*N.H.* xxxvii. 40), because it did not approximate to the colour of wine, or because its possession was supposed to be an antidote against inebriety. There are similar Greek epigrams in *Pal. Anth.* ix. 748 and 752.

CLV.—*Lanae Albae*

VELLERIBUS primis Apulia, Parma secundis
nobilis : Altinum tertia laudat ovis.

CLVI.—*Lanae Tyriae*

Nos Lacedaemoniae pastor donavit amicae:
deterior Ledae purpura matris erat.

CLVII.—*Lanae Pollentinae*

NON tantum pullo lugentes vellere lanas,
sed solet et calices haec dare terra suos.

CLVIII.—*Idem*

LANA quidem tristis sed tonsis apta ministris,
quales non primo de grege mensa citat.

CLIX.—*Tomentum Leuconicum*

OPPRESSAE nimium vicina est fascia plumae ?
vellera Leuconicis accipe rasa sagis.

CLX.—*Tomentum Circense*

TOMENTUM concisa palus Circense vocatur.
haec pro Leuconico stramina pauper emit.

---

[1] *cf.* Plin. *N. H.* viii. 73.
[2] A *municipium* in Venetia on the road between Patavium
(Padua) and Aquileia (now Altino) : *cf.* IV. xxv. 1.
[3] Paris gave to Helen.
[4] Laconian purple was the finest produced in Europe, that
of Tyre the finest in Asia : Plin. *N. H.* ix. 60. The latter
was superior to the former.
[5] A town in Liguria, now Polenza. It was famed for its
wool, which was black : Plin. *N. H.* viii. 73.

CLV.—*White Wool*

APULIA is renowned for the finest wool,[1] Parma for second quality; its sheep, third in rank, commend Altinum.[2]

CLVI.—*Tyrian Wools*

Us the shepherd gave to his Lacedaemonian mistress:[3] of less worth was the purple of her mother Leda.[4]

CLVII.—*Wool from Pollentia* [5]

THIS land is wont to supply not only wool that mourns with its black fleece: it supplies also its native chalices.

CLVIII.—*The Same*

MY wool is indeed sad in hue, but 'tis fit for close-clipt attendants,[6] such as—but not from the first rank of slaves—the table summons.

CLIX.—*Leuconian Bed-stuffing*

IS the bed-girth [7] too near the feather pillow you crush down? Accept fleeces shorn for Leuconian [8] cloaks.

CLX.—*Circensian Bed-stuffing*

MARSH-REED chopped up is called Circensian [9] stuffing. This litter the poor man buys in lieu of Leuconian.

---

[6] The smarter attendants often had their hair long : *cf.* II. lvii. 5 ; III. lviii. 31.

[7] *cf.* v. lxii. 6.

[8] *Leuconicum* was a wool much used as a stuffing : *cf.* XI. xxi. 8 and lvi. 9. It came from the Leucones, a Gaulish people.

[9] So called because it was used in the circus on seats by the common people : *cf.* Sen. *De Vit. Beat.* xxv. 2.

CLXI.—*Pluma*

LASSUS Amyclaea poteris requiescere pluma,
  interior cycni quam tibi lana dedit.

CLXII.—*Faenum*

FRAUDATA tumeat fragilis tibi culcita mula.
  non venit ad duros pallida cura toros.

CLXIII.—*Tintinabulum*

REDDE pilam : sonat aes thermarum. ludere pergis ?
  Virgine vis sola lotus abire domum.

CLXIV.—*Discus*

SPLENDIDA cum volitant Spartani pondera disci,
  este procul, pueri : sit semel ille nocens.

CLXV.—*Cithara*

REDDIDIT Eurydicen vati : sed perdidit ipse,
  dum sibi non credit nec patienter amat.

CLXVI.—*Idem*

DE Pompeiano saepe est eiecta theatro
  quae duxit silvas detinuitque feras.

---

[1] A city of Laconia. The feathers are called Amyclaean
because Jupiter appeared to Spartan Leda in the shape of a
swan.

[2] *cf.* Hor. *Od.* III. i. 21 for a similar idea.

CLXI.—*Feathers*

TIRED you may rest on feathers of Amyclae [1] which the swan's inner down has given you.

CLXII.—*Hay*

LET your rustling mattress swell with thefts from your mule: pale Care comes not to hard couches. [2]

CLXIII.—*A Bell*

GIVE up the ball: the bell of the warm baths is sounding. Do you go on playing? You want to go home after a bath in the Virgin water only. [3]

CLXIV.—*A Quoit*

WHILE the burnished weight of the Spartan quoit is flying, keep far off, ye boys: let that quoit be guilty only once. [4]

CLXV.—*A Cithern*

IT restored Eurydice to her bard; but he himself lost her, trusting not himself, nor loving with patience.

CLXVI.—*The Same*

OFTEN has that been driven [5] from Pompey's theatre, which drew after it woods and stayed wild beasts. [6]

---

[3] The hot baths will be full, or closed, and he will have to content himself with a cold bath from the *aqua Virgo*: cf. v. xx. 9.   [4] cf. clxxiii. *post*.

[5] *i.e.* hissed off by the audience.

[6] *i.e.* when played by Orpheus: cf. *Spect.* xxi.

CLXVII.—*Plectrum*

Fervida ne trito tibi pollice pusula surgat,
  exornent docilem candida plectra lyram.[1]

CLXVIII.—*Trochus*

Inducenda rota est : das nobis utile munus :
  iste trochus pueris at mihi canthus erit.

CLXIX.—*Idem*

Garrulus in laxo cur anulus orbe vagatur ?
  cedat ut argutis obvia turba trochis.

CLXX.—*Signum Victoriae Aureum*

Haec illi sine sorte datur cui nomina Rhenus
  vera dedit.   deciens adde Falerna, puer.

CLXXI.—Βρούτου παιδίον *Fictile*

Gloria tam parvi non est obscura sigilli :
  istius pueri Brutus amator erat.

   [1] *garrula βγ.*

---

[1] An instrument for striking the strings.

[2] Rings were often strung round the orbit of a boy's hoop :
see a picture taken from a sepulchral bas-relief at Tivoli
reproduced in Rich's *Dict. Ant. s.v.* "Anulus." How the
hoop was able to run is very obscure. Perhaps loose rings
were supported in position by the *clavis*, or hook, for
trundling the hoop. Or perhaps the rings were attached to
the inner circumference.

CLXVII.—*A Quill for Playing the Lyre*

THAT an angry blister may not arise on your chafed thumb, let an ivory quill[1] embellish your responsive lyre.

CLXVIII.—*A Hoop*

THE wheel must be fitted with a tyre: you give me a useful present; this to boys will be a hoop, but to me a tyre.

CLXIX.—*The Same*

WHY do noisy rings wander round the wide orbit? That the crowd that meets them may give way to tinkling hoops.[2]

CLXX.—*A Golden Statue of Victory*[3]

SHE is given without a drawn lot to him to whom Rhine has given a true victor's name. Ten times[4] pour Falernian, boy.

CLXXI.—*A Clay Image of "Brutus' Boy"*

THE renown of so small a statue[5] is not unknown. Of this boy was Brutus the lover.

---

[3] This, and the following, describe *sigilla* (statuettes), which were frequently given at the Saturnalia, *i.e.* on the last two days, which were called *Sigillaria*: *cf.* Aus. *De Fer. Rom.* v. 32 (*Festa sigillorum nomine dicta colunt*).

[4] To represent the letters of Germanicus (Domitian): *cf.* IX. xciii. 7, 8.

[5] *cf.* II. lxxvii. 4 ; IX. l. The statuette was by Strongylion, a Greek sculptor of the fifth century B.C.: Plin. *N.H.* xxxiv. 19 (21).

THE EPIGRAMS OF MARTIAL

CLXXII.—*Sauroctonos Corinthius*

Ad te reptanti, puer insidiose, lacertae
parce ; cupit digitis illa perire tuis.

CLXXIII.—*Hyacinthus in Tabula Pictus*

Flectit ab inviso morientia lumina disco
Oebalius, Phoebi culpa dolorque, puer.

CLXXIV.—*Hermaphroditus Marmoreus*

Masculus intravit fontis : emersit utrumque :
pars est una patris, cetera matris habet.

CLXXV.—*Danae Picta*

Cur a te pretium Danae, regnator Olympi,
accepit, gratis si tibi Leda dedit ?

CLXXVI.—*Persona Germana*

Sum figuli lusus russi persona Batavi.
quae tu derides, haec timet ora puer.

CLXXVII.—*Hercules Corinthius*

Elidit geminos infans nec respicit anguis.
iam poterat teneras hydra timere manus.

---

[1] On a replica of a work of Praxiteles representing the
young Apollo with an arrow watching a lizard. It was
called Σαυροκτόνος : cf. Plin. *N.H.* xxxiv. 19 (10).

[2] Apollo, when playing at quoits with Hyacinthus, killed
him by accident. From his blood sprang the hyacinth
inscribed with the Greek αἰαῖ (alas): cf. Milton's "Sanguine
flower inscribed with woe." The picture alluded to may be
a copy of the one by Antidotus of the fourth century B.C.,
the original of which was transported to Rome by Augustus
on the capture of Alexandria : Plin. *N.H.* xxxv. 40 (28).

CLXXII.—*The Lizard-slayer in Corinthian Bronze*

SPARE the lizard, treacherous boy, as it creeps up to you; it longs to perish by your hands.[1]

CLXXIII.—*A Picture of Hyacinthus*

FROM the hated quoit he turns his dying eyes, the Oebalian boy, the reproach and sorrow of Phoebus.[2]

CLXXIV.—*A Marble Hermaphroditus*

MALE, he entered the fount;[3] he came forth both male and female: one part of him is his sire's, all else has he of his mother.

CLXXV.—*A Picture of Danae*

WHY of you, Ruler of Olympus, did Danae[4] receive her price, if Leda unbought was kind to you?

CLXXVI.—*A German Mask*

I AM a freak of the potter, the mask of a red-haired Batavian. This face you deride a boy dreads.[5]

CLXXVII.—*Hercules in Corinthian Bronze*

THE infant throttles[6] the two serpents, nor does he glance on them. Already might the hydra[7] fear youthful hands.

---

[3] Salmacis: *cf.* VI. lxviii. 9; and see Ovid, *Met.* iv. 285.

[4] Possibly a copy of Artemon's picture of Danae *mirantibus eam praedonibus*: *cf.* Plin. *N.H.* xxxv. 40 (32).

[5] To him it is a bogey.

[6] The Goddess Hera, jealous of Alcmena the mother of Hercules, sent two serpents to kill him in his cradle: *cf.* Verg. *Aen.* viii. 289.

[7] The Lernaean hydra, or water-snake, was one of the monsters slain by Hercules: *cf.* *Spect.* xxvii. 5; IX. ci. 9.

CLXXVIII.—*Hercules Fictilis*

Sum fragilis: sed tu, moneo, ne sperne sigillum:
non pudet Alciden nomen habere meum.

CLXXIX.—*Minerva Argentea*

Dic mihi, virgo ferox, cum sit tibi cassis et hasta,
quare non habeas aegida. "Caesar habet."

CLXXX.—*Europe Picta*

Mutari melius tauro, pater optime divum,
tunc poteras, Io cum tibi vacca fuit.

CLXXXI.—*Leandros Marmoreus*

Clamabat tumidis audax Leandros in undis
"Mergite me, fluctus, cum rediturus ero."

CLXXXII.—*Sigillum Gibberi Fictile*

Ebrius haec fecit terris, puto, monstra Prometheus:
Saturnalicio lusit et ipse luto.

---

[1] The statuette was called Hercules Fictilis: *cf.* Plin.
N.H. xxxv. 45. It was by Turianus of Fregellae in the time
of Tarquinius Priscus.

[2] See the description of Domitian's breastplate, VII. i. and ii.

[3] The original was in the *Porticus Pompeii*, painted by
Antiphilus, the rival of Apelles: Plin. *N.H.* xxxv. 37.

[4] As a bull J. would have escaped the hundred eyes of
Argus set to watch Io: *cf.* lxxxv. 2.

CLXXVIII.—*A Hercules in Clay*

FRAGILE am I, but do not you, I charge you, despise my small statue : it shames not Alcides to bear my name.[1]

CLXXIX.—*A Minerva in Silver*

TELL me, gallant maid, whereas thou hast thy helm and thy spear, why hast thou not thine aegis? "Caesar has it."[2]

CLXXX.—*A Picture of Europa*[3]

BETTER, most excellent Father of the Gods, couldst thou have been changed into a bull when Io was to thee a heifer.[4]

CLXXXI.—*A Marble Leander*

DARING Leander cried amid the swelling waters: "Drown me, ye waves, when I am turning home."[5]

CLXXXII.—*A Clay Statuette of a Hunchback*

'TWAS a drunken Prometheus,[6] I fancy, made for the earth this monster; he himself, too, played with Saturnalian clay.[7]

---

[5] *Spect.* xxv. B is on the same subject.
[6] *i.e.* the potter : *cf.* Juv. iv. 133.
[7] The original Prometheus (*ipse*) made men out of clay (*cf.* x. xxxix. 4), and had a taste for making grotesque figures. Statuettes of dwarfs and monstrosities were doubtless often made, and given as presents at the Saturnalia, the taste for slaves of this type being common : *cf.* the Polyphemus and Scylla of VII. xxxviii.

CLXXXIII.—*Homeri Batrachomachia*

PERLEGE Maeonio cantatas carmine ranas
et frontem nugis solvere disce meis.

CLXXXIV.—*Homerus in Pugillaribus Membranis*

ILIAS et Priami regnis inimicus Ulixes
multiplici pariter condita pelle latent.

CLXXXV.—*Vergili Culix*

ACCIPE facundi Culicem, studiose, Maronis,
ne nucibus positis "Arma virumque" legas.

CLXXXVI.—*Vergilius in Membranis*

QUAM brevis inmensum cepit membrana Maronem!
ipsius vultus prima tabella gerit.

CLXXXVII.—Μενάνδρου Θαΐς

HAC primum iuvenum lascivos lusit amores;
nec Glycera pueri, Thais amica fuit.

CLXXXVIII.—*Cicero in Membranis*

SI comes ista tibi fuerit membrana, putato
carpere te longas cum Cicerone vias.

---

[1] "If Homer can unbend, I can be excused."
[2] *Culex*, an early poem of Vergil's.
[3] With which they gambled at the Saturnalia : *cf.* XIV.
i. 12.

CLXXXIII.—*Homer's "Battle of Frogs and Mice"*

READ through the story of the frogs sung in Homer's lay, and learn to smooth your brow by means of my trifles.[1]

CLXXXIV.—*Homer in Parchment Handybooks*

THE *Iliad* and the tale of Ulysses, foe to Priam's realm, both lie stored in many-folded skins.

CLXXXV.—*Virgil's Gnat*

RECEIVE, studious reader, the Gnat[2] of eloquent Maro; you need not then lay aside your nuts[3] to read "Arms and the Man."

CLXXXVI.—*Virgil in Parchment*

How short a parchment[4] has comprised the mighty Maro! The features of the man himself the first leaf bears.

CLXXXVII.—*The Thais of Menander*

WITH this first he lightly touched youth's wanton love, and Glycera was not the mistress of his boyhood: 'twas Thais.[5]

CLXXXVIII.—*Cicero in Parchment*

IF this parchment shall be your travelling companion, imagine you are taking a long journey with Cicero.

---

[4] Parchment being very expensive, books were often copied in small characters : *cf.* cxc.

[5] From this play came the line quoted by St. Paul, φθείρουσιν ἤθη χρήσθ' ὁμιλίαι κακαί.

THE EPIGRAMS OF MARTIAL

CLXXXIX.—*Monobyblos Properti*

Cynthia, facundi carmen iuvenale Properti,
  accepit famam; non minus ipsa dedit.

CXC.—*Titus Livius in Membranis*

Pellibus exiguis artatur Livius ingens,
  quem mea non totum bybliotheca capit.

CXCI.—*Sallustius*

Hic erit, ut perhibent doctorum corda virorum,
  primus Romana Crispus in historia.

CXCII.—*Ovidi Metamorphosis in Membranis*

Haec tibi multiplici quae structa est massa tabella,
  carmina Nasonis quinque decemque gerit.

CXCIII.—*Tibullus*

Ussit amatorem Nemesis lasciva Tibullum,
  in tota iuvit quem nihil esse domo.

CXCIV.—*Lucanus*

Sunt quidam qui me dicant non esse poetam:
  sed qui me vendit bybliopola putat.

CXCV.—*Catullus*

Tantum magna suo debet Verona Catullo,
  quantum parva suo Mantua Vergilio.

---

[1] The first book of Propertius was published by him at the
age of twenty. It was called *Cynthia*, and in some MSS. is
headed "Monobiblos." But whether M. alludes to this is
uncertain.

CLXXXIX.—*Propertius in a Single Volume*

CYNTHIA,[1] the theme of eloquent Propertius' youthful song, won from him fame; no less she herself bestowed.

CXC.—*Titus Livius in Parchment*

NARROWED into scanty skins is bulky Livy, the whole of whom my library does not contain.[2]

CXCI.—*Sallust*

HERE will be Crispus, first of Roman historians, as the judgment of learned men declares.

CXCII.—*Ovid's "Metamorphoses" in Parchment*

THIS bulk, that has been formed of many a leaf, contains the fifteen books of Naso's poems.

CXCIII.—*Tibullus*

WANTON Nemesis[3] fired her lover Tibullus, whom it pleased to be "of no account in his own house."

CXCIV.—*Lucan*

SOME are there that say I am no poet: but the bookseller that sells me thinks I am.

CXCV.—*Catullus*

As much great Verona owes to her Catullus as small Mantua owes to her Virgil.

---

[2] It is too small to hold Livy in his ordinary shape. L. wrote 142 books of annals.

[3] It was Delia of whom Tib. (I. v. 30) writes "*At juvet in tota me nihil esse domo*" Nemesis was his second love.

CXCVI.—*Calvi de Aquae Frigidae Usu*

Haec tibi quae fontes et aquarum nomina dicit
ipsa suas melius charta natabit aquas.

CXCVII.—*Mulae Pumilae*

His tibi de mulis non est metuenda ruina:
altius in terra paene sedere soles.

CXCVIII.—*Catella Gallicana*

Delicias parvae si vis audire catellae,
narranti brevis est pagina tota mihi.

CXCIX.—*Asturco*

Hic brevis ad numeros rapidum qui colligit unguem,
venit ab auriferis gentibus Astur equus.

CC.—*Canis Vertragus*

Non sibi sed domino venatur vertragus acer,
inlaesum leporem qui tibi dente feret.

CCI.—*Palaestrita*

Non amo quod vincat, sed quod succumbere novit
et didicit melius τὴν ἐπικλινοπάλην.

---

¹ Licinius Calvus, an orator and poet of the age of Cicero.
He is praised by Catullus, Propertius, and Ovid; but M.
suggests that this particular work is fit only to be thrown
away: *cf.* I. v. 2.   ² *cf.* M.'s description of Issa (I. cix.).
³ *cf. Non vulgaris in cursu gradus, sed mollis alterno
crurum explicatu glomeratio*: Plin. *N.H.* viii. 67. This trot
or amble was taught: *ibid.*

CXCVI.—*Calvus'* [1] *Poem on the Use of Cold Water*

THESE sheets, that speak to you of fountains and of the names of rivers, themselves will better swim in the waters they tell of.

CXCVII.—*Dwarf Mules*

FROM these mules no fall is to be apprehended : you are used to sit almost higher on the ground.

CXCVIII.—*A Gallic Lapdog*

IF you wish to hear the tricks of a small lapdog, for the telling a whole page of mine is too short.[2]

CXCIX.—*A Jennet*

THIS little horse, that picks up its hurrying hoof in measured time,[3] has come from tribes rich in gold, an Asturian steed.

CC.—*A Greyhound* [4]

NOT for himself, but for his master, hunts the keen greyhound, who will bring you a hare unwounded by his tooth.

CCI.—*A Wrestler*

I DO not like him because he wins, but because he knows how to yield, and has learned the better art of recovering himself.[5]

---

[4] The word is by some translated "tumbler," a dog that inveigled game by careless gambols, or by rolling himself into a heap, and so disguising his shape. It is alluded to in *Hudibras*.

[5] There is probably an obscene sense here : *cf.* Suet. *Dom.* 22 (*assiduitatem concubitus velut exercitationis genus clinopalen vocabat*).

CCII.—*Simius*

CALLIDUS emissas eludere simius hastas,
  si mihi cauda foret, cercopithecus eram.

CCIII.—*Puella Gaditana*

TAM tremulum crisat, tam blandum prurit, ut ipsum
  masturbatorem fecerit Hippolytum.

CCIV.—*Cymbala*

AERA Celaenaeos lugentia Matris amores
  esuriens Gallus vendere saepe solet.

CCV.—*Puer*

SIT nobis aetate puer, non pumice, levis,
  propter quem placeat nulla puella mihi.

CCVI.—*Cestos*

COLLO necte, puer, meros amores,
  ceston de Veneris sinu calentem.

CCVII.—*Idem*

SUME Cytheriaco medicatum nectare ceston:
  ussit amatorem balteus iste Iovem.

---

[1] The *cercopithecus* came from Aethiopia : Plin. *N.H.* viii.
30. In Egypt it was a sacred animal : Juv. xv. 4.
[2] Who rejected the advances of his stepmother, Phaedra,
the wife of his father Theseus.

CCII.—*A Monkey*

A MONKEY cunning to avoid darts hurled at me,
I should be a "long-tailed ape"[1] had I a tail.

CCIII.—*A Girl from Gades*

SALTEGGIA con si minuto tremito, ed eccita con
tanta lusinga, che Ippolito[2] stesso si masturberebbe.

CCIV.—*Cymbals*

THE brazen cymbals that mourn for the boy of
Celaenae,[3] the darling of the Great Mother, her
priest is often wont to sell when hungry.

CCV.—*A Young Slave*

MAY I have a boy with a cheek smooth with youth,
not with pumice, for whose sake no maid would
please me.

CCVI.—*A Cestus*

ROUND thy neck twine, boy, love's very essence,[4]
a cestus[5] warm from the bosom of Venus.

CCVII.—*The Same*

TAKE thou the cestus imbued with Cytherea's
nectar: this girdle fired[6] the lover Jove.

---

[3] Attis, the love of Cybele: *cf.* II. lxxxvi. 4.
[4] A phrase from Catullus xiii. 9.
[5] *cf.* VI. xiii. 5.
[6] Hera borrowed from Aphrodite her *cestus* to inflame the
ardour of Zeus: Hom. *Il.* xiv. 214, 312.

CCVIII.—*Notarius*

CURRANT verba licet, manus est velocior illis:
  nondum lingua suum, dextra peregit opus.

CCIX.—*Concha*

LEVIS ab aequorea cortex Mareotica concha
  fiat: inoffensa curret harundo via.

CCX.—*Morio*

NON mendax stupor est nec fingitur arte dolosa.
  quisquis plus iusto non sapit, ille sapit.

CCXI.—*Caput Vervecinum*

MOLLIA Phrixei secuisti colla mariti.
  hoc meruit, tunicam qui tibi, saeve, dedit?

CCXII.—*Pumilus*

SI solum spectes hominis caput, Hectora credas:
  si stantem videas, Astyanacta putes.

CCXIII.—*Parma*

HAEC, quae saepe solet vinci, quae vincere raro,
  parma tibi, scutum pumilionis erit.

---

[1] This epigram explains the small price at which M.'s
poems could be sold by Tryphon: *cf.* XIII. iii. 2. A number
of slaves as shorthand writers could copy books cheaply.

[2] Papyrus, Mareotis being a part of Egypt. Pliny (*N.H.*
xiii. 25) says that papyrus was smoothed by an instrument
or by a shell, but that the writing fades.

[3] *cf.* VI. xxxix.; VIII. xiii.; XII. xciii.

[4] The ram with the golden fleece that carried Phryxus

CCVIII.—*A Shorthand Writer*

ALBEIT the words speed, the hand is swifter than they: not yet has the tongue, the hand has finished its work.[1]

CCIX.—*A Sea-shell*

LET the rind of the Mareotic rush[2] be made smooth by the sea-shell: the reed-pen will run on an unimpeded path.

CCX.—*A Natural*[3]

HIS dulness is not assumed, or pretended by crafty art. He that has wits no more than is enough has his wits.

CCXI.—*A Ram's Head*

YOU have cut the soft throat of the lord of the flock, a ram of Phryxus;[4] did he deserve this who gave you, cruel man, your tunic?

CCXII.—*A Dwarf*

IF you regard the man's head alone you would believe him Hector; if you saw him standing you would deem him Astyanax.[5]

CCXIII.—*A Small Shield*

THIS, which is wont oft to be overcome, rarely to win,[6] will be to you a small buckler, but a dwarf's great shield.

and Helle through the air, and whose fleece was afterwards carried off by the Argonauts from Colchis: *cf.* vi. iii. 6; viii. li. 9.   [5] The young son of Hector: *cf.* viii. vi. 16.

[6] Domitian favoured the *scutarii*, gladiators who fought with the ordinary large oblong shield, as against the gladiators called "Thracians," who wore a smaller shield of a round shape: *cf.* ix. lxviii. 8.

513

CCXIV.—*Comoedi Pueri*

Non erit in turba quisquam Μισούμενος ista :
sed poterit quivis esse Δὶς ἐξαπατῶν.

CCXV.—*Fibula*

Dic mihi simpliciter, comoedis et citharoedis,
fibula, quid praestas?   "Carius ut futuant."

CCXVI.—*Accipiter*

Praedo fuit volucrum : famulus nunc aucupis idem
deicit et captas non sibi maeret aves.

CCXVII.—*Opsonator*

Dic quotus et quanti cupias cenare, nec unum
addideris verbum : cena parata tibi est.

CCXVIII.—*Auceps*

Non tantum calamis sed cantu fallitur ales,
callida dum tacita crescit harundo manu.

CCXIX.—*Cor Bubulum*

Pauper causidicus nullos referentia nummos
carmina cum scribas, accipe cor, quod habes.

---

[1] The two mentioned are comedies of Menander. In the
latter occurs the celebrated line ὃν οἱ θέοι φιλοῦσιν ἀποθνήσκει
νέος.   [2] cf. VII. lxxxii. 1, 2.
[3] The removal of the clasp has to be paid for : *cf. Solvitur
his magno comoedi fibula* (Juv. vi. 73).
[4] Birds are caught not only by a limed cane but also by an
imitation of their note, or by the note of a decoy bird. As

CCXIV.—*Boy Comic Actors*

IN all this troupe will be no one "The Hated";
but any one of them can be "The Double Deceiver."[1]

CCXV.—*A Singer's Clasp*

TELL me candidly, O clasp, what do you guarantee
to comedians and harp-players?[2] "The greater
value of their favours."[3]

CCXVI.—*A Hawk*

HE preyed once upon birds; the servant of the
fowler now, he strikes them down, and is sad the
birds are not taken for his own behoof.

CCXVII.—*A Caterer*

SAY with how many and at what cost you want to
dine, and do not add another word: your dinner is
ready for you.

CCXVIII.—*Bird-catching Rods*

NOT only by canes, but by a bird's note also is
the bird deceived while the cunning reed is being
lengthened by the noiseless hand.[4]

CCXIX.— *A Bullock's Pluck*

SEEING that you, a poor lawyer, write poems that
do not bring you in a penny, take from me pluck
like your own.[5]

to the cane, *cf.* IX. liv. 3; and, as to the decoy, see the
engraved gem in Rich's *Dict. Antiq. s.v.* " Arundo."

[5] There is a play on two meanings of the word *cor*, viz.
"heart" and " sense": *cf.* VI. lxiv. 18. " Pluck " is a
butcher's name for the heart, liver and lights of an animal :
see Skeat's *Etym. Dict. s.v.* ; and also means " courage."

CCXX.—*Cocus*

Non satis est ars sola coco: servire palatum
nolo: cocus domini debet habere gulam.

CCXXI.—*Craticula cum Verubus*

Rara tibi curva craticula sudet ofella;
spumeus in longa cuspide fumet aper.

CCXXII.—*Pistor Dulciarius*

Mille tibi dulces operum manus ista figuras
extruet: huic uni parca laborat apis.

CCXXIII.—*Adipata*

Surgite: iam vendit pueris ientacula pistor
cristataeque sonant undique lucis aves.

INCERTAE SEDIS EPIGRAMMA

Flavia gens, quantum tibi tertius abstulit heres!
paene fuit tanti non habuisse duos.

Hoc epigramma extat apud scholiastam in Iuvenalem S.
iv. 38. Vulgo in fine libri spectaculorum legitur, libro xi.
adsignatur a Friedl.

BOOK XIV. ccxx–ccxxiii

CCXX.—*A Cook*

INSUFFICIENT is his art alone for a cook: I would not have his palate that of a slave; a cook ought to possess the taste of his master.

CCXXI.—*A Gridiron with Spits*

LET your grated gridiron be unctuous with the rounded cutlet; on the long pointed spit let a foaming boar smoke.

CCXXII.—*The Confectioner*

A THOUSAND toothsome shapes of handiwork that hand will construct for you; for him alone labours the frugal bee.

CCXXIII.—*Rich Dainties*

GET up: already the baker is selling to boys their breakfast, and the crested fowls of dawn are crowing on all sides.

AN EPIGRAM OF UNCERTAIN POSITION

O FLAVIAN family, of how much glory has thy third heir robbed thee! Well nigh had it stood us in stead not to have possessed the twain![1]

[1] These lines (which are amplified by Ausonius, *Caes.* xii.) mean that Domitian was so evil that it had been better for Rome not to have had Flavian Emperors at all, even good ones like Vespasian and Titus.

EPIGRAMS ASCRIBED TO MARTIAL

EPIGRAMMATA QUAEDAM
M. VAL. MARTIALI AFFICTA

I.—*De Rusticatione*

Rure morans quid agam, respondeo pauca, rogatus.
  luce deos oro ; famulos, post arva reviso,
partibus atque meis iustos indico labores.
inde lego, Phoebumque cio, Musamque lacesso.
hinc oleo corpusque frico mollique palaestra   5
stringo libens, animo gaudens, ac foenore liber.
prandeo, poto, cano, ludo, lavo, coeno, quiesco.
dum parvus lychnus modicum consumat olivi,
haec dat nocturnis nox lucubrata Camoenis.

II.—*In Varum*

Ad coenam nuper Varus me forte vocavit :
  ornatus dives, parvula coena fuit.
auro, non dapibus, oneratur mensa : ministri
  apponunt oculis plurima, pauca gulae.
tunc ego, "Non oculos, sed ventrem, pascere veni : 5
  aut appone dapes, Vare, vel aufer opes."

---

¹ These are partly gathered from MSS. and old glossaries, partly embodied in his works by Hadrianus Junius and others.

Hadr. Jun. (Adrien de Jonghe, 1512–1575) was a Dutch physician and savant, one of the most learned men of the

EPIGRAMS ASCRIBED TO MARTIAL [1]

I.—*Life in the Country*

As you ask me what I do while staying in the country I reply shortly. At daybreak I pray to the gods; I visit my servants and afterwards my fields, and to my staff I assign their proper tasks. Then I read and call on Phoebus, and challenge the Muses. After this I rub my body with oil, and with mild gymnastics gladly brace myself, happy in my mind and free from moneylenders. I lunch, drink, sing, play, bathe, dine, go to bed. Provided my small lamp consume but little oil, such lucubrations as these night furnishes to the nocturnal Muses.

II.—*Against Varus*

VARUS happened to invite me lately to dinner: his appointments were rich, his dinner was scanty. The table is loaded with gold plate, not with meats; the attendants set before us much to please the eye, little to tickle the palate. Then I said: "I did not come to stuff my eyes, but my stomach; either provide your provender, Varus, or remove your property."

age. Among his works were commentaries on Plautus, Horace, Petronius, Seneca, and Martial; and a Philippid, or *Epithalamium* on the marriage of Philip and Mary. He was the Rector of the College of Harlem, and his library was pillaged by the Spaniards.

EPIGRAMS ASCRIBED TO MARTIAL

III.—*In Ponticum*

PONTICE, per reges discurris, et omnia lustras:
    magna quidem sequeris, Pontice: magnus homo es.
Pontice, si qua facis, sine teste facis, sine turba;
    non adhibes multos, Pontice: cautus homo es.
Pontice, te celebrem forma natura creavit: 5
    dignus eras Helena, Pontice: pulcher homo es.
Pontice, voce tua posses adamanta movere:
    vox tua dulce sonat, Pontice: dulcis homo es.
Pontice, sic alios, sic te quoque decipit error:
    vis dicam verum, Pontice?   Nullus homo es.   10

IV.—*De Vetula*

TACTA places, audita places: si non videare,
    tota places: neutro, si videare, places.

V.—*De Milone*

MILO domi non est: peregre Milone profecto
    arva vacant: uxor non minus inde parit.
cur sit ager sterilis, cur uxor fertilis, edam:
    quo fodiatur ager non habet, uxor habet.

VI.—*De Histrionis Poena*

ANTE Iovis statuam crepuit satur histrio: poenam
    Iuppiter indixit, vivere de proprio.

III.—*Against Ponticus*

PONTICUS, you run about among great lords, and have an eye for everything going; you pursue, indeed, great things, Ponticus; you are a great man. Ponticus, if you do anything, you do it without a witness, without a crowd round you; you don't make confidants of many, Ponticus; you are a cautious man. Ponticus, nature has fashioned you of remarkable beauty; you would have been worthy of Helen, Ponticus; you are a handsome man. Ponticus, with that voice of yours you might stir adamant; your voice is sweet-toned, Ponticus; you are a sweet man. Ponticus, this error deceives you too as it does other men. Would you have me tell you the truth, Ponticus? You are not a man at all.

IV.—*On an Old Woman*

To the touch you are pleasing, listened to you are pleasing; if you are not seen, you are wholly pleasing; in neither way if you are seen are you pleasing.

V.—*On Milo*

MILO is not at home; Milo has gone abroad, and his fields are neglected; yet his wife is no less fruitful since. Why his land is sterile, why his wife is fertile, I will declare: his land has no cultivator, his wife has.

VI.—*On an Actor's Punishment*

A FULL-FED actor broke wind before Jove's statue. Jupiter declared the penalty, to live at his own expense.[1]

---

[1] XII. lxxvii. is an epigram on the same subject.

EPIGRAMS ASCRIBED TO MARTIAL

VII.—*In Effrontem*

Os atavi, patris nasum, duo lumina patris,
  et matris gestus dicis habere tuae.
cum referas priscos, nullamque in corpore partem
  mentiris; frontem, dic mihi, cuius habes?[1]

VIII.—*Ad Mattum*

Qui negat esse domi se, tunc cum limina pulsas,
  quid dicat, nescis? Dormio, Matte, tibi.

IX.—*Ad Milonem*

Tura, piper, vestes, argentum, pallia, gemmas,
  vendere, Milo, soles; cum quibus emtor abit.
coniugis utilior merx est: quae vendita saepe,
  vendentem nunquam deserit aut minuit.

X

Nec volo me summis fortuna nec applicet imis,
  sed medium vitae temperet illa gradum.
invidia excelsos, inopes iniuria vexat:
  quam felix vivit, quisquis utroque caret!

---

[1] *i.e.* whose "cheek"? The forehead was the seat of shame: cf. Pers. v. 103 (*frontem perisse de rebus*) and Shak. *R. and J.* III. ii. 91, "upon his brow Shame is ashamed to sit."

VII.—*Against a Shameless Person*

You say you have your fourth grandfather's mouth, your father's nose, both your father's eyes, and your mother's carriage. Since you recall your ancestors —and do not describe incorrectly any part of your body—tell me, whose forehead [1] have you?

VIII.—*To Mattus*

Don't you know what he says who denies himself just when you knock at his door? "To you, Mattus, I am asleep." [2]

IX.—*To Milo*

Frankincense, pepper, garments, silver plate, cloaks, jewels you are accustomed to sell, Milo, and the buyer goes off with them. Your wife is as merchandise more useful to you : she, though often sold, never leaves the seller or diminishes his estate.

X.—*On a Middle Station*

I would not have Fortune set me in the highest or in the lowest place; rather let her moderation grant life's middle station. Envy assails the high, wrong the weak : how happy does he live who escapes both !

[2] An allusion to the proverb "*Non omnibus dormio*," said of those that are willing to be blind to the doings of some others, but not of everybody : Fest. xii. 487 ; Cic. *Ep.* vii. 24. Erasmus (*Adag. s.v.*) tells the story of one Galba, who pretended to sleep while Maecenas toyed with his wife, but woke up when a slave began to steal his wine.

EPIGRAMS ASCRIBED TO MARTIAL

XI.—*Ad Scaevolam*

SCAEVOLA, tu coenas apud omnes, nullus apud te :
  alterius siccas pocula, nemo tua.
aut tu redde vices, aut desine velle vocari :
  dedecus est semper sumere, nilque dare.

XII.—*Ad Auctum*

EXIGIS a nobis, quem nulli solvis, amorem :
  quam nulli praestas, exigis, Aucte, fidem.
exigis a nobis, quem non merearis, honorem :
  mirum est, quod non das, id tibi velle dari.

XIII.—*De Filo*

PALLIA Filus habet, digitos circumligat auro :
  sed tamen est Filus paupere pauperior.
sunt Tyriae chlamydes, mille instrumenta, clientes
  Filo : sed tamen est paupere pauperior.
atria sunt Filo regali consita cultu :   5
  sed tamen est Filus paupere pauperior.
esurit atque sitit, gemmis instructus et auro ;
  Cyclade vestitus esurit atque sitit.
pondus adesse famis, pallor maciesque loquuntur :
  aurea bulla negat pondus adesse famis.   10
ergo miser se servitio pro pane locabit :
  sed ne sit servus aurea bulla facit.
si vero quenquam pulsabit supplice voto,
  ut non exoret, serica vestis adest.

---

[1] *cf.* III. xxvii.
[2] The epigram is on a miserly rich man.
[3] The *bulla* was an ornament in the shape of a heart worn
by children up to the age of seventeen, and then consecrated

XI.—*To Scaevola*

SCAEVOLA, you dine with everybody, no one with you; another man's cups you drain, no one drains yours. Either make return, or give over looking for invitations: it is a disgrace always to take and give nothing.[1]

XII.—*To Auctus*

You claim from us what you pay to no one, love; what you accord to no man you claim, Auctus, trust. You claim from us what you don't deserve, honour; it is wonderful that what you don't give you expect to be given you.

XIII.—*On Filus*

FILUS possesses cloaks, he surrounds his fingers with gold, but yet Filus is poorer than the poor.[2] Filus has Tyrian mantles, a thousand appointments, clients, but yet he is poorer than the poor. Filus has a hall furnished in royal style, but yet Filus is poorer than the poor. He hungers and thirsts while he is arrayed in jewels and gold; though he is clad in an embroidered robe he hungers and thirsts. His pallor and emaciation bespeak a load of hunger; his gold brooch says there is no load of hunger. The wretched man will then hire himself out in slavery for bread, but his gold amulet prevents him being a slave.[3] If, indeed, he assails any man with suppliant prayers, his silken garb is at hand to prevent him

to the *Lares*, or Household Gods. It was gold in the case of children of free birth, leather in the case of children of freedmen. It enclosed an amulet (a *phallus*) against the evil eye; hence it was worn by a victorious general during a triumph: Macrob. *Sat.* i. 6.

ergo ne pereat, fiat de divite pauper: 15
pauper enim factus ditior esse potest.

XIV.—*Ad Aulum*

Non sanguis, non oris honor, non gloria census,
non gravitas morum proderit, Aule, tibi.
pauper enim tu semper eris, quia pauper es: et te
colligit ulterior ulteriore gradus.

XV.—*Ad Regulum*

Praedicat Hermagoras, non omnibus esse placendum.
elige de multis, Regule, cui placeas.

XVI.—*Ad Aulicum*

Multa mihi donas, vereor ne multa requiras.
nolo mihi dones, Aulice, si repetas.

XVII.—*Ad Germanicum*

Exaltas in lite tuam, Germanice, vocem,
ut furias mentis vox furiosa sonet.

XVIII.—*Ad Bassum*

Omnis amicus amat, sed non qui amat omnis amicus:
sed quem, Basse, tu ames, esto et amicus ei.

---

[1] v. lxxxi. has a similar sentiment.
[2] A Greek rhetorician who came to Rome in the time of
Augustus.

prevailing. So, that he may not perish, let him from rich become poor; for a man become poor may acquire riches.

XIV.—*To Aulus*

NOT blood, not beauty of face, not proud estate, not weight of character will avail you, Aulus. For you will be always poor because you are poor: [1] and a grade lower than the lowest includes you.

XV.—*To Regulus*

HERMAGORAS [2] preaches that one need not please everybody. Choose, Regulus, [3] some one out of many to please.

XVI.—*To Aulicus*

YOU make me many presents: I am afraid you will require many in return. I don't want you, Aulicus, to give me anything if you claim an equivalent.

XVII.—*To Germanicus*

YOU raise your voice, Germanicus, in court that a furious voice may echo to the fury of your mind.

XVIII.—*To Bassus*

EVERY friend loves, but not every man who loves is a friend: but do you, Bassus, be also a friend to the man you love.

[3] An eminent advocate, many times alluded to by Martial, but in more complimentary terms : *cf.* IV. xvi. 6.

XIX.—*In Turgidum*

In noctem prandes, in noctem, Turgide, coenas,
   multimodoque mades nocte dieque mero.
cumque cuti studeas, uxorem ducere non vis :
   cum nolis, dicis, Vita pudica placet.
Turgide, mentiris.   Non est haec vita pudica.   5
   vis dicam, quae sit vita pudica ?   Modus.

XX.—*In Chloen*

Lascivo Ganymede cales : te quilibet intrat :
   Hippolytos etiam reddis amore graves.
plurimus interea tibi limen servat adulter :
   exposita es cuivis : quam populare sapis !
Demophilem cuperem te dicere, te nisi mater   5
   esse Chloen vellet.   Non sapit atque sapit.

XXI.—*In Laïdem*

Formosissima Laï feminarum,
dum noctis pretium tibi requiro,
magnum continuo petis talentum :
tanti non emo, Laï, poenitere.

XXII.—*In Macrinum*

Defungi fungis homines, Macrine, negabas :
   boleti leti causa fuere tui.

---

[1] *cf.* viii. xlvi. 2.   [2] *i.e.* loved by the people.
[3] The point of the epigram is very obscure.
[4] The Attic talent of 60 *minae* of silver, about £240.

XIX.—*Against Turgidus*

TILL nightfall you lunch, till nightfall, Turgidus, you dine, and with all sorts of wine day and night you reek. And, although you are careful of your person, you are unwilling to take a wife; your unwillingness says: " A chaste life pleases me." Turgidus, you lie; this is not a chaste life. Would you have me tell you what is a chaste life? Moderation.

XX.—*Against Chloe*

YOU are hot for a wanton Ganymede; you are every man's goods; even Hippolytuses [1] you make heavy with lust. In the meantime many an adulterer hangs about your threshold; you are exposed for sale to anyone: how popular is your taste! I should have wished to have called you Demophile,[2] had not your mother wished you should be Chloe: she is unwise and wise.[3]

XXI.—*Against Lais*

LAIS, most beautiful of women, when I ask you what is the price of your favours, you at once require a great [4] talent. At such a cost, Lais, I do not buy repentance.[5]

XXII.—*Against Macrinus*

YOU used to deny, Macrinus, that men could become defunct through funguses: mushrooms made room for *your* heirs! [6]

[5] This is the answer said to have been made by Demosthenes to Lais, the Corinthian courtesan : Gell. i. 8. Perhaps the epigram is put in the mouth of D.

[6] The pun on *leti* and *boleti* can only be paraphrased.

XIX.—*Against Prodigals.*

You might all day long, till nightfall, Porphias,
you dine, and with all sorts of wine day and night
you reek. And although you are careful of your
person, you see nothing to take a wife; your unwillingness says, "A chaste life pleases me." Pur-
nisher, you do lie; this is not a chaste life. Would you
have me tell you what is a chaste life? Moderation.

XX.—*Against Chloe.*

You are hot for a wanton Ganymede; you are
every man's prude, even Hippolytus; if you make
heavy with lust. If the meantime haply an adulterer
bangs about your threshold; you are exposed for
sale to anyone; how peculiar is your taste; I should
have wished to have called you Hermophila, had not
your mother wished you should be Chloe; she is
unchaste and wise.

XXI.—*Against Lais.*

Lais, most beautiful of women, when I ask you
what is the price of your favours, you at once require
a great talent. At such a cost Lais, I do not buy
repentance.

XXII.—*Against Meneius.*

You used to deny, Meneius, that men could become deterred through foul tongues; mushrooms made
room for your facts.

¹ This is the second said to have been made by Turnus
against Lais, the Goethian epigram being i.e. Perhaps
the epigram is put in the mouth of it.
² The pun on χεω and φερω can only be paraphrased.

INDEXES

INDEX OF PROPER NAMES

Apicius, M. Gabius, a noted gourmand of the time of Tiberius. According to Seneca (*Ad Helv.* x.) after spending in gluttony one hundred million sesterces (£800,000), he found himself oppressed by debt, looked into his accounts, and, discovering he had remaining only ten millions committed suicide. Martial alludes to this (III. xxii.), giving the sums as sixty millions and ten respectively. Pliny (*N.H.* ix. 30) speaks of him as *ad omne luxus ingenium mirus,* and (*N.H.* x. 68) calls him *nepotum omnium altissimus gurges.* Athenæus (l. 12) tells how that, hearing lobsters were very large in Libya, he set off at once, but finding from samples that they were of ordinary size, he returned without landing

Apollinaris, Domitius, a learned friend of M. and a favourable critic of his epigrams (IV. lxxvi ; VII. xxvi.). M. (X. xxx.) describes his villa at Formiae. **He is** perhaps the A. alluded to by Pliny (*Ep.* ix. 13) as *consul designatus* in A.D. 97

Auctus, Pomponius, a learned lawyer, and admirer of Martial, whose works he knew by heart, VII. li.

Avitus, Stertinius, Consul A.D. 92. He placed a bust of M. in his library, of which M. writes (IX. *Introd. Ep.*) the inscription. M. addresses to him an epigram (X. xcvi.) on the charms of country life in Spain

Baetis, the Guadalquivir, the principal river in Hispania Baetica, according to Pliny (iii. 3) the most fertile province in Spain. It flows past Corduba and Hispalis (Cordova and Seville) and falls into the Atlantic N. of Gades (Cadiz). The district was renowned for olives (XII. lxiii. 2 ; XII. xcviii. 1), which Martial thinks superior to those of Venafrum : VII. xxviii. 3 ; and Statius to Attic, *Silv.* II. vii. 29 ; whereas Pliny (xv. 3) thinks the olives of Venafrum superior to those of Baetica and Istria. The province of Baetica was also celebrated for its wool, to which the waters of the Baetis gave a golden hue, often alluded to by Martial

Bilbilis, the second city of Hispania Tarraconensis, on the high road between Emerita and Caesar Augusta (Merida and Saragossa). Was a *municipium* in Imperial times. It stood on a rocky height surrounded by the Salo, a river famed for tempering iron. Its site is at or near Bambola, near Calatayud, a Moorish City built by Ayub, the nephew of Musa, the Governor of N.W. Africa at the time of the Arab invasion, who used the remains of Bilbilis as a quarry. Bilbilis was also the scene of a battle between A. Metellus and the insurgent Sertorius in B.C. 74

Castricus, some friend of Martial, who **is** addressed in several

535

character of his epigrams. Nothing more is known of him

Festus, a friend of the Emperor, who died of a cancer in the face, I. lxxviii. If he be the same as the Valerius Festus, spoken of by Pliny (*Ep.* iii. 7) as guilty *per summum facinus* of the murder in A.D. 69 of Piso the proconsul of Africa (see Tac. *Hist.* iv. 49) M. is hardly justified in speaking of his *indignas fauces* and *pia ora.* Tacitus, *supra,* describes him as *sumptuosae adulescentiae, neque modica cupiens*

Flaccus, a native of Patavium, is addressed by Martial in many epigrams ; he is a guest in X. xlviii., and in XII. lxxiv. Martial makes him a present of " dreadnought " glass. He appears to have been a poet, I. lxi. and lxxvi. Some commentators, on the strength of the two epigrams mentioned, have identified him with Valerius Flaccus, the epic poet of the *Argonautica.* But it is not certain that Valerius Flaccus was born at Patavium ; Setia in Campania contends for the honour of being his birthplace, and the Vatican MS. has appended the words " Setinus Balbus." And Quintilian says (X. i. 90) *multum in Valerio Flacco nuper amisimus* ; consequently V. Flaccus must have died before A.D. 90 or 91, the probable date of Quintilian's great work, in which case none of Martial's last six books at least can refer to him. The notes to IX. lv. 2 and XI. lxxx. 3 should be corrected. It is noticeable also that Martial never refers—as might have been expected—to the *Argonautica,* as he does to the *Punica* of Silius.

Frontinus, *Sextus Julius,* succeeded Petilius Cerealis, and was succeeded by Agricola, as Governor of Britain. Tacitus (*Ag.* 17) describes him as " a great man so far as he was permitted to

be," i.e. by the Emperor's jealousy. He subdued the powerful and warlike Silures in South Wales in spite of the difficulties of the country (Tac. *supra*). In A.D. 97 he was *curator aquarum,* and in 98 Consul (according to M.) for the second time ; but his name does not appear in the Fasti (Hoffm. *Lex. Univ.*). He had been Praetor Urbanus in 70 (Tac. *Hist.* iv. 39), an office he resigned to Domitian, not then Emperor. He wrote a treatise on the art of war called *Strategemata,* and a work on the Roman aqueducts, both of which are extant. He died in 106, saying in his will *impensa monumenti supervacua est ; memoria nostri durabit si vita meruimus*

Fronto, described by M. (I. lv.) as a distinguished lawyer and soldier. Perhaps the same as T. Catius Fronto, consul in 96, and alluded to by Pliny (*Ep.* iv. 9 and vi. 13) as an orator

Fuscus, apparently a lawyer of some eminence and wealth whom Martial (VII. xxviii) begs to read and criticise his seventh book. He is not the Cornelius Fuscus who fell in the Dacian war, VI. lxxvi ; and perhaps not the Fuscus whom M. courts in I. liv.

Ianthis, or Violentilla, the wife of Stella the poet. Martial (VI. xxi.) as well as Statius (*Silv.* I. ii.) celebrates her marriage. The name is taken from *ἴον,* the Greek form of *viola.* Statius calls her Asteris

Latinus, a celebrated mime, or comic actor. He was a favourite of Domitian, and a *delator,* Schol on Juv. iv. 53. Martial writes an epigram (IX. xxviii). on his portrait. Suetonius (*Dom.* 15) tells a story how Latinus, when dining with Domitian before the murder of the latter, had disturbed the Emperor, who had been alarmed by various

INDEX OF PROPER NAMES

Marsus, Domitius, a poet of the Augustan age, frequently mentioned by Martial, together with Pedo and Catullus, with whom he compares himself, v. v. 6 ; VII. xcix. 7. He wrote epics. Ov. *Ex. P.* IV. xvi. 5 ; and Martial alludes to an *Amazonis* (IV. xxix. 8) which, however, he regards as inferior to the satires of Persius. Marsus is chiefly distinguished for his epigrams, which were licentious and biting, one of his books being called *cicuta* (hemlock). An epitaph of his on Tibullus is extant

Martialis, Julius, a friend for 33 years of the poet, by whom he is addressed in some of the finest epigrams, I. xv. ; V. xx., X. xlvii, and XII. xxxiv. Martial also describes his villa on the Janiculum, IV. lxiv ; and his library, VII. xvii. Paley identifies him with the Julius Martialis mentioned by Tacitus (*Hist.* i. 28 and 82) as *tribunus legionis,* when Otho was aspiring to the purple, and as being suspected of complicity with the plot. He appears to have been a good critic, VI. i ; and Martial sends him his sixth book, *ibid.* ; and he is probably also the Martialis to whom is sent the third book from Forum Cornelii, III. v.

Maternus, a jurisconsult, whom Martial describes as a fellow-townsman of Bilbilis, and an old friend, x. xxxvii. 1, 3. In the same epigram M. compares the charm of life in Spain with life in a Roman villa

Melior, Atedius, a *bon vivant* of the time, called *nitidus,* IV. liv. 8. Martial praises him (VIII. xxxviii) for his liberality to the Guild of Scribes in memory of his friend Blaesus ; and both Martial (VI. xxviii and xxix), and Statius (*Silv.* II. i.) have written on the death of his freedman Glaucias

Messalla Corvinus, M. Valerius, the friend of Horace and patron of Tibullus. Was Consul B.C. 31 and Praefectus Urbi in 27. He was a patron of learning and the arts, and was himself a poet, a grammarian, historian, and orator. He took the side of Brutus and Cassius in the civil war, but was afterwards reconciled to Augustus. His tomb (alluded to by Martial, VIII. iii. 5 and X. ii. 9) was, like that of Licinus, celebrated for its splendour

Nomentum, now La Mentana, a town in the Sabine Country, 14½ Roman miles N.E. of Rome. Originally a Latin town, a colony from Alba, it was taken by Tarquinius Priscus, the fifth king of Rome. Martial, and also Seneca, had a house here, VI. xliii. 4, IX. xviii. 2 ; and here M. retired when he wanted quiet, XII. lvii. 27. Nomentum was celebrated for its wine, which, when it was old, M. praises, I. cv., and offers to his guests in X. xlviii. 19 ; but the poet in other respects depreciates his property, x. xciv. His fields, he says (VII. xxxi. 8) " produced nothing but himself "

Ovidius, Q., Martial's friend and neighbour at Nomentum. He had accompanied Caesonius Maximus into exile when the former was banished by Nero, for which Martial (VII. xliv. and xlv.) praises him. In his old age he accompanied a friend to Britain, apparently in fulfilment of a promise, or from affection, x. xliv. Martial writes two epigrams (IX. lii. and liii) on his birthday

Paris, a mime or comic actor, for whom Martial writes an epitaph (XI. xiii). He had great influence at Court, and was the darling of the Roman people. Domitian, on suspicion of his intrigue with

539

INDEX OF PROPER NAMES

energetic in action, ready of tongue, a master of the art of sowing the seeds of suspicion against other men, influential in discords and seditions, a plunderer, a briber, in peace most vile, in war not to be despised," *Hist.* ii. 86. "He had a ready audacity," *Ann.* xiv. 40; and "glibness of speech, and skill and influence in soothing the common herd," *Hist.* iii. 10. "He was of an arrogance impatient of an equal, much more of a superior," *Hist.* iv. 80; "success in the case of such a character laid bare his avarice, his insolence, and his other hidden vices," *Hist.* iii. 49

Priscus, Terentius, a fellow-countryman of Martial, to whom he dedicates, on Priscus' return to Spain, the twelfth book. In XII. lxii. he addresses Saturn on the same subject. Martial calls him (XII. iv.) his Maecenas. In VIII. xlv. he celebrates Priscus's return from Sicily; and in another epigram (XII. xiv.) warns him against the danger of too reckless hunting

Proculus, G. Julius, a friend of Martial, to whom he sends (I. lxx.) his first book, and whose recovery from illness he commemorates, XI. xxxvi.

Pudens, Aulus, of Sassina in Umbria, a friend of Martial, and a centurion. He served in Pannonia. Martial celebrates his marriage with Claudia, IV. xiii.; and prays (VI. lviii. 10) that he may return from his campaigns with primipilar rank and the rank of a knight. It may be inferred from I. xxxi. 3, as compared with V. xlviii. 1, that he attained the former honour at least

Quintianus, some rich friend of M. (v. xviii. 9) to whom M. says that, being poor, he will only send his books. In I. lii. M.

appeals to him against a plagiarist

Quintilianus, M. Fabius, was born at Calagurris (Calahorra) in Spain. He was the most celebrated of Roman rhetoricians. Educated at Rome, he returned to Spain, and came back with Galba in 68. He practised at the Bar, but is chiefly known as a teacher of eloquence, the younger Pliny (*Ep.* ii. 14; vi. 6) being one of his pupils. He held the chair of rhetoric founded by Vespasian; and was granted by Domitian the insignia of a consul, to which Juvenal (vii. 197) may perhaps sarcastically allude. After twenty years' tenure of the chair he retired about 89 A.D., and in two years had completed the work for which he is principally known, the *Institutiones Oratoriae* in twelve books. He advised Martial to take up a profession, II. xc.

Rabirius, the architect of Domitian's palace, VII. lvi. Martial has an epigram on the death of R.'s parents, and praises his filial piety, X. lxxi.

Regulus, M. Aquillius, a celebrated advocate. He was a delator under Nero and Domitian, and attained great wealth. He is disliked by Pliny, but is flattered by Martial, who praises his character (I. cxi.). Pliny ridicules even his oratorical power (*Ep.* iv. 7), and his extravagant grief for the death of his son, "a boy of a quick but inscrutable disposition, who yet might have followed the right, had he not been like his father," *Ep.* iv. 2. M. congratulates him in two epigrams (I. xii. and lxxxii.) on his escape from death. Pliny describes him as "rich, factious, courted by many, feared by more; and fear is generally stronger than love," *Ep.* i. 5;

541

INDEX OF PROPER NAMES

and whose tomb he regarded as a temple. He committed suicide by voluntary starvation in his seventy-sixth year because of an incurable cancer. As a poet Martial (VII. lxiii.) calls him immortal, but Pliny says that his works showed more scholarly care than genius. He is known by his *Punica*, an epic on the second Punic war in seventeen books, of which Prof. Mackail says : " His *Punic War* may fairly contend for the distinction of being the worst epic ever written . . . its author the most striking instance in Latin literature of the incorrigible amateur . . . without any inventive or constructive power of his own. Silius copies with tasteless pedantry all the outworn traditions of the heroic epic." He is only once referred to in the fifth century ; then he fell into complete oblivion till he was discovered in the fifteenth

Stella, L. Arruntius, of Patavium, a patron and friend of Martial and Statius, who dedicates to him the first book of the *Silvae*. Both Martial (VI. xxi.) and Statius (*Silv.* i. 2) write epithalamia on Stella's marriage with Violentilla, whom M. calls Ianthis, and Statius Asteris. Stella gave games to celebrate the conclusion of the Sarmatian war, VIII. lxxviii. ; and was consul A.D. 101 ; an honour for which M. (IX. xlii.) had solicited Apollo. Statius (*Silv.* I. ii. 177) also says that he was a *quindecimvir librorum sibyllinorum*. He was also a poet. M. alludes to his *Columba*, a poem on the death of Ianthis' pet dove, I. vii. 1 ; VII. xiv. 5 ; and writes several epigrams (*e.g.* VI. xlvii.) on a spring in Stella's house

Sulpicia, a poetess of the time, of whom nothing is known, X. xxxv. She was the wife of Calenus, X. xxxviii. She is mentioned by Ausonius and by Sidonius Apolli-

naris ; and a satirical poem on the expulsion by Domitian of the philosophers from Rome is commonly attributed to her. Paley ascribes to her the poems often contained in the editions of Tibullus

Sura, Licinius, of Hispania Tarraconensis, held offices under Nerva and Trajan, being under the latter three times consul. Martial speaks (VII. xlvii. 1) of his learning, and (VI. lxiv. 13) appreciation of M.'s poems, and in the first epigram, one of the best, of his unexpected recovery from severe illness. He would seem to have been a natural philosopher, for Pliny (*Ep.* IV. xxx.) consults him as to the unexplained ebb and flow of a spring. On his death Trajan gave him a public funeral, and built baths in his memory. He is perhaps the Sura of I. xlix. 40, but this Sura may be Palfurius Sura, who was removed from the Senate by Vespasian, became a Stoic, was a delator under Domitian, and was after his death condemned by the Senate, Schol. in Juv. iv. 53

Tullus, Cn. Domitius Curvius, the brother of Lucanus (*q.v.*). He held high office under Vespasian and Domitian. He was a rich man like his brother, and Pliny (*Ep.* viii. 18) speaks of the disappointment of the *captatores* when his will was opened, and says of the two brothers that it seemed ordained by fate that they should be enriched even against the will of the donors. He had played upon the expectations of legacy-hunters (*se captandum praebuisset*) during his life, and by his will left his property to his relations, thus showing himself *longe melior morte quam vita*. He was a cripple, unable even to brush his own teeth, complaining that " he daily licked

543

the fingers of his slaves," Pliny, *l.c.* Pliny speaks of the devotion of his wife

Vestinus, perhaps the Lucius V. described by Tacitus (*Hist.* iv. 53) as *equestris ordinis virum, sed auctoritate famaque inter proceres*, to whom Vespasian gave the duty of restoring the Capitol ; and perhaps also the son of the consul Vestinus who, being marked for death by Nero, committed suicide by opening his veins in a bath (Tac. *Ann.* xv. 69). Martial praises him (IV. lxxiii.) for dividing his property amongst his friends when he was on the point of death. Paley suggests that his motive was to avoid making the Emperor his heir, or joint heir ; and cites the example of Agricola (Tac. *Ag.* 43), who had made Domitian joint heir with his own wife and daughter

Zoilus, an anonymous person frequently attacked by M., and to whom is attributed every vice. He had been a slave (III. xxix.) and a runaway one (XI. liv.), and had afterwards become a knight (III. xxix.) It is not improbable that M. borrowed the name from the original Zoilus, a grammarian of Amphipolis who flourished in the time of Philip of Macedon and Alexander the Great, and whose name, because of his attacks on Homer, Plato, and others, became one synonymous with malignant criticism, Ov. *Rem. Am.* 366. He was called κυὼν ῥητορικός, and ὁμηρομάστιξ, and remains, in the words of Swinburne (*Cont. of Shak.* II.) "eternally alive (or in Browning's characteristically audacious phrase) 'immortally immerded.'" Aelian (*V.H.* xi. 10) reports a remark of his that he always spoke evilly of men because he could not do them evil

INDEX OF FIRST LINES

A

INDEX OF FIRST LINES

INDEX OF FIRST LINES

C

547

INDEX OF FIRST LINES

548

INDEX OF FIRST LINES

INDEX OF FIRST LINES

INDEX OF FIRST LINES

INDEX OF FIRST LINES

INDEX OF FIRST LINES

INDEX OF FIRST LINES

INDEX OF FIRST LINES

K

L

INDEX OF FIRST LINES

556

INDEX OF FIRST LINES

N

INDEX OF FIRST LINES

INDEX OF FIRST LINES

559

INDEX OF FIRST LINES

INDEX OF FIRST LINES

INDEX OF FIRST LINES

INDEX OF FIRST LINES

INDEX OF FIRST LINES

S

INDEX OF FIRST LINES

INDEX OF FIRST LINES

INDEX OF FIRST LINES

567

INDEX OF FIRST LINES

PRINTED IN GREAT BRITAIN BY RICHARD CLAY AND COMPANY, LTD.,
BUNGAY, SUFFOLK

THE LOEB CLASSICAL LIBRARY

VOLUMES ALREADY PUBLISHED

Latin Authors

AMMIANUS MARCELLINUS. Translated by J. C. Rolfe. 3 Vols.

APULEIUS: THE GOLDEN ASS (METAMORPHOSES). W. Adlington (1566). Revised by S. Gaselee.

ST. AUGUSTINE: CITY OF GOD. 7 Vols. Vol. I. G. H. McCracken. Vol. VI. W. C. Greene.

ST. AUGUSTINE, CONFESSIONS OF. W. Watts (1631). 2 Vols.

ST. AUGUSTINE, SELECT LETTERS. J. H. Baxter.

AUSONIUS. H. G. Evelyn White. 2 Vols.

BEDE. J. E. King. 2 Vols.

BOETHIUS: TRACTS and DE CONSOLATIONE PHILOSOPHIAE. Rev. H. F. Stewart and E. K. Rand.

CAESAR: ALEXANDRIAN, AFRICAN and SPANISH WARS. A. G. Way.

CAESAR: CIVIL WARS. A. G. Peskett.

CAESAR: GALLIC WAR. H. J. Edwards.

CATO: DE RE RUSTICA; VARRO: DE RE RUSTICA. H. B. Ash and W. D. Hooper.

CATULLUS. F. W. Cornish; TIBULLUS. J. B. Postgate; PERVIGILIUM VENERIS. J. W. Mackail.

CELSUS: DE MEDICINA. W. G. Spencer. 3 Vols.

CICERO: BRUTUS, and ORATOR. G. L. Hendrickson and H. M. Hubbell.

[CICERO]: AD HERENNIUM. H. Caplan.

CICERO: DE ORATORE, etc. 2 Vols. Vol. I. DE ORATORE, Books I. and II. E. W. Sutton and H. Rackham. Vol. II. DE ORATORE, Book III. De Fato; Paradoxa Stoicorum; De Partitione Oratoria. H. Rackham.

CICERO: DE FINIBUS. H. Rackham.

CICERO: DE INVENTIONE, etc. H. M. Hubbell.

CICERO: DE NATURA DEORUM and ACADEMICA. H. Rackham.

CICERO: DE OFFICIIS. Walter Miller.

CICERO: DE REPUBLICA and DE LEGIBUS; SOMNIUM SCIPIONIS. Clinton W. Keyes.

CICERO: DE SENECTUTE, DE AMICITIA, DE DIVINATIONE. W. A. Falconer.

CICERO: IN CATILINAM, PRO FLACCO, PRO MURENA, PRO SULLA. Louis E. Lord.

CICERO: LETTERS TO ATTICUS. E. O. Winstedt. 3 Vols.

CICERO: LETTERS TO HIS FRIENDS. W. Glynn Williams. 3 Vols.

CICERO: PHILIPPICS. W. C. A. Ker.

CICERO: PRO ARCHIA POST REDITUM, DE DOMO, DE HARUS-PICUM RESPONSIS, PRO PLANCIO. N. H. Watts.

CICERO: PRO CAECINA, PRO LEGE MANILIA, PRO CLUENTIO, PRO RABIRIO. H. Grose Hodge.

CICERO: PRO CAELIO, DE PROVINCIIS CONSULARIBUS, PRO BALBO. R. Gardner.

CICERO: PRO MILONE, IN PISONEM, PRO SCAURO, PRO FONTEIO, PRO RABIRIO POSTUMO, PRO MARCELLO, PRO LIGARIO, PRO REGE DEIOTARO. N. H. Watts.

CICERO: PRO QUINCTIO, PRO ROSCIO AMERINO, PRO ROSCIO COMOEDO, CONTRA RULLUM. J. H. Freese.

CICERO: PRO SESTIO, IN VATINIUM. R. Gardner.

CICERO: TUSCULAN DISPUTATIONS. J. E. King.

CICERO: VERRINE ORATIONS. L. H. G. Greenwood. 2 Vols.

CLAUDIAN. M. Platnauer. 2 Vols.

COLUMELLA: DE RE RUSTICA. DE ARBORIBUS. H. B. Ash, E. S. Forster and E. Heffner. 3 Vols.

CURTIUS, Q.: HISTORY OF ALEXANDER. J. C. Rolfe. 2 Vols.

FLORUS. E. S. Forster; and CORNELIUS NEPOS. J. C. Rolfe.

FRONTINUS: STRATAGEMS and AQUEDUCTS. C. E. Bennett and M. B. McElwain.

FRONTO: CORRESPONDENCE. C. R. Haines. 2 Vols.

GELLIUS, J. C. Rolfe. 3 Vols.

HORACE: ODES and EPODES. C. E. Bennett.

HORACE: SATIRES, EPISTLES, ARS POETICA. H. R. Fairclough.

JEROME: SELECTED LETTERS. F. A. Wright.

JUVENAL and PERSIUS. G. G. Ramsay.

LIVY. B. O. Foster, F. G. Moore, Evan T. Sage, and A. C. Schlesinger and R. M. Geer (General Index). 14 Vols.

LUCAN. J. D. Duff.

LUCRETIUS. W. H. D. Rouse.

MARTIAL. W. C. A. Ker. 2 Vols.

MINOR LATIN POETS: from PUBLILIUS SYRUS to RUTILIUS NAMATIANUS, including GRATTIUS, CALPURNIUS SICULUS, NEMESIANUS, AVIANUS, and others with "Aetna" and the "Phoenix." J. Wight Duff and Arnold M. Duff.

OVID: THE ART OF LOVE and OTHER POEMS. J. H. Mozley.

2

OVID: FASTI. Sir James G. Frazer.

OVID: HEROIDES and AMORES. Grant Showerman.

OVID: METAMORPHOSES. F. J. Miller. 2 Vols.

OVID: TRISTIA and EX PONTO. A. L. Wheeler.

PERSIUS. Cf. JUVENAL.

PETRONIUS. M. Heseltine; SENECA: APOCOLOCYNTOSIS.
W. H. D. Rouse.

PLAUTUS. Paul Nixon. 5 Vols.

PLINY: LETTERS. Melmoth's Translation revised by W. M. L.
Hutchinson. 2 Vols.

PLINY: NATURAL HISTORY. H. Rackham and W. H. S. Jones.
10 Vols. Vols. I.–V. and IX. H. Rackham. Vols. VI. and
VII. W. H. S. Jones.

PROPERTIUS. H. E. Butler.

PRUDENTIUS. H. J. Thomson. 2 Vols.

QUINTILIAN. H. E. Butler. 4 Vols.

REMAINS OF OLD LATIN. E. H. Warmington. 4 Vols. Vol. I.
(ENNIUS AND CAECILIUS.) Vol. II. (LIVIUS, NAEVIUS,
PACUVIUS, ACCIUS.) Vol. III. (LUCILIUS and LAWS OF XII
TABLES.) (ARCHAIC INSCRIPTIONS.)

SALLUST. J. C. Rolfe.

SCRIPTORES HISTORIAE AUGUSTAE. D. Magie. 3 Vols.

SENECA: APOCOLOCYNTOSIS. Cf. PETRONIUS.

SENECA: EPISTULAE MORALES. R. M. Gummere. 3 Vols.

SENECA: MORAL ESSAYS. J. W. Basore. 3 Vols.

SENECA: TRAGEDIES. F. J. Miller. 2 Vols.

SIDONIUS: POEMS and LETTERS. W. B. Anderson. 2 Vols.

SILIUS ITALICUS. J. D. Duff. 2 Vols.

STATIUS. J. H. Mozley. 2 Vols.

SUETONIUS. J. C. Rolfe. 2 Vols.

TACITUS: DIALOGUES. Sir Wm. Peterson. AGRICOLA and
GERMANIA. Maurice Hutton.

TACITUS: HISTORIES AND ANNALS. C. H. Moore and J. Jackson.
4 Vols.

TERENCE. John Sargeaunt. 2 Vols.

TERTULLIAN: APOLOGIA and DE SPECTACULIS. T. R. Glover.
MINUCIUS FELIX. G. H. Rendall.

VALERIUS FLACCUS. J. H. Mozley.

VARRO: DE LINGUA LATINA. R. G. Kent. 2 Vols.

VELLEIUS PATERCULUS and RES GESTAE DIVI AUGUSTI. F. W.
Shipley.

VIRGIL. H. R. Fairclough. 2 Vols.

VITRUVIUS: DE ARCHITECTURA. F. Granger. 2 Vols.

Greek Authors

ACHILLES TATIUS. S. Gaselee.

AELIAN: ON THE NATURE OF ANIMALS. A. F. Scholfield. 3 Vols.

AENEAS TACTICUS, ASCLEPIODOTUS and ONASANDER. The Illinios Greek Club.

AESCHINES. C. D. Adams.

AESCHYLUS. H. Weir Smyth. 2 Vols.

ALCIPHRON, AELIAN, PHILOSTRATUS: LETTERS. A. R. Benner and F. H. Fobes.

ANDOCIDES, ANTIPHON, Cf. MINOR ATTIC ORATORS.

APOLLODORUS. Sir James G. Frazer. 2 Vols.

APOLLONIUS RHODIUS. R. C. Seaton.

THE APOSTOLIC FATHERS. Kirsopp Lake. 2 Vols.

APPIAN: ROMAN HISTORY. Horace White. 4 Vols.

ARATUS. Cf. CALLIMACHUS.

ARISTOPHANES. Benjamin Bickley Rogers. 3 Vols. Verse trans.

ARISTOTLE: ART OF RHETORIC. J. H. Freese.

ARISTOTLE: ATHENIAN CONSTITUTION, EUDEMIAN ETHICS, VICES AND VIRTUES. H. Rackham.

ARISTOTLE: GENERATION OF ANIMALS. A. L. Peck.

ARISTOTLE: METAPHYSICS. H. Tredennick. 2 Vols.

ARISTOTLE: METEROLOGICA. H. D. P. Lee.

ARISTOTLE: MINOR WORKS. W. S. Hett. On Colours, On Things Heard, On Physiognomies, On Plants, On Marvellous Things Heard, Mechanical Problems, On Indivisible Lines, On Situations and Names of Winds, On Melissus, Xenophanes, and Gorgias.

ARISTOTLE: NICOMACHEAN ETHICS. H. Rackham.

ARISTOTLE: OECONOMICA and MAGNA MORALIA. G. C. Armstrong; (with Metaphysics, Vol. II.).

ARISTOTLE: ON THE HEAVENS. W. K. C. Guthrie.

ARISTOTLE: ON THE SOUL. PARVA NATURALIA. ON BREATH. W. S. Hett.

ARISTOTLE: ORGANON—Categories, On Interpretation, Prior Analytics. H. P. Cooke and H. Tredennick.

ARISTOTLE: ORGANON—Posterior Analytics, Topics. H. Tredennick and E. S. Foster.

ARISTOTLE: ORGANON—On Sophistical Refutations. On Coming to be and Passing Away, On the Cosmos. E. S. Forster and D. J. Furley.

ARISTOTLE: PARTS OF ANIMALS. A. L. Peck; MOTION AND PROGRESSION OF ANIMALS. E. S. Forster.

ARISTOTLE: PHYSICS. Rev. P. Wicksteed and F. M. Cornford. 2 Vols.

ARISTOTLE: POETICS and LONGINUS. W. Hamilton Fyfe; DEMETRIUS ON STYLE. W. Rhys Roberts.

ARISTOTLE: POLITICS. H. Rackham.

ARISTOTLE: PROBLEMS. W. S. Hett. 2 Vols.

ARISTOTLE: RHETORICA AD ALEXANDRUM (with PROBLEMS. Vol. II.). H. Rackham.

ARRIAN: HISTORY OF ALEXANDER and INDICA. Rev. E. Iliffe Robson. 2 Vols.

ATHENAEUS: DEIPNOSOPHISTAE. C. B. Gulick. 7 Vols.

ST. BASIL: LETTERS. R. J. Deferrari. 4 Vols.

CALLIMACHUS: FRAGMENTS. C. A. Trypanis.

CALLIMACHUS, Hymns and Epigrams, and LYCOPHRON. A. W. Mair; ARATUS. G. R. Mair.

CLEMENT of ALEXANDRIA. Rev. G. W. Butterworth.

COLLUTHUS. Cf. OPPIAN.

DAPHNIS AND CHLOE. Thornley's Translation revised by J. M. Edmonds; and PARTHENIUS. S. Gaselee.

DEMOSTHENES I.: OLYNTHIACS, PHILIPPICS and MINOR ORATIONS. I.–XVII. AND XX. J. H. Vince.

DEMOSTHENES II.: DE CORONA and DE FALSA LEGATIONE. C. A. Vince and J. H. Vince.

DEMOSTHENES III.: MEIDIAS, ANDROTION, ARISTOCRATES, TIMOCRATES and ARISTOGEITON, I. AND II. J. H. Vince.

DEMOSTHENES IV.–VI.: PRIVATE ORATIONS and IN NEAERAM. A. T. Murray.

DEMOSTHENES VII.: FUNERAL SPEECH, EROTIC ESSAY, EXORDIA and LETTERS. N. W. and N. J. DeWitt.

DIO CASSIUS: ROMAN HISTORY. E. Cary. 9 Vols.

DIO CHRYSOSTOM. J. W. Cohoon and H. Lamar Crosby. 5 Vols.

DIODORUS SICULUS. 12 Vols. Vols. I.–VI. C. H. Oldfather. Vol. VII. C. L. Sherman, Vols. IX. and X. R. M. Geer. Vol. XI. F. Walton.

DIOGENES LAERITIUS. R. D. Hicks. 2 Vols.

DIONYSIUS OF HALICARNASSUS: ROMAN ANTIQUITIES. Spelman's translation revised by E. Cary. 7 Vols.

EPICTETUS. W. A. Oldfather. 2 Vols.

EURIPIDES. A. S. Way. 4 Vols. Verse trans.

EUSEBIUS: ECCLESIASTICAL HISTORY. Kirsopp Lake and J. E. L. Oulton. 2 Vols.

GALEN: ON THE NATURAL FACULTIES. A. J. Brock.

THE GREEK ANTHOLOGY. W. R. Paton. 5 Vols.

GREEK ELEGY AND IAMBUS with the ANACREONTEA. J. M. Edmonds. 2 Vols.

THE GREEK BUCOLIC POETS (THEOCRITUS, BION, MOSCHUS). J. M. Edmonds.

GREEK MATHEMATICAL WORKS. Ivor Thomas. 2 Vols.

HERODES. Cf. THEOPHRASTUS: CHARACTERS.

HERODOTUS. A. D. Godley. 4 Vols.

HESIOD AND THE HOMERIC HYMNS. H. G. Evelyn White.

HIPPOCRATES and the FRAGMENTS OF HERACLEITUS. W. H. S. Jones and E. T. Withington. 4 Vols.

HOMER: ILIAD. A. T. Murray. 2 Vols.

HOMER: ODYSSEY. A. T. Murray. 2 Vols.

ISAEUS. E. W. Forster.

ISOCRATES. George Norlin and LaRue Van Hook. 3 Vols.

ST. JOHN DAMASCENE: BARLAAM AND IOASAPH. Rev. G. R. Woodward and Harold Mattingly.

JOSEPHUS. H. St. J. Thackeray and Ralph Marcus. 9 Vols. Vols. I.–VII.

JULIAN. Wilmer Cave Wright. 3 Vols.

LUCIAN. 8 Vols. Vols. I.–V. A. M. Harmon. Vol. VI. K. Kilburn.

LYCOPHRON. Cf. CALLIMACHUS.

LYRA GRAECA. J. M. Edmonds. 3 Vols.

LYSIAS. W. R. M. Lamb.

MANETHO. W. G. Waddell: PTOLEMY: TETRABIBLOS. F. E. Robbins.

MARCUS AURELIUS. C. R. Haines.

MENANDER. F. G. Allinson.

MINOR ATTIC ORATORS (ANTIPHON, ANDOCIDES, LYCURGUS, DEMADES, DINARCHUS, HYPEREIDES). K. J. Maidment and J. O. Burtt. 2 Vols.

NONNOS: DIONYSIACA. W. H. D. Rouse. 3 Vols.

OPPIAN, COLLUTHUS, TRYPHIODORUS. A. W. Mair.

PAPYRI. NON-LITERARY SELECTIONS. A. S. Hunt and C. C. Edgar. 2 Vols. LITERARY SELECTIONS (Poetry). D. L. Page.

PARTHENIUS. Cf. DAPHNIS AND CHLOE.

PAUSANIAS: DESCRIPTION OF GREECE. W. H. S. Jones. 4 Vols. and Companion Vol. arranged by R. E. Wycherley.

PHILO. 10 Vols. Vols. I.–V.; F. H. Colson and Rev. G. H. Whitaker. Vols. VI.–IX.; F. H. Colson.

PHILO: two supplementary Vols. (*Translation only.*) Ralph Marcus.

PHILOSTRATUS: THE LIFE OF APOLLONIUS OF TYANA. F. C. Conybeare. 2 Vols.

PHILOSTRATUS: IMAGINES; CALLISTRATUS: DESCRIPTIONS. A. Fairbanks.

PHILOSTRATUS and EUNAPIUS: LIVES OF THE SOPHISTS. Wilmer Cave Wright.

PINDAR. Sir J. E. Sandys.

PLATO: CHARMIDES, ALCIBIADES, HIPPARCHUS, THE LOVERS, THEAGES, MINOS and EPINOMIS. W. R. M. Lamb.

PLATO: CRATYLUS, PARMENIDES, GREATER HIPPIAS, LESSER HIPPIAS. H. N. Fowler.

PLATO: EUTHYPHRO, APOLOGY, CRITO, PHAEDO, PHAEDRUS. H. N. Fowler.

PLATO: LACHES, PROTAGORAS, MENO, EUTHYDEMUS. W. R. M. Lamb.

PLATO: LAWS. Rev. R. G. Bury. 2 Vols.

PLATO: LYSIS, SYMPOSIUM, GORGIAS. W. R. M. Lamb.

PLATO: REPUBLIC. Paul Shorey. 2 Vols.

PLATO: STATESMAN, PHILEBUS. H. N. Fowler; ION. W. R. M. Lamb.

PLATO: THEAETETUS and SOPHIST. H. N. Fowler.

PLATO: TIMAEUS, CRITIAS, CLITOPHO, MENEXENUS, EPISTULAE. Rev. R. G. Bury.

PLUTARCH: MORALIA. 15 Vols. Vols. I.-V. F. C. Babbitt. Vol. VI. W. C. Helmbold. Vol. VII. P. H. De Lacy and B. Einarson. Vol. IX. E. L. Minar, Jr., F. H. Sandbach, W. C. Helmbold. Vol. X. H. N. Fowler. Vol. XII. H. Cherniss and W. C. Helmbold.

PLUTARCH: THE PARALLEL LIVES. B. Perrin. 11 Vols.

POLYBIUS. W. R. Paton. 6 Vols.

PROCOPIUS: HISTORY OF THE WARS. H. B. Dewing. 7 Vols.

PTOLEMY: TETRABIBLOS. Cf. MANETHO.

QUINTUS SMYRNAEUS. A. S. Way. Verse trans.

SEXTUS EMPIRICUS. Rev. R. G. Bury. 4 Vols.

SOPHOCLES. F. Storr. 2 Vols. Verse trans.

STRABO: GEOGRAPHY. Horace L. Jones. 8 Vols.

THEOPHRASTUS: CHARACTERS. J. M. Edmonds. HERODES, etc. A. D. Knox.

THEOPHRASTUS: ENQUIRY INTO PLANTS. Sir Arthur Hort, Bart. 2 Vols.

THUCYDIDES. C. F. Smith. 4 Vols.

TRYPHIODORUS. Cf. OPPIAN.

XENOPHON: CYROPAEDIA. Walter Miller. 2 Vols.

XENOPHON: HELLENICA, ANABASIS, APOLOGY, and SYMPOSIUM. C. L. Brownson and O. J. Todd. 3 Vols.

XENOPHON: MEMORABILIA and OECONOMICUS. E. C. Marchant.

XENOPHON: SCRIPTA MINORA. E. C. Marchant.

IN PREPARATION

Greek Authors

ARISTOTLE: HISTORY OF ANIMALS.   A. L. Peck.
PLOTINUS: A. H. Armstrong.

Latin Authors

BABRIUS AND PHAEDRUS.   Ben E. Perry.

DESCRIPTIVE PROSPECTUS ON APPLICATION

London   WILLIAM HEINEMANN LTD
Cambridge, Mass.   HARVARD UNIVERSITY PRESS